D1747004

Subsidia et Instrumenta Linguarum Orientis

(SILO)

Herausgegeben von / Edited by
Reinhard G. Lehmann

1

2010
Harrassowitz Verlag · Wiesbaden

Johanna Brankaer

Coptic
A Learning Grammar (Sahidic)

2010
Harrassowitz Verlag · Wiesbaden

Text on the cover: Gospel of Thomas 2, 92a, 94:
Jesus said: let him who seeks not stop
seeking until he finds.
And when he finds, he will be disturbed.
And when he is disturbed, he will be astonished
And he will rule over the all.
Jesus said: seek and you will find.
Jesus said: he who seeks will find
And he who knocks, it will be opened to him.

Bibliografische Information der Deutschen Nationalbibliothek
Die Deutsche Nationalbibliothek verzeichnet diese Publikation in der Deutschen
Nationalbibliografie; detaillierte bibliografische Daten sind im Internet
über http://dnb.d-nb.de abrufbar.

Bibliographic information published by the Deutsche Nationalbibliothek
The Deutsche Nationalbibliothek lists this publication in the Deutsche
Nationalbibliografie; detailed bibliographic data are available in the internet
at http://dnb.d-nb.de.

For further information about our publishing program consult our
website http://www.harrassowitz-verlag.de
© Otto Harrassowitz GmbH & Co. KG, Wiesbaden 2010
This work, including all of its parts, is protected by copyright.
Any use beyond the limits of copyright law without the permission
of the publisher is forbidden and subject to penalty. This applies
particularly to reproductions, translations, microfilms and storage
and processing in electronic systems.
Printed on permanent/durable paper.
Logo: Semitic inscription on the top of a foundation nail. Period of the Amorite
Kingdoms (2004–1595 BCE). Larsa, Babylon. © akg-images/Erich Lessing.
Printing and binding: AZ Druck und Datentechnik GmbH, Kempten
Printed in Germany
ISSN 1867-8165
ISBN 978-3-447-05894-0

Table of contents

Acknowledgments	VII
Introduction	1
References	7
PART I: ELEMENTS	**13**
Pronouns and determiners	15
Nouns	19
Numerals	29
Prepositions	31
Adverbs	35
Verbs	37
PART II: CONSTRUCTIONS	**45**
Nominal articulation	47
The nominal sentence	51
The durative sentence	57
The suffixically conjugated verboid	65
The existential and the indicational sentence	67
The non-durative sentence	69
The causative infinitive	81
Part III: COMPLEX SENTENCES	**83**
Main clauses	85
Subordinate clauses	87
Relative clauses	95
Cleft sentences	99
PART IV: EXERCISES	**101**
Exercise 1	103
Exercise 2	105
Exercise 3	106
Exercise 4	108
Exercise 5	108
Exercise 6	109
Exercise 7	110
Exercise 8	111
Exercise 9	112
Exercise 10	112
Exercise 11	112

PART V: SELECTION OF TEXTS **113**
Luke 15:11–32: the prodigal son 115
The apophthegmata patrum 117
A catechesis of Theodorus 122
The *Homily on the Church of the Rock*, attributed to Timothy Æluros 125
Anti-chalcedonian fragment 129
Shenoute, on the Ethiopian invasions 131
Shenoute, On women's piety 133
The three steles of Seth (NHC VII, 5) 136
The Gospel of Mary (BG 1) 139

GLOSSARIES & INDEX **143**
Coptic glossary 145
Greek glossary 175
Glossary of proper nouns 185
Glossary of nomina sacra 186
Grammatical index 187

CONCORDANCES & PARADIGMS **191**
Concordance with some existing grammars 193
Concordance of grammatical terms 197
Grammatical paradigms 199

Acknowledgments

A first version of this textbook has been conceived as a syllabus for the course Coptic, elementary level, at the Oriental Institute of the Université Catholique de Louvain-la-Neuve. It was prepared under the direction of Jean-Marie Sevrin, whom I'd like to thank for taking the initiative for this book. While working at this project we had many stimulating discussions, which I'm also grateful for.

I would also like to thank Hans-Gebhard Bethge and Uwe Karsten-Plisch who have both supported me with their revision of the text, their suggestions and critical remarks.

Katharina Greschat has been a great supervisor in both allowing me to write this grammar and encouraging me from the beginning till the end.

Diane Abs revised the English text of this grammar, which I am really greatful for. Any remaining mistakes are mine own.

I am furthermore grateful to the people of Harrassowitz-Verlag, especially Julia Guthmüller, who made this text look good.

I would also like to thank my editor, Reinhard Lehmann, chief editor of the series SILO, for accepting this book in this great series and for supporting me during the whole preparation of the learning grammar.

I am finally indebted to all my students of Coptic, at the Université Catholique de Louvain-la-Neuve and at the Humboldt-Universität zu Berlin, who allowed me to test and improve this method.

Jena and Overijse, November 2009   Johanna Brankaer

Introduction

About this book

Initially, a French version of this book was conceived as a textbook for the course Coptic I taught at the Université Catholique de Louvain (30 hours). It should be useful as well for teaching Coptic as for learning it yourself.

The book consists of five parts. The first three are concerned with learning Coptic grammar. Part four consists of exercises to apply what you have learned in the corresponding grammatical chapters. Finally there is a selection of texts, which will allow you to gain more in-depth knowledge of the language as well as of some aspects of Coptic culture. Both the exercises and the texts have cross-references to the grammatical part of this book.

The grammatical part is conceived as a systematic synthesis of what one finds in the existing basic grammars, textbooks and some unpublished workbooks. Since this book was conceived first, the Coptic Grammar by Bentley Layton has established itself as *the* reference grammar. In order to make it easier for students to use this grammar, the same terminology has been used here. In annex, however, you will find a glossary with the equivalents of some terms used in other grammars and textbooks.

The grammatical part of this textbook consists of three main sections, elements, constructions and complex sentences. I suggest that in a teaching context, you start with the constructions and learn the elements as they show up in the constructions and the complex sentences. This will allow you to progress steadily without having too much baggage to carry along from the start. A system of cross-references makes it possible to 'commute' between both grammar parts and the exercises and texts. The elements are in way the building stones you use when learning Coptic sentence constructions. The exercises are also conceived in this way. They follow the rhythm of the constructions. If you work in this way, you will also have dealt with all the elements at the end of the constructions. The systematic presentation of elements and constructions is also conceived for later reference. This book should be useful as a basic grammar for students who have already familiarised themselves with the Coptic language.

This course is meant to familiarize the students progressively with the different kinds of Coptic sentences. This is done in the constructions part, after a first chapter on nominal articulation.

All of the examples given in this book are analysed. The separators used to distinguish all elements are ≠ for the prepersonal bound state, - for the prenominal bound state and a full stop to separate all other elements (e.g. article and noun).

There is no method to learn the Coptic vocabulary in this book. At the end you will find a glossary of all the Coptic and Greek words used in the book, in the grammatical examples as well as in the exercises and texts. It is recommended to learn the vocabulary gradually as you find it in the examples and exercises, so you can draw up a list of the words you have encountered.

Coptic

The term 'Coptic'
The word 'Coptic' is derived from the Arabic term *qubti*, which was used by the Arabs to refer to the (mostly Christian) inhabitants of Egypt. The Arabic is on its turn a loan word from the Greek, αἰγύπτιος (*Aigyptios*). Originally the term Coptic referred to the descendants of the ancient Egyptians, to distinguish them from foreign, more recent, groups of the population. The Coptics from Antiquity referred to their language as T.MN̄T-PM̄.N̄-KHME (*tementremenkême*), which signifies an *abstract category* (MN̄T-) in relation to *the humans* (PM̄) of *Egypt* (KHME).

The term Coptic gradually lost its ethnic and linguistic meaning to refer specifically to the Christians of Egypt – in order to distinguish them from e.g. Muslims. The Egyptian Church played an important role in the first centuries of the Christian era. The patriarchs of Alexandria were among the most powerful. The monachism that was born on Egyptian soil with inspiring figures, such as Anthony, influenced similar movements all over the Christian world. In the aftermath of the Council of Chalcedon (451) the Egyptian church was the first 'national church' to break with byzantine authority. The term 'national church' does not imply that the authority of this church was confined to the borders of Egypt. It extended to Libya (the region of Pentapolis) and Ethiopia (around Axum).

One should take care not to identify the Coptic church with the Coptic language. In Antiquity the official language of the 'Coptic' church remained Greek, even though important texts, like the Easter Letters of the Alexandrian bishops were immediately translated into Coptic for the use of the local bishops. An important part of Coptic literature of all sorts was actually translated from Greek. It was above all the monastic environment that produced a rich original Coptic literature, as it was the case with the Pachomian monasteries in Tabbenese and Pbow and the White monastery of Shenoute.

The use of the Coptic language was progressively abandoned in favour of Arabic after the muslim conquest of Egypt (642). After the 10th century, Coptic documents become very rare. From the 13th century onwards, however, there was a growing interest from Arabic scholars in the Coptic language. They published Coptic grammars in Arabic, as well as works dealing with philological, literary and cultural topics. The last important examples of Coptic as a spoken language have been attested in the 15th century[1]. Most of the Copts today speak Arabic. Only in liturgy some traces of Coptic (mixed up with Greek formulas) are preserved. The situation of Coptic in Egypt is in a way similar to that of Latin in the Christian West.

---

1   Cf. J. Vergote, *Grammaire Copte*, t. Ia, 1–2.

The Coptic language

From a linguistic point of view Coptic represents the last stage of ancient Egyptian (ca. 300–1000 A.D.). Egyptian is a linguistic group in itself, which presents some affinities with Semitic languages and some African languages.

One should not confound the Coptic language and the Coptic writing (that is, the Greek alphabet with some supplementary signs). Language and writing have not evolved simultaneously in Egypt[2]. The most ancient writing systems, hieroglyphic and hieratic, were still used in later periods, up to the Ptolemaic, Roman and Byzantine time (332 B.C. – 641 B.C.). From the late Empire on, Middle Egyptian was at that time still used as a literary language, but it was not spoken anymore. From the New Empire onwards (ca. 1570 B.C.) New Egyptian became the dominant language, which evolved into Demotic (the 'popular' language) and eventually into Coptic in Christian times. There are, however, already before that period some attestations of Egyptian in Greek writing. Linguistically this language does not correspond with the Coptic stage, but still with Demotic, even though these texts or words are often qualified as 'Old Coptic'. Greek letters were mostly used instead of Egyptian signs where pronunciation matters. The previous Egyptian writing systems have no notation of vowels. It is thus no surprise to find 'Coptic' writing in e.g. magic texts.

Coptic is of great interest for the study of the Egyptian language. It is the first time in its history that the vowels are written. The use of a simple writing system, consisting of the Greek alphabet with some supplementary signs, made written Egyptian more accessible than it was before.

As the final stage of the Egyptian language, Coptic has also been considerably influenced by Greek, which was the official language of the Coptic church. This influence is mostly limited to the vocabulary. Greek words are not only used for technical terms or in translations. They also very often occur in orginal Coptic writings, such as the works of Shenoute. On a purely grammatical level the influences are less conspicuous. Some Greek conjunctions are used to introduce certain Coptic adverbial subordinate clauses.

Later Coptic texts can also show an influence of Arabic. This has however very few consequences for the vocabulary and was never as important as the Greek influence.

Dialects

Coptic dialectology has developed over the last decades into a discipline in itself. There was hardly any real standardisation in Coptic. Many dialects existed next to one another. Each one of these dialects has its own variants and many texts have a very mixed dialectical profile. The overview you find here is limited to the dialects mentioned in Crum's *Coptic Dictionary*.

S   Sahidic is the main southern dialect of Egypt, but it spread very quickly to the entire Nile Valley. It became the dominant literary language in the 'classical' period. The oldest Sahidic texts are dated around 300 A.D. Of all Coptic dialects Sahidic has the least particularities and the most in common with the others. It therefore offers a good introduction in Coptic.

---

2   Cf. Cl. Obsomer, *Égyptien hiéroglyphique. Grammaire pratique du moyen égyptien et exercices d'application* (Langues et cultures anciennes, 1), Bruxelles 2003, 10–11.

B   Bohairic is the main northern dialect, spoken originally in the Nile Delta. It is played a predominant role from the 9th century onwards, due to the importance of the monasteries in the Wadi Natrun. Since the 11th century, Bohairic is the official language of the Coptic liturgy.

F   Fayumic is the dialect spoken in the oasis of Fayum (ⲠⲒⲞⲘ).

M   Middle Egyptian or Oxyrhynchic was mainly spoken around Oxyrynchus.

A^2 or L Subakhmimic or Lycopolitanic was a southern dialect that was probably overshadowed by the spread of Sahidic.

A   Akhmimic is another southern dialect. It represents probably the most ancient linguistic stage of all known Coptic dialects. It is probably originary from the surroundings of the Town of Akhmim (Nord of Thebes). Like A^2/L this dialect has probably been abandoned in favour of Sahidic.

Alphabet and orthography

Coptic uses the Greek alphabet with some supplementary signs taken from Demotic. The letters can also have numeral value (cf. 085). The order of the Greek alphabet is preserved. The supplementary Coptic signs are put at the end. Here is a list with the alphabet, the names of the individual letters and their English equivalents.

ⲁ	alpha	a
ⲃ	beta	b (v)
ⲅ	gamma	g
ⲇ	delta	d
ⲉ	epsilon	e
ⲍ	zeta	z
ⲏ	eta	ê
ⲑ	theta	th
ⲓ	iota	i
ⲕ	kappa	k
ⲗ	lambda	l
ⲙ	mu	m
ⲛ	nu	n
ⲝ	xi	x
ⲟ	omicron	o
ⲡ	pi	p
ⲣ	rho	r
ⲥ	sigma	s
ⲧ	tau	t
ⲩ	upsilon	u
ⲫ	phi	ph
ⲭ	khi	kh
ⲯ	psi	ps
ⲱ	oméga	ô

ϣ	shai	ch
ϥ	phai	f
ᮛ	khai	kh (only in B)
ϧ	khai	kh (only in A)
ϩ	hori	h
ϫ	djandja	dj
ϭ	kjima	tch, ky (palatalyzed)
ϯ	ti	ti

The superlinear stroke is another orthographical element. When it is written above a consonant (e.g. N̄), it indicates the existence of a muted vowel preceding this consonant. In many manuscripts the use of the superlinear stroke is not entirely consistent. Sometimes the superlinear stroke seems interchangeable with ϵ.

Γ, Δ and Z only occur in words of Greek origin. In some cases Z is used as an equivalent of C (ΔNCHBϵ and ΔNZHBϵ, *school*). Γ can also be used instead of K (often after N, e.g. Γ for K, the suffix pronoun of the 2nd pers. m. sg.).

Some letters are the equivalent of two other letters:
Θ = T + ϩ
Φ = Π + ϩ
X = K + ϩ
ξ = K + C
Ψ = Π + C
ϯ = T + I.

ΦO = Π.ϨO, *the face*; POX = POKϨ, *to be burned*; ΛΩξ = ΛΩKC, *to bite*; ϯPHNH = T.ϵIPHNH, *the peace*

In Greek words these letters usually keep their original value and they are not necessarily counted as two letters (this is important e.g. in knowing which article has to be used).

I and ϵI can both represent the phoneme [i] (ϵINϵ, *to bring*; CIBT, *pea*) or the semivocal [j] (ϵIΩT, *father*; XOI, *ship*).

OY can also function as a vowel (MOYN, *to stay*) and as semivocal (OYΔ, *a, one*). The semivocal is written as a simple Y after Δ, ϵ and H (NΔY, *to see*).

N is assimilated before M, Π, Ψ, Φ and becomes M (M̄.MΔΘHTHC M̄-MΩYCHC, *Moses' disciples*). There is no assimilation when M or Π have the superlinear stroke (N.M̄CΔϨ, *the crocodiles*) or if the M was originally a N.

N can be completely assimilated before B, P or Λ (P̄.PΩMϵ for N̄.PΩMϵ, *the humans*).

Haplography: a doubled consonant is often only written once (MN̄TH for MN̄T-TH, *fifteen*).

Dittography: more rarely a consonant is doubled for no apparent reason. This is often the case of N followed by a vowel.

Bibliography

Textbooks and Grammars

Aufrère, Sydney H./Bosson, Nathalie (eds.), *Guillaume Bonjour, Elementa linguae copticae, grammaire inedite du XVIIe siècle* (Cahiers d'orientalisme 24), Genève 2005.
Lambdin, Thomas O., *Introduction to Sahidic Coptic*, Macon, GA, Mercer University Press, 1983.
Layton, Bentley, *A Coptic Grammar*, (Porta Linguarum Orientalium, 20), Wiesbaden 2000; Second Edition, Revised and Expanded, Wiesbaden 2004.
—, *Coptic in 20 Lessons*. Introduction to Sahidic Coptic with Exercises and Vocabularies, Leuven/Paris/Dudley, MA 2007.
Mallon, Alexis, *Grammaire Copte. Bibliographie. Chrestomathie. Vocabulaire*, Quatrième édition revue par M. Malinine, Beyrouth 1956 (1907).
Plisch, Uwe-Karsten, *Einführung in die Koptische Sprache. Sahidischer Dialekt,* (Sprachen und Kulturen des Christlichen Orients, 5), Wiesbaden, 1999.
Polotsky, Hans Jakob, *Collected papers*, Jerusalem 1971.
—, *Grundlagen des koptischen Satzbaus* (American Studies in Papyrology 27–28), Decatur, Georgia 1987, 1990.
Shisha-Halevy, Ariel, Coptic Grammatical Categories. Structural studies in the syntax of Shenoutean Sahidic (Analecta Orientalia 53), Roma 1986.
—, *Coptic Grammatical Chrestomathy,* (Orientalia Lovaniensa Analecta, 30), Leuven 1988.
Steindorff, Georg, *Koptische Grammatik mit Chrestomathie , Wörterverzeichnis und Literatur* (Porta Linguarum Orientalium, 14), Hamburg 1979 (Berlin 1894).
Sterling, Gregory E., *Coptic Paradigms: A Summary of Sahidic Coptic Morphology*, Leuven 2008.
Stern, Ludwig, *Koptische Grammatik*, Osnabrück 1971 (Leipzig 1880).
Till, Walter C., *Koptische Grammatik (saïdischer Dialekt),* Leipzig 1955, 1961[2], 1966[3], 1986[6].
—, *Koptische Dialektgrammatik*, München 1961[2].
Vergote, J., *Grammaire Copte I a/b, II a/b (Parties synchronique et diachronique),* Leuven 1973, 1983.
Walters, C.C., *An Elementary Coptic Grammar of the Sahidic Dialect,* Oxford 1972.

Garitte, G., *Cours de copte* (unpublished syllabus), Université catholique de Louvain.
Quaegebeur, J., *Koptisch: elementaire grammatica van het Sahidisch* (unpublished syllabus), Katholieke Universiteit Leuven 1994.

Dictionaries

Crum, W. E., *A Coptic Dictionary,* Oxford, Clarendon Press 1939 (reprint en 2000).
Kasser, Rodolphe, *Compléments au Dictionnaire Copte de Crum,* (Bibl. d'Etudes Coptes 7), Le Caire 1964.
Smith, Richard H., *A Concise Coptic Dictionary* (SBL dissertation series 13), Grand Rapids, Michigan 1983.
Westendorf, Wolfhart, *Koptisches Handwörterbuch,* Heidelberg 1965–1977.

Cerny, Jaroslav, *Coptic Etymological Dictionary,* Cambridge 1976.
Vycichl, Werner, *Dictionnaire Etymologique de la Langue Copte,* Leuven 1983.

Böhlig, Alexander, *Ein Lexikon der Griechischen Wörter im Koptischen* (Studien zur Erforschung des christlichen Aegyptens), München 1958[3].
Förster, Hans, Wörterbuch der griechischen Wörter in den koptischen dokumentarischen Texten (Texte und Untersuchungen zur Geschichte der altchristlichen Literatur 148), Berlin 2002.

References

Acts	Horner, G., *The Coptic Version of the New Testament in the Southern Dialect Otherwise Called Sahidic and Thebaic*, 1–7, Oxford, 1911–1924, vol 6.
Aeg	Lagarde, P. de, *Aegyptiaca*, Göttingen, 1883.
1ApocJames	Brankaer, J./Bethge, H.-G., *Codex Tchacos* (Texte und Untersuchungen zur Geschichte der altchristlichen Literatur 161), Berlin 2007.
2ApocJames	Funk, W.-P., Die zweite Apokalypse des Jakobus aus Nag-Hammadi-Codex V (Texte und Untersuchungen zur Geschichte der altchristlichen Literatur 119), Berlin 1976.
ApocPeter	Havelaar, H.W., *The Coptic Apocalypse of Peter (nag-Hammadi-Codex VII,3)* (Texte und Untersuchungen zur Geschichte der altchristlichen Literatur 144), Berlin 1999.
Apoph.Patr.	Chaîne, M., *Le manuscrit de la version copte en dialecte sahidique des «Apophthegmata patrum»* (Institut français d'archéologie orientale, Bibliothèque d'études coptes, 4), Le Caire, 1960.
Besa	Kuhn, K.H., *Letters and Sermons of Besa* (Corpus scriptorum Christianorum orientalium, 313), Louvain, 1970.
BG	Till, W., *Die gnostische Schriften des koptischen Papyrus Berolinensis 8502*, Berlin, 1955.
BHom	Budge, E.A.W., *Coptic Homilies in the Dialect of Upper Egypt*, London, 1910.
BMis	Budge, E.A.W., *Miscellaneous Coptic Texts in the Dialect of Upper Egypt*, London, 1915.
Br	Schmidt, C., *Gnostische Schriften in koptischer Sprache aus dem Codex Brucianus* (Texte und Untersuchungen zur Geschichte der altchristlichen Literatur 8, 1/2), Leipzig, 1892.
C.O.	Crum, W.E., *Coptic Ostraca* (Special Extra Publication of the Egypt Exploration Fund), London, 1902.
1Cor	Horner, G., *The Coptic Version of the New Testament in the Southern Dialect Otherwise Called Sahidic and Thebaic*, 1–7, Oxford, 1911–1924, vol. 4.
2Cor	Horner, G., *The Coptic Version of the New Testament in the Southern Dialect Otherwise Called Sahidic and Thebaic*, 1–7, Oxford, 1911–1924, vol. 4.
Deut	Ciasca, A., *Sacrorum Bibliorum fragmenta copto-sahidica Musei Borgiani issu et sumptibus S. Congregationis de Propaganda Fide edita*, vol. 1, Roma, 1885; Kasser, R., *Papyrus Bodmer XVIII : Deutéronome I–X, 7 en sahidique*, Cologny-Genève, 1962.
DialSav	Létourneau, P., *Le dialogue du sauveur (NH III,5)* (Bibliothèque Copte de Nag Hammadi, section Textes 29), Québec/Louvain-Paris 2003.

References

Eph	Horner, G., *The Coptic Version of the New Testament in the Southern Dialect Otherwise Called Sahidic and Thebaic*, 1–7, Oxford, 1911–1924, vol. 5.
ExAn	Kulawik, C., *Die Erzählung über die Seele (Nag-Hammadi Codex II,6)* (Texte und Untersuchungen zur Geschichte der altchristlichen Literatur 155), Berlin 2006.
Gal	Horner, G., *The Coptic Version of the New Testament in the Southern Dialect Otherwise Called Sahidic and Thebaic*, 1–7, Oxford, 1911–1924, vol. 5.
Gen	Ciasca, A., *Sacrorum Bibliorum fragmenta copto-sahidica Musei Borgiani issu et sumptibus S. Congregationis de Propaganda Fide edita*, vol. 1, Roma, 1885; Maspero, G., *Fragments de la version thébaine de l'Ancien Testament* (Mémoires publiés par les membres de la mission archéologique française au Caire, 4/1), Paris, 1892; Wessely, C., *Griechische und koptische Texte theologischen Inhalts*, vol. 4 (Studien zur Palaeographie und Papyruskunde, 15), Leizig, 1914.
GosJud	Brankaer, J./Bethge, H.-G., *Codex Tchacos* (Texte und Untersuchungen zur Geschichte der altchristlichen Literatur 161), Berlin 2007.
GreatSeth	Painchaud, L., *Le deuxième traité du grand Seth (NH VII,2)* (Bibliothèque Copte de Nag Hammadi, section Textes 6), Québec 1982.
Heb	Horner, G., *The Coptic Version of the New Testament in the Southern Dialect Otherwise Called Sahidic and Thebaic*, 1–7, Oxford, 1911–1924, vol. 5.
HM	Till, W., *Koptische Heiligen- und Martyrerlegenden : Texte, Übersetzungen und Indices*, 1–2 (Orientalia christiana analecta 102, 108), Roma, 1935, 1936.
Jas	Horner, G., *The Coptic Version of the New Testament in the Southern Dialect Otherwise Called Sahidic and Thebaic*, 1–7, Oxford, 1911–1924, vol 7.
Jer	Feder, F., *Biblia Sahidica: Ieremias, Lamentationes (Threni), Epistula Ieremiae et Baruch* (Texte und Untersuchungen zur Geschichte der altchristliche Literatur, 147), Berlin-New York, 2002.
John	Horner, G., *The Coptic Version of the New Testament in the Southern Dialect Otherwise Called Sahidic and Thebaic*, 1–7, Oxford, 1911–1924, vol. 3.
1John	Horner, G., *The Coptic Version of the New Testament in the Southern Dialect Otherwise Called Sahidic and Thebaic*, 1–7, Oxford, 1911–1924, vol. 7.
3John	Horner, G., *The Coptic Version of the New Testament in the Southern Dialect Otherwise Called Sahidic and Thebaic*, 1–7, Oxford, 1911–1924, vol. 7.
Job	Ciasca, A., *Sacrorum Bibliorum fragmenta copto-sahidica Musei Borgiani issu et sumptibus S. Congregationis de Propaganda Fide edita*, vol. 2, Roma, 1889
Judg	Thompson, H., *A Coptic Palimpsest containing Joshua, Judges, Ruth, Judith, and Esther in the Sahidic Dialect*, London, 1911.
K	Unpublished Coptic text from the Wiener Papyrussammlung, taken from Till.
LetPetPhil	Bethge, H.-G., *Der Brief des Petrus an Philippus. Ein neutestamentliches Apokryphon* (Texte und Untersuchungen zur Geschichte der altchristlichen Literatur 141), Berlin 1997

LibThom	Schenke, H.-M., *Das Thomas-Buch (Nag-Hammadi-Codex II,7)* (Texte und Untersuchungen zur Geschichte der altchristlichen Literatur 138), Berlin 1989.
Luke	Horner, G., *The Coptic Version of the New Testament in the Southern Dialect Otherwise Called Sahidic and Thebaic*, 1–7, Oxford, 1911–1924, vol. 2.
Mark	Horner, G., *The Coptic Version of the New Testament in the Southern Dialect Otherwise Called Sahidic and Thebaic*, 1–7, Oxford, 1911–1924, vol. 1.
Morgan	Manuscript from the Pierpont Morgan Library (New York), taken from Layton.
Matt	Horner, G., *The Coptic Version of the New Testament in the Southern Dialect Otherwise Called Sahidic and Thebaic*, 1–7, Oxford, 1911–1924, vol. 1.
Mun	Munier, H., *Catalogue général des antiquités égyptiennes du musée du Caire, n° 9201–9304: manuscrits coptes*, Le Caire, 1916.
Num	Schleifer, J., *bruchstücke der Sahidischen Bibelübersetzung* (Sitzungsberichte der kaiserl. Akademie der Wissenschaften in Wien, philosophisch-historische Klasse, 170/1), Wien, 1909, 1911, 1912.
P	Paris, Bibliothèque Nationale, fonds copte (unpublished manuscripts).
Pach	Lefort, L.Th., *S. Pachomii vitae sahidice scriptae* (Corpus scriptorum Christianorum orientalium, 99), Paris, 1933.
ParSem	Roberge, M., *La paraphrase de Sem* (Bibliothèque Copte de Nag Hammadi, section Textes 25), Québec/Louvain-Paris 2000.
1Pet	Horner, G., *The Coptic Version of the New Testament in the Southern Dialect Otherwise Called Sahidic and Thebaic*, 1–7, Oxford, 1911–1924, vol. 7.
2Pet	Horner, G., *The Coptic Version of the New Testament in the Southern Dialect Otherwise Called Sahidic and Thebaic*, 1–7, Oxford, 1911–1924, vol. 7.
PCod	Crum, W.E., *Der Papyruscodex saec. VI–VII der Philippsbibliothek in Cheltenham* (Schriften der Wissenschaftlichen Gesellschaft in Straßburg, 18. Heft), Straßburg, 1915.
Phil	Horner, G., *The Coptic Version of the New Testament in the Southern Dialect Otherwise Called Sahidic and Thebaic*, 1–7, Oxford, 1911–1924, vol. 5.
ProtTrim	Poirier, P.-H., *La Pensée première à la triple forme (NH XIII,1)* (Bibliothèque Copte de Nag Hammadi, section Textes 32), Québec/Louvain-Paris 2006.
Prov	Worrell, W., *The Proverbs of Solomon in Sahidic Coptic according to the Chicago Manuscript* (University of Chicago, Oriental Institue Publications, 12), Chicago, 1931.
Ps	Budge, E.A.W., *The Earliest Known Coptic Psalter: The Text, in the Dialect of Upper Egypt, Edited from the Unique Papyrus Codex Oriental 5000 in the British Museum*, London, 1889; Worrell, W., *The Coptic Psalter in the Freer collection*, New York, 1916.
PS	Schmidt, C., *Pistis Sophia* (Coptica 2), Kobenhagen, 1925.
PSFA	Elanskaya, A.I., Coptic literary texts of the Pushkin State Fine Arts Museum in Moscow (Studia Aegyptiaca 13), Budapest 1991.

Rev	Horner, G., *The Coptic Version of the New Testament in the Southern Dialect Otherwise Called Sahidic and Thebaic*, 1–7, Oxford, 1911–1924, vol. 7.
Rom	Horner, G., *The Coptic Version of the New Testament in the Southern Dialect Otherwise Called Sahidic and Thebaic*, 1–7, Oxford, 1911–1924, vol. 4.
Rossi	Rossi, I., *I papiri copti del Museo egizio di Torino*, Torino, 1887–1892.
1Sam	Kuhn, K.H., *The Coptic (Sahidic) Version of Kingdoms I, II (Samuel I, II)* (Corpus scriptorum Christianorum orientalium, 313), Louvain, 1970.
Sextus	Poirier, P.-H., *Les sentences de Sextus (NH XII,1), Fragments (NH XII,3);* Painchaud, L., *Platon, Fragment de la République (NH VI,5)* (Bibliothèque Copte de Nag Hammadi, section Textes 11), Québec 1983.
ShIII	Leipoldt, J., *Sinuthii Archimandritae Vita et Opera Omnia* (Corpus scriptorum Christianorum orientalium, 42), Paris, 1908.
ShIV	Leipoldt, J., *Sinuthii Archimandritae Vita et Opera Omnia* (Corpus christianorum orientalium, 73), Louvain, 1954.
ShAmél	Amélineau, E., *Œuvres de Schenoudi*, 1–2, Paris, 1907, 1914.
ShChass	Chassinat, E., *Le quatrième livre des entretiens et épîtres de Shenouti* (Institut français d'archéologie orientale du Caire, Mémoires, 23), le Caire, 1911.
ShEnch	Shisha-Halévy, A., "Unpublished Shenoutiana in the Britisch Library", *Enchoria* 5, 1975, p. 149–185.
ShLefort	Lefort, L.Th., "Catéchèse christologique de Chenoute", *Zeitschrift für aegyptische Sprache und Altertumskunde*, 80, 1955, p. 40–45.
ShMiss	Amélineau, E., *Monuments pour servir à l'histoire de l'Egypte chrétienne aux ive et ve siècles* (Mission Archéologique Française au Caire, Mémoires, 4), Paris, 1888.
ShOr	Shisha-Halévy, A., "Two new Shenoute Texts from the British Library", *Orientalia* 44, 1975, p. 149–185.
ShRE	Guérin, H., "Sermons inédits de Senouti", dans *Revue Égyptologique* 10, 1902, p. 148–164.
Silv	Zandee, J., *The Teachings of Silvanus (Nag Hammadi Codex VII,4), Text, Translation, Commentary*, Leiden 1991.
Sir	Thompson, H., *The Coptic (Sahidic) Version of certain books of the Old Testament from a papyrus in the British Museum*, Oxford, 1908
Song	Thompson, H., *The Coptic (Sahidic) version of certain books of the Old Testament from a Papyrus in the British Museum*, London, 1908.
StelesSeth	Claude, P., *Les trois steles de Sèth* (Bibliothèque Copte de Nag Hammadi, section Textes 8), Québec 1983.
1Thess	Horner, G., *The Coptic Version of the New Testament in the Southern Dialect Otherwise Called Sahidic and Thebaic*, 1–7, Oxford, 1911–1924, vol. 5.
Till	Till, W.C., *Koptische Grammatik*, Leipzig, 1961^2.

References

1Tim	Horner, G., *The Coptic Version of the New Testament in the Southern Dialect Otherwise Called Sahidic and Thebaic*, 1–7, Oxford, 1911–1924, vol. 5.
2Tim	Horner, G., *The Coptic Version of the New Testament in the Southern Dialect Otherwise Called Sahidic and Thebaic*, 1–7, Oxford, 1911–1924, vol. 5.
Tob	Maspero, G., *Fragments de la version thébaine de l'Ancien Testament* (Mémoires publiés par les membres de la mission archéologique française au Caire, 4/1), Paris, 1892.
TT	Crum, W.E., *Theological Texts from Coptic Papyri* (Anecdota Oxoniensia), Oxford, 1913.
V.A.	Garitte, G., *S. Antonii vitae versio Sahidica* (Corpus scriptorum Christianorum orientalium, 117), Paris, 1949.
Wess	Wessely, C., *Griechische und Koptische Texte theologischen Inhalts*, 1–5 (Studien zur Paläographie und Papyruskunde 9, 11, 12, 15, 18), 1909–1917.
Z	Zoega, G., *Catalogus codicum copticorum manu scriptorum qui in Museo Borgiano Velitris adservantur : Avec une introduction historique et des notes bibliographiques par Joseph-Marie Sauget*, Hildesheim, 1973 (Roma, 1810).
Za	Maspero, G., *Fragments de la version thébaine de l'Ancien Testament* (Mémoires publiés par les membres de la mission archéologique française au Caire, 4/1), Paris, 1892.

Part I: Elements

Pronouns and determiners

A. The personal pronoun

The independent personal pronoun

001. The independent personal pronouns are only used in apposition to make the subject explicit or to emphasize it (cf. 202). They can also express the predicate (cf. 208).

002. The independent personal pronoun can in some cases be used instead of the suffixed pronoun. This can imply a shift in meaning. E.g. ⲚⲤⲀ ⲚⲦⲞϤ (*except for him*) and ⲚⲤⲰ≠ϥ (*after him*).

003. These are the full forms of the independent personal pronoun:

	sg.	pl.
1	ⲀⲚⲞⲔ	ⲀⲚⲞⲚ
2 m.	ⲚⲦⲞⲔ	ⲚⲦⲰⲦⲚ
2 f.	ⲚⲦⲞ	
3 m.	ⲚⲦⲞϤ	ⲚⲦⲞⲞⲨ
3 f.	ⲚⲦⲞⲤ	

004. The unstressed (reduced) form of the independent personal pronoun is used as the prefixed subject of the nominal sentence (cf. 191, 200).

	sg.	pl.
1	ⲀⲚⲄ	ⲀⲚ(Ⲛ)
2 m.	ⲚⲦⲔ	ⲚⲦⲈⲦⲚ
2 f.	ⲚⲦⲈ	
3 m.	ⲚⲦϤ	(ⲚⲦⲞⲞⲨ)
3 f.	(ⲚⲦⲞⲤ)	

The prefixed personal pronoun

005. These personal pronouns are used for the subject of the durative sentence (cf. 224).

	sg.	pl.
1	ϯ	ⲦⲚ
2 m.	Ⲕ (Ⲅ)	ⲦⲈⲦⲚ
2 f.	ⲦⲈ (Ⲧⲣ)	
3 m.	ϥ	ⲤⲈ
3 f.	Ⲥ	

006. The Ⲕ of the 2nd pers. sg. is often assimilated to Ⲅ after the Ⲛ of negation.

The personal suffixes

007. The pronominal suffixes can be attached to:
- prepositions in the prepersonal state (cf. 093);
- certain common nouns (cf. 048);
- transitive infinitives (cf. 119);
- the possessive pronoun and article (cf. 020, 021);
- the conjugation bases of the non-durative sentence (cf. 308);
- the conjugation bases of the four converters (cf. 145–148).

1 sg.	⸗I	after a simple vowel
	⸗T	after a doubled consonant (after T: ⲡⲁⲧ⸗T > ⲡⲁⲧ)
2 sg. m.	⸗K	(after N often Г)
2 sg. f.	Ø	after a simple vowel
	⸗E	after a consonant
	⸗TE	after a doubled vowel
3 sg. m.	⸗ϥ	
3 sg. f.	⸗C	
1 pl.	⸗N	
2 pl.	⸗TN̄	
	⸗THYTN̄	
3 pl.	⸗OY	

008. For the 2nd pers. pl. a short vowel preceding the suffix ⸗TN̄ becomes long. ⲉ-, ⲉⲣⲟ⸗ (prep. *to*) > ⲉⲣⲱ⸗ⲧⲛ̄

009. The suffix THYTN̄ for the 2nd pers. pl. is usually used after T. It can express a reflexive meaning (ϨⲰⲦⲦⲎⲨⲦⲚ̄, *you yourselves*). Normally THYTN̄ is treated as a nomen after the prenominal status.

010. The suffix for the 3rd pers. pl. ⸗OY sis written ⸗Y after ⲁ, ⲉ, and ⲏ.

011. The suffix ⸗ⲤⲞⲨ, ⸗ⲤⲈ for the 3rd pers. pl. is used with certain verbs (ⲬⲞⲞⲨ, *to send*; ⲦⲚ̄ⲚⲞⲞⲨ, *to send*; ⲦⲞⲞⲨ, *to buy*) and with the imperatives ⲀⲠⲒ⸗, *do!*, and ⲀⲚⲒ⸗, *bring!* (cf. 136). It is also used for the object of ⲞⲨⲚ̄Ⲧⲁ⸗/ⲘⲚ̄Ⲧ⸗ (cf. 157).

B. Demonstrative pronouns and articles

The demonstrative pronoun

012. There are two sets of demonstrative pronouns in Coptic. Each set has three forms:
- masculine starting with ⲡ;
- feminine starting with ⲧ;
- plural (both masculine and feminine) starting with ⲛ.

There is a whole set of determiners following this pattern (cf. 018–021).

Pronouns and determiners

013. The independent demonstrative pronouns are:
- ⲠⲀⲒ, ⲦⲀⲒ, ⲚⲀⲒ (*this, these*)
- ⲠⲎ, ⲦⲎ, ⲚⲎ for a more remote person or object (*that, those*)

014. There is also an unstressed form (without emphasis) of this pronoun:
ⲠⲈ, ⲦⲈ, ⲚⲈ
This form of the demonstrative pronoun is used for the 3rd pers. subject of the nominal sentence (cf. 191, 206).

The demonstrative article

015. The demonstrative article is always placed before a (common) noun. Its forms are:
- ⲠⲈⲒ, ⲦⲈⲒ, ⲚⲈⲒ (*this, these*)
- ⲠⲒ, ϯ, ⲚⲒ (*that, those*)

016. The unstressed form of the demonstrative article is Ⲡ/ⲠⲈ Ⲧ/ⲦⲈ Ⲛ/ⲚⲈ. This form is actually the definite article (cf. 054).

Other demonstrative elements

017. The relative sentence ⲈⲦⲘ̄ⲘⲀⲨ (*that is there*) is used to refer to a more distant person or thing. It can be preceded by the article.

C. Possessive pronouns and articles

The possessive pronoun

018. The possessive pronoun is always followed by the possessor. This can be a noun (with article) or a personal pronoun (suffixed).

019. In the pronominal state the possessive pronoun has the form of the possessive prefix:
ⲠⲀ-, ⲦⲀ-, ⲚⲀ-.
The possessive pronoun is followed by a noun with article (article phrase). This form is used to express filiation and is often an element of proper nouns.
ⲠⲀ-Ⲡ.ⲢⲞ, *doorkeeper (the one of the door)*
ⲠⲀ-Ⲧ.ϢⲈⲖⲈⲈⲦ, *bridegroom (the one of the bride)*
ⲠⲀ-ⲘⲒⲚ, *Pamin (the one of Min)*
ⲚⲀ-ⲚⲈⲤⲦⲞⲢⲒⲞⲤ, *the doctrines of Nestorius*.

020. The prepersonal state of the possessive pronoun is:
ⲠⲰ⸗, ⲦⲰ⸗, ⲚⲞⲨ⸗.
The pronominal suffix refers to the possessor (cf. 007).
ⲚⲞⲨ⸗Ⲓ ⲐⲎⲢ⸗ⲞⲨ ⲚⲞⲨ⸗Ⲕ ⲚⲈ (John 17:10). *Everything that is mine is yours.*

The possessive article

021. The possessive article expresses the possessor of the word it determines. It consists basically of the article ⲡⲉ⸗, ⲧⲉ⸗, ⲛⲉ⸗ with the personal suffixes (cf. 007).

	m.	f.	pl.
1 sg.	ⲡⲁ	ⲧⲁ	ⲛⲁ
2 sg. m.	ⲡⲉ⸗ⲕ	ⲧⲉ⸗ⲕ	ⲛⲉ⸗ⲕ
2 sg. f.	ⲡⲟⲩ	ⲧⲟⲩ	ⲛⲟⲩ
3 sg. m.	ⲡⲉ⸗ϥ	ⲧⲉ⸗ϥ	ⲛⲉ⸗ϥ
3 sg. f.	ⲡⲉ⸗ⲥ	ⲧⲉ⸗ⲥ	ⲛⲉ⸗ⲥ
1 pl.	ⲡⲉ⸗ⲛ	ⲧⲉ⸗ⲛ	ⲛⲉ⸗ⲛ
2 pl.	ⲡⲉ⸗ⲧⲛ̄	ⲧⲉ⸗ⲧⲛ̄	ⲛⲉ⸗ⲧⲛ̄
3 pl.	ⲡⲉ⸗ⲩ	ⲧⲉ⸗ⲩ	ⲛⲉ⸗ⲩ

022. At first sight there might be some confusion between the possessive pronoun in the pronominal state and the possessive article of the 1st pers. sg. The possessive pronoun is always followed by an article.

ⲡⲁ-ⲡ.ⲉⲓⲱⲧ, *the one belonging to the Father (the one of the father)*
ⲡⲁ.ⲉⲓⲱⲧ, *my father*

D. Interrogative and indefinite elements

Interrogative elements

023. These are some of the most common interrogative pronouns and modifiers (cf. 401, 402):
ⲛⲓⲙ, *who?*
ⲟⲩ, *what?*
ⲁϣ, *which? what?*
ⲁϩⲣⲟ⸗, *what about...? why?* (ⲁϩⲣⲟ⸗ⲕ, *What about you?*)

Indefinite elements

024. The following are the most common indefinite pronouns and modifiers:
ⲕⲉ (ϭⲉ) (m.), ⲕⲉⲧⲉ (f.), ⲕⲟⲟⲩⲉ (pl.), *other* (cf. 075)
...ⲛⲓⲙ, *every* ... (cf. 078)
ⲗⲁⲁⲩ, *someone, something*; with negation *nobody, nothing*
ⲟⲩⲟⲛ, *someone, something*
ⲟⲩⲁ/ⲟⲩⲉⲓ (cf. 85), *someone*; ⲟⲩⲁ ⲟⲩⲁ, *each*
ϩⲟⲉⲓⲛⲉ, *some*

Nouns

025. The noun is a lexeme (LAYTON) or semanteme (VERGOTE), that is, an element of the vocabulary with specific meaning. There are but two classes of semantemes in Coptic: the noun and the verb. Though both classes are distinct, there are some interesting correspondences between them. Just like the verb some nouns also exist in a prenominal and/or a prepersonal state. Just like the object of a verb the genitive can be directly connected or through the preposition ⲛ̄-. On top of that, most infinitives can also function as a noun.

026. Nouns are lexemes or semantemes that can be actualized in two ways:
– independently (with an article or other determining element). The noun then refers to a thought object (to be distinguished from a process, action, or relation).
– as attribute.

A. Substantives and adjectives

027. There are only a small amount of 'real' adjectives in Coptic. One could therefore refer to gendered nouns and non–gendered nouns (LAYTON) instead of substantives and adjectives. In fact many 'substantives' can also function as 'adjectives'.
ⲤϨⲒⲘⲈ (f.), *woman, wife*; ⲈⲒⲰⲦ (m.), *father*; ⲂⲰⲰⲚ, *bad, wicked*; ⲚⲞϬ, *big*.

028. One should distinguish between a denotative function and a descriptive function of a noun.
The denotative function can only be fulfilled by gendered nouns, proper nouns and possessives. They denote one or more entities as particular instances of a class or a unique individual.
The descriptive function can be fulfilled by gendered nouns and non–gendered nouns. In this function they describe an entity referring to one or more of its characteristics.

029. Only gendered nouns can fulfil both functions. Normally however, they have a denotative function. When these nouns have a descriptive function the article does not necessarily correspond with the grammatical gender of the noun. E.g. ⲘⲈ (*truth*) is a feminine noun, but one can find the form Ⲡ.ⲘⲈ, which translates the Greek adjective ὁ ἀλητινός, *the truthful*.

030. As for the Greek words, the substantives are gendered nouns, the adjectives non–gendered.

031. The neuter form of the Greek adjectives is however used to refer to 'inanimates' or things, the masculine form (or the feminine) is used with regard to persons.
ⲆⲀⲒⲘⲞⲚⲒⲞⲚ (m.), *demon*; ϨⲈⲖⲠⲒⲤ (f.), *hope* (=ἔλπις); ⲠⲒⲤⲦⲞⲤ, *faithful*

ⲛ̄.ⲉⲡⲓⲑⲩⲙⲓⲁ ⲛ̄-ⲥⲁⲣⲕⲓⲕⲟⲛ (1Pet 2:11), *carnal desires.*
ⲟⲩ.ⲯⲩⲭⲏ ⲙ̄-ⲡⲓⲥⲧⲏ ⲛ̄-ⲁⲅⲁⲑⲏ (Sextus 30:19f) *a faithful good soul*

Comparative and superlative

032. There are no distinct forms for the comparative and the superlative in Coptic. They can mostly be inferred from the context.
The second member of the comparison can be introduced by the prepositions ⲉ-, ⲉⲣⲟ⸗ and ⲡⲁⲣⲁ-, ⲡⲁⲣⲁⲣⲟ⸗.

033. The preposition ⲉ- can be emphasized by the word ϩⲟⲩⲟ (*more*). We find the following combinations: ⲛ̄-ϩⲟⲩⲟ ⲉ-, ⲛ̄-ϩⲟⲩⲉ, ⲉ-ϩⲟⲩⲟ ⲉ-, or ⲉ-ϩⲟⲩⲉ.

ⲁϣ ⲡⲉ ⲡ.ⲛⲟϭ (Matt 23:17). *Which one is the biggest?*
ⲡ.ⲕⲟⲩⲓ ⲉⲣⲟ⸗ϥ (Luke 7:28). *The one who is smaller than him.*
ϥ.ϭⲙ̄ϭⲟⲙ ⲛ̄-ϩⲟⲩⲉ ⲉⲣⲟ⸗ⲛ (BHom 54:11). *He is stronger than us.*

B. Gender and number

034. Gender and number of a noun can normally be inferred from the article or some other determiner.

Gender

035. There are two genders in Coptic: masculine and feminine.

036. Masculine Coptic nouns often end on a consonant or a short vowel, feminine nouns on ⲉ or a long vowel.

037. Greek masculine and feminine nouns keep their gender in Coptic. Greek neuter substantives are treated as masculine.
ⲡ⸥ⲥⲱⲙⲁ (m.), *the body* (the Greek σῶμα is neuter).

038. The infinitive as a verbal noun is masculine.
ⲡⲉ⸗ϥ.ϫⲡⲟ, *his birth.*

039. A certain number of Coptic nouns have masculine as well as feminine forms:

ⲥⲟⲛ	brother	ⲥⲱⲛⲉ	sister
ϣⲏⲣⲉ	son	ϣⲉⲉⲣⲉ	daughter
ϩⲟϥ	snake	ϩⲱϥ	snake
ⲥⲁⲃⲉ	wise man	ⲥⲁⲃⲏ	wise woman
ϩⲗ̄ⲗⲟ	old man	ϩⲗ̄ⲗⲱ	old woman
ⲛⲟⲩⲧⲉ	god	ⲛ̄ⲧⲱⲣⲉ	goddess

040. A noun is only gendered when it has a denotative function! (cf. 028)

Number

041. In most cases the plural of a noun is only indicated by the article or some other determiner.

042. There are, however, a number of nouns that have a separate form for the plural. In some cases this plural form exists as an alternative to the unchanged form and can express a specific nuance.

043. This list contains some of the most frequent plural forms:

ⲡⲉ	ⲡⲏⲩⲉ	heaven
ⲁⲡⲉ	ⲁⲡⲏⲩⲉ	head
ⲣ̄ⲡⲉ	ⲣ̄ⲡⲏⲩⲉ	temple
ϣⲏⲣⲉ	ϣⲣⲏⲩ	child
	(often ⲛ̄.ϣⲏⲣⲉ)	
ⲣⲟⲙⲡⲉ	ⲣ̄ⲙ̄ⲡⲟⲟⲩⲉ	year
ϩⲱⲃ	ϩⲃⲏⲩⲉ	work, thing
ⲉⲓⲱⲧ	ⲉⲓⲟⲧⲉ	father
ⲥⲟⲛ	ⲥⲛⲏⲩ	brother
ⲥϩⲓⲙⲉ	ϩⲓⲟⲙⲉ	woman, wife

044. Most of the Greek nouns do not have a special plural form. The frequent plural ending –ⲟⲟⲩⲉ can however also be used for Greek words.
ⲯⲩⲭⲟⲟⲩⲉ, *souls*
ⲉⲡⲓⲥⲧⲟⲗⲟⲟⲩⲉ, *letters*

045. The dual form as such does no longer exist in Coptic. There are however some traces of the use of the dualis. Some words, expressing a duality, can be treated as a singular or as a plural form.

ⲥⲡⲟⲧⲟⲩ	lips
ⲡⲁϩⲟⲩ	buttocks
ⲟⲩⲉⲣⲏⲧⲉ	feet
ϣⲏⲧ	two hundred
	(dualis of ϣⲉ)

C. Bound state

046. There are three bound states in Coptic: the absolute state, the prenominal state and the prepersonal state. A noun can have one or more of these forms, which are listed under the absolute state in a dictionary.
The absolute state is the noun in itself, independently.
A noun in the prenominal state is followed by another noun that determines it. This is the genitive, expressing the possessor of the first noun. The prenominal state is indicated by the marker -.

A noun in the prepersonal state has a personal pronoun immediately suffixed to it. This suffix often refers to the possessor. The prepersonal liaison is represented by the marker ⸗.

047. Most of the Coptic nouns only exist in the absolute state

048. A limited number of Coptic nouns have a prenominal and/or prepersonal state. They only occur in combination with a determiner, that is another noun, or, more often, the personal pronoun suffix. This category of nouns can be referred to as 'possessed nouns' (LAYTON 138–140). The possessor and the possessed are linked by an inherent, unalienable possession (SHISHA–HALEVY 1.1.1).

This construction is however often replaced by the indirect genitive construction with the preposition ⲛ- (cf. 175–178).

Many of these words are used in the construction of complex prepositions (cf. 100).

absolute	prenominal	prepersonal	translation
		ⲁⲛⲁ⸗	will
		ⲁⲡⲏⲭ(ⲛ̄)⸗	end
ⲃⲟⲗ	ⲃⲗ̄-, ⲃⲁⲛ̄-	ⲃⲗ̄ⲗⲁ⸗	outside
ⲉⲓⲁ	(ⲉⲓⲉⲣ-, ⲉⲓⲁⲛ̄-)	ⲉⲓⲁⲧ⸗	eye
		ⲕⲟⲩⲛ(ⲧ)⸗, ⲕⲟⲩⲟⲩⲛ⸗	bosom
		ⲗⲓⲕⲧ⸗	cover
ⲣⲟ	ⲣⲛ̄-	ⲣⲱ⸗	mouth
ⲣⲁⲛ	ⲣⲉⲛ-	ⲣⲛ̄ⲧ⸗	name
		ⲣⲁⲧ⸗	foot
ⲥⲟⲩⲉⲛ		ⲥⲟⲩⲛ̄ⲧ⸗	worth
ⲧⲱⲣⲉ	ⲧⲛ̄-, ⲧⲉ-	ⲧⲟⲟⲧ⸗	hand
	ⲧⲟⲩⲛ̄-	ⲧⲟⲩⲱ⸗	breast, womb
ϣⲁ		ϣⲁⲛⲧ⸗	nose
ϩⲏ		ϩⲏⲧ⸗	foreside
ϩⲏ		ϩⲏⲧ⸗	belly
ϩⲟ	ϩⲣ̄ⲛ̄-, ϩⲛ̄-	ϩⲣⲁ⸗	face
ϩⲣⲟⲟⲩ	ϩⲣⲟⲩⲛ̄-	ϩⲣⲁ⸗	voice
ϩⲏⲧ	(ϩ)ⲧⲉ-, (ϩ)ⲧⲛ̄-	ϩⲏⲧ⸗	heart
		ϩⲧⲏ⸗	peak, spike
	ϫⲛ̄-	ϫⲱ⸗	head

D. Composite nouns

049. There are many composite nouns that consist of a noun in the prenominal state followed by a (non–gendered) noun. Here are some of the more frequent examples.

> ⲘⲚⲦ- (used to build abstract nouns):
> ⲘⲚⲦϨⲖⲞ, *(old) age*; ⲘⲚⲦϨⲈⲂⲢⲀⲒⲞⲤ, *Hebrew*
> ⲘⲚⲦϢⲀ ⲈⲚⲈϨ, *eternity*
> ⲘⲚⲦⲢ̄ⲢⲞ, *rule, kingdom*
>
> ⲠⲘⲚ- (ⲢⲰⲘⲈ Ⲛ̄-), *man of*:
> ⲠⲘⲚ̄ⲔⲎⲘⲈ, *Egyptian*
> ⲠⲘ̄ⲢⲀⲔⲞⲦⲈ, *man from Alexandria*
> ⲠⲘⲚ̄ⲚⲞⲨⲦⲈ, *god–loving, pious*
>
> ϢⲂⲢ̄- (ϢⲂⲎⲢ, *friend, companion*):
> ϢⲂⲢ̄Ⲙ̄ϨⲀⲖ, *fellow slave* (σύνδουλος)
> ϢⲂⲢ̄ⲘⲀⲐⲎⲦⲎⲤ, *classmate*

ⲈⲒⲈⲠ- (ⲈⲒⲞⲠⲈ, *work*) (can also be linked to a noun with the preposition Ⲛ̄-) :
ⲈⲒⲈⲠϢⲈ, *wooden, timber*; ⲈⲒⲈⲠϢⲰⲦ, *commerce, merchandise*

ⲈⲒⲈϨ- (ⲈⲒⲰϨⲈ, *field*) :
ⲈⲒⲈϨⲈⲖⲞⲞⲖⲈ, *vineyard*; ⲈⲒⲈϨϢⲎⲚ, *orchard*

ⲢⲀ- (is used in words expressing a place or substantives with general meaning):
ⲢⲀⲦⲎⲨ, *air, heaven*; ⲢⲀ, *state, condition*

ⲤⲦ- (ⲤⲦⲞⲒ, *odour*):
ⲤⲦⲚⲞⲨϤⲈ, *perfume*; ⲤⲦⲂⲰⲰⲚ, *bad smell, stench*

ϢⲞⲨ- (ϢⲀⲨ, *useful, valuable*):
ϢⲞⲨⲘⲈⲢⲒⲦϤ, *amiable*; Ⲡ.ϢⲞⲨⲦⲢⲈϤⲘⲞⲨ, *he who deserves to die*

ϢⲚ̄- (ϢⲎⲢⲈ, *child*) sometimes ϢⲢ̄- :
ϢⲚ̄ⲤⲞⲚ, *son of a brother (nephew)*; ϢⲢ̄ⲂⲰⲰⲚ, *bad son*

ϢⲤ̄Ⲛ- (ⲤⲀϢ, *blow, strike, wound*) sometimes ⲤϢ- :
ϢⲤ̄ⲚⲀⲀⲤ, *punch*; ϢⲤ̄ⲚⲖⲞⲄⲬⲎ, *lance stab*

ϨⲀⲘ-, *worker*:
ϨⲀⲘϢⲈ, *carpenter*; ϨⲀⲘⲚⲞⲨⲂ, *goldsmith*

ⲀⲚ-, *chief*:
ⲀⲚⲬⲰⲬ, *chief, captain*

050. Other words are composed with the preposition Ⲛ̄-.

> ⲂⲰ, *tree*:
> ⲂⲰ Ⲛ̄-ⲔⲚ̄ⲦⲈ, *fig–tree*; ⲂⲰ Ⲛ̄-ⲈⲖⲞⲞⲖⲈ, *vine*

> ⲙⲁ, *place*:
> ⲙⲁ ⲙ̄-ⲡⲱⲧ, *refuge*; ⲙⲁ ⲛ̄-ⲉⲗⲟⲟⲗⲉ, *vineyard*

ⲙⲁⲥ, *small, little*:
ⲙⲁⲥ ⲙ̄-ⲙⲟⲩⲓ, *lion cub*

ⲥⲁ, *man of*:
ⲥⲁ ⲛ̄-ⲛⲉϩ, *oil merchant*; ⲥⲁ ⲛ̄-ϫⲓ-ϭⲟⲗ, *liar*

051. Still other words are composed with a prefix that is not a noun on itself.

> ⲁⲧ (negation), *un–, without*:
> ⲁⲑⲏⲧ (ⲁⲧ-ϩⲏⲧ), *foolish, unwise*
> ⲁⲧⲛⲁⲩ ⲉⲣⲟ⸗ϥ, *invisible* (m.)
>
> ϭⲓⲛ- (+ infinitive; forms feminine nouns):
> ϭⲓⲛϣⲁϫⲉ, *word, conversation, story*
> ϭⲓⲛϣⲱⲛⲉ, *illness*
>
> ⲣⲉϥ- (+ infinitive), *man who…*:
> ⲣⲉϥϯ-ϩⲁⲡ, *judge*; ⲣⲉϥⲣ̄-ⲛⲟⲃⲉ, *sinner*
> ⲣⲉϥϫⲓ-ϭⲟⲗ, *liar*

052. **The construct participle** is a descriptive noun ('adjective') that expresses a generic verbal action. It is used to build non–gendered nouns. It is always applied to the category of animates. Usually, it is linked with a noun without article (undetermined) (cf. 069).

Here are some of the most common examples (the infinitive is given in brackets)

> ⲙⲁⲓ- (ⲙⲉ, *to love*):
> ⲙⲁⲓⲛⲟⲩⲧⲉ, *pious (loving God)*
>
> ϫⲁⲥⲓ- (ϫⲓⲥⲉ, *to elevate*):
> ϫⲁⲥⲓ ϩⲏⲧ, *arrogant (high hearted)*

ⲙⲁⲥⲧ- (ⲙⲟⲥⲧⲉ, *to hate*):
ⲙⲁⲥⲧⲛⲟⲩⲧⲉ, *impious (hating God)*

ⲟⲩⲁⲙ- (ⲟⲩⲱⲙ, *to eat*):
ⲟⲩⲁⲙⲣⲱⲙⲉ, *cannibal (eating men)*

ϥⲁⲓ- (ϥⲓ, *to carry*):
ϥⲁⲓⲛⲁϩⲃ, *beast of burden (carrying a yoke)*

ϩⲁⲗϭ- (ϩⲗⲟϭ, *to be sweet*):
ϩⲁⲗϭϣⲁϫⲉ, *eloquent (of sweet words)*

053. The construction with invariable ⲡⲉⲧ- (substantivated relative sentence, cf. 466) is another way to build nouns.
ⲡ.ⲉⲧ.ⲛⲁⲛⲟⲩ⸗ϥ, *the good (that, which is good)*

E. Determiners

The definite article

054. The definite article is the unstressed form of the demonstrative pronoun (cf. 016).

 m. ⲡ (ⲡⲉ)
 f. ⲧ (ⲧⲉ)
 pl. ⲛ (ⲛⲉ)

055. One should pay attention to some particularities of Coptic orthography:

ⲡ+ⲋ = ⲫ
ⲧ+ⲋ = ⲑ
ⲧ+ⲓ = ϯ

Assimilation: ⲛ becomes ⲙ when followed by ⲡ/ⲃ/ⲯ/ⲙ.
Before ⲃ, ⲗ and ⲣ, the definite article can be completely assimilitated to ⲃ, ⲗ or ⲣ.

056. The longer forms ⲡⲉ-/ⲧⲉ-/ⲛⲉ- are used when the following noun begins with two consonants. ⲡⲉ.ϩⲧⲟ, *the horse*.
ⲟⲩ and ⲓ (ⲉⲓ) are considered as consonants: ⲡⲉ-ⲟⲩ > ⲡⲉⲩ.
ⲑ, ⲫ, ⲭ, ⲯ, ϩⲣ are considered as two consonants. ⲛⲉ.ⲑⲩⲥⲓⲁ, *the offerings*
ϭ, ϫ are each considered as one consonant.
If one of the initial consonants is a sonant, both ⲡ and ⲡⲉ are possible.
ⲡ.ⲣ̄ⲡⲉ/ⲡⲉ.ⲣ̄ⲡⲉ *the temple*
ⲣ̄ⲣⲟ (*king*) and ϩⲗ̄ⲗⲟ (*old man*) always have ⲡ.
Words composed with ⲙⲛ̄ⲧ and ⲣⲙ̄ (cf. 049) always have ⲡ.

057. The longer forms are also used with a number of words expressing time:
ⲡⲉ.ⲟⲩⲟⲉⲓϣ, *the time*; ⲧⲉ.ⲣⲟⲙⲡⲉ, *the year*; ⲡⲉ.ϩⲟⲟⲩ, *the day*; ⲧⲉ.ⲩϣⲏ, *the night*; ⲧⲉ.ⲩⲛⲟⲩ, *the hour*.

058. Exception: ⲡ.ⲛⲁⲩ, *the time*

The use of the definite article

059. The definite article is used to determine gender and number of nouns or nominal expressions.
ⲫⲱⲃ (ⲡ.ϩⲱⲃ), *the thing, the work*
ⲧ.ⲙⲉ, *the truth*
ⲡ.ⲡⲉⲧ.ⲟⲩⲁⲁⲃ, *the saint (the one who is saint)*

060. The definite article is used with certain proper nouns when these are familiar to the interlocutor.
ⲧ.ⲥⲁⲙⲁⲣⲓⲁ, *Samaria*

061. The definite article is used before the names of gods.
ⲡ.ⲛⲟⲩⲧⲉ, *God*
ⲡ.ⲁⲡⲟⲗⲗⲱⲛ, *Apollo*

062. The definite article is also used with a vocative.
ⲧⲉ.ⲥϩⲓⲙⲉ (John 2:4), *Wife!*

The indefinite article

063. The indefinite article is derived from some indefinite pronouns.
sg. ⲟⲩ (< ⲟⲩⲁ, *one*) (cf. 085)
pl. ϩⲉⲛ (< ϩⲟⲉⲓⲛⲉ, *some*) (cf. 024)

064. Please pay attention to Coptic orthography:
ⲉ/ⲁ + ⲟⲩ > ⲉⲩ/ⲁⲩ

The use of the indefinite article

065. The indefinite article is used with abstract nouns:
ⲟⲩ.ⲕⲁⲕⲉ, *darkness*
ⲟⲩ.ⲙⲛⲧⲁⲧⲧⲁⲕⲟ, *indestructibility*

066. It is often used with material nouns:
ⲟⲩ.ⲙⲟⲟⲩ, *water*

067. It is also used in adverbial expressions introduced by the preposition ϩⲛ̄- (cf. 098):
ϩⲛ̄-ⲟⲩ.ⲙⲉ, *truly*.

068. The indefinite article is also used with the predicate of the nominal sentence (cf. 192):
ⲁⲛⲅ ⲟⲩ.ⲡⲣⲟⲫⲏⲧⲏⲥ, *I am a prophet(ess)*

Zero–determiner, the absence of an article

069. There is no article used before the second term in composites (prenominal state of a verb or noun followed by an undetermined noun or construct participle [cf. 052]). In some cases also after the preposition ⲛ̄–:
ⲡ.ⲣⲉϥ.ϫⲓ-ϣⲟϫⲛⲉ, *adviser*

070. The negated term in negative sentences has no article. This is especially the case of non-existence or deprivation.
ϩⲉⲛ.ⲡⲏⲅⲏ... ⲉⲙⲛ̄-ⲙⲟⲟⲩ ⲛ̄ϩⲏⲧ⸗ⲟⲩ (2Pet 2:17), *springs without water*
ⲛ̄ⲅ-ⲧⲙ̄.ϫⲓⲧ⸗ⲛ̄ ⲉϩⲟⲩⲛ ⲉ-ⲡⲉⲓⲣⲁⲥⲙⲟⲥ (Matt 6:13). *And lead us not in temptation.*
ⲙⲉⲣⲉ.ⲣⲉϥϫⲓⲟⲩⲉ ϩⲱⲛ ⲉⲣⲟ⸗ϥ (Luke 12:33). *No thief came close to him.*

071. Undetermined elements in enumerations have no article:
ⲉⲓⲧⲉ ⲕⲟⲩⲓ ⲉⲓⲧⲉ ⲛⲟϭ (HM I 159:9), *either small or big*.

072. After certain prepositions, followed by undetermined elements, there is no article:
ϣⲁ-ⲉⲛⲉϩ, *forever, until eternity*

073. The predicate, after the preposition of identity ⲛ- has no article:
ⲁⲁ⸗ⲕ ⲛ̄-ⲣⲙⲙⲁⲟ (ShChass 85:34). *Make yourself rich.*
ⲧⲁⲁ⸗ⲩ ⲙ̄-ⲙⲛ̄ⲧⲛⲁ (Luke 12:33). *Give them as alms.*

074. After the preposition ϩⲱⲥ (*like, just as*), there is no article:
ϩⲱⲥ ⲟⲓⲕⲟⲛⲟⲙⲟⲥ (HM II 11:22), *as manager*.

Other determiners

075. ⲕⲉ, *other*
pl. ϩⲉⲛ.ⲕⲉ
ⲡ.ⲕⲉ, *the other*
ⲕⲉ can also mean *also, too* or *more*. It can also be used in combination with numerals (cf. 086).
ⲕⲉ.ϫⲱⲱⲙⲉ, *another book*
ⲡ.ⲕⲉ.ⲟⲩⲁ, *the other (one)*
ⲛⲉⲩ.ⲕⲉ.ⲥⲁⲣⲝ, *their flesh too*

076. The possessive article (cf. 015)

077. The demonstrative article (cf. 021)

078. …ⲚⲒⲘ: *every*
ⲞⲨⲞⲚ ⲚⲒⲘ, *everyone*
ϨⲰⲂ ⲚⲒⲘ, *everything*

079. The suffixed personal pronoun (cf. 007).

Numerals

A. Cardinal numbers

080. Just like in Greek, the letters are also used with numeric value. They have a supralinear stroke when used as numbers. For the number six, the Greek sign stigma (ϛ) is used.

081. The numbers from 1 to 9 and 10, 20, and 30 have distinct forms for the feminine and the masculine.

082. Some numbers have a secondary form (VERGOTE: état construit), which is a kind of prenominal form used in composed numbers.

083. The numbers 1–9 have a special form, which is used in combination with decades. It is immediately attached to the preceeding decades. If the decade has a secondary form, this is used in the composite number.

084. The multiples of 100 and 1000 are written with the secondary form of the cipher followed by ϣⲉ/ϣⲟ, or with the absolute form of the cipher followed by the preposition ⲛ̄- and ϣⲉ/ϣⲟ.

085. Table:

		m	f.	secondary form	with decades
1	ⲁ̄	ⲟⲩⲁ	ⲟⲩⲉⲓ	ⲟⲩ-	ⲟⲩⲉ (m)/ⲟⲩⲉⲓ (f.)
2	ⲃ̄	ⲥⲛⲁⲩ	ⲥⲛ̄ⲧⲉ		ⲥⲛⲟⲟⲩⲥ (m.)/ ⲥⲛⲟⲟⲩⲥⲉ (f.)
3	ⲅ̄	ϣⲟⲙⲛ̄ⲧ	ϣⲟⲙⲧⲉ	ϣⲙ̄ⲧ-, ϣⲙⲛ̄ⲧ-	ϣⲟⲙⲧⲉ
4	ⲇ̄	ϥⲧⲟⲟⲩ	ϥⲧⲟ(ⲉ)	ϥⲧⲟⲩ-, ϥⲧⲉⲩ-	ⲁϥⲧⲉ
5	ⲉ̄	ϯⲟⲩ	ϯ(ⲉ)		ⲧⲏ
6	ϛ̄	ⲥⲟⲟⲩ	ⲥⲟ(ⲉ)	ⲥⲉⲩ-	ⲁⲥⲉ
7	ⲍ̄	ⲥⲁϣϥ̄	ⲥⲁϣϥⲉ		ⲥⲁϣϥ(ⲉ)
8	ⲏ̄	ϣⲙⲟⲩⲛ	ϣⲙⲟⲩⲛⲉ		ϣⲙⲏⲛⲉ
9	ⲑ̄	ⲯⲓⲥ/ⲯⲓⲧ	ⲯⲓⲧⲉ/ⲯⲓⲥⲉ		
10	ⲓ̄	ⲙⲏⲧ	ⲙⲏⲧⲉ	ⲙⲛ̄ⲧ-	
20	ⲕ̄	ϫⲟⲩⲱⲧ	ϫⲟⲩⲱⲧⲉ	ϫⲟⲩⲧ-	
30	ⲗ̄	ⲙⲁⲁⲃ	ⲙⲁⲁⲃⲉ	ⲙⲁⲃ-	
40	ⲙ̄		ϩⲙⲉ	ϩⲙⲉ-, ϩⲙⲉⲧ-	
50	ⲛ̄		ⲧⲁⲉⲓⲟⲩ	ⲧⲁⲉⲓⲟⲩ-	

		m./f.	secondary form
60	x̄	ⲥⲉ	ⲥⲉ-, ⲥⲉⲧ-
70	ō	ϣϥⲉ/ϣⲃⲉ/ⲥϣϥⲉ	ϣϥⲉ-
80	π̄	ϩⲙⲉⲛⲉ	ϩⲙ(ⲉ)ⲛⲉ-, ϩⲙⲉⲛⲉⲧ-
90	ϥ̄	ⲡⲥⲧⲁⲓⲟⲩ	ⲯⲁⲓⲧ-, ⲡⲥⲧⲁⲓⲟⲩ-
100	r̄	ϣⲉ	
200	c̄	ϣⲏⲧ	
300	t̄	ϣⲙⲛ̄ⲧ-ϣⲉ	
400	ȳ	ϥⲧⲟⲟⲩ ⲛ̄-ϣⲉ, ϥⲧⲉⲩ-ϣⲉ	
1000	ā	ϣⲟ	
2000	b̄	ϣⲟ ⲥⲛⲁⲩ	
3000	ḡ	ϣⲟⲙⲛ̄ⲧ ⲛ̄-ϣⲟ, ϣⲙⲛ̄ⲧ-ϣⲟ	
10 000		ⲧⲃⲁ	

086. The cardinal number is normally linked with the noun it determines with the preposition ⲛ̄- (cf. 170). In this construction, the noun always has a singular form. The number can be determined by the definite article or some other determiner.

087. The number 2 is always placed immediately after the substantive it determines (without the preposition ⲛ̄-).

ϯⲟⲩ ⲛ̄-ⲟⲉⲓⲕ ⲙⲛ̄-ⲧⲃ̄ⲧ ⲥⲛⲁⲩ. (Matt 14:17), *five loaves of bread and two fishes*
ⲡⲉϥ.ⲙⲛ̄ⲧ-ⲥⲛⲟⲟⲩⲥ ⲙ̄.ⲙⲁⲑⲏⲧⲏⲥ (Matt 10:1), *his 12 disciples*
ⲧ.ⲡⲓⲥⲧⲓⲥ ⲑⲉⲗⲡⲓⲥ ⲧ.ⲁⲅⲁⲡⲏ ⲡⲉⲓ.ϣⲟⲙⲛ̄ⲧ (1Cor 13:13), *(The) belief, (the) hope, and (the) love, these three...*
ⲕⲉ.ⲥⲁϣϥ̄ ⲙ̄-ⲡ̄ⲛ̄ⲁ̄ (Matt 12:45), *seven other spirits*

088. An approximate number is preceded by the prefix ⲁ or ⲛⲁ.
ⲛⲁ.ϥⲧⲟⲩ-ϣⲉ ⲧⲁⲓⲟⲩ ⲛ̄-ⲣⲟⲙⲡⲉ (Acts 13:20), *about 450 years*

B. Ordinal numbers

089. ϣⲟⲣⲡ(ⲉ) and ϩⲟⲩⲉⲓⲧ(ⲉ) mean *first*.

090. The other ordinal numbers are composed of ⲙⲉϩ + cardinal number.

091. ⲙⲉϩ is the prenominal form of the verb ⲙⲟⲩϩ, which means *to fill*.

092. The ordinal number is linked to the noun by the attributive preposition ⲛ̄-. Normally the number precedes the noun in this construction, but the inverse order is also possible.
ⲡⲉ.ϩⲟⲩⲉⲓⲧ ⲛ̄-ⲣⲱⲙⲉ (BG 29:10), *the first man*
ⲡ.ⲙⲉϩ-ⲥⲛⲁⲩ ⲛ̄-ϩⲟⲟⲩ (Num 7:18), *the second day*
ⲡ.ⲙⲉϩ-ⲧⲁⲓⲟⲩ ⲙⲛ̄ ⲟⲩⲁ ⲙ̄-ⲯⲁⲗⲙⲟⲥ, *Psalm 51*
ⲡ.ⲙⲟⲩ ⲙ̄.ⲙⲉϩ-ⲥⲛⲁⲩ (Rev 2:11), *the second death*
ⲙ̄-ⲡ.ⲙⲉϩ-ⲥⲉⲡ ⲥⲛⲁⲩ (Deut 9:18), *the second time*

Prepositions

093. Prepositions normally have a nominal or pronominal complement. They usually have two bound states: (1) the prenominal state, when they introduce a noun, a nominal locution or an independent pronoun (except for the personal pronoun); (2) the prepersonal state when they introduce a personal pronoun suffix.

094. There are however some 'defective' prepositions, that is preposition that do not have both bound states. They are linked with their complement by a periphrastic expression for the missing bound state. (cf. 101–102)

095. There are two sorts of prepositions: (1) the simple prepositions (cf. 98–99); and (2) prepositions composed of a simple preposition in combination with a noun (cf. 100).

096. Both bound states of certain prepositions might have another origin, e.g. ϨⲚ-, ϨⲎⲦⲚ⸗ (*in*). In this case, the form of the prepersonal state is the prepersonal form of ϨⲎ, *belly*.

097. Preposition that have a prepersonal bound state ending in a short vowel, often have a long vowel before the suffix of the 2nd pers. pl.
ⲘⲘⲞ⸗ > ⲘⲘⲰⲦⲚ
ⲚⲀ⸗ > ⲚⲎⲦⲚ.

A. Simple prepositions

098. This is a list of the most common simple pepositions, which should be memorized.
ⲀϪⲚ-, ⲀϪⲚⲦ⸗ (often ⲈϪⲚ-): *without*
Ⲉ-, ⲈⲢⲞ⸗: *to; for; than* (second term of the comparison); introduces the object of some verbs denoting sense perception (cf. 282).
ⲈⲦⲂⲈ-, ⲈⲦⲂⲎⲎⲦ⸗: *about, because of*
Ⲛ-, ⲘⲘⲞ⸗: *in, on, from* (locative); *at, in* (temporal); *by, through* (instrumental), *of* (partitive genitive, cf. 178); link with the object of many verbs (cf. 280); attribution and identity (cf. 161, 165–172).
Ⲛ-, ⲚⲀ⸗: *for, to* (dative).
ⲘⲚ-, ⲚⲘⲘⲀ⸗: *with; and* (cf. 186).
ⲞⲨⲂⲈ-, ⲞⲨⲂⲎ⸗: *against*
ⲞⲨⲦⲈ-, ⲞⲨⲦⲰ⸗: *between; in the middle of*
ϢⲀ-, ϢⲀⲢⲞ⸗: *to, till*
ϨⲀ-, ϨⲀⲢⲞ⸗: *under, from under; outside of; starting with; with regard to; about*
ϨⲎⲦ⸗: *before, in front of*
Ϩⲓ-, ϨⲓⲰ(Ⲱ)⸗: *upon; and* (cf. 187)
ϨⲚ-, ⲚϨⲎⲦ⸗: *in*
ϪⲒⲚ-: *from... on*

099. A number of Greek prepositions are also used in Coptic. Most of them only have the prenominal state.
ⲀⲚⲦⲒ-: *against; instead of*
ⲈⲒⲘⲎⲦⲒ (Ⲉ)-: *except, unless*
ⲔⲀⲦⲀ-, ⲔⲀⲦⲀⲢⲞ⸗: *after, following*
ⲠⲀⲢⲀ-, ⲠⲀⲢⲀⲢⲞ⸗: *in comparison, more than*
ⲠⲢⲞⲤ-, ⲠⲢⲞⲤⲢⲞ⸗: *corresponding to, more than*
ⲬⲰⲢⲒⲤ-: *without*
ϨⲰⲤ-: *as, like*

B. Composite prepositions

100. Many preposition are made up of a simple preposition followed by a noun at the prenominal or prepersonal state (cf. 048). These nouns are usually body parts, but lose their concrete meaning to assume a more abstract sense.

(ⲂⲞⲖ) *outside*
ⲚⲂⲖ̄-, ⲚⲂⲖ̄ⲖⲀ⸗: *except for; further than*

(ⲈⲒⲀⲦ⸗) *eye*
ϨⲀⲈⲒⲀⲦ⸗: *before, in front of*

(ⲖⲒⲔⲦ⸗) *cover*
Ⲛ̄ⲖⲒⲔⲦ⸗: *on top of, covering*

(ⲢⲞ) *mouth*
ⲈⲢⲚ̄-, ⲈⲢⲰ⸗: *towards, to*
ϨⲀⲢⲚ̄-, ϨⲀⲢⲰ⸗: *under; in front of*
ϨⲒⲢⲚ̄-, ϨⲒⲢⲰ⸗: *towards, to*

(ⲢⲀⲦ⸗) *foot*
ⲈⲢⲀⲦ⸗: *towards, to* (a person)
ϨⲀⲢⲀⲦ⸗: *under, underneath*
ϨⲒⲢⲀⲦ⸗: *towards, to*

(ⲤⲀ) *side*
Ⲛ̄ⲤⲀ-, Ⲛ̄ⲤⲰ⸗: *after; except for*
Ⲙ̄Ⲛ̄ⲚⲤⲀ-, Ⲙ̄Ⲛ̄ⲚⲤⲰ⸗: *after*

(ⲦⲰⲢⲈ) *hand*
ⲈⲦⲚ̄-, ⲈⲦⲞⲞⲦ⸗: *towards, to*
Ⲛ̄ⲦⲚ̄- (ⲚⲦⲈ-), Ⲛ̄ⲦⲞⲞⲦ⸗: *in, at, by, with, next to, from*
ϨⲀⲦⲚ̄-, ϨⲀⲦⲞⲞⲦ⸗: *next to, with*
ϨⲒⲦⲚ̄-, ϨⲒⲦⲞⲞⲦ⸗: *by* (agens)*; from, of*

(ⲦⲞⲨⲰ-) *bosom*
ⲈⲦⲞⲨⲚ̄-, ⲈⲦⲞⲨⲰ⸗: *next to; for; with*
ϨⲒⲦⲞⲨⲚ- (ϨⲒⲦⲞⲨⲈ-, ϨⲒⲦⲞⲨⲈⲚ-), ϨⲒⲦⲞⲨⲰ⸗: *next to*

(ϨH) *front*
ⲈϨⲎⲦ⸗: *in front of*
ϨⲎⲦ⸗: *in front of*

(ϨH) *belly*
(ϨⲚ̄-) Ⲛ̄ϨⲎⲦ⸗: *in, at, on* (the prenominal state is the simple preposition ϨⲚ-, cf. 098)

(Ϩⲟ) *face*
ⲈϨⲢⲚ̄- (ⲈϨⲚ̄-/ϨⲚ̄-), ⲈϨⲢⲀ⸗: *toward; facing; between*
ⲚⲀϨⲢⲚ̄-, ⲚⲀϨⲢⲀ⸗: *in the presence of, facing, in front of*

(ϨⲎⲦ) *heart*
ϨⲀϨⲦⲚ̄- (ϨⲀϨⲦⲈ-/ϨⲀⲦⲚ̄-/ϨⲀⲦⲈ-), ϨⲀϨⲦϨ⸗ (ϨⲀⲦϨ⸗): *with, near to*

(ⲬⲚ̄-) *head*
ⲈⲬⲚ̄- (ⲬⲰ-), ⲈⲬⲰ⸗: *on; for; against; to; after*
ϨⲀⲬⲰ⸗: *before, in front of*
ϨⲒⲬⲚ̄- (ϨⲒⲬⲰ-), ϨⲒⲬⲰ⸗: *on, upon, on top of; in, at; next to; from above*

C. Remarks

Defective prepositions

101. If a preposition has no prenominal bound state, the noun can be attached through a periphrastic expression: the preposition has the personal suffix corresponding to its complement. This suffix is connected to the complement by the attributive preposition Ⲛ̄- (which expresses identity in this case, cf. 161).
ϨⲀⲢⲀⲦ⸗ϥ Ⲙ̄-ⲠⲦⲞⲞⲨ (Mark 5:11), *on the mountain* (on it, that is the mountain)
ϨⲀⲢⲞ⸗ⲞⲨ Ⲛ̄-ⲚⲈ⸗ⲦⲚ.ⲞⲨⲈⲢⲎⲦⲈ (Mark 6:11), *under your (pl.) feet* (under them, that is, your feet)

102. There are some prepositional expressions that only exist in the absolute state. The nominal or personal complement is then linked through the preposition Ⲛ̄-, Ⲙ̄ⲘⲞ⸗.
Ⲛ̄-Ⲧ.ⲠⲈ Ⲙ̄ⲘⲞ⸗Ⲥ (Heb 9:5), *above her*
Ϩⲓ ⲠⲀϨⲞⲨ Ⲙ̄ⲘⲞ⸗Ⲓ (Till 208), *behind me*

Preposition + adverb

103. Some prepositions can be accompanied by an adverb that modifies or emphasises its original meaning. The most common adverbs are:
ⲂⲞⲖ: *(towards the) outside*; with Ⲛ̄ϨⲎⲦ: *(to the) out(side) of*
ⲈϨⲞⲨⲚ *(towards the) inside*
(Ⲉ)ϨⲢⲀⲒ *up, down*

ϨⲘ̄-Ⲡ.ⲎⲒ, *in the house*
ⲈⲂⲞⲖ ϨⲘ̄-Ⲡ.ⲎⲒ, *out of the house*
ⲈϨⲞⲨⲚ Ⲉ-Ⲡ.ⲎⲒ, *into the house*
ϨⲢⲀⲒ ϨⲚ̄-Ⲧ.ⲠⲈ, *in (the) heaven, above*

Adverbs

A. Adverbs

104. There is only a limited number of 'real' adverbs in Coptic.
ⲖⲀⲀⲨ: *... at all* (cf. 024)
ⲞⲚ: *again*
ⲦⲰⲚ: *where? wherefrom? how?*
ⲦⲰⲚⲞⲨ/ⲦⲰⲚⲈ: *very, certainly*
ⲦⲚⲀⲨ/ⲦⲚ̄ⲚⲀⲨ: *when?*
ϬⲈ: *more*
ⲦⲀⲒ: *here*, only occurs in the relative expression ⲈⲦ.ⲦⲀⲒ: *...who is here.*

105. Some Greek adverbs are used in Coptic.
ⲆⲒⲔⲀⲒⲰⲤ: *rightly*
ⲠⲞⲖⲖⲀⲔⲒⲤ: *often*
ⲤⲰⲘⲀⲦⲒⲔⲰⲤ: *physically*
ϨⲞⲖⲰⲤ: *completely*
ⲠⲰⲤ: *how?*

106. Some composites consisting of a preposition (cf. 098) and a noun are used as adverbs.
ⲈⲂⲞⲖ: *outside* (can also be used in combination with other adverbs and verbs from which it takes its meaning).
ⲈⲘⲀⲦⲈ: *very*
ⲈⲘⲀⲨ: *there* (dynamic)
ⲈⲚⲈϨ: *always, eternally*
ⲈⲠⲈⲤⲎⲦ: *down*
ⲈϨⲞⲨⲚ: *inside*
(Ⲉ)ϨⲢⲀⲒ: *up, down* (these are actually homonymes. The orthographic difference between both adverbs has disappeared in Sahidic. In Bohairic there is a distinction between ⲈϨⲢⲀⲒ, *up*, and ⲈϦⲢⲀⲒ, *down*.)
Ⲙ̄ⲘⲀⲦⲈ: *only, exclusively*
Ⲙ̄ⲘⲀⲨ: *there* (static)

B. Prepositional locutions

107. The syntactic function of the adverb can also be fulfilled by a locution introduced by the preposition Ⲛ̄-.
Ⲛ̄-ⲖⲀⲀⲨ: *in nothing, no way*
Ⲙ̄-ⲘⲎⲚⲈ: *daily*
Ⲙ̄-ⲠⲈ.ϨⲞⲞⲨ: *by day, during the day*

ⲛ-ⲁⲣⲭⲁⲓⲟⲥ: *in the past*
ⲛ̄-ⲟⲩ.ⲙⲁ: *somewhere* (ⲕⲉ.ⲙⲁ: *elsewhere*)
ⲛ̄-ⲑⲉ (ⲛ̄-ⲧ.ϩⲉ): *so, thus, in this way*
ⲛ̄-ⲧⲉ.ⲩϣⲏ: *by night, during the night*

108. Adverbial expressions of mode or manner are often composed with the preposition ϩⲛ̄- followed by a noun or an infinitive with the indefinite article.
ϩⲛ̄-ⲟⲩ.ⲙⲉ: *truly*
ϩⲛ̄-ⲟⲩ.ⲙⲛ̄ⲧ.ⲁⲧ.ⲥⲟⲟⲩⲛ̄: *unconsciously, without knowing*
ϩⲛ̄-ⲟⲩ.ϭⲉⲡⲏ: *fast, in a hurry*
ϩⲛ̄-ⲟⲩ.ϩⲟⲧⲉ ⲙⲛ̄-ⲟⲩ.ⲛⲟϭ ⲛ̄-ⲣⲁϣⲉ (Matt 28:8), *with fear and great joy.*

109. The negative equivalent of this expression uses the preposition ⲁϫⲛ̄-. In this case the noun or infinitive have no article.
ⲁϫⲛ̄-ⲛⲟⲙⲟⲥ: *illegally*
ⲁϫⲛ̄-ϩⲟⲧⲉ: *without fear*

C. Nouns

110. When the adverbial use is clear from the context, there can be apheresis of the preposition ⲛ̄-. In this case a noun can function as adverb. This is mostly the case with nouns expressing a notion of time. Iteration of a noun has often a distributive significance.
ⲗⲁⲁⲩ: *not at all, no way*
ⲕⲉ.ⲙⲁ: *elsewhere* (cf. 075)
ⲧⲉ.ⲛⲟⲩ: *now* (ⲛ̄ⲧⲉ-ⲩⲛⲟⲩ: *immediately*)
ⲧⲉ.ⲣⲟⲙⲡⲉ: *yearly, during a year* (ἐνιαύσιος)
ⲡⲟⲟⲩ: *today* (also ⲙ̄-ⲡⲟⲟⲩ)

ⲟⲩⲇⲉ ⲡⲉ.ϩⲟⲟⲩ ⲟⲩⲇⲉ ⲧⲉ.ⲩϣⲏ (ApophPatr 231), *neither by day, nor by night*
ϩⲟⲟⲩ ϩⲟⲟⲩ, *every day, from day to day*
ⲕⲟⲩⲓ ⲕⲟⲩⲓ, *little by little*
ϣⲏⲙ ϣⲏⲙ, *little by little*
ⲟⲩⲁ ⲟⲩⲁ, *one by one*

Verbs

A. The infinitive

111. The infinitive is a verbal noun that expresses an action. It can occur in different constructions, where it has either the value of a noun (cf. 025) or the predicate of the durative sentence (cf. 231) and as conjugated verb in the non-durative sentence (cf. 308).

112. An infinitive can be active as well as passive. Only the context allows to distinguish between both. To avoid ambiguity and in translations from Greek texts, a periphrastic construction is used with the 3rd person plural as subject and the subject of the passive clause as object. When the agent is mentioned, there is no ambiguity as to the passive meaning.
Ν̄-2ΜΕ Ν̄-2ΟΟΥ Ε/Υ.ΠΕΙΡΑΖΕ Μ̄ΜΟ/Ҁ 2ΙΤΜ̄ Π.ΔΙΑΒΟΛΟC (Luke 4:4), *40 days, being temped by the devil.*

113. There are two infinitive forms in Coptic. These are remnants from ancient Egyptian and most of the verbs have maintained only one form. The first class of infinitives expresses an action or an event, (e.g. ΚѠ, *to place, put;* ΜΟΥΚ̄2, *to afflict, to oppress;* CѠΤΜ̄, *to hear, to listen*). The second class of infinitives have inchoative meaning and express the adoption of a condition or state (e.g. Μ̄ΚΑ2, *to be[come] sad;* 2ΛΟ6, *to be sweet;* Μ̄ΤΟΝ, *to take rest*). Both classes of infinitives are accentuated in different ways.

114. There is a class of verbs beginning with Τ that have causative meaning:
TCΒ̄ΚΟ: *to diminish, make small* (CBOK, *to be small*)
ΘΒ̄ΒΙΟ: *to humiliate* (2Β̄ΒΕ, *to be small, humble*)
Τ2Μ̄ΚΟ: *to make sad* (Μ̄ΚΑ2, *to be sad*)
ΧΠΟ: *to generate, to give birth* (ѠѠΠΕ, *to become*)
ΤΑΙΟ: *to honour* (ΑΙΑΙ, *to grow*)
ΤΑѠΟ: *to increase* (ΑѠΕ, *to be many*)
ΤΜ̄ΜΟ: *to nourish* (ΟΥѠΜ, *to eat*)

115. Many verbs consist of a verb and a noun. The following verbs occur frequently in such constructions:
ΕΙΡΕ, *to do;* Τ̄, *to give;* ΧΙ, *to take;* ΚѠ, *to put, place;* ϤΙ, *to carry;* Ο Ν̄-, *to be*
Ρ̄-2ΑΠ: *to give justice, to go to law*
Τ̄-2ΑΠ: *to do justice*
ΧΙ-2ΑΠ: *to be judged, condemned*
Ρ̄-2ΟΤΕ, Ο Ν̄-2ΟΤΕ: *to have fear*
Τ̄-2ΟΤΕ: *to frighten*

Verbs composed with ϯ often have a 'passive' equivalent with ϫⲓ, e.g. ϯ-/ϫⲓ-ϩⲁⲡ.

116. Many Greek verbs are used in Coptic. These verbs have a simplified form based on the Greek imperative of the 2nd pers. sg. ⲕⲣⲓⲛⲉ, *to decide, to judge;* ⲙⲉⲧⲁⲛⲟⲉⲓ, *to repent*; ⲡⲁⲣⲁⲇⲓⲇⲟⲩ, *to hand over*.

117. Greek verbs are usually preceded by ⲣ̄- in Coptic. This is the prenominal bound state of the infinitive ⲉⲓⲣⲉ, *to do*.

118. The negation of the infinitive is ⲧⲙ̄.
ⲡ.ⲧⲙ.ϯ-ϭⲱⲛⲧ ⲇⲉ ⲛⲁ⸗ϥ (ShAmél II 233:13), *not to make him angry*

Bound states

119. The infinitive has three bound states: the absolute state, the prenominal state and the prepersonal state. The absolute state is used when there is no direct object or when this is introduced by a preposition (as is often the case in the durative sentence, cf. 280).
The prenominal state is used when the infinitive is immediately followed by a nominal object. In dictionaries the prenominal bound state is indicated by -.
The prepersonal state is used when the infinitive is immediately followed by a personal subject. In dictionaries the prepersonal bound state is indicated by ⸗.
Here are some examples of common verbs that have the three bound states:

ⲥⲱⲧⲡ	ⲥⲉⲧⲡ-	ⲥⲟⲧⲡ⸗	*to choose*
ⲕⲱ	ⲕⲉ-	ⲕⲁⲁ⸗	*to put, to place*
ⲕⲱⲧ	ⲕⲉⲧ-	ⲕⲟⲧ⸗	*to build, to construct*
ⲉⲓⲣⲉ	ⲣ-	ⲁⲁ⸗	*to do, to work*
ϫⲓⲥⲉ	ϫⲉⲥⲧ-	ϫⲁⲥⲧ⸗	*to elevate, to exalt*

120. Greek verbs only have the absolute state. This means the object cannot be immediately attached to the verb. They are connected through the preposition ⲛ̄-/ⲙ̄ⲙⲟ⸗.

B. The stative

121. The stative expresses the state in which the subject is. In lexica and dictionaries it is indicated with the sign †.

122. There are two sorts of statives in Coptic. One class has no particular ending. These were originally male forms. The other one has the ending –ⲧ. These were originally female forms. Both forms have lost their gender in Coptic.

123. Here is a list of some common statives. They usually express the state that is the result of the verb they are derived from. In the case of verbs of movement, we usually find the stative in the durative sentence.

ⲃⲱⲕ	*to go*	ⲃⲏⲕ†	*to have gone*
ⲃⲱⲗ	*to detach*	ⲃⲏⲗ†	*to be detached*

ⲕⲱ	to put, lay	ⲕⲏ†	to lie
ⲙⲟⲩⲕϩ	to blow, strike	ⲙⲟⲕϩ†	to be sick
ⲙⲟⲩ	to die	ⲙⲟⲟⲩⲧ†	to be dead
ⲟⲩⲱⲛ	to open	ⲟⲩⲏⲛ†	to be open
ⲥⲟⲗⲥⲗ̄	to comfort	ⲥⲗ̄ⲥⲱⲗ†	to be comforted
ϫⲓⲥⲉ	to lift	ϫⲟⲥⲉ†	to be exalted

124. Some statives don't have an attested infinitive.
ϩⲟⲟⲩ, *to be bad*.

125. The stative of the verb ⲉⲓ (*to go*) is ⲛⲏⲩ†. It often has a future meaning.

126. The stative can only be used as a predicate in the durative sentence (cf. 225). In other kinds of sentences a periphrastic locution with ϣⲱⲡⲉ ⲉ- or ⲉⲓ ⲉ- can be used.
ϥ.ⲛⲁ.ϣⲱⲡⲉ ⲉ⸗ϥ.ⲙⲏⲣ ϩⲛ̄-ⲙ̄.ⲡⲏⲩⲉ (Matt 16,19). *It will be bound in the heavens*.

127. Some rare statives however can function as infinitives.
ϩⲙⲟⲟⲥ, *to sit down, to sit*; ⲁϩⲉ, *to get up, to be upright*.

128. Since the stative expresses a state, it is always intransitive; it cannot have an object.

C. The causative infinitive

129. The causative infinitive is actually composed of two infinitives. The first infinitive is ⲧⲣⲉ-, the causative infinitive (beginning with ⲧ) of ⲉⲓⲣⲉ (*to do*). The second infinitive expresses the thing one is made to do. The subject of the second infinitive is actually the object of the first one: it is the person/thing that *is made to do* something. It can be a noun or a suffixed personal pronoun.
ⲧⲣⲉ-/ⲧⲣⲉ⸗ (*to make ... do*) – noun, or personal pronoun – infinitive
ⲧⲣⲉ⸗ϥ.ⲥⲱⲧⲡ̄, *to make him choose*

130. The form of the causative infinitive with the 1st person sg. is ⲧⲣⲁ.

131. The form of the causative infinitive with the 2nd pers. f. sg. is ⲧⲣⲉ.

132. The negation of the causative infinitive is ⲧⲙ̄. It precedes ⲧⲣⲉ if ⲧⲣⲉ functions as a conjugated verb. When the causative infinitive functions as a noun, ⲧⲙ̄ is placed before the second infinitive.
ϥ-ⲧⲣⲉ⸗ϥ.ⲥⲱⲧⲡ̄ > ϥ.ⲧⲙ̄.ⲧⲣⲉ⸗ϥ.ⲥⲱⲧⲡ̄, *he does not make him choose*.
ϩⲙ̄-ⲡ.ⲧⲣⲉ⸗ϥ.ⲥⲱⲧⲡ̄ > ϩⲙ̄-ⲡ.ⲧⲣⲉ⸗ϥ.ⲧⲙ̄.ⲥⲱⲧⲡ̄, *by making him not choose*

133. The causative infinitive can be used as a noun or as a conjugated verb. In the second case, it has its own subject (different from the subject of the second infinitive it consists of).
ⲁ⸗ϥ.ⲧⲣⲉ⸗ϥ.ⲥⲱⲧⲡ̄, *he has made him choose*.

134. In spite of its name, the causative infinitive does not always confer a causative meaning. It is often used instead of the simple infinitive, e.g. when there is a need to express the subject of this infinitive (the second infinitive in the construction of the causative infinitive) (cf. 391–394).

D. The imperative

135. Most of the Coptic verbs do not have a special form for the imperative. They use the same form as for the infinitive. Moreover there is no distinction between the 2nd pers. sg. and pl.
ⲂⲰⲔ, *go!*
ⲘⲈⲢⲈ ⲠⲬⲞⲈⲒⲤ, *love the Lord!*
ⲘⲈⲢⲒⲦ⸗ϥ, *love him!*

136. A limited number of verbs do have a special form for the imperative. The most common ones are:

ⲈⲒ	ⲀⲘⲞⲨ (m.)			*come!*
	ⲀⲘⲎ (f.)			
	ⲀⲘⲎⲈⲒⲦⲚ̄ (pl.)			
ⲈⲒⲚⲈ	ⲀⲚ(Ⲉ)ⲒⲚⲈ	ⲀⲚⲒ-	ⲀⲚⲒ⸗	*bring!*
ⲈⲒⲢⲈ	ⲀⲢⲒⲢⲈ	ⲀⲢⲒ-	ⲀⲢⲒ⸗	*do!*
ⲖⲞ	ⲀⲖⲞⲔ (m.)			*stop!*
	ⲀⲖⲞ (f.)			
	ⲀⲖⲰⲦⲚ̄ (pl.)			
ⲚⲀⲨ	ⲀⲚⲀⲨ			*look!*
ϯ	ⲘⲀ		ⲘⲀ⸗	*give!*
ⲞⲨⲰⲚ	ⲀⲨⲰⲚ			*open!*
ⲬⲰ		ⲀⲬⲒ-	ⲀⲬⲒ⸗	*say!*

137. The composite verbs with Ⲣ̄- have ⲀⲢⲒ- in the imperative.
ⲀⲢⲒ-ⲘⲚ̄ⲦⲢⲈ, *testify!*

138. Composite verbs with ϯ- can alternatively have ⲘⲀ- or ϯ- in the imperative.
ϯ-ϨⲦⲎ⸗Ⲕ, *pay attention!*
ⲘⲀ-ⲠⲚⲞⲂⲚⲈϬ, *blame!*

139. Causative infinitives with Ⲧ- can also have ⲘⲀ- in the imperative.
ⲘⲀ-ⲦⲤⲀⲂⲞ⸗Ⲓ, *teach me!*

140. The imperatives ϢⲰⲠⲈ Ⲉ- (*become! be!*) and ⲀⲢⲒ- (*do!*) occur in a periphrastic construction which allows to make an imperative for predicates other than the infinitive, e.g. the stative, or an adverbial expression. The Ⲉ- introduces the circumstantial conversion (cf. 146).
ϢⲰⲠⲈ Ⲉ⸗ⲦⲈⲦⲚ̄.ⲞⲨⲀⲀⲂ (1Pet 1:16). *Become saints!*

ⲀⲢⲒ-ϨⲒϨⲎ Ⲙ-Ⲡ.ⲬⲞⲈⲒⲤ ϨⲚ̄-ⲞⲨⲰⲚϨ ⲈⲂⲞⲖ (Ps 146 (147):7). *Be revealed in front of the Lord!*

141. The imperative of a nominal sentence uses the verb ϢⲰⲠⲈ Ⲛ̄- followed by the predicate of the nominal sentence. The same construction can be used for a prepositional predicate.

    ϢⲰⲠⲈ ⲆⲈ Ⲛ̄-ⲢⲈϥ-ⲈⲒⲢⲈ Ⲙ̄-Ⲡ.ϢⲀϪⲈ (Jas 1:22). *Become practitioners of the Word!*

    ϢⲰⲠⲈ Ⲛ̄-ⲦⲀ.ϨⲈ (Gal 4:12). *Become like me (in my way)!*

142. The negation of the imperative is Ⲙ̄ⲠⲢ̄-.

    Ⲙ̄ⲠⲢ̄-Ⲣ̄-ϨⲞⲦⲈ (Matt 14:27). *Don't be afraid!*

143. There is also a construction Ⲙ̄ⲠⲰⲢ Ⲉ- + infinitive. It expresses an emotive negative imperative.

    Ⲙ̄ⲠⲰⲢ ϬⲈ ⲠⲀ.ⲤⲞⲚ Ⲉ-ⲤⲞⲢⲘ⸗Ⲉⲕ ⲘⲀⲨⲀⲀ⸗Ⲕ (Besa, fr. 28). *I beg you, my brother, do not go astray alone!*

E. Conversions

144. Many sentences can be converted in order to assume a different function, like the circumstantial and relative conversion, or to a modified meaning: past meaning for the preterit conversion and the emphasis on an element other than the subject and the predicate or the main verb.

    These conversions are marked by fixed modifiers, a kind of 'conjugation bases', that is, prenominal or prepersonal elements that are placed before the subject.

145. The preterit conversion is used to modify a sentence in a sentence in a past tense. The modifier is always ⲚⲈ-, ⲚⲈ⸗. This construction is often accompanied by an invariable ⲠⲈ, which remains untranslated.

146. The circumstantial conversion transforms an independent sentence in a subordinate sentence indicating the circumstances of the main clause. It can have causal, temporal, concessive, etc. meaning, and is used in a way similar to Greek participes. It is always introduced by ⲈⲢⲈ-, Ⲉ⸗.

147. The relative conversion transforms a sentence in a relative clause, which determines a nominal element. It is usually introduced by ⲈⲦⲈⲢⲈ-, ⲈⲦ⸗. In the affirmative past tense, the modifier is Ⲛ̄ⲦⲈ-, Ⲛ̄ⲦⲀ⸗.

148. The focalising conversion emphasises an element in the sentence other than the subject or the (verbal) predicate. The modifier is generally ⲈⲢⲈ-, Ⲉ⸗. The affirmative past tense has Ⲛ̄ⲦⲈ-, Ⲛ̄ⲦⲀ⸗.

F. Suffixically conjugated verboids

149. As a remnant from an anterior phase of the Egyptian language, some Coptic verboids – so called by LAYTON, because they belong to another class than the Coptic verb – only exist in a conjugated form. The subject is not attached to a conjugation base, but it is immediately attached to the verb. The verb can have a prepersonal or a prenominal bound state. They generally have a present meaning (except for ⲡⲉϫⲉ-, which often has a past meaning).

Only the verbs expressing a quality also have the preterit conversion and relative conversion (cf. 462). To express a time other than the present a periphrastic construction with ϣⲱⲡⲉ ⲉ- is used.

ⲡⲉϫⲉ-	ⲡⲉϫⲁ⸗	*to say* (with past meaning) (2nd f. sg.: ⲡⲉϫⲉ)
ϩⲛⲉ-	ϩⲛⲁ⸗	*to want*
ⲙⲉϣⲉ-	ⲙⲉϣⲁ⸗	*to ignore, to be ignorant* (ⲙⲉϣⲁ⸗ⲕ: *maybe*).

150. Many suffixically conjugated verboids (beginning with ⲛⲉ/ⲛⲁ) express some quality:

ⲛⲁⲁ-/ⲛⲁⲉ-	ⲛⲁⲁ(ⲁ)⸗	*to be big, great*
	ⲛⲁⲓⲁⲧ⸗	*to be blessed*
ⲛⲁⲛⲟⲩ-	ⲛⲁⲛⲟⲩ⸗	*to be good*
ⲛⲉⲥⲉ-	ⲛⲉⲥⲱ⸗	*to be beautiful*
	ⲛⲉⲥⲃⲱⲱ⸗	*to be intelligent, wise*
ⲛⲁϣⲉ-	ⲛⲁϣⲱ⸗	*to be many*
ⲛⲉϥⲣ̄-		*to be good*
	ⲛⲉϭⲱ⸗	*to be ugly*

151. The subject of these verboids is always definite.

152. The impersonal verboid ⲟⲩⲛ̄- and its negation ⲙ̄ⲛ- or ⲙ̄ⲙⲛ̄- have often an indefinite subject (cf. 302–304). They are translated: *there is(n't)*
ⲟⲩⲛ̄- ⲕⲉ.ⲧⲟⲡⲟⲥ ⲟⲛ (Br 231:5). *There is also another place.*
ⲙ̄ⲛ-ⲁⲧⲛⲟⲃⲉ (BMis 148:15). *There is no (one) without sin.*

153. The forms ⲟⲩⲛ̄-/ⲙ̄ⲛ- are used in the durative sentence with an indefinite subject (cf. 267–268).
ⲟⲩⲛ̄-ⲣⲱⲙⲉ ⲛ̄-ⲡⲉⲓ.ⲙⲁ (Z 352:17). *Is anyone (a man) here (in this place)?*
ⲟⲩⲛ̄-ⲟⲩ.ⲥⲟⲛ ϩⲙ̄-ⲡ.ϩⲓ (TILL, 288). *There is a Brother in the house.*
ⲙ̄ⲛ-ⲗⲁⲁⲩ ⲛ̄.ⲣⲱⲙⲉ ⲥⲟⲟⲩⲛ ⲛ̄-ⲛⲁⲓ (Z 346:3). *Nobody knows these things.*

The forms ⲟⲩⲛ̄ⲧⲉ-, ⲟⲩⲛ̄ⲧⲁ⸗ and ⲙ̄ⲛ̄ⲧⲉ-, ⲙ̄ⲛ̄ⲧⲁ⸗

154. The form ⲟⲩⲛ̄-/ⲙ̄ⲛ- can be combined with the preposition ⲛ̄ⲧⲉ-, ⲛ̄ⲧⲁ⸗. Literally it means: "*there is y for x*", but it usually can be translated: "*x has y*". The complement of ⲛ̄ⲧⲉ-, ⲛ̄ⲧⲁ⸗ is the possessor. The possessed (object) follows after the subject.

ⲞⲨⲚ̄Ⲧⲉ-, ⲞⲨⲚ̄ⲦⲀ⸗ and (Ⲙ̄)ⲘⲚ̄Ⲧⲉ-, (Ⲙ̄)ⲘⲚ̄ⲦⲀ⸗ can be considered as a suffixically conjugated verboid meaning "*to have*".

155. ⲞⲨⲚ̄Ⲧⲉ, ⲞⲨⲚ̄ⲦⲀ⸗ and ⲘⲚ̄Ⲧⲉ-, ⲘⲚ̄ⲦⲀ⸗ are often accompanied by the adverb Ⲙ̄ⲘⲀⲨ (*there*), which can normally remain untranslated.

156. If the object of this expression is a noun, the entire expression (ⲞⲨⲚ̄ⲦⲀ + the suffix) is at the prenominal state. The forms are the following:

1 sg.	ⲞⲨⲚ̄ⲦⲀⲒ	ⲞⲨⲚ̄Ⲧ︥-
2 sg. (m)	ⲞⲨⲚ̄ⲦⲀⲔ	ⲞⲨⲚ̄ⲦⲔ̄-
2 sg. (f)	ⲞⲨⲚ̄Ⲧⲉ	ⲞⲨⲚ̄Ⲧⲉ-
3 sg. (m.)	ⲞⲨⲚ̄ⲦⲀϤ	ⲞⲨⲚ̄ⲦϤ-
3 sg. (f.)	ⲞⲨⲚ̄ⲦⲀⲤ	ⲞⲨⲚ̄ⲦⲤ-
1 pl.	ⲞⲨⲚ̄ⲦⲀⲚ	ⲞⲨⲚ̄ⲦⲚ̄-
2 pl.	ⲞⲨⲚ̄ⲦⲎⲦⲚ̄	ⲞⲨⲚ̄ⲦⲉⲦⲚ̄-
3 pl.	ⲞⲨⲚ̄ⲦⲀⲨ	ⲞⲨⲚ̄ⲦⲞⲨ-

ⲞⲨⲚ̄Ⲧⲉ-Ⲡ.ⲉⲒⲰⲦ Ⲡ.ⲰⲚ̄Ϩ (John 5:26). *The Father has the life.*
ⲞⲨⲚ̄ⲦⲀ⸗Ⲩ Ⲛⲉ⸗Ⲩ.ⲘⲀϨ (Matt 8:20). *They have their nests.*
Ⲛⲉ.ⲨⲚ̄Ⲧ⸗ⲞⲨ-ϨⲉⲚ.Ⲕⲉ.ϢⲎⲘ ⲆⲈ Ⲛ̄-ⲦⲂⲦ̄ (Mark 8:7). *They had also some little fishes.*

157. The object (the possessed) can also be a personal pronoun. In that case it is suffixed to the first pronoun (the possessor). These are the secondary suffixes (see also: double object 285–287):

	sg.	pl.
1	-Ⲧ	-ⲤⲚ
2 m.	-Ⲕ, -ⲤⲔ, -ⲦⲔ	-ⲐⲎⲨⲦⲚ̄
f.	/ (?)	
3 m.	-Ϥ, -ⲤϤ	-Ⲥⲉ, -ⲤⲞⲨ
f	-Ⲥ	

Ⲛ.ⲉⲦⲉ.ⲞⲨⲚ̄ⲦⲀ⸗Ⲥ⸗Ⲥⲉ ⲦⲎⲢⲞⲨ (Mark 5:26), *all (the things) that she has*

Part II: Constructions

Nominal articulation

A. The apposition

158. Generally, the apposition comes after the term it extrapolates.
Exception: the apposition of the subject in many nominal sentences with three members (cf. 210–212).

159. If the apposition is an appellative (common noun), it has the article or another determiner.
The meaning of an apposition might be very close to that of an attribute.
ⲡ.ⲛⲟⲩⲧⲉ ⲡ.ⲛⲟϭ *the great God* (literally: *the God, the great one*).

160. If the apposition is a proper noun it has no article. A proper noun in apposition to a common name or a pronoun might be introduced by the conjunction ϫⲉ (*that is*), which is also used to introduce direct and indirect speech (cf. 405).

161. The apposition can be linked to a preceding noun or pronoun through the attributive preposition ⲛ̄-, which expresses identity.

162. The following words can also be considered as appositions:
ϩⲱⲱ⸗, *-self, too*
ⲙⲁⲩⲁⲁ(ⲧ)⸗/ⲟⲩⲁⲁ(ⲧ)⸗, *alone*
ⲧⲏⲣ⸗, *entirely, all of...*

ⲁⲃⲣⲁϩⲁⲙ ⲡ.ⲡⲁⲧⲣⲓⲁⲣⲭⲏⲥ (Heb 7:4), *Abraham, the patriarch.*
ⲡⲉ⸗ⲛ.ⲉⲓⲱⲧ ⲁⲃⲣⲁϩⲁⲙ (Luke 3:8), *our father, Abraham.*
ⲟⲩ.ⲣⲱⲙⲉ ⲇⲉ ϫⲉ ⲁⲛⲁⲛⲓⲁⲥ (Acts 22:12), *and a man, that is Ananias.*
ⲡ.ⲛⲟⲩⲧⲉ ⲙⲁⲩⲁⲁ⸗ϥ (BHom 50:8), *God alone.*
ⲛ̄.ⲣⲉϥ-ⲣ ⲛⲟⲃⲉ ϩⲱ⸗ⲟⲩ (Luke 6:33), *the sinners too.*
ⲡ.ⲕⲁϩ ⲧⲏⲣ⸗ϥ (Till 194), *the entire earth.*

Iteration

163. The iteration of a term often has a distributive meaning in Coptic.
The iteration of definite nouns is translated: *every*.
The iteration of words with a zero-determiner are translated: ... *by* ... (distributive) (cf. SHISHA-HALEVY 2.3).
ⲡ.ⲟⲩⲁ ⲡ.ⲟⲩⲁ, *every one*
ⲙ̄-ⲡⲉ.ϩⲟⲟⲩ ⲡⲉ.ϩⲟⲟⲩ (Tob 10:1), *every day*
ϣⲏⲙ ϣⲏⲙ, *little by little*

B. Attribution

164. There are 2 attributive constructions in Coptic: (1) noun and attribute are linked through the attributive preposition ⲛ̄-, (2) noun and attribute are immediately linked without any preposition.
For the numerals, cf. 086, 087.

Attributive preposition ⲛ̄-

165. We find the following construction with the attributive preposition ⲛ̄-:
article – noun – ⲛ̄- – attribute.

166. The attribute can be a noun, without the article.
This is the sole construction where gendered nouns can be used as attribute (with a descriptive function).

167. The same construction is used with the Greek (substantivated) adjective. The adjective takes the masculine or feminine form for persons and animals, the neuter form for inanimates (cf. 037).

ⲧ.ϣⲉⲉⲣⲉ ⲛ̄-ⲥⲁⲃⲏ (Sir 22:4), *the wise daughter*
ⲟⲩ.ⲣⲱⲙⲉ ⲛ̄-ⲇⲓⲕⲁⲓⲟⲥ (Mark 6:20), *a righteous man*
ϩⲉⲛ.ⲟⲩⲱϣ ⲛ̄-ⲥⲁⲣⲕⲓⲕⲟⲛ (PSFA 710:114a), *fleshly lusts.*

168. Some prepositional expressions can also be attributed to a noun through the preposition ⲛ̄-.
ⲟⲩ.ⲱⲛϩ̄ ⲛ̄-ϣⲁ ⲉⲛⲉϩ (Matt 25:46), *an eternal life.*

169. When the first noun has the article ...ⲛⲓⲙ, the construction is:
noun – ⲛⲓⲙ ⲛ̄- – attribute.
ⲣⲱⲙⲉ ⲛⲓⲙ ⲛ̄-ⲥⲟⲫⲟⲥ, *every wise man*

170. Alternatively, the construction with the attribute preceding the noun is possible in some cases (cf. numerals 087):
article – attribute – ⲛ̄- – noun.

171. This construction occurs frequently with the following attributes:
ⲛⲟϭ, *great, big*; ⲕⲟⲩⲓ, *small, little*: ϣⲏⲙ, *little*; ⲙⲉⲣⲓⲧ, *(be-)loved*; ϣⲟⲣⲡ, *first*; ϩⲁⲉ, *last*; ϩⲁϩ, *many* (without article: cf. 071). These attributes however can also follow the noun.
ⲧ.ⲛⲟϭ ⲛ̄-ϭⲟⲙ (Acts 8:10), *the great power*
ⲡ.ϩⲁⲉ ⲛ̄-ϩⲟⲟⲩ ⲛ̄-ⲛⲟϭ (John 7:37), *the last great day*

172. The construction with ...ⲛⲓⲙ is:
attribute – ⲛⲓⲙ – ⲛ̄ – noun.
ⲕⲟⲩⲓ ⲛⲓⲙ ⲛ̄-ϣⲏⲣⲉ, *every little child.*

Attribution without the preposition N̄-

173. A very limited number of adjectives is written immediately after the noun, without any intermediating preposition:
article – noun – attribute.

174. This construction is *always* used with the adjective ϢΗΜ (*small, little*).
It also occurs with ΚΟΥΙ and ΝΟϬ, but more rarely. In those cases it might express some nuance.
Τ.ϢΕΕΡΕ ϢΗΜ (Matt 9, 24), *the little girl*

175. The construction with …ΝΙΜ is:
noun – attribute – ΝΙΜ
ϢΗΡΕ ϢΗΜ ΝΙΜ, *every little child*

Other constructions used to express a quality or characteristic

176. The relative clause with a stative or a verb expressing a quality (cf. 147, 150, 243).

177. The circumstantial clause (cf. 146).

C. The genitive

178. The genitive or nominal complement can be expressed by a bound state, whereby the possessed has the prenominal or prepersonal state and is immediately followed by the possessor. This construction is however only possible for a very limited number of nouns (cf. 048)

179. Usually the genitive is expressed with one of the following prepositions:
N̄- (M̄ΜΟ⸗)
N̄ΤΕ-(N̄ΤΑ⸗)

The genitive with N̄-(M̄ΜΟ⸗)

180. The construction of the genitive is as follows:
noun (*regens*) – N̄- – article/determiner – possessor (*rectum*).
Π.ΡΑΝ Μ̄-Π.ΧΟΕΙⲤ (Till 111), *the name of the Lord.*

181. Sometimes we cannot tell the difference between a *genitivus explicativus*, and the expression of identity (through the attributive particle N̄-, cf. 161).
Π.ΚΑϨ N̄-ΚΗΜΕ, *the land (of) Egypt.*

182. If the possessed noun (*regens*) has the prepersonal state it takes the (kataphoric) suffix corresponding to the possessor (*rectum*). When the possessor is a noun, the whole construction is followed by N̄- and the possessor.
ϨΗΤ⸗Ⲥ N̄-ΤΕ⸗Ϥ.ΜΑΑΥ (Luke 1:15), *the belly of his mother.*

183. Certain specialists distinguish between the construction with N̄- and the construction with N̄-/M̄ΜΟ⸗ (LAYTON 203). The latter preposition is used for the partitive genitive.

NIM M̄-ⲠⲤⲀϢϤ (Matt 22:28), *which of the seven?*
NIM M̄MⲰTN̄, *which one of you (pl.)?*

The genitive with N̄TE

184. The construction of the genitive is as follows:
noun (*regens*) – N̄TE – determiner – possessor (*rectum*)

185. This construction is used in the following cases:
– the noun (*regens*) has the indefinite or demonstrative article;
– the possessor (*rectum*) is separated from the noun (*regens*) by another element.

ⲞⲨ.ϤⲀⲒϢⲒⲚⲈ N̄TE Ⲡ.ⲘⲞⲨ (Prov 16, 14), *a ship of death*
ⲠⲈⲒ.ϢⲎⲢⲈ N̄TE Ⲡ.ⲢⲰⲘⲈ (John 12, 34), *this son of man*
Ⲡ.ⲘⲞⲞⲨ ⲈⲦ.ⲞⲚϨ N̄TE Ⲡ.ⲞⲨⲞⲈⲒⲚ (BG 26, 20), *the living water of the light*

D. Nominal coordination

186. The most common way to coordinate common nouns with an article or with another determiner or proper nouns with each other is through the preposition MN̄-, NM̄MⲀ⸗ (*with*).

187. A noun without determiner is linked to another noun through the preposition ϨⲒ- (*on, upon*).

188. The conjunction ⲀⲨⲰ can be used for the coordination of nouns as well as for the coordination of clauses. When ⲀⲨⲰ is used, articles and prepositions are repeated before every noun.

189. The conjunctions Ϫ(Ⲓ)Ⲛ et Ⲏ are used for disjunctive coordination.

ⲠⲈⲦⲢⲞⲤ MN̄-ⲒⲀⲔⲰⲂⲞⲤ MN̄-ⲒⲰϨⲀⲚⲚⲎⲤ MN̄-ⲀⲚⲆⲢⲈⲀⲤ (Matt 13:3), *Peter, (and) James, (and) John, and Andrew.*
ⲤⲀⲢⲜ ϨⲒ-ⲤⲚⲞϤ (BMis 51:16), *flesh and blood.*
ⲂⲀⲢⲀⲂⲂⲀⲤ ϪN̄-ⲒⲤ̄ (Matt 27:17), *Barabbas or Jesus?*

190. In some rare cases ⲀⲨⲰ is used in an enumeration in concurrence with MN̄- or ϨⲒ-. Sometimes ⲀⲨⲰ precedes MN̄- or ϨⲒ-.
Ⲡ.ⲚⲞϬ N̄-ⲞⲨⲞⲈⲒⲚ ⲀⲨⲰ MN̄-ⲘⲨⲤⲦⲎⲢⲒⲞⲚ (PS 18:12), *the great light and the mystery.*

See exercise 1

The nominal sentence

A. Some general observations

Subject

191. The subject of the simple nominal sentence can be a personal pronoun (cf. 004) or a demonstrative pronoun (cf. 014). In the first case, with a 1st or 2nd pers. subject, we have an interlocutive sentence. The subject is the person speaking or the person spoken to. When the subject is a 3rd pers. pronoun, the sentence is delocutive. The subject is not implicated in the exchange between author and reader, but a person spoken about.
In both cases the subject can be expanded by a term in extraposition, which can be an independent personal pronoun, another pronoun, a proper noun, or a common noun.
In the nominal sentence with three members the demonstrative ⲡⲉ/ⲧⲉ/ⲛⲉ connects two elements. For this type of sentences there might remain some ambiguity as to which element is the subject and which the predicate.

Predicate

192. If the subject is a personal pronoun the predicate can be a common noun (preceded by an article or some other demonstrative or possessive element), an indefinite (ⲟⲩⲁ/ⲟⲩⲉⲓ) or an interrogative pronoun (ⲛⲓⲙ). A noun has often an indefinite article (cf. 064), in which case it often expresses a quality (cf. 068).

193. If the subject is the demonstrative pronoun ⲡⲉ/ⲧⲉ/ⲛⲉ (cf. 014) the predicate can be a proper noun, a common noun (cf. 035–053), a pronoun (personal, demonstrative, possessive, indefinite, interrogative, cf. 003, 013, 01–020, 023, 024), a number, an infinitive, a causative infinitive or a completive clause introduced by ϫⲉ.

194. Predicates that cannot be used in the nominal sentence of the first type can be connected with the subject in verbal constructions using ⲟ ⲛ̄-... or ⲡ̄-..., meaning *to be*.
ⲉⲕ.ⲟ ⲛ̄-ϣⲙ̄ⲙⲟ ⲉ-ⲑⲓⲉⲣⲟⲩⲥⲁⲗⲏⲙ (Luke 24:18) ...*since you are a stranger in Jerusalem.*

Negation

195. The negation of the nominal sentence is (ⲛ̄-)... ⲁⲛ.

Conversions

196. The preterit conversion: if the nominal sentence expresses a past reality it is introduced by ⲛⲉ.
ⲛⲉ.ⲟⲩ.ⲕⲟⲩⲓ ⲡⲉ ϩⲛ̄-ⲧⲉϥ.ϭⲟⲧ (Luke 19:3). *He was small of his sort.*

197. The circumstantial conversion: the nominal sentence can function as a circumstantial sentence introduced by ⲉ.

198. It indicates the circumstances under which the principal clause takes place. Thus a subordinate clause of time, manner, cause, condition, goal or consequence can be obtained (cf. 422, 433, 444, 451). The circumstantial conversion can also function as a completive clause after verbs of incomplete predication, which can be completed by a predicative complement, expressing a wish, command, beginning, end, etc. (cf. 412) or as a relative clause determining an indefinite antecedent (cf. 471). It can be used as the equivalent of a Greek participle.
ⲉ.ⲁⲛⲟⲛ ⲡ.ⲅⲉⲛⲟⲥ ϭⲉ ⲙ̄-ⲡ.ⲛⲟⲩⲧⲉ (Acts 17:29) *...since we are the race of God.*

199. The relative conversion: the nominal sentence can be converted into a relative clause introduced by ⲉⲧⲉ.
The relative clause modifies a preceding element (= antecedent) (cf. 453).
ⲛ.ⲁⲥⲉⲃⲏⲥ ⲛⲁ.ⲙⲉ ⲉⲧⲉ-ϩⲉⲛ.ⲃⲟⲧⲉ ⲙ-ⲡ.ϫⲟⲉⲓⲥ ⲛⲉ ⲛⲉⲩ.ϩⲓⲟⲟⲩⲉ (ShIV 10: 14–15). *The real impious whose ways are abominations for the Lord.*

B. The subject is a personal pronoun (interlocutive)

Structure

200. subject – predicate
The subject is the unstressed form of the independent personal pronoun of the first or second person (cf. 004). The subject always precedes the predicate.
If the predicate is a noun, it always has an article (definite, indefinite, possessive, or ⲛⲓⲙ).
ⲁⲛⲅ̄ ⲟⲩ.ⲡⲣⲟⲫⲏⲧⲏⲥ. (Rev 2:20) *I am a prophetess.*

201. This construction rarely occurs with the 3rd pers.
ⲛ̄ⲧϥ̄ ⲡⲁ-ⲡⲉ.ⲭⲥ̄. (2Cor 10:7) *He belongs to Christ (he is the one of the Christ).*

Extraposition (apposition of the subject)

202. This construction can be preceded by the independent, emphatic form of the independent personal pronoun. The pronoun in extraposition stresses the subject.
ⲛ̄ⲧⲟⲕ ⲛ̄ⲧⲕ̄ ⲟⲩ.ⲡⲣⲟⲫⲏⲧⲏⲥ. (John 4:19) *You* (m. sg.)*, you are a prophet.*

203. The pronoun in extraposition can itself be accompanied by another element in extraposition (cf. 158–162).

Conversions

204. This type of sentence can be converted into a circumstantial clause.
ⲉ.ⲁⲛⲟⲛ ⲡ.ⲅⲉⲛⲟⲥ ϭⲉ ⲙ̄-ⲡ.ⲛⲟⲩⲧⲉ. (Acts 17:29) *...since we are the race of God.*

205. The preterit conversion of this sentence type only occurs with a sense of irreality or regret.

ϨΑΜΟΙ ΝΕ.ΑΝΟΝ ΟΥΑ ΜΜΟ̅ΟΥ. (ShIV 92:18) *It would have been good if we were one of them.*

C. The subject is a demonstrative pronoun (delocutive)

Structure

206. predicate – ΠΕ/ΤΕ/ΝΕ (= subject)

ΠΕ͞Ν.ΝΟΥΤΕ ΠΕ. (John 8:54) *He is our God.*
Π.ϢΩΜ ΠΕ. (ShIV 110:22) *It is summer.*
ΑΝΟΚ ΠΕ. *It is me.*

207. We can distinguish between a personal locution and an impersonal one. In the first case the subject, the demonstrative pronoun ΠΕ/ΤΕ/ΝΕ, normally agrees with the predicate (cf. 014).
The subject of the impersonal construction is the invariable ΠΕ.
In the first case ΠΕ/ΤΕ/ΝΕ is an anaphoric pronoun: it refers to an element that is not included in the predicate. In the second case ΠΕ is an endophoric pronoun: it refers to an element that is implied in the predicate (LAYTON 266–267).

208. The predicate can also be a personal pronoun (emphatic form of the independent pronoun). There is some plasticity as to the actual sense of this locution. The predicate might in some cases be translated as subject.

D. The nominal sentence with three members

209. A term or phrase in extraposition can accompany the demonstrative pronoun ΠΕ/ΤΕ/ΝΕ, the subject of the nominal sentence. In some cases the term or phrase in apposition seems to function as the real subject of the phrase. The usual word order of the nominal sentence (predicate – subject) is not obligatory in this kind of sentences. In many cases therefore there is some ambiguity as to what is the subject and what is the predicate.
These are the possible patterns:

210. apposition of the subject – predicate – ΠΕ/ΤΕ/ΝΕ (subject)
ΝΕΙ.ΡΩΜΕ ϨΕΝ.ΙΟΥΔΑΙ ΝΕ (Acts 16:20). *These men are Jews (these men, they are Jews).*
ΠΕ/ΤΕ/ΝΕ is anaphoric in this construction: it refers to what precedes and agrees with it in gender and number.

211. predicate – ΠΕ/ΤΕ/ΝΕ – (apposition of the) subject
ΟΥ.ΜΕ ΠΕ Π.ΝΟΥΤΕ (John 3:33). *God is true.*
ΠΕ/ΤΕ/ΝΕ is cataphoric (prospective): il refers to what follows.

212. (apposition of the) subject – ⲡⲉ/ⲧⲉ/ⲛⲉ – predicate
ⲡⲉⲓ.ⲁⲡⲟⲧ ⲡⲉ ⲧ.ⲇⲓⲁⲑⲏⲕⲏ ⲙ̄-ⲃⲣ̄ⲣⲉ (1Cor 11:25). *This cup, it is the new alliance.*

213. The terms in extraposition can be proper nouns, common nouns, pronouns, completive clauses (subject clause), etc.

Conversions

214. The preterit conversion is introduced by ⲛⲉ.
ⲛⲉ.ⲡ.ⲛⲁⲩ ⲇⲉ ⲡⲉ ⲛ̄-ⲭⲡ̄-ϣⲟⲙⲧⲉ (Mark 15:25). *It was the moment of the third hour.*

215. If the predicate is preceded by an extraposition determining the subject, the ⲛⲉ of the preterit conversion can be intercalated between the term in extraposition and the predicate or it can precede the term in extraposition.
ⲛⲉ.ⲧⲉ⸗ϥ.ⲉⲓⲟⲡⲉ ⲧⲱ⸗ⲟⲩ ⲧⲉ (Acts 18:3). *He had the same craft as them (his craft was theirs).*
ⲧ.ⲡⲉⲧⲣⲁ ⲅⲁⲣ ⲛⲉ.ⲡⲉ.ⲭ̄ⲥ̄ ⲡⲉ (ShIII 51:28). *Because the rock was Christ.*

216. The circumstantial conversion is introduced by ⲉ.
ⲟⲩ.ⲣⲱⲙⲉ... ⲉ.ⲡⲉ⸗ϥ.ⲣⲁⲛ ⲡⲉ ⲙⲁⲑⲑⲁⲓⲟⲥ (Matt 9:9). *A man... whose name is Matthew.*

217. If the predicate is preceded by an extraposition determining the subject, the ⲉ of the circumstantial conversion is intercalated between the term in extraposition and the predicate.
ⲟⲩ.ⲙⲟⲟⲩ ⲉ.ⲙ.ⲡⲱ⸗ⲕ ⲁⲛ ⲡⲉ (ShOr 155:42–44). *Water that isn't yours.*

218. The relative conversion is introduced by ⲉⲧⲉ.
ⲡ.ⲉⲧⲉ ⲙ̄.ⲡⲱ⸗ⲧⲛ̄ ⲁⲛ ⲡⲉ (Lk 16:12). *That which isn't yours (pl.).*

E. Stylistic remarks

Iteration

219. The predicate can be repeated, usually followed by ⲟⲛ. The iteration expresses invariable identity.
ⲡⲓ.ⲥⲁⲧⲁⲛⲁⲥ ⲡⲓ.ⲥⲁⲧⲁⲛⲁⲥ ⲟⲛ ⲡⲉ (ShAmél II 290:8). *Satan always remains Satan (Satan is Satan again).*
ⲛ̄.ⲥⲟⲃⲧ ⲇⲉ ⲛ̄ⲧⲟⲟⲩ ⲛ̄ⲧⲟⲟⲩ ⲟⲛ ⲡⲉ (ShChass 143:20–22). *The walls remain always the same (the walls, they are always themselves).*

Intercalated ⲡⲉ/ⲧⲉ/ⲛⲉ

220. If the predicate consists of a noun and a modifier, the subject ⲡⲉ/ⲧⲉ/ⲛⲉ can be intercalated.
ϩⲉⲛ.ⲣⲱⲙⲉ ⲛⲉ ⲛ̄.ⲣⲉϥ-ϫⲓ-ⲙⲁⲉⲓⲛ (Za 3:8). *These are fortune-tellers (men receiving signs).*

Extraposition

221. Even if the subject (ⲡⲉ/ⲧⲉ/ⲛⲉ) already has an extraposition, this term in extraposition can itself also be preceded by another term in extraposition.

ⲡ.ⲕⲟⲩⲓ ⲛϨⲏⲧ⸱ⲑⲩⲧⲛ̄ ⲧⲏⲣ⸱ⲧⲛ̄ ⲡⲁⲓ ⲡⲉ ⲡ.ⲛⲟϭ (Luke 9:48). *The smallest one among you all, that is the greatest one.*

Other elaborations

222. Every element of the nominal sentence can be accompanied by a complement (nominal compliment or genitive, attributive complement, apposition, relative clause, adverbial expression). The complement normally follows immediately after the element it accompanies.

This does not mean that they cannot be separated by one or more other elements (e.g. particles).

ⲡⲁⲓ ⲟⲩ.ⲙⲉ ⲡⲉ ⲛ̄ⲧⲁ.ϫⲟⲟ⸱ϥ (John 4:18). *This is true, what you* (f. sg.) *have told me.*

ⲡ.ⲟⲓⲕ ⲇⲉ ⲉ.ϯ.ⲛⲁ.ⲧⲁⲁ⸱ϥ ⲁⲛⲟⲕ ⲡⲉ ⲧⲁ.ⲥⲁⲣⲝ Ϩⲁ-ⲡ.ⲱⲛϨ ⲙ̄-ⲡ.ⲕⲟⲥⲙⲟⲥ (John 6:51). *The bread that I will give, it is my flesh for the life of the world.*

ⲕⲁⲧⲁ-ⲟⲩ.ⲟⲓⲕⲟⲛⲟⲙⲓⲁ ⲙⲉⲛ ⲧⲉ⸱ϥ.ⲙⲁⲁⲩ ⲧⲉ (ShLefort 42:21–22). *According to the economy she is his mother.*

See exercise 2

The durative sentence

A. Some general observations

223. The durative sentence is a bipartite construction. There are three types: the pseudo-tenses of present (also called present I) and future (future I) and the durative sentence with adverbial predicate. These sentences express a durative or situational sense.

The subject
224. According to the type of the sentence, the subject can be (1) personal, (2) definite or (3) indefinite. In the latter case a construction with ⲟⲩⲛ-, ⲙⲛ̄- is used. If the subject is a personal pronoun, it takes the form of the proclitic personal pronoun (cf. 005).

The predicate
225. The predicate can be (1) the infinitive, (2) the stative, (3) the future auxiliary ⲛⲁ- followed by an infinitive, or (4) an adverbial expression.
The infinitive can have an object, which is either immediately attached to a bound state of the infinitive, or introduced by the preposition ⲛ̄-/ⲙ̄ⲙⲟ⸗ (cf. 279–280). The stative is always intransitive (cf. 128).

Negation
226. The negation is (ⲛ̄-)… ⲁⲛ.
ⲁⲛ comes after the predicate. The subject can be preceded by ⲛ̄-.

Conversions
227. Preterit conversion: if the durative sentence expresses a reality in the past it is preceded by ⲛⲉⲣⲉ-/ⲛⲉ⸗.

228. Circumstantial conversion: the durative sentence can be used as a circumstantial sentence. It is then preceded by ⲉⲣⲉ-/ⲉ⸗ (ⲉⲧⲉ when the subject is indefinite).

229. Relative conversion: the durative sentence can function as a relative sentence when it is preceded by ⲉⲧⲉⲣⲉ-/ⲉⲧ⸗ (ⲉⲧⲉ before ⲟⲩⲛ̄-).

230. Focalising conversion: the focalising conversion of the durative sentence, which emphasises an element other than subject or predicate, is introduced by ⲉⲣⲉ-/ⲉ⸗.

B. The durative sentence with personal or definite subject

I. The present
Structure

231. definite subject – predicate (= infinitive/stative)
ϥ.ⲥⲱⲧⲙ̄, *he chooses*
ⲡ.ⲣⲱⲙⲉ ⲥⲱⲧⲙ̄, *the man chooses*

Negation

232. The negation is (ⲛ̄)… ⲁⲛ.

The subject

233. If the subject is a noun or a syntactic equivalent, enclitic conjunctions (ⲇⲉ, ⲅⲁⲣ, ⲟⲉ) or elements determining the subject can be intercalated between the subject and the predicate.
If the subject is a personal pronoun, it is immediately followed by the predicate.
ⲙ̄.ⲡⲉ⸗ⲕ.ϩⲏⲧ ⲅⲁⲣ ⲥⲟⲩⲧⲱⲛ ⲁⲛ (Acts 8:21). *Your heart is not right.*

234. The subject can be emphasised or explicitated by an apposition.
ⲛ̄ⲧⲱⲧⲛ̄ ⲛ̄ⲧⲉⲧⲛ̄.ϣⲟⲃⲉ ⲉ-ϩⲁϩ ⲛ̄-ϫⲁϫ (Matt 10:31). *You (pl.), you are more worth than a multitude of sparrows.*

235. The apposition of the subject can also come after the predicate. When the subject is a 3rd person it is normally introduced by ⲛ̄ϭⲓ-.
ϥ.ⲥⲟⲟⲩⲛ ⲅⲁⲣ ⲛ̄ϭⲓ-ⲡⲉ⸗ⲧⲛ̄.ⲉⲓⲱⲧ ⲉⲧ.ϩⲛ̄-ⲙ.ⲡⲏⲩⲉ (Matt 6:32). *For he knows, your (pl.) Father who is in the heavens = for your Father… knows.*

236. Rarely, the apposition immediately follows the predicate.
ϥ.ϫⲱ ⲅⲁⲣ ⲙ̄ⲙⲟ⸗ⲥ ⲛ̄ⲧⲟϥ ⲡ.ϫⲟⲉⲓⲥ. (ShIII 60:4–5). *For the Lord has said it.*

237. When the subject is a 1st or 2nd person, the apposition comes after the predicate.
†.ϣⲓⲛⲉ ⲉⲣⲱ⸗ⲧⲛ̄ ϩⲙ̄-ⲡ.ϫⲟⲉⲓⲥ ⲁⲛⲟⲕ ⲧⲉⲣⲧⲓⲟⲥ (Rom 16:22). *I greet you (pl.) in the Lord, I, Tertius.*

Conversions

238. The preterit conversion (imperfect) is introduced by ⲛⲉⲣⲉ-/ⲛⲉ⸗.
ⲡ.ϣⲁϫⲉ ⲛⲉ⸗ϥ.ϣⲟⲟⲡ ⲛ̄ⲛⲁϩⲣⲛ̄-ⲡ.ⲛⲟⲩⲧⲉ (John 1:1). *The Word was with God.*

239. The negation is (ⲛ̄)… ⲁⲛ.

240. An invariable ⲡⲉ can occur in the clause with preterit conversion. This does not have to be translated.
ⲛⲉ⸗ϥ.ⲟⲩⲉϣ ⲛⲁⲩ ⲅⲁⲣ ⲉⲣⲟ⸗ϥ ⲡⲉ (Luke 23:8). *For he wanted to see him.*

241. The preterit conversion can be converted into a circumstantial clause introduced by ⲉ.
ϩⲙ̄-ⲡⲉ.ⲩⲟⲉⲓϣ ⲧⲏⲣ⸗ϥ ⲉ.ⲛⲉ⸗ⲩ.ϣⲟⲟⲡ ϩⲓϫⲙ̄-ⲡ.ⲕⲁϩ (ShAmél II 539:14–15). *All the time they were on the earth…*

242. The circumstantial conversion is introduced by ⲉ-/ⲉ⸗.
ⲟⲩ.ⲙⲩⲥⲧⲏⲣⲓⲟⲛ ⲉ⸗ϥ.ϩⲏⲡ (1ApocJames 28:3), *the hidden mystery (the mystery that is hidden)*
ⲁ⸗ϥ.ⲉⲓ ⲉϩⲣⲁⲓ ⲉ-ⲧ.ⲡⲉⲣⲓⲭⲟⲣⲟⲥ ⲧⲏⲣⲥ̄ ⲙ̄-ⲡ.ⲓⲟⲣⲇⲁⲛⲏⲥ ⲉ⸗ϥ.ⲕⲩⲣⲓⲥⲥⲁⲓ ⲙ̄-ⲡ.ⲃⲁⲡⲧⲓⲥⲙⲁ ⲙ̄-ⲙⲉⲧⲁⲛⲟⲓⲁ ⲛ̄-ⲕⲁ-ⲛⲟⲃⲉ ⲉⲃⲟⲗ (Luke 3:3). *He went to the whole region of the Jordan, preaching the baptism of repentence of forgiveness of sins.*

243. The relative sentence is introduced by ⲉⲧⲉ-/ⲉⲧ⸗.
ⲧ.ⲅⲉⲛⲉⲁ ⲉⲧ.ϫⲟⲟⲣ ⲁⲩⲱ ⲉⲧ.ⲟⲩⲁⲁⲃ (GosJud 36:25s.), *the strong and holy race (the race that is strong and that is holy)*
ⲡ.ⲉⲧ.ⲥⲱⲧⲙ̄ ⲉⲣⲱ⸗ⲧⲛ̄ ⲉ⸗ϥ.ⲥⲱⲧⲙ̄ ⲉⲣⲟ⸗ⲓ (Luke 10:16). *He who listens to you* (pl.), *he is listening to me.*

244. The focalising conversion (present II) is introduced by ⲉⲣⲉ-/ⲉ⸗
ⲉ⸗ⲩ.ⲕⲣⲓⲛⲉ ⲙ̄ⲙⲟ⸗ⲓ ⲉⲧⲃⲉ ⲑⲉⲗⲡⲓⲥ ⲙⲛ̄ ⲧ.ⲁⲛⲁⲥⲧⲁⲥⲓⲥ ⲛ̄-ⲛ.ⲉⲧ.ⲙⲟⲟⲩⲧ (Acts 23:6). *It is because of the hope and the resurrection of the dead that I am judged (that they judge me).*

245. The negation is ⲛ̄... ⲁⲛ.

246. The pronominal conjugation base with the suffix of the 2nd pers. f. sg. is ⲉⲣⲉ.

II. The future

Structure

247. definite subject — ⲛⲁ — infinitive
ϥ.ⲛⲁ.ⲥⲱⲧⲡ̄, *he will choose*
ⲡ.ⲣⲱⲙⲉ ⲛⲁ.ⲥⲱⲧⲡ̄, *the man will choose*

248. The negation is ⲛ̄... ⲁⲛ.

249. Remarks: cf. present (cf. 233–237).
ⲡ.ⲕⲁⲕⲉ ⲛⲁ.ⲡⲁⲣⲁⲅⲉ (1John 2:8). *The darkness will pass by.*
ⲛ̄.ϥ.ⲛⲁ.ⲙⲟⲩ ⲁⲛ (Luke 2:26). *He will not die.*

250. The future can also express an approximation
ⲉ⸗ⲩ.ⲛⲁ.ⲣ̄ ⲟⲩ.ⲧⲃⲁ ⲟⲩ.ϣⲟⲥ ⲛ̄-ⲣⲱⲙⲉ (Judg 8:10). *They are about 15,000 men.*

Conversions

251. The preterit conversion (imperfect of the future) is introduced by ⲛⲉⲣⲉ-/ⲛⲉ⸗
ⲁⲩⲱ ⲥⲁⲃⲏⲗ ϫⲉ ⲁ⸗ϥ.ϫⲓ ⲛ̄ⲛ-ⲟⲩ.ⲃⲟⲏⲑⲉⲓⲁ ⲉⲃⲟⲗ ⲛ̄-ⲧ.ⲡⲉ ⲛⲉ⸗ϥ.ⲛⲁ.ϣ.ⲕⲟⲧ⸗ϥ ⲁⲛ ⲉ-ⲡⲉ⸗ϥ.ϯⲙⲉ (ExAn 136:33–35). *And if he had not received help from heaven, he would not return to his town.*

252. The negation is ...ⲁⲛ.

253. Just like the preterit conversion of the present (cf. 240), the preterit conversion of the future can be accompanied by an invariable ⲡⲉ.
ⲛⲉ⸗ϥ.ⲛⲁ.ⲙⲟⲩ ⲡⲉ (John 4:47). *He was going to die.*

254. The circumstantial conversion is introduced by ⲉ-/ⲉ⸗.
ⲛⲓⲙ ⲛ̄-ⲣ̄ⲣⲟ ⲉ⸗ϥ.ⲛⲁ.ⲃⲱⲕ ⲉ-ⲙⲓϣⲉ ⲙⲛ̄ ⲕⲉ.ⲣ̄ⲣⲟ (Luke 14:31), *which king, going to war with another king…*

255. The relative conversion is introduced by ⲉⲧⲉ-/ⲉⲧ⸗.
ⲡ.ⲉⲧ.ⲛⲁ.ⲥⲱⲧⲙ̄ ⲉ-ⲡⲉⲧⲛ̄.ϣⲁϫⲉ, *the one who will hear your* (pl.) *words…*
ⲡ.ⲏⲓ ⲇⲉ ⲉⲧⲉⲧⲛ̄.ⲛⲁ.ⲃⲱⲕ ⲉϩⲟⲩⲛ ⲉⲣⲟ⸗ⲥ (Luke 10:5), *the house in which you* (pl.) *will go.*

256. The focalising conversion of the future (future II) is introduced by ⲉⲣⲉ-/ⲉ⸗
ⲉ⸗ⲓ.ⲛⲁ.ⲕⲣⲓⲛⲉ ⲙ̄ⲙⲟ⸗ⲕ ⲉⲃⲟⲗ ϩⲛ̄ ⲣⲱ⸗ⲕ (Luke 19:22). *It is by your mouth that I judge you.*
ⲙⲏ ⲉⲣⲉ ⲧⲁ.ⲯⲩⲭⲏ ⲛⲁ.ϩⲩⲡⲟⲧⲁⲥⲥⲉ ⲁⲛ ⲙ̄-ⲡ.ⲛⲟⲩⲧⲉ (Ps 61:2). *Isn't it to God that my soul will submit?*

257. The negation is …ⲁⲛ.

258. The pronominal form of the conjugation base with the suffix of the 2nd pers. f. sg. is ⲉⲣⲉ.

259. This tense generally expresses an intention, a supposition or a perspective.

III. The durative sentence with adverbial predicate
Structure

260. Definite subject – predicate (adverb or prepositional expression)

261. The negation is (ⲛ̄-)… ⲁⲛ

262. After the ⲛ̄ of the negation the personal pronoun of the 2nd pers. m. sg. can be ⲅ instead of ⲕ.
ⲡⲁ.ⲛⲟⲃⲉ ⲙ̄-ⲡⲁ.ⲙ̄ⲧⲟ ⲉⲃⲟⲗ ⲛ̄-ⲟⲩⲟⲉⲓϣ ⲛⲓⲙ (Ps 50 (51):3). *My sin is always in front of me.*
ⲕ.ⲙ̄-ⲡⲉⲓ.ⲙⲁ (Z 353:11). *You are here (in this place).*
ⲛ̄.ⲧ.ⲙⲉ ϩⲙ̄-ⲡⲁⲓ ⲁⲛ (1John 2:4). *The truth is not in him (this).*

Conversions

263. The preterit conversion is introduced by ⲛⲉⲣⲉ-/ⲛⲉ⸗.
It is often accompanied by an invariable ⲡⲉ.
ⲛⲉ⸗ϥ.ϩⲙ̄-ⲡ.ⲕⲟⲥⲙⲟⲥ ⲡⲉ (John 1:10). *He was in the world.*

264. The circumstantial conversion is introduced by ⲉⲣⲉ-/ⲉ⸗.
ⲁ⸗ⲥ.ⲉⲓ ⲉⲧⲓ ⲉⲣⲉ-ⲡ.ⲕⲁⲕⲉ ⲃ̄ⲃⲟⲗ (John 20:1). *She came while it was dark outside.*

265. The relative conversion is introduced by ⲉⲧⲉⲣⲉ-/ⲉⲧ⸗.
ⲛ.ⲉⲧⲉⲣⲉ-ⲡ.ⲥⲁϩⲟⲩ ϩⲣⲁⲓ ϩⲓϫⲱ⸗ⲟⲩ (ShIII 189:15). *Those on which the curse rests (is).*

266. The focalising conversion is introduced by ⲉⲣⲉ-/ⲉ⸗.

ⲉⲣⲉ-ⲧ.ⲡⲏⲅⲏ ⲙ̄-ⲡ.ⲱⲛ̄ϩ ϩⲛ̄-ⲧ.ϭⲓϫ ⲙ̄-ⲡ.ⲇⲓⲕⲁⲓⲟⲥ (Prov 10:11). *The source of life is in the hand of the righteous.*

C. The durative sentence with indefinite subject

267. In the preceding durative sentences the subject was always definite or personal. In the case of an indefinite subject, a periphrastic construction with ⲟⲩⲛ̄- (negation ⲙⲛ̄-) is used.
This includes relative propositions with a general meaning, even when they are preceded by a definite article.
For the conversions of the present and the future one also finds construction without ⲟⲩⲛ̄- (cf. 277).

Structure

268. ⲟⲩⲛ̄-/ⲙⲛ̄- – indefinite subject – predicate

269. After ⲉ ⲟⲩⲛ̄ is written ⲩⲛ̄.
ⲙⲏ ⲟⲩⲛ̄-ⲙⲉⲉⲩⲉ ⲡⲟⲗⲩⲙⲉⲓ ⲛⲙ̄ⲙⲁⲕ (ApophPatr 181). *Aren't there thoughts (that) fight against you?*
ⲛⲁⲙⲉ ⲟⲩⲛ̄-ⲁⲅⲁⲑⲟⲛ ⲛⲓⲙ ⲛⲁ.ϣⲱⲡⲉ ⲛⲁϥ (ShIV 188:1–2). *Really, everything good will happen to him.*
ⲙⲏ ⲙⲛ̄-ⲙⲛ̄ⲧⲥⲛⲟⲟⲩⲥ ⲛ̄-ⲟⲩⲛⲟⲩ ϩⲛ̄-ⲡⲉ.ϩⲟⲟⲩ (John 11:9). *Aren't there 12 hours in a day?*

270. ⲟⲩⲟⲛ ⲛⲓⲙ and ...ⲛⲓⲙ can occur as subject of this construction, but they can also be used in the definite present and future sentence (cf. 024, 078).

271. The predicate can be (1) an infinitive, (2) a stative, (3) the auxiliary ⲛⲁ- followed by an infinitive, or (4) an adverbial construction.
Subject and predicate are not bound. Other elements can be intercalated.
ⲟⲩⲛ̄-ϭⲉ ⲇⲉ ⲕⲱⲧ ⲉϫⲱⲥ (1Cor 3:10). *But someone else builds upon it.*

Conversions

272. The preterit conversion is introduced by ⲛⲉ.
ⲛⲉ.ⲩⲛ̄ ⲟⲩⲟⲉⲓⲛ ϣⲟⲟⲡ ⲙⲛ̄ ⲟⲩ.ⲕⲁⲕⲉ ⲁⲩⲱ ⲛⲉ-ⲩⲛ̄ ⲟⲩ.ⲡ̄ⲛ̄ⲁ ϩⲛ̄ ⲧ.ⲟⲩ.ⲙⲏⲧⲉ (ParSem 1:24–28). *There existed light and darkness and there was spirit in their midst.*

273. The circumstantial conversion is introduced by ⲉ.
ⲡ.ⲭ̄ⲥ̄ ⲡⲁⲓ ⲉ.ⲩⲛ̄ ϭⲟⲙ ⲙ̄ⲙⲟϥ ⲉ-ⲃⲟⲗⲕ̄ ⲉⲃⲟⲗ (Silv 96:20s.), *the Christ, the one who is able to set you free.*

274. The relative conversion is preceded by ⲉⲧⲉ.
ⲛ̄ⲧⲟⲕ ⲉⲧⲉ ⲟⲩⲛ̄-ϭⲟⲙ ⲙ̄ⲙⲟⲕ ϩⲙ ⲙⲁ ⲛⲓⲙ (StelesSeth 119:30s.), *you, who have power (to you) in every place.*

275. The focalizing conversion is preceded by ⲉ.

ⲉ.ⲙⲛ̄-ϣϭⲟⲙ ⲉⲛⲉϩ ⲉ-ϫⲱⲕ ⲉⲃⲟⲗ ⲛ̄-ⲛ̄.ⲉⲧ.ϯ-ⲡⲉ⸗ⲩ.ⲟⲩⲟⲓ ⲉⲣⲟ⸗ⲟⲩ (Heb 10:1).
It can never make perfect those who draw near.

276. For the focalizing conversion of a negative sentence introduced by ⲙⲛ̄-, there is a variant introduced by ⲉⲧⲉ.
ⲉⲧⲉ.ⲙⲛ̄-ϭⲱⲣϭ ⲇⲉ ⲛⲏⲩ ⲉϫⲛ̄-ⲛⲓⲙ ⲉⲃⲟⲗ ϩⲓⲧⲟⲟⲧ⸗ϥ (Job 25:3). *And upon whom a hunt will not come through his hand?*

277. For the conversions of the affirmative propositions there are also variants without ⲟⲩⲛ̄-.
The preterit conversion is in that case introduced by ⲛⲉⲣⲉ-.
ⲛⲉⲣⲉ-ⲟⲩ.ⲛⲟϭ ⲛ̄-ⲱⲛⲉ ⲧⲁⲗⲏⲩ ⲉⲣⲟ⸗ϥ (BMis 474:17–18). *A big stone was placed on him.*
The circumstantial proposition is introduced by ⲉⲣⲉ-.
ϩⲱⲥ ⲉⲣⲉ-ⲟⲩ.ⲥϯⲭⲁⲣⲓⲟⲛ ⲧⲟ ϩⲓⲱⲱ⸗ϥ (ApophPatr 180). *…as if he was wearing a tunica.*
ⲉⲣⲉ.ⲛⲓⲙ ⲛⲁ.ⲛⲁ ⲛⲁ⸗ⲛ (P 131⁵4v *a*14). *Who will have mercy on us?*
The relative proposition is introduced by ⲉⲧⲉⲣⲉ-.
ⲡ.ⲙⲁ ⲅⲁⲣ ⲉⲧⲉⲣⲉ.ⲥⲛⲁⲩ ⲏ ϣⲟⲙⲛ̄ⲧ ⲥⲟⲟⲩϩ ⲉⲣⲟ⸗ϥ ⲉ-ⲡⲁ.ⲣⲁⲛ (Matt 18:20). *The place where two or three gather in my name…*

D. The object

278. In the durative sentence, the object can be immediately attached to a bound state of the infinitive under certain conditions. When the object is a noun, the infinitive has the prenominal state. When the object is a personal pronoun, it has the prepersonal state. The object can also be connected to the verb by the mediating preposition ⲛ̄-/ⲙ̄ⲙⲟ⸗. The way in which the object is connected depends on the nature of the object. This is explained in the Stern-Jernstedt rule.

The Stern-Jernstedt rule:
Direct connection

279. In the durative sentence the nominal object can only be directly attached to the verb (in the prenominal state) if it has no article or if it is an indefinite pronoun. It can thus not be a pronominal object.
ⲉ⸗ϥ.ⲛⲉϫ-ⲇⲁⲓⲙⲟⲛⲓⲟⲛ ⲉⲃⲟⲗ ϩⲛ̄-ⲃⲉⲉⲗⲍⲉⲃⲟⲩⲗ (Luke 11:15). *It is by Beelzeboul that he chases demons.*

Indirect connection

280. In the durative sentence every object that does not belong to the above mentioned categories is indirectly attached to the verb with the preposition ⲛ̄-/ⲙ̄ⲙⲟ⸗. This includes pronominal objects.
ⲛⲉ⸗ϥ.ⲛⲟⲩϫⲉ ⲇⲉ ⲉⲃⲟⲗ ⲛ̄-ⲟⲩ.ⲇⲁⲓⲙⲟⲛⲓⲟⲛ (Luke 11:14). *He threw out a demon.*

281. The infinitive that completes the future auxiliary ⲛⲁ- is not considered as a durative infinitive. (Only the auxiliary itself is durative.) In non-durative conjugations the object can optionally be connected to a bound state infinitive or to the preposition ⲛ̄-/ⲙ̄ⲙⲟ⸗.

282. The object can also be introduced by other prepositions:
ⲉ-/ⲉⲣⲟ⸗ is often used with verbs that express an intension or sense perception (e.g. ⲛⲁⲩ, *to see*; ⲥⲱⲧⲙ̄, *to hear*; ϫⲱϩ, *to touch*), but also with some other verbs (e.g. ⲙⲟⲩⲧⲉ, *to call*; ϭⲉ, *to find*; ⲉⲓⲙⲉ, *to know*; ⲥⲙⲟⲩ, *to bless*; ϩⲁⲣⲉϩ, *to protect*).

The prepositions ⲛ̄ⲥⲁ-/ⲛ̄ⲥⲱ⸗ (e.g. ϣⲓⲛⲉ, *to search*; ⲡⲱⲧ, *to persecute*; ⲥⲱⲃⲉ, *to mock*; ϩⲱⲧⲃ̄, *to kill*) and ϩⲁ-/ϩⲁⲣⲟ⸗ (e.g. ϥⲓ, *to carry*; ⲧⲱⲟⲩⲛ̄, *to lift*) normally modify the sense of the verb.

ⲛⲉ⸗ⲩ.ϣⲓⲛⲉ ⲛ̄ⲥⲱ⸗ⲓ (PS 48:23). *They searched for me.*
ⲛⲉ⸗ⲩ.ϣⲓⲛⲉ ⲙ̄ⲙⲟ⸗ⲓ. *They interrogated me.*
ⲛⲉ⸗ⲩ.ϣⲓⲛⲉ ⲉⲣⲟ⸗ⲓ. *They visited me.*

Exceptions

283. ⲟⲩⲉϣ-, ⲟⲩⲁϣ⸗ (*to want, desire, love*) always has the object immediately attached.

284. ⲣ̄-ⲡ.ⲙⲉⲉⲩⲉ ⲛ̄- (*to remember*) can have both constructions in the durative sentence ⲉⲓⲣⲉ ⲙ̄-ⲡ.ⲙⲉⲉⲩⲉ or ⲣ-ⲡ.ⲙⲉⲉⲩⲉ.

ⲉ⸗ⲓ.ⲟⲩⲉϣ-ⲟⲩ.ⲛⲁ ⲉϩⲟⲩⲉ-ⲟⲩ.ⲑⲩⲥⲓⲁ (Matt 9:13). *More than a sacrifice, it is mercy that I need.*
ⲉ⸗ⲉⲓ.ⲉⲓⲣⲉ ⲙ̄-ⲡ.ⲙⲉⲉⲩⲉ ⲛ̄-ⲛⲉ⸗ⲕ.ⲣⲙ̄ⲉⲓⲏ (2Tim 1:4). *When I remember your (sg.) tears.*
ⲛ̄.ⲧⲉⲧⲛ̄.ⲣ̄-ⲡ.ⲙⲉⲉⲩⲉ ⲁⲛ ⲙ̄-ⲡ.ϯⲟⲩ ⲛ̄-ⲟⲉⲓⲕ (Matt 16:9). *Don't you (pl.) remember the 5 breads?*

Double object

285. A limited number of verbs can have a double object. Among these are principally the causative verbs with ⲧ (e.g. ⲧⲙ̄ⲙⲟ, *to make to eat*; ⲧⲥⲟ, *to make to drink*; ⲧⲧⲟ, *to make to give*) (cf. 114).
ⲁ⸗ⲩ.ⲧⲥⲟ ⲙ̄-ⲡⲉ⸗ⲩ.ⲉⲓⲱⲧ ⲛ̄-ⲟⲩ.ⲏⲣⲡ̄ (Gen 19:33). *They made their father drink wine.*

286. If the object of a non-durative sentence (cf. 279–280) is a personal pronoun, it can be immediately attached to the infinitive. The second object can be attached directly to this construction, or indirectly with the preposition ⲛ̄-. In the first case the infinitive is in the reduced pronominal state. (LAYTON 172).
ⲧⲙ̄ⲙⲉ⸗ϥ-ⲟⲉⲓⲕ (ShIII 106:18). *Make him eat bread!*
ⲁ⸗ϥ.ⲧⲙ̄ⲙⲟ⸗ⲕ ⲙ̄-ⲡ.ⲙⲁⲛⲛⲁ (Deut 8:3). *He made you (sg.) eat the manna.*

287. If the second object (of a non-durative sentence) is also a personal pronoun, it takes the form of the second suffix (cf. 157):

1	-ⲧ	-ⲥⲛ
2 m.	-ⲕ, -ⲥⲕ̄, -ⲧⲕ̄	-ⲧⲏⲩⲧⲛ̄
2 f.	?	
3 m.	-ϥ, -ⲥϥ̄	-ⲥⲉ, -ⲥⲟⲩ
3 f.	-ⲥ	

ⲁ⸗ϥ.ⲧⲥⲟ⸗ϥ⸗ⲥϥ̄. *He made him drink it.*

288. The verb ϯ-ⲛⲁ⸗ (*to give to*) has two objects, both of which are immediately attached to the verb. The first object is always a personal pronoun and expresses the person to whom something is given. The second object refers to the thing given. If the second object is a personal pronoun, it has the form of the second suffixes (cf. 157, 287).
ϥ.ⲛⲁ.ϯ-ⲛⲁ⸗ⲕ⸗ⲥⲉ ⲙ̄.ⲡⲟⲟⲩ (Sir 20:15). *He will give them to you today.*
This verb is a rare variant for the construction with dative ϯ ⲛ̄-/ⲙ̄ⲙⲟ⸗ ⲛ̄-/ⲛⲁ⸗.

289. The suffix of the 3rd pers. pl., -ⲥⲟⲩ/-ⲥⲉ, is also used for the object of a limited number of verbs (e.g. ⲥϩⲁⲓ⸗, *to write*; ⲧⲟⲟⲩ⸗, *to buy*; ⲧⲛ̄ⲛⲟⲟⲩ⸗, *to send*; ϫⲟⲟⲩ⸗, *to send*; ϭⲟⲟⲩ⸗, *to narrow*). It is also used after ϯⲛⲁ⸗, certain imperatives (ⲁⲛⲓ⸗, *bring!*; ⲁⲣⲓ⸗, *do! make!*; ⲁⲩⲉⲓ⸗, *give!*; ⲁϫⲓ⸗, *say!*) and for the personal subject of ⲟⲩⲛ̄ⲧⲁ⸗/ⲙⲛ̄ⲧⲁ⸗ (cf. 154–157).

Reflexivity and reciprocity

290. To express reflexivity the personal pronoun corresponding to the subject is used for the object.
ⲡ.ⲥⲁⲉⲓⲛ ⲁⲣⲓ-ⲡⲁϩⲣⲉ ⲉⲣⲟ⸗ⲕ (Luke 4:23). *Doctor, heal yourself!*

291. To emphasise the reflexivity the object can be accompanied by the inflected modifier ⲙ̄ⲙⲓⲛⲙ̄ⲙⲟ⸗.

292. To express reciprocity ⲉⲣⲏⲩ preceded by the possessive article is used.
ⲁⲛⲟⲛ ⲙ̄.ⲙⲉⲗⲟⲥ ⲛ̄-ⲛⲉⲛ.ⲉⲣⲏⲩ (Rom 12:5). *We are the members of one another.*
ⲡⲁⲣⲁⲕⲁⲗⲉⲓ ⲛ̄-ⲛⲉⲧⲛ̄.ⲉⲣⲏⲩ (1Thess 5:11). *Exhort one another (pl.).*

See exercise 3

The suffixically conjugated verboid

293. The suffixically conjugated verboid has its subject attached to it (cf. 149–157). It always occurs in the prenominal or prepersonal bound state. It normally expresses a present tense (with the exception of ⲡⲉϫⲁ⸗ϥ). The verbs expressing a quality can also have past meaning when they are converted into a preterit. For other verbs a periphrastic construction with ϣⲱⲡⲉ is used when a time other then present is expressed.

294. The negation is rare. Its construction is: (ⲛ̄) – verboid – subject – ⲁⲛ.

Conversions

295. The verbs expressing a quality have the preterit conversion introduced by ⲛⲉ (often accompanied by an invariable ⲡⲉ, cf. 207).
ⲛⲉ.ⲛⲉⲥⲱ⸗ϥ ⲡⲉ ⲛ̄-ⲡ.ⲛⲟⲩⲧⲉ (Acts 7:20). *He was beautiful to God.*

296. The circumstantial conversion is introduced by ⲉ-.
ⲣⲁϣⲉ… ⲉ.ⲛⲁⲁ⸗ϥ ⲉ-ⲡⲁⲓ (3John 4). *A joy… bigger than this one.*

297. The relative conversion is introduced by ⲉⲧ(ⲉ).
ⲡⲉ.ϭⲣⲟϭ ⲉⲧ.ⲛⲁⲛⲟⲩ⸗ϥ (Matt 13:38). *The seed that is good (the good seed).*

298. The focalising conversion is introduced by ⲉ.
ϩⲓⲧⲛ̄-ⲟⲩ ⲉ.ⲛⲁⲁ⸗ⲩ ⲉ-ⲛⲉ⸗ⲩ.ⲉⲣⲏⲩ (ShChass 135:44–46). *How is it that some are greater than the others?*

ϩⲛⲉ-, ϩⲛⲁ⸗ has the circumstantial, the relative and the focalising conversion.
ⲉ.ⲛ.ϩⲛⲁ⸗ⲓ ⲁⲛ ⲉ-ϫⲟⲟ⸗ϥ (ShAmél II 191:11). *Even though I don't want to say it…*
ⲕⲁⲧⲁ-ⲡ.ⲉⲧⲉ.ϩⲛⲉ-ⲧⲉ⸗ⲕ.ⲯⲩⲭⲏ (Deut 12:15). *According to what your soul wants.*
ⲉ.ϩⲛⲉ-ⲡ.ϫⲟⲉⲓⲥ ϩⲛ̄-ⲛ.ⲉⲧ.ⲣ̄-ϩⲟⲧⲉ ϩⲏⲧ⸗ϥ (Ps 146:11). *It is in those which fear him, that the Lord takes pleasure.*

299. ⲟⲩⲛ̄/ⲙⲛ̄- and ⲟⲩⲛ̄ⲧⲉ- ⲙⲛ̄ⲧⲉ- have the four conversions (just like other durative constructions, cf. 238–246 and 251–259).
ⲛⲉ.ⲟⲩⲛ̄ⲧ⸗ⲥ ⲟⲩ.ϩⲙ̄ϩⲁⲗ (Gen 16:1). *She had a servant.*
ⲉ.ⲙⲛ̄-ⲛⲟⲙⲟⲥ (Rom 5:13). *When there is no Law…*
ⲛ̄-ⲑⲉ ⲅⲁⲣ ⲉⲧⲉ.ⲩⲛ̄ⲧⲉ-ⲡ.ⲓⲱⲧ ⲡ.ⲱⲛϩ̄ (John 5:26). *For in the same way that the Father has the life…*
ⲉ.ⲙⲛ̄ϯ-ⲟⲩ.ϩⲱⲃ ⲇⲉ ⲙ̄ⲙⲁⲩ ⲉ⸗ϥ.ⲟⲣϫ ⲉ-ⲥϩⲁⲓ ⲙ̄-ⲡ.ⲣ̄ⲣⲟ ⲉⲧⲃⲏⲏⲧ⸗ϥ (Acts 25:26). *But I have nothing definite to write to the emperor about him.*

See exercise 4

The existential and the indicational sentence

300. An existential sentence can be expressed in Coptic by means of the construction with ⲞⲨⲚ̄-/ⲘⲚ̄- (*there is/there isn't*). An indicational sentence can begin with ⲈⲒⲤ- (*look! behold!*). With a noun ⲈⲒⲤ- can also mean *there is*.
ⲈⲒⲤ-ⲞⲨ.ⲤⲂⲰ Ⲃ̄-ⲂⲢ̄ⲢⲈ (Mark 1:27). *Look, there is a new teaching!*

301. This construction can as well occur with a noun as with a sentence.

302. ⲞⲨⲚ̄-, ⲘⲚ̄- can occur with a noun or with a durative sentence.
Ⲙ̄ⲘⲚ̄-Ⲡ.ⲈⲦ.ⲚⲈⲀ∕ϥ ⲈⲢⲞⲒ (GreatSeth 64:20). *There is no one who is greater than me.*
ⲚⲈ.ⲞⲨⲚ̄ ⲞⲨ.ⲚⲞϬ Ⲛ̄-ϢⲦⲞⲢⲦⲢ̄ ϢⲞⲞⲠ ϨⲘ̄ ⲠⲒ.ⲦⲞⲠⲞⲤ ⲦⲎⲢϥ̄ Ⲛ̄-ⲔⲞⲤⲘⲒⲔⲞⲚ (GreatSeth 52:10–12). *There was a great confusion in the whole cosmic place.*

303. Before a noun, ⲈⲒⲤ- occurs alone. Before a pronoun or a verb, ⲈⲒⲤ ϨⲎⲎⲦⲈ (*look, behold*) is normally used instead of ⲈⲒⲤ.
ⲈⲒⲤ ⲞⲨ.ⲢⲰⲘⲈ Ⲉ∕ϥ.ⲘⲈϨ Ⲛ̄-ⲤⲰⲂⲀϨ (Luke 5:12). *Behold, there was a man full of (filled with) leprosy.*
ⲈⲒⲤϨⲎⲎⲦⲈ ϬⲈ Ⲁ-ⲦⲈ.ⲠⲖⲀⲚⲎ Ⲛ̄-Ⲛ.ⲔⲞⲞⲨⲈ ⲞⲨⲀⲚϨ̄ ⲈⲂⲞⲖ (ShOrig 413). *Behold, the error of the others is manifest.*
ⲈⲒⲤ-Ⲡ.ϪⲞⲈⲒⲤ Ⲁ∕ϥ.ⲤⲰⲦⲘ̄ Ⲉ-Ⲡ.ⲀϢⲔⲀⲔ Ⲙ̄-ⲠⲀ.ⲢⲒⲘⲈ (ExAn 137:20s.). *Behold, the Lord, he has listened to the cry of my tears.*

304. ⲞⲨⲚ̄- with a durative sentence always has an indefinite subject (cf. 267).
ⲀⲨⲰ ⲈϢⲰⲠⲈ ⲞⲨⲚ̄-ⲞⲨ.ⲘⲈⲖⲞⲤ ϢⲰⲚⲈ (1Cor 12:26). *And when one of the members is sick...*
ⲘⲚ̄-ⲀⲚⲀⲤⲦⲀⲤⲒⲤ ⲚⲀϢⲰⲠⲈ (Mk 12:18). *There will be no resurrection.*

305. A verbal sentence starting with ⲈⲒⲤ (ϨⲎⲎⲦⲈ) can have either a definite or an indefinite subject.
ⲀⲨⲰ ⲈⲒⲤ ϨⲎⲦⲈ ⲈⲒⲤ ⲒⲀⲔⲔⲰⲂⲞⲤ Ⲁ∕ϥ.Ⲣ̄-ⲆⲒⲀⲔⲞⲚⲈⲒ ϨⲒϪⲚ̄ ⲠⲦⲞⲞⲨ (1ApocJames CT 17,7f.). *Behold, James did his service on the mountain.*
ⲈⲒⲤ-ⲞⲨ.ⲘⲚⲦϪⲀϪⲈ Ⲉ-Ⲡ.ⲚⲞⲨⲦⲈ ⲚⲀ.ⲘⲈ (ShIII 75:7). *Here is truly a hostility against God.*

306. For the conversions of ⲞⲨⲚ̄-, ⲘⲚ̄- cf. 272–276.

307. The construction with ⲈⲒⲤ- has no conversions.

See exercise 5

The non-durative sentence

308. The non-durative sentence consists of three elements: a conjugation base, followed by the subject and the predicate. The conjugation base has a bound state depending on the subject, which can be definite, indefinite or personal (cf. 007). The predicate is an infinitive. The object of the infinitive can indiscriminately be attached to the bound state of the infinitive as to the preposition N̄-/M̄MO⸗ (or another preposition, cf. 282). There are two sets of conjugation bases: (1) those forming a main clause, and (2) those forming a subordinate clause.

A. Main clause bases

309. This category consists of five 'tenses' which can be used in main clauses (principal sentences). Four of the five conjugations have different conjugation bases for the affirmative and for the negative conjugation (the past, the aorist, the optative and the jussive). The 5th only exists as a negative conjugation base (*not yet*).

I. The past
Structure

310. Affirmative
ⲁ-/ⲁ⸗ – subject – infinitive
ⲁ⸗ϥ.ⲥⲱⲧⲡ̄, *he chose*
ⲁ-ⲡ.ⲣⲱⲙⲉ ⲥⲱⲧⲡ̄, *the man chose*

311. Negative
ⲙ̄ⲡⲉ-/ⲙ̄ⲡ(ⲉ)⸗ – subject – infinitive
ⲙ̄ⲡ⸗ϥ.ⲥⲱⲧⲡ̄, *he didn't choose*
ⲙ̄ⲡⲉ-ⲡ.ⲣⲱⲙⲉ ⲥⲱⲧⲡ̄, *the man didn't choose*

Use

312. This form normally expresses a past reality without the connotation duration. It is the tense normally used in narration. If the conjugation base ⲁ is followed by ⲟⲩ (indefinite article or the 3rd pers. pl. suffix pronoun) it is usually written ⲁⲩ.
ⲁ⸗ϥ.ϫⲓ ⲛ̄-ⲟⲩ.ⲟⲉⲓⲕ ⲁ⸗ϥ.ⲥⲙⲟⲩ ⲉⲣⲟ⸗ϥ ⲁ⸗ϥ.ⲡⲟϣ⸗ϥ ⲁⲩⲱ ⲁ⸗ϥ.ⲧⲁⲁ⸗ϥ ⲛⲁ⸗ⲩ (Mark 14, 22). *He took the bread, blessed it, broke it and gave it to them.*
ⲁ-ϩⲁϩ ⲡⲓⲥⲧⲉⲩⲉ ⲉⲣⲟ⸗ϥ (John 7:31). *Many believed in him.*
ⲁⲛⲟⲕ ⲁ⸗ⲓ.ⲉⲓ ϩⲙ̄-ⲡ.ⲣⲁⲛ ⲙ̄-ⲡⲁ.ⲓⲱⲧ ⲁⲩⲱ ⲙ̄ⲡⲉ⸗ⲧⲛ̄.ϫⲓⲧ (John 5:43). *I have come in the name of my Father and you* (pl.) *haven't received me.*

Conversions

313. The preterit conversion is introduced by ⲛⲉ.ⲁ-, ⲛⲉⲁ⸗ and ⲛⲉ.ⲙⲡⲉ, ⲛⲉ.ⲙⲡ⸗.
ⲛⲉ.ⲁ⸗ϥ.ⲉⲓ ⲉⲃⲟⲗ ϩⲙ̄-ⲡ.ⲉⲓⲟⲟⲣ ⲁⲩⲱ ⲛⲉ⸗ϥ.ⲙⲉϩ ⲛ-ⲙ̄ⲥⲁϩ… ⲛ̄ⲧⲟϥ ⲇⲉ ⲁ⸗ϥ.ϣⲗⲏⲗ ⲁ⸗ϥ.ϫⲓⲟⲟⲣ (VA 21:7–9). *He had come by the canal and this was filled with crocodiles…, but he prayed and crossed (it).*

314. The circumstantial conversion is normally preceded by ⲉ. The orthography of he circumstantial conversion of the negative past might be reduced to the superlinear stroke.
ⲟⲩ.ⲉⲡⲓⲥⲧⲟⲗⲏ ⲉ.ⲁ⸗ϥ.ⲥⲁϩ⸗ⲥ̄ ϣⲁ-ⲛⲉ.ⲥⲛⲏⲩ ⲉⲧ-ϩⲛ̄-ⲧⲉ.ⲝⲩⲛⲉ (VA 1:3–4). *A letter he has written to the brethren abroad.*
ⲛ̄ⲛⲉ⸗ⲩ.ⲉϣ.ⲣ̄-ⲗⲁⲁⲩ ⲛ̄-ϩⲱⲃ ⲉϫⲱ⸗ⲟⲩ ⲙ̄ⲡ⸗ⲟⲩ.ϫⲛⲟⲩ⸗ⲟⲩ (ShIV 44:27). *They won't be able to do anything unless they ask it to them.*

315. The relative conversion is introduced by (ⲉ)ⲛ̄ⲧ.ⲁ-, (ⲉ)ⲛ̄ⲧⲁ⸗ and ⲉⲧⲉ.ⲙⲡⲉ-, ⲉⲧⲉ.ⲙⲡ⸗.
ⲡ.ϫⲟⲉⲓⲥ ⲉⲛⲧ.ⲁ⸗ⲕ.ϫⲓ.ⲟⲩⲁ ⲉⲣⲟ⸗ϥ (ShChass 42:34–35). *The Lord whom you cursed.*
ⲡ.ⲣⲱⲙⲉ ⲉⲧⲉ.ⲙ̄ⲡ⸗ϥ̄.ⲃⲱⲕ ϩⲙ̄-ⲡ.ϣⲟϫⲛⲉ ⲛ̄-ⲛ.ⲁⲥⲉⲃⲏⲥ (Ps 1:1). *The man who has not walked according to the advice of the impious.*

316. The focalising conversion is introduced by (ⲉ)-ⲛ̄ⲧⲉ-/(ⲉ)-ⲛ̄ⲧⲁ⸗.
ⲡⲉⲓ.ϩⲱⲃ ⲛⲧⲁ⸗ⲓ.ⲛⲁⲩ ⲉⲣⲟ⸗ϥ ϩⲙ̄-ⲡ.ⲉⲃⲟⲧ ⲉⲡⲏⲡ (ShIV 198:15). *It is in the month Epep that I have sent this thing.*

317. The negation of the focalising conversion is … ⲁⲛ
ⲛ̄ⲧⲁ⸗ⲓ.ⲥⲟⲩⲱⲛ⸗ⲉ ⲅⲁⲣ ⲁⲛ ⲛ̄-ⲃⲣ̄ⲣⲉ ⲁⲗⲗⲁ ϯ-ⲥⲟⲟⲩⲛ ⲙ̄ⲙⲟ ϫⲓⲛ-ⲛ̄.ϣⲟⲣⲡ (ShIII 21). *It is not recently that I've come to know you (f. sg.), but I know you since the beginning.*

318. In a negative sentence one might find the normal form of the past tense instead of an expected focalising conversion (alternatively the relative conversion ⲉⲧⲉ ⲙ̄ⲡⲉ might be used).
ⲉⲧⲉ.ⲙⲡⲉ.ϫⲱϩⲙ̄ ϩⲛ̄-ⲁϣ ⲙ̄-ⲙⲁ (Jer 3:2). *Where (in which place) haven't you (f.sg.) been defiled?*

II. "Not yet"

Structure

319. ⲙ̄ⲡⲁⲧⲉ-/ⲙ̄ⲡⲁⲧ⸗ – subject – infinitive
ⲙ̄ⲡⲁⲧ⸗ϥ.ⲥⲱⲧⲡ̄, *he hasn't chosen yet*
ⲙ̄ⲡⲁⲧⲉ-ⲡ.ⲣⲱⲙⲉ ⲥⲱⲧⲡ̄, *the man hasn't chosen yet*

320. This tense is always negative.
ⲙ̄ⲡⲁⲧⲉ-ⲧⲁ.ⲟⲩⲛⲟⲩ.ⲉⲓ (John 2:4). *My hour has not yet come.*

Conversions

321. The preterit conversion is introduced by ⲛⲉ. It can be accompanied by an invariable ⲡⲉ (cf. 207).

ⲛⲉ.ⲙⲡⲁⲧ⳱ⲟⲩ.ⲛⲉϫ-ⲓⲱϩⲁⲛⲛⲏⲥ ⲅⲁⲣ ⲡⲉ ⲉ-ⲡⲉ.ϣⲧⲉⲕⲟ (John 3:24). *For John had not yet been thrown in prison.*

322. The circumstantial conversion is usually introduced by ⲉ. Orthographically this can be reduced to the superlinear stroke. The circumstantial conversion is translated: *before.*
ⲁ-ⲧⲉ⳱ϥ.ⲯⲩⲭⲏ ⲣ̄-ⲛⲟⲃⲉ ⲉ.ⲙⲡⲁⲧⲉ⳱ⲥ̄.ⲉⲓ ⲁ-ⲡⲉ⳱ϥ.ⲥⲱⲙⲁ (Wess 9, 144c). *His soul has sinned before it came to his body.*
ⲙ̄ⲡⲁⲧⲉ-ⲟⲩ.ⲁⲗⲉⲕⲧⲱⲣ ⲙⲟⲩⲧⲉ ⲛ̄-ⲥⲉⲡ ⲥⲛⲁⲩ ⲕ.ⲛⲁ-ⲁⲡⲁⲣⲛⲁ ⲙ̄ⲙⲟ⳱ⲓ ⲛ̄-ϣⲙⲛ̄ⲧ-ⲥⲱⲱⲡ (Mark 14:72). *Before a cock crows twice, you will deny me thrice.*

323. The relative conversion is introduced by ⲉⲧⲉ.
ⲟⲩⲟⲛ ⲅⲁⲣ ⲛⲓⲙ ⲉⲧⲉ.ⲙ̄ⲡⲁⲧ⳱ⲟⲩ.ⲥⲟⲩⲱⲛ⳱ⲅ ⲙⲛ̄-ⲛⲉ⳱ⲕ.ⲙⲁⲅⲓⲁ (ShIII 77). *For everyone who didn't know you yet, you and your magic tricks...*

III. The aorist
Structure

324. Affirmative
ϣⲁⲣⲉ-/ϣⲁ⳱ – subject – infinitive
ϣⲁ⳱ϥ.ⲥⲱⲧⲡ̄, *he is used to choose, he chooses*
ϣⲁⲣⲉ-ⲡ.ⲣⲱⲙⲉ ⲥⲱⲧⲡ̄, *the man is used to choose, chooses*

325. Negative
ⲙⲉⲣⲉ/ⲙⲉ⳱ – subject – infinitive
ⲙⲉ⳱ϥ.ⲥⲱⲧⲡ̄, *he is not used to choose, he doesn't choose*
ⲙⲉⲣⲉ-ⲡ.ⲣⲱⲙⲉ.ⲥⲱⲧⲡ̄, *the man is not used to choose, doesn't choose*

Use

326. This tense expresses a repeated action, a habit or a general truth without implying any temporal aspect. The negation can also express incapacity (Till 305).
ϣⲁⲣⲉ-ⲟⲩ.ϣⲏⲣⲉ ⲛ̄-ⲥⲟⲫⲟⲥ ⲉⲩⲫⲣⲁⲛⲉ ⲙ̄-ⲡⲉ⳱ϥ.ⲉⲓⲱⲧ (Prov 10:1). *A wise child pleases his father.*
ⲡ.ⲥⲟⲟⲩⲛ̄ ϣⲁ⳱ϥ.ϫⲓⲥⲉ ⲧ.ⲁⲅⲁⲡⲏ ⲇⲉ ϣⲁ⳱ⲥ.ⲕⲱⲧ (1Cor 8:1). *Knowledge elevates and love builds.*
ⲙⲉⲣⲉ-ⲓⲟⲩⲇⲁⲓ ⲧⲱϩ ⲙⲛ̄-ⲥⲁⲙⲁⲣⲓⲧⲏⲥ (John 4:9). *Jews do not mix with the Samaritans.*

Conversions

327. The preterit conversion is introduced by ⲛⲉ.
ⲛ̄ⲧⲟⲕ ⲇⲉ ⲛⲉ.ϣⲁ⳱ⲕ.ⲡⲱⲣϫ̄ ⲉⲃⲟⲗ ⲙ̄ⲙⲟ⳱ⲛ (LetPetPhil 133:1s.). *But you were separated from us.*

328. The circumstantial conversion is introduced by ⲉ.
ⲛ̄-ⲑⲉ ⲇⲉ ⲛ̄-ⲛ̄.ⲧⲃⲛⲟⲟⲩⲉ ⲉϣⲁⲣⲉ-ⲡ⳱ⲟⲩ.ⲥⲱⲙⲁ ⲧⲉⲕⲟ ⲧⲉⲉⲓ ⲧⲉ ⲑⲉ ⲛ̄-ⲛⲉⲉⲓ.ⲡⲗⲁⲥⲙⲁ (LibThom 139:6–8). *In the way of the beasts when their body is destructed, in that way these moulded figures (will).*

329. The relative conversion is introduced by ⲉⲧⲉ (or ⲉ).

ⲡ.ⲧⲟⲟⲩ ⲉⲧⲉ.ϣⲁ⸗ⲩ.ⲙⲟⲩⲧⲉ ⲉⲣⲟ⸗ϥ ϫⲉ ⲡⲁ-ⲛⲓ.ϫⲟⲉⲓⲧ (LetPetPhil 133:14s.). *The mountain that is called the one of the olives.*

330. The focalising conversion is introduced by ⲉ. It is only attested for the affirmative form.
ⲉⲃⲟⲗ ϩⲓⲧⲟⲟⲧ ⲉ.ϣⲁ⸗ⲥ.ⲉⲓ ⲛ̄ϭⲓ-ϯ.ⲅⲛⲱⲥⲓⲥ (ProtTrim 36,9s.). *It is through me that the gnosis comes.*

IV. The optative

Structure

331. Affirmative
ⲉⲣⲉ-/ⲉ⸗ – subject – ⲉ – infinitive
ⲉ⸗ϥ.ⲉ.ⲥⲱⲧⲡ̄, *he shall choose*
ⲉⲣⲉ-ⲡ.ⲣⲱⲙⲉ ⲥⲱⲧⲡ̄, *the man shall choose*

332. The prepersonal conjugation base with the suffix of the 2nd pers. f. sg. is ⲉⲣⲉ.

333. With a nominal subject the ⲉ before the infinitive might be omitted. In that case the optative has the same form as the focalising conversion of the present.
ⲉⲣⲉ-ⲡ.ϫⲟⲉⲓⲥ ⲧⲱⲱⲃⲉ ⲛⲁ⸗ϥ ⲕⲁⲧⲁ-ⲛⲉ⸗ϥ.ϩⲃⲏⲩⲉ (2Tim 4:14). *The Lord will requite him according to his works.*

334. In this case, the predicate might help to distinguish between both forms. If it is a stative or an adverbial expression, we certainly deal with the focalising conversion of the present. If the predicate is an infinitive which has the prepersonal bound state, or a causative infinitive, we certainly deal with an optative. In other cases the ambiguity remains.

335. Negative
ⲛ̄ⲛⲉ-/ⲛ̄ⲛⲉ⸗ – subject – infinitive
ⲛ̄ⲛⲉ⸗ϥ.ⲥⲱⲧⲡ̄, *he shall not choose*
ⲛ̄ⲛⲉ-ⲡ.ⲣⲱⲙⲉ ⲥⲱⲧⲡ̄, *the man shall not choose*

336. The usual form of the prepersonal conjugation base with the suffix of the 1st pers. sg. is ⲛ̄ⲛⲁ (ⲛ̄ⲛⲉ⸗ⲓ is a rare variant).
After ϫⲉⲕⲁ(ⲁ)ⲥ one might find the variant ⲉⲛⲛⲉ⸗.

Use

337. This tense expresses a future reality without connection to the actual situation of the speaker. This use includes orders, promises, predictions, wishes, etc. In a main clause it is used to formulate a precept, an order or a moderate prohibition. It also expresses a deliberative question at the 1st person.
In the subordinate clause introduced by ϫⲉ or ϫⲉⲕⲁ(ⲁ)ⲥ it expresses a goal or result (cf. 447).
ⲉ⸗ⲓ.ⲉ.ⲕⲱ ⲛ̄-ⲟⲩ.ⲙⲛ̄ⲧ-ϫⲁϫⲉ ϩⲛ̄-ⲧⲉ⸗ⲕ.ⲙⲏⲧⲉ ⲙⲛ̄-ⲧⲉ⸗ⲕ.ⲥϩⲓⲙⲉ (Gen 3:15). *I will put animosity between you and your wife.*
ⲛ̄ⲛⲉ⸗ⲕ-ϩⲱⲧⲃ̄ (Deut 5:17). *You shall not kill.*

ⲘⲠⲢ̄-ⲔⲢⲒⲚⲈ ϪⲈⲔⲀⲤ Ⲛ̄ⲚⲈ⸌Ⲩ.ⲔⲢⲒⲚⲈ Ⲙ̄ⲘⲰ⸌ⲦⲚ̄ (Matt 7:1). *Do not judge in order not to be judged.*
ⲀⲖⲖⲀ ϪⲈⲔⲀⲤ Ⲉ⸌Ⲩ.Ⲉ.ϪⲰⲔ ⲈⲂⲞⲖ Ⲛ̄ϬⲒ-ⲚⲈ.ⲄⲢⲀⲪⲎ (Mark 14:49). *But in order that the Scriptures are fulfilled...*

338. In the works of Shenoute and other Sahidic authors the focalising conversion of the future can be used with the same meaning (cf. 256–259).
Ⲉ⸌Ⲩ.ⲚⲀ.ⲦⲀⲀ⸌ϤⲚⲀ⸌Ⲩ Ϩ̄Ⲙ̄-Ⲡ.ϢⲒ ⲈⲦ-ⲦⲎϢ (ShIV 55:20). *It will be given to them in the fixed measure.*

Conversions

339. There are no conversions of the positive form.

340. The negative form can be converted to a circumstantial sentence introduced by Ⲉ (which can be omitted for orthographic reasons).
Ⲉ⸌Ϥ.ⲦⲰⲘ Ⲛ̄-ⲚⲈ⸌ⲦⲚ̄.ⲘⲀⲀϪⲈ ϪⲈⲔⲀⲀⲤ Ⲉ.ⲚⲈ⸌Ⲩ.ⲤⲰⲦⲘ̄ Ⲉ-ⲦⲈ.ⲤⲘⲎ Ⲛ̄ⲦⲈ-ⲠⲀ.ϢⲀϪⲈ (2ApocJames 60:7–10). *He closes your (pl.) ears so that you may not hear the sound of my word.*

341. The relative conversion of the negative form is introduced by ⲈⲦⲈ (ⲈⲦⲈ.Ⲛ̄ⲚⲈ⸌ with a variant orthography ⲈⲦⲈ ⲚⲈ⸌).
Ⲡ.ⲈⲦⲈ.Ⲛ̄ⲚⲈ⸌Ϥ.ⲤⲞⲨⲚ̄-Ⲧ.ⲚⲞⲨⲚⲈ Ⲛ̄-Ⲧ.ⲔⲀⲔⲒⲀ Ⲛ̄-ⲞⲨ.ϢⲘ̄ⲘⲞ ⲈⲢⲞ⸌Ⲥ ⲀⲚ ⲠⲈ (DialSav 134:17–19). *The one who will not have known the root of the darkness, he will be no stranger to it.*

V. The jussive

Structure

342. Affirmative
ⲘⲀⲢⲈ-/ⲘⲀⲢ(Ⲉ)⸌ – subject – infinitive
ⲘⲀⲢⲈ⸌Ϥ.ⲤⲰⲦⲠ̄, *may he choose*
ⲘⲀⲢⲈ-Ⲡ.ⲢⲰⲘⲈ ⲤⲰⲦⲠ̄, *may the man choose*

343. This tense is only used for the 1st and 3rd persons. For the 2nd person the imperative is used instead (cf. 135–143).

344. An Ⲉ is intercalated in the prepersonal conjugation base of the 3rd pers. m. and f. sg.

345. Negative
ⲘⲠⲢ̄-ⲦⲢⲈ-/ⲘⲠ.Ⲣ̄-ⲦⲢⲈ⸌
ⲘⲠⲢ̄-ⲦⲢⲈ⸌Ϥ.ⲤⲰⲦⲠ̄, *may he not choose*
ⲘⲠⲈⲢ̄-ⲦⲢⲈ-Ⲡ.ⲢⲰⲘⲈ ⲤⲰⲦⲠ̄, *may the man not choose*

346. The negative form is actually the negation of the causative infinitive (cf. 132).

347. The prepersonal conjugation base with the suffix of the 1st pers. sg. is ⲘⲠⲢ̄-ⲦⲢⲀ.

348. There exists also an absolute form of the negative jussive: ⲘⲠⲰⲢ Ⲉ-ⲦⲢⲈ.

Use

349. The jussive normally expresses an order at the 1st or 3rd person. With the 1st person it often has an exhortative meaning. Sometimes it has a causative meaning. It rarely expresses a wish.

ⲙⲁⲣⲉ⸗ϥ.ⲣ̄-ⲟⲩⲟⲉⲓⲛ ⲛ̄ϭⲓ-ⲡⲉ⸗ⲧⲛ̄.ⲟⲩⲟⲉⲓⲛ (Matt 5:16). *That your* (pl.) *light might shine!*

ⲙ̄ⲡⲣ̄.ⲧⲣⲉ⸗ⲛ.ⲥⲱϣ ⲛ-ⲧⲉ.ⲭⲁⲣⲓⲥ ⲁⲗⲗⲁ ⲙⲁⲣ⸗ⲛ.ϯ-ⲉⲟⲟⲩ ⲛ̄ⲧⲟϥ ⲙ̄-ⲡ.ⲛⲟⲩⲧⲉ ⲡ.ⲉⲛⲧⲁ⸗ϥ.ⲕⲁⲁ⸗ⲛ ϩⲁ-ⲡⲉ⸗ⲛ.ⲁⲩⲧⲉϩⲟⲩⲥⲓⲟⲛ (ShIV 24:8–10). *Let us not despise the grace, but let us praise God, who has put us under our free will.*

Conversions

350. There are no conversions.

See exercise 6

B. Subordinate clause bases

351. The 'tenses' belonging to this category normally occur in subordinate sentences. They express 'relative time' (LAYTON 343) or an adverbial relation to the main clause (e.g. goal, condition).

352. The conjunctive bases are used to continue or extend other constructions. Unlike the precursive, the conditional and the limitative they can't precede the main clause.
Some of these tenses can also be used in an independent sentence.

353. The conjugation bases of this category have no separate negative forms. The negation ⲧⲙ̄- is intercalated after the personal subject or before the nominal subject.

354. The subordinate clause conjugations have no conversions.

I. The precursive

Structure

355. ⲛ̄ⲧⲉⲣⲉ-/ⲛ̄ⲧⲉⲣ(ⲉ)⸗ – subject – infinitive
ⲛ̄ⲧⲉⲣⲉ⸗ϥ.ⲥⲱⲧⲡ̄, *when he has/had chosen*
ⲛ̄ⲧⲉⲣⲉ-ⲡ.ⲣⲱⲙⲉ ⲥⲱⲧⲡ̄, *when the man has/had chosen*

356. The prepersonal conjugation base with the suffix of the 2nd pers. f. sg. is ⲛ̄ⲧⲉⲣⲉ or ⲛ̄ⲧⲉⲣⲉⲣ.

Use

357. This construction expresses a singular event preceding the reality expressed in the main clause (cf. 422) or a concomitant circumstance. The main clause with the precursive occurs normally has a past tense (past or a preterit conversion) or the verb ⲡⲉϫⲉ (cf. 149).
ⲁⲩⲱ ⲛⲉ⸗ⲩ.ⲣ̄-ϣⲡⲏⲣⲉ ⲛ̄ⲧⲉⲣⲉ⸗ϥ.ⲱⲥⲕ ϩⲛ̄-ⲡ.ⲉⲣⲡⲉ (Luke 1:21). *And they were wondering, when he had been delayed in the sanctuary.*
ⲡⲁⲓ ⲉ-ⲁ-ⲇⲁⲩⲉⲓⲇ ⲁⲁ⸗ϥ ⲛ̄ⲧⲉⲣⲉ⸗ϥ.ϩⲕⲟ (Luke 6:3). *... that what David has done when he was hungry.*
ⲛ̄ⲧⲉⲣⲉ-ϩⲧⲟⲟⲩⲉ ⲇⲉ ϣⲱⲡⲉ ⲛⲉ.ⲩⲛ̄-ⲟⲩ.ⲛⲟϭ ⲛ̄-ϣⲧⲟⲣⲧⲣ̄ ϣⲟⲟⲡ ϩⲛ̄-ⲙ̄.ⲙⲁⲧⲟⲓ (Acts 12:18). *When the morning had come there was a great confusion among the soldiers.*

II. The conditional

Structure

358. ⲉⲣ(ⲉ)ϣⲁⲛ- – subject / ⲉ⸗ – subject – ϣⲁⲛ – infinitive
ⲉ⸗ϥ.ϣⲁⲛ.ⲥⲱⲧⲡ̄, *if he chooses/chose*
ⲉⲣϣⲁⲛ-ⲡ.ⲣⲱⲙⲉ ⲥⲱⲧⲡ̄, *if the man chooses/chose*

359. The prepersonal conjugation base with the suffix of the 2nd pers. f. sg. is ⲉⲣϣⲁⲛ or ⲉⲣⲉϣⲁⲛ.

360. There exists a shorter form ⲉ⸗. This form rarely occurs and if so, mostly with negation.

ⲉ⸗ⲧⲉⲧⲛ̄.ⲧⲙ̄.ⲟⲩⲱⲙ ⲛ̄-ⲧ.ⲥⲁⲣⲝ ⲛ̄-ⲡ.ϣⲏⲣⲉ ⲙ̄-ⲡ.ⲣⲱⲙⲉ... ⲙⲛ̄ⲧⲏ⸗ⲧⲛ̄ ⲙ̄ⲙⲁⲩ ⲙ̄-ⲡ.ⲱⲛϩ ⲛ̄ϩⲏⲧ⸗ⲧⲏⲩⲧⲛ̄ (John 6:53). *If you (pl.) do not eat the flesh of the Son of Man... you (pl.) will not have the life in yourselves.*

Use

361. The conditional can have a conditional or a temporal meaning.

362. When it has conditional meaning it can be introduced by the conjunctions ⲉⲓⲙⲏⲧⲓ, ⲉϣⲱⲡⲉ, ⲉϣⲭⲉ, ⲕⲁⲛ (cf. 429, 440).

ⲡ.ⲥⲃ̄ⲃⲉ ⲅⲁⲣ ⲣ̄-ⲛⲟϥⲣⲉ ⲉ⸗ⲕ.ϣⲁⲛ.ⲣ̄-ⲡ.ⲛⲟⲙⲟⲥ (Rom 2:25). *For the circumcision is useful if you practice the Law.*

ⲕⲁⲛ ⲉ⸗ⲓ.ϣⲁⲛ.ⲕⲣⲓⲛⲉ ⲇⲉ ⲁⲛⲟⲕ ⲧⲁ-ⲕⲣⲓⲥⲓⲥ ⲟⲩ.ⲙⲉ ⲧⲉ (John 8:16). *Even if I judge, my judgement is true.*

ⲉϣⲱⲡⲉ ⲇⲉ ⲉ⸗ⲥ.ϣⲁⲛ.ⲡⲱⲣⲝ ⲙⲁⲣⲉ⸗ⲥ.ϭⲱ ⲛ̄-ⲧⲉⲓ.ϩⲉ (1Cor 7:11). *But when she divorces, let her remain like this.*

363. When the conditional is used in a temporal clause it expresses a general meaning, contrary to the precursive (cf. 425).

ϩⲁϩ ⲛ̄-ⲥⲟⲡ ⲉ⸗ⲓ.ϣⲁⲛ.ⲧⲱⲟⲩⲛ... ϣⲁ⸗ⲓ.ϣⲧⲟⲣⲧⲣ̄ ϩⲣⲁⲓ ⲛϩⲏⲧ ϩⲛ̄-ⲟⲩ.ⲙⲕⲁϩ ⲛ̄ϩⲏⲧ (ShIII 150:14–17). *Often when I stood up... I was troubled by suffering.*

ⲁⲩⲱ ⲉⲣϣⲁⲛ-ⲡⲉ.ⲡ̄ⲛ̄ⲁ̄ ⲙ̄-ⲡⲟⲛⲏⲣⲟⲛ ⲉⲓ ⲉϩⲣⲁⲓ ⲉⲝⲛ̄-ⲥⲁⲟⲩⲗ ⲇⲁⲩⲉⲓⲇ ϣⲁ⸗ϥ.ⲭⲓ ⲛ̄-ⲧⲉ⸗ϥ.ϭⲓⲛⲏⲣⲁ ϩⲛ̄-ⲧⲉ⸗ϥ.ϭⲓⲝ ⲉ⸗ϥ.ⲯⲁⲗⲗⲉⲓ (1Sam 16:23). *And each time an evil spirit comes unto Saul, David takes his lyre in his hand and sings.*

III. The limitative

Structure

364. ϣⲁⲛⲧⲉ-/ϣⲁⲛⲧ⸗ – subject – infinitive
ϣⲁⲛⲧ⸗ϥ.ⲥⲱⲧⲡ̄, *until he chooses/chose*
ϣⲁⲛⲧⲉ-ⲡ.ⲣⲱⲙⲉ ⲥⲱⲧⲡ̄, *until the man chooses/chose*

365. The prepersonal form of the conjugation base with the suffix of the 2nd pers. sg. f. is ϣⲁⲛⲧⲉ.

366. The persersonal form of the conjugation base with the suffix of the 1st pers. sg. is ϣⲁⲛϯ, but there is also a variant ϣⲁⲛⲧⲁ.

Use

367. This construction denotes a temporal limitation. It has the same temporal value as the main clause. It is usually translated *"until"*.

ϣⲁⲛⲧⲉ can also be used to express a goal or consequence (cf. 450).

ϣⲁ⸗ⲓ.ϣⲗⲏⲗ ϣⲁⲛϯ.ⲛⲁⲩ ⲉ-ⲡ.ϩⲟ ⲙ̄-ⲡⲉ.ⲭ̄ⲥ̄ (ShAmél I 467:8–9). *I usually pray until I see the face of Christ.*

ϣⲁⲛⲧⲉ-ⲟⲩ ϣⲱⲡⲉ ⲡ.ϫⲟⲉⲓⲥ ⲉⲧ.ⲟⲩⲁⲁⲃ ⲙ̄-ⲙⲉ ⲉ.ⲛ-ⲅ.ⲕⲣⲓⲛⲉ ⲁⲛ (Rev 6:10). *Until what happens, Lord, saint and truthful, do you not judge?*

ⲟⲩ.ⲡ.ⲉⲧ⸗ⲛ̄.ⲛⲁ.ⲁⲁ⸗ϥ ϣⲁⲛⲧ⸗ⲟⲩ ⲡⲟⲟⲛⲉ⸗ϥ ⲉⲃⲟⲗ ϨⲚ̄ Ⲛ̄-ⲕⲟⲗⲁⲥⲓⲥ (PS 276).
What will we do in order to make the punishments stop?

IV. The conjunctive

Structure

368. Ⲛ̄ⲧⲉ-/Ⲛ̄⸗ – subject – infinitive
Ⲛ̄⸗ϥ.ⲥⲱⲧⲡ̄, *he (will) choose(s)*
Ⲛ̄ⲧⲉ-ⲡ.ⲣⲱⲙⲉ ⲥⲱⲧⲡ̄, *the man (will) choose(s)*

369. The prepersonal forms are as follows:

1	Ⲛ̄ⲧⲁ/ⲧⲁ	Ⲛ̄⸗ⲧⲛ̄
2 m.	Ⲛ̄⸗ⲅ/Ⲛ̄⸗ⲅ/ⲛⲉ⸗ⲕ	Ⲛ̄⸗ⲧⲉⲧⲛ̄
2 f.	Ⲛ̄ⲧⲉ	
3 m.	Ⲛ̄⸗ϥ/Ⲛ̄⸗ϥ̄/ⲛⲉ⸗ϥ	Ⲛ̄⸗ⲥⲉ
3 f.	Ⲛ̄⸗ⲥ/Ⲛ̄⸗ⲥ/ⲛⲉ⸗ⲥ	

Use

370. The conjunctive occurs in coordination with some other element. In itself it has no connotation of time or mode. It takes the aspect of time or mode from the verb it extends. The conjunctive can occur after a verbal construction or after some other element.

After a verbal construction:

371. The conjunctive can follow after a certain number of verbal constructions. It can be preceded by a paratactic conjunction like ⲁⲗⲗⲁ, ⲁⲩⲱ, ⲉ-ⲡ.ⲙⲁ, ⲏ, ⲧⲟⲧⲉ, but more often it is connected to the preceding clause without any conjunction (asyndeton).

The conjunctive is used to describe an action that immediately follows the preceding verb or is similar to it. It can also express a goal or result (cf. 445).

372. The following constructions can be followed by a conjunctive:
– a non-durative sentence (except the past and Ⲙ̄ⲡⲁⲧⲉ);
– an imperative: in this case the conjunctive makes the gender or number implied in the imperative explicit;
– the infinitive as a noun, including the use in prepositional expressions (cf. 111);
– the future and ⲚⲎⲨ (the stative of ⲉⲓ, which has often a future meaning).

ⲉ⸗ϥ.ϣⲁⲛ.†-ϨⲎⲞⲨ Ⲙ̄-ⲡ.ⲕⲟⲥⲙⲟⲥ ⲧⲏⲣ⸗ϥ Ⲛ̄⸗ϥ̄.ⲥⲟⲣⲙ⸗ⲉϥ ⲇⲉ Ϩⲱⲱ⸗ϥ Ⲏ Ⲛ̄⸗ϥ̄.†-ⲟⲥⲉ Ⲙ̄ⲙⲟ⸗ϥ (Luke 9:25). *If he gains the entire world, but looses himself, or lays fine upon himself....*

ϣⲁⲣⲉ-ⲡ.ⲣⲉϥⲣ̄-ⲛⲟⲃⲉ ϫⲓ ⲉϫⲱ⸗ϥ Ⲛ̄⸗ϥ̄.ⲧⲙ̄.ⲧⲁⲁ⸗ⲩ (Ps 36 (37):21). *The sinner borrows and does not render.*

ⲥⲱⲧⲉ Ⲙ̄ⲙⲟ⸗ⲓ Ⲛ̄⸗ⲅ̄.ⲛⲁ ⲛⲁ⸗ⲓ (Ps 25 (26):11). *Save me and have mercy on me.*

ⲉ⸗ⲓ.ⲛⲁ.ⲣ̄-ⲟⲩ ⲧⲁ.ⲕⲗⲏⲣⲟⲛⲟⲙⲓ Ⲙ̄-ⲡ.ⲱⲛϨ ϣⲁ-ⲉⲛⲉϨ (Luke 18:18). *What shall I do to inherit the eternal life?* (This construction can also be identified as a future conjunctive cf. 382.)

ΟΥ.ΝΟΒЄ ΠЄ ΟΥШΜ-Π.ΟЄΙΚ N̄-ΟΥ.ΡШΜЄ N̄⸗Γ.Τ̄Μ.Ρ̄-ΠЄ⸗Ϥ.ϨШΒ (ShChass 104:28–31). *It is a sin to eat the bread from a man and not to do his work (and that you do not do his work).*

ΤЄ.ΝΑ.Ш N̄ΤЄ.ΧΠΟ (Luke 1:31). *You will conceive and give birth.*

ΝЄ⸗Ϥ.ΝΑ.ΡΟЄΙC ΠЄ N⸗Ϥ.Τ̄Μ.ΚΑΑ⸗Υ Є-ϬШΤϨ Є-ΠЄ⸗Ϥ.ΗΙ (Matt 24:43). *He would have kept guard and he would not have let them intrude his house.*

ϨΗΛΙΑC ΜЄΝ ΝΗΥ N⸗Ϥ.ΑΠΟΚΑΘΙCΤΑ N̄-ϨШΒ ΝΙΜ (Matt 17:11). *Eliah will come and he will restore everything*

373. In a circumstantial or relative subordinate clause, or a clause introduced by ЄϢΧЄ or ЄϢШΠЄ, the conjunctive can also extend the past tense, Μ̄ΠΑΤЄ, a durative sentence in the present, and ΟΥΝ̄ΤЄ (cf. 154).

Μ̄ΠΑΤ-ΟΥШΜ (= Є.ΜΠΑΤ⸗ΟΥ.ΟΥШΜ) ЄΒΟΛ ϨΜ̄-Π.ΟЄΙΚ ΑΥШ N⸗CЄ.CШ ЄΒΟΛ Μ̄-Π.ΑΠΟΤ (ShIV 66:17–18). *...before eating bread and drinking the cup.*

ΟΥ.ΑΘΗΤ ΔЄ ΠЄ Π.ЄΤЄ.ΟΥΝ̄ΤΑ⸗Ϥ.COΥ N⸗Ϥ.Τ̄Μ.ΝΑ N̄ϨΗΤ⸗ΟΥ (ShChass 194:57–195:2). *It is a fool who possesses them (richnesses) and doesn't give alms from them.*

After other elements:

374. The conjunctive can be used in subordinate clauses introduced by certain conjunctions (Є-Π.ΜΑ, *instead of*; ЄΙΜΗΤΙ, *if not, except*; Η, *or*; ΚΑΝ, *even if*; ΜΗΠШC, *lest, in order not to*; ΜΗΠΟΤЄ, *so that not*; ΜΝ̄Ν̄CΑ, *after*; N̄CΑΒΗΛ, *if not, except*; ϨΙΝΑ, *order to, so that*; ϨШCΤЄ, *so that*).

ΑΛΛΑ ΚΑΝ ΑΝΟΝ Η ΟΥ.ΑΓΓЄΛΟC ЄΒΟΛ ϨΝ̄-Τ.ΠЄ N⸗Ϥ.ΤΑϢЄ-ΟЄΙϢ ΝΗ⸗ΤN̄ Π.ΒΟΛ Μ̄-Π.ЄΝΤ.Α⸗Ν.ΤΑϢЄ-ΟΙϢ Μ̄ΜΟ⸗Ϥ ΝΗ⸗ΤN̄ ΜΑΡЄ⸗Ϥ.ϢШΠЄ Є⸗Ϥ.ΒΗΤ (Gal 1:8). *But if we (ourselves) or an angel from heaven announces to you (pl.) another (Gospel) than the one we have announced to you, let him be damned..*

375. The conjunctive can be used after ΧЄΚΑ(Α)C instead of the optative when an adverbial construction or a subordinate proposition is intercalated between ΧЄΚΑ(Α)C and the verb.

ΧЄΚΑΑC Є.Α⸗ΤЄΤN̄.ΝΑΥ ЄΡΟ⸗Ϥ N̄-ΤЄΤN̄.ΡΑϢЄ ΟΝ (Phil 2:28). *That, once having seen him again, you may rejoice.*

376. The conjunctive can be used in a completive clause where it makes the subject or the object of the preceding expression explicit (Α⸗C.ϢШΠЄ, *it has happened*; ΑΛΛΟ... ΑΛΛΟ, *on the one hand, ... on the other*; ΓЄΝΟΙΤΟ, *might...* (wish); ΚЄ.ΚΟΥΙ ΠЄ, *still a little more (time) and...*; ΜΗ.ΓЄΝΟΙΤΟ, *might... not*; ΝΑΝΟΥ⸗C ΠЄ, *it is good/better*; ΟΥ.ΜΟΙϨЄ ΤЄ/ΟΥ.ϢΙΠЄ ΠЄ/...*, it is a miracle/a shame*; ϨΑΜΟΙ, *it should be*).

ΚЄ.ΚΟΥЄΙ ΠЄ N̄-ΤЄΤN̄.ΛΟ Є⸗ΤЄΤN̄.ΝΑΥ ЄΡΟ⸗ЄΙ (John 16:16). *A little more (time) and you will cease to see me.*

377. The conjunctive can also occur in a main clause. In this case it is usually preceded by a particle or an adverb (ΑΡΑ, ΑΡΗΥ, ΜΟΓΙC, ΜЄϢΑΚ).

ΑΡΑ N̄ΤЄ-ΟΥ.ΟΥΧΑΙ ϢШΠЄ N̄-ϨΑϨ (ShChass 168:7–9). *Will salvation come for the many?*

378. The conjunctive can function as apodosis after a subordinate clause expressing a factual presupposition.
ⲉⲣⲉ.ϣⲓⲛⲉ ⲛⲥⲁ-ⲣⲓⲙⲉ ⲉ-ⲟⲩ.ⲥⲱⲛⲉ ⲛⲧⲉ.ⲧⲟⲉⲓⲧ ⲉⲣⲟ-ⲙ̄ⲙⲓⲛⲙ̄ⲙⲟ (ShAmél I 204:14–205:1). *When you are busy* (f. sg.) *crying over a sister, you are mourning yourself.*

379. The conjunctive can substitute a (causative) infinitive.
ⲁⲉⲓ.ϯ ⲛⲏⲧⲛ̄ ⲛ̄-ⲧ.ⲉⲝⲟⲩⲥⲓⲁ ⲉ-ϩⲱⲙ ⲉϫⲛ̄ ⲛ̄-ϩⲟϥ... ⲛ̄ⲧⲉ.ⲧⲙ̄ ⲗⲁⲁⲩ ϫⲓⲧϥ(ⲧ)ⲏⲧⲛ̄ ⲛ̄-ϭⲟⲛⲥ̄ (Luke 10:19). *I have given you* (pl.) *the power to walk on serpents ... and to feel no pain at all.*
ϩⲙ̄-ⲡ.ⲧⲣⲉϥⲥⲱⲧⲙ̄ ⲉⲣⲟϥ ⲁⲩⲱ ⲛ̄-ⲥⲉ.ⲛⲁⲩ ⲉ-.ⲙ.ⲙⲁⲉⲓⲛ (Acts 8:6). *While they heard him and saw the signs.*

V. The future conjunctive
Structure

380. ⲧⲁⲣⲉ-/ⲧⲁⲣ(ⲉ)ϥ – subject – infinitive
ⲧⲁⲣⲉϥ.ⲥⲱⲧⲙ̄, *in order that he may choose*
ⲧⲁⲣⲉ-ⲡ.ⲣⲱⲙⲉ ⲥⲱⲧⲙ̄, *in order that the man may choose*

381. There is a rare variant ⲛ̄ⲧⲁⲣ(ⲉ).

382. The 1st pers. sg. ⲧⲁⲣⲓ is rarely used and often replaced by the conjunctive ⲛ̄ⲧⲁ (or ⲧⲁ).

383. In a subordinate clause the future conjunctive normally only occurs in the affirmative sense.

384. The optative is commonly used to express the negation.

Use

385. The future conjunctive can extend a positive order or a rhetorical question. It then expresses a promise, the reassurances of the speaker that an event will take place.
ⲙⲁⲣⲛ̄.ⲡⲣⲟⲥⲉⲭⲉ ⲉ-ⲛⲉϥ.ϣⲁϫⲉ ⲧⲁⲣⲛ̄.ⲉⲓⲙⲉ ⲉ-ⲡ.ⲉⲧⲛ̄.ϣⲓⲛⲉ ⲛ̄ⲥⲱϥ (ShLefort 41:9). *Let's pay attention to his words and we will know what we are looking for (or: in order to know...).*
ⲉϥ.ⲧⲱⲛ ⲡ.ⲟⲩⲱⲛϣ ⲧⲁⲣⲉ-ϣⲱⲥ ⲡⲱⲧ ⲛ̄ⲥⲱϥ (ShAmél II 510:7–8). *Where is the wolf? (Say it) and the shepherds will persecute it (or: so the shepherds might persecute it).*
ⲁⲟⲩⲱⲛ ⲛ̄.ⲛⲁ.ⲃⲁⲗ ⲧⲁ.ⲛⲁⲩ ⲉ-ⲛⲓ.ϣⲡⲏⲣⲉ (Ps 118:18). *Open my eyes and I will see the marvels (or: so that I see...).*

386. The future conjunctive can complete verbs of incomplete predication (cf. 412).
ⲕⲁ-ⲛⲁⲓ ⲧⲁⲣϥⲟⲩ.ⲃⲱⲕ (John 18:8). *Let them all go.*

387. The future conjunctive rarely expresses a goal after a narrative verb or in a question (cf. 445).

ⲁϥ.ⲙⲟⲩⲛ ⲇⲉ ⲉⲃⲟⲗ ⲉϥ.ϣⲗⲏⲗ ϩⲁⲣⲟ⸗ⲥ ⲧⲁⲣⲉ⸗ⲥ.ⲟⲩϫⲁⲓ ⲁⲩⲱ ⲁ-ⲡ.ⲛⲟⲩⲧⲉ ⲥⲱⲧⲙ̄ ⲉⲣⲟ⸗ϥ (ApophPatr 240). *He continued praying in order for her to get well and God heard him.*

ⲛ̄ⲧⲁ ⲡⲟⲩ.ⲥⲟⲛ ⲃⲱⲕ ⲉ-ⲧⲱⲛ ⲧⲁⲣⲉ⸗ⲛ.ⲕⲱⲧⲉ ⲛ̄ⲥⲱ⸗ϥ (Song 6:1). *Where has your (f. sg.) brother gone, so we might look for him?*

388. The 1st pers. pl. of the future conjunctive can be used in a main clause with a deliberative meaning (expression a hesitating question, a demand for permission). In this case the negation ⲧⲙ̄ can occur.

ⲡ.ϫⲟⲉⲓⲥ ⲧⲁⲣ⸗ⲛ̄.ϩⲓⲟⲩⲉ ⲛ̄-ⲧ.ⲥⲏϥⲉ (Luke 22:49). *Lord, will we slay with the sword?*

ⲧⲁⲣ⸗ⲛ̄.ϯ ϫⲛ̄ ⲧⲁⲣ⸗ⲛ̄.ⲧⲙ̄.ϯ (Mark 12:14). *Shall we give or shall we not give?*

See exercise 7

The Causative infinitive

389. The causative infinitive can be used in sentences as a conjugated verb. It can also function as a verbal noun. In the latter case it often replaces the simple infinitive and looses its causative meaning (cf. 129–134).

A. The causative infinitive as (conjugated) verb

390. The causative infinitive can occur in durative and non-durative sentences. It can also complete some auxiliaries, like (ⲉ)ϣ, *to be able, can*, and ⲟⲩⲱϣ, *to want*. It has always causative meaning, except when it is the complement of ⲟⲩⲱϣ.

ⲁⲩⲱ ⲉ⸗ⲕ.ⲧⲣⲉ-ϩⲉⲛ.ⲕⲟⲟⲩⲉ ⲁⲡⲁⲧⲁ ⲛ̄ⲙⲙⲁ⸗ⲕ (ShIII 81:23). *And you let the others go astray with you.*

ⲕⲁⲛⲁ ⲛ̄-ⲧ.ⲅⲁⲗⲓⲗⲁⲓⲁ ⲡ.ⲙⲁ ⲉⲛⲧ.ⲁ⸗ϥ.ⲧⲣⲉ-ⲡ.ⲙⲟⲟⲩ ⲣ-ⲏⲣⲡ (John 4:46). *Cana in Galilea, where he changed water in wine* (where he made the water become wine).

ⲙ̄ⲡ⸗ϥ.ⲉϣ.ⲧⲣⲉ-ⲣⲱⲙⲉ ⲣ̄-ⲛⲟⲃⲉ ⲡⲁⲣⲁ-ⲡⲉ⸗ϥ.ⲟⲩⲱϣ (ShChass 74:45–58). *He could not make a man sin against his will.*

ⲡ.ⲛⲟⲩⲧⲉ ⲡⲉ⸗ⲛ.ⲥⲱⲧⲏⲣ ⲡⲁⲓ ⲉⲧ-ⲟⲩⲉϣ.ⲧⲣⲉ-ⲣⲱⲙⲉ ⲛⲓⲙ ⲱⲛϩ̄ (1Tim 2:3–4). *God, our Saviour, the one who wants that every man lives.*

B. The causative infinitive as verbal noun

391. The causative infinitive can be a masculine noun. In that case, it has no causative meaning.

392. It can also be used after certain prepositions. The most common ones are the following: ⲁⲛⲧⲓ-, *against, in exchange for*; ⲁϫⲛ̄-, *without*; ⲉ-, *in order to, for*; ⲉⲓⲥ-, *towards, for*; ⲉ-ⲡ.ⲙⲁ ⲉ-, *instead of*; ⲉⲓⲙⲏⲧⲓ ⲉ-, *without, if not*; ⲙⲛ̄ⲛ̄ⲥⲁ- (ⲉ), *after*; ⲭⲱⲣⲓⲥ-, *without*; ϩⲁⲑⲏ ⲉ-, *before*; ϩⲛ̄-, *while*; ϩⲱⲥⲧⲉ ⲉ-, *so that*; ϩⲓⲧⲙ̄, *because of, through*.

ⲛⲁⲛⲟⲩ-ⲧⲣⲉ-ⲡ.ⲣⲱⲙⲉ ⲙⲟⲩ ⲛ̄ϩⲟⲩⲟ ⲉ-ⲱⲛϩ̄ ⲉ⸗ϥ.ⲣ-ⲛⲟⲃⲉ (ShAmél I 52:59). *It is better for the human to die than to live in sin* (while sinning).

ⲉⲓⲥ-ⲡⲉⲉ(ⲓ).ⲧⲣⲉ⸗ⲧⲛ̄.ⲗⲩⲡⲓ ⲅⲁⲣ ⲕⲁⲧⲁ-ⲡ.ⲛⲟⲩⲧⲉ ⲁ⸗ϥ.ⲣ̄-ϩⲱⲃ ⲛⲏ⸗ⲧⲛ̄ ⲉ-ⲩ.ⲛⲟϭ ⲛ̄-ⲥⲡⲟⲩⲇⲏ (2Cor 7:11). *Behold, that you (pl.) suffer according to God has made you very zealous.*

ϩⲙ̄-ⲡ.ⲧⲣⲉ⸗ⲩ.ⲛ̄ⲕⲟⲧⲕ ⲇⲉ ⲛ̄ϭⲓ-ⲛ̄.ⲣⲱⲙⲉ ⲁ⸗ϥ.ⲉⲓ ⲛ̄ϭⲓ-ⲡⲉ⸗ϥ.ϫⲁϫⲉ (Matt 13:25). *While the people slept, his enemy came.*

393. The expression ⲉ-ⲧⲣⲉ- is often used to build a subordinate clause of goal or consequence (cf. 449).
ⲧⲟⲧⲉ ⲁ⸗ϥ.ⲉⲓ ⲛ̄ϭⲓ-ⲓ̄ⲥ̄ ⲉⲃⲟⲗ ϩⲛ̄-ⲧ.ⲅⲁⲗⲓⲗⲁⲓⲁ ⲉϩⲣⲁⲓ ⲉϫⲙ̄-ⲡ.ⲓⲟⲣⲇⲁⲛⲏⲥ ϣⲁ-ⲓⲱϩⲁⲛⲛⲏⲥ ⲉ-ⲧⲣⲉ⸗ϥ.ϫⲓ-ⲃⲁⲡⲧⲓⲥⲙⲁ ⲉⲃⲟⲗ ϩⲓⲧⲟⲟⲧ⸗ϥ̄ (Matt 3:13). *Jesus then went from Galilea to the Jordan, to John, in order to be baptised by him.*

394. ⲉ-ⲧⲣⲉ- can also complete verbs of incomplete predication. These are verbs that need to be completed by another verb (cf 412) (LAYTON 363). It can also be used to extend the optative or the imperative (LAYTON 341).
ⲁ⸗ϥ.ⲟⲩⲉϩ-ⲥⲁϩⲛⲉ ⲇⲉ ⲉ-ⲧⲣⲉ-ⲙ̄.ⲙⲏⲏϣⲉ ⲛⲟϫ⸗ⲟⲩ ⲉϩⲣⲁⲓ ⲉϫⲙ̄-ⲡⲉ.ⲭⲟⲣⲧⲟⲥ (Matt 14:19). *He ordered the crowd to sit down on the grass.*

See exercise 8

Part III: Complex sentences

Main clauses

Cf. *supra*: the nominal sentence (191–194), the durative sentence (223–225), the non-durative sentence (308).

A. Coordination

395. Different sentences can be connected with each other by mere juxtaposition, without a conjunction. Asyndetic linkage is often encountered in narrative, especially with the past tense (which can follow another past tense or the precursive).
The asyndeton can express a closer link between both sentences than the coordination with a conjunction.
ⲁ-ⲛ.ⲇⲁⲓⲙⲱⲛⲓⲟⲛ ⲥⲟⲟⲩⲛ-ⲡ.ϫⲟⲉⲓⲥ ⲙ-ⲡⲉⲓ.ⲟⲩⲟⲉⲓϣ ⲁⲩ.ⲡⲁϩⲧⲟⲩ ⲁⲩ. ⲟⲩⲱϣⲧ ⲛⲁϥ ⲁⲩ.ⲁϣⲕⲁⲕ ⲉⲃⲟⲗ ϩⲛ-ⲟⲩ.ⲛⲟϭ ⲛ̄-ⲥⲙⲏ (ShIII 85:23–86:1). *At that moment the demons recognized the Lord, kneeled, worshipped him, and cried out with a loud voice.*

396. Different sentences can also be linked with conjunctions, such as ⲁⲩⲱ (*and*), ⲏ (*or*), ⲉⲓⲧⲉ (*either, or*), ϫⲛ̄- (*or else, whether*), ⲟⲩⲇⲉ (*nor*), ⲁⲗⲗⲁ (*but*), ⲇⲉ (*and, but*), ⲟⲛ (*also*).

397. ⲁⲩⲱ can also occur at the beginning of a main clause, even if it is preceded by a subordinate clause (apodotic ⲁⲩⲱ).

ⲙⲡⲣ̄.ⲧⲣⲉⲛ.ⲛ̄ⲕⲟⲧⲕ̄ ⲁⲩⲱ ϯϩⲉ ⲁⲩⲱ ϭⲱ ϩⲛ̄-ⲡ.ⲕⲁⲕⲉ (ShChass 165:30–33). *Let's not fall asleep, let's not get drunk and let's not stay in the dark.*
ⲏ ⲅⲁⲣ ϥ.ⲛⲁ.ⲙⲉⲥⲧⲉ-ⲟⲩⲁ ⲛϥ̄.ⲙⲉⲣⲉ-ⲟⲩⲁ ⲏ ⲛϥ̄.ϭⲟⲗϥ̄ ⲛ̄-ⲟⲩⲁ ⲛϥ̄.ⲕⲁⲧⲁ-ⲫⲣⲟⲛⲉⲓ ⲛ̄-ⲡ.ⲕⲉ.ⲟⲩⲁ (Matt 6:24). *For either he will hate the one and love the other, or he'll devote himself to the one and despise the other.*
ⲕⲉⲧⲟⲓ ⲛⲉ.ⲟⲩⲛ̄ⲧⲁⲛ ϩⲁϩ ⲙ̄ⲙⲁⲩ ⲡⲉ ⲁⲩⲱ ⲛⲉⲩ.ⲣⲱϣⲉ ⲙ̄ⲙⲟⲛ ⲁⲛ (Z 328:4). *Even though we had many, they were not enough for us.*

B. The interrogative sentence

398. The full interrogative sentence usually has the same form as the affirmative sentence.

399. It can however be indicated by the presence of interrogative particles, such as ⲉⲓⲉ, ⲉϣϫⲉ, ⲁⲣⲁ, ⲙⲏ (rhetorical questions), ⲙⲏⲧⲓ (expresses wonder or doubt).

400. A deliberative question at the first person can be expressed by the optative (cf. 337).

ⲡⲁⲓ ⲡⲉ ⲡⲉ⸗ⲧⲛ̄.ϣⲏⲣⲉ (John 9:19). *Is this your* (pl.) *son?*
ⲉⲓⲉ ⲛ̄.ⲁⲅⲅⲉⲗⲟⲥ ⲁⲣⲁ ⲟⲩⲛ̄ ⲥⲁⲣⲝ ⲙ̄ⲙⲟ⸗ⲟⲩ (Pcod 6:8). *Do the angels have flesh?*
ⲉϣϫⲉ ⲕ.ⲥⲟⲟⲩⲛ̄ (Matt 25:26). *Do you know?*
ⲙⲏ ⲉ⸗ϥ.ⲛⲁ.† ⲛⲁ⸗ϥ ⲛ̄-ⲟⲩ.ⲱⲛⲉ (Matt 7:9). *Wouldn't he give him a stone?*
ⲙⲏ† ⲉ⸗ϥ.ⲛⲁ.ⲙⲟⲩⲟⲩⲧ ⲙ̄ⲙⲟ⸗ϥ (John 8:22). *He wouldn't kill himself, would he?*

401. In a partial question interrogative pronouns (cf. 023) and adverbs (cf. 104) take the place of their syntactic equivalents in the sentence.

402. If an interrogative pronoun (ⲟⲩ, ⲁϣ, ⲛⲓⲙ) or adverb (ⲡⲱⲥ, ⲧⲱⲛ, ⲧⲛⲁⲩ) occurs after the verb, the latter has the focalising conversion.
ⲉⲧⲃⲉ-ⲟⲩ ⲧⲉⲧⲛ̄.ϣⲓⲛⲉ ⲛ̄ⲥⲱ⸗ⲓ (Luke 2:49). *Why are you* (pl.) *looking for me?*
ⲉ⸗ⲧⲉⲧⲛ̄.ϣⲓⲛⲉ ⲛ̄ⲥⲁ ⲛⲓⲙ (John 18:4). *Who are you looking for?*

403. The conjunction ϫⲛ̄ (ϫⲉⲛ, ϫⲓⲛ) (*or*) can be used to separate the different parts of a disjunctive question. The disjunctive conjunction ⲏ is less frequent.
ϫⲛ̄ ⲙ̄ⲙⲟⲛ. *Or not?*
ⲛ̄ⲧⲟⲕ ⲡ.ⲉⲧ.ⲛⲏⲩ ϫⲛ̄ ⲉ⸗ⲛ.ⲛⲁ.ϭⲱϣⲧ ϩⲏⲧ⸗ϥ̄ ⲛ̄-ⲕⲉ.ⲟⲩⲁ (Luke 7:19). *Are you the one who will come or shall we look out for another one?*

404. There is no formal difference between the direct and the indirect question.
ⲛ̄⸗ϥ.ⲛⲁ.ϩⲙⲟⲟⲥ ⲁⲛ ⲛ̄-ϣⲟⲣⲡ̄ ⲛ̄⸗ϥ.ϫⲓ-ϣⲟϫⲛⲉ ϫⲉ ⲟⲩⲛ̄ ϭⲟⲙ ⲙ̄ⲙⲟ⸗ϥ ⲉ-ⲧ.ⲙ̄ⲛⲧ ⲛ̄-ⲟⲩ.ⲧⲃⲁ ⲉ-ⲡ.ⲉⲧ.ⲛⲏⲩ ⲉϫⲱ⸗ϥ ⲙⲛ̄ ⲧⲃⲁ ⲥⲛⲁⲩ (Luke 14:31). *Will he not sit first and take counsel whether it is possible for him to meet with a 10 000 him who comes upon him with two 10 000's?*

See exercise 9

Subordinate clauses

A. The completive clause

Object clause

405. The object clause is generally introduced by the conjunction ϫⲉ.
This conjunction can also introduce indirect as well as direct speech.
ϯ.ⲛⲁⲩ ϫⲉ ⲛ̄ⲧⲟⲕ ⲛ̄ⲧⲕ ⲟⲩ.ⲡⲣⲟⲫⲏⲧⲏⲥ (John 4:19). *I see that you are a prophet.*

406. When it expresses a goal the object clause can take the form of a final clause introduced by ϫⲉⲕⲁ(ⲁ)ⲥ (cf. 447).
This is mostly the case with the main verb expressing some application, effort, or care.
ⲁ⸗ϥ.ⲥⲉⲡⲥⲱⲡ⸗ϥ ϫⲉⲕⲁⲥ ⲉ⸗ϥ.ⲉ.ⲉⲓ (John 4:47). *He prayed him to come (that he might come).*

407. The completive clause after verbs expressing fear is usually introduced by ⲙⲏⲡⲱⲥ, ⲙⲏⲡⲟⲧⲉ, sometimes combined with ϫⲉ.
ⲁ-ⲡ.ⲭⲓⲗⲓⲁⲣⲭⲟⲥ ⲣ̄-ϩⲟⲧⲉ ⲙⲏⲡⲱⲥ ⲛ̄⸗ⲥⲉ.ⲙⲟⲩⲟⲩⲧ ⲙ̄-ⲡⲁⲩⲗⲟⲥ (Acts 23:10). *The tribune was afraid that Paul might be killed.*

408. The conjunctive can have the value of an object clause (cf. 376).
ⲧⲉⲧⲛ̄.ⲟⲩⲱϣ ϭⲉ ⲧⲁ.ⲕⲱ ⲛⲏ⸗ⲧⲛ̄ ⲉⲃⲟⲗ ⲙ̄.ⲡ.ⲣ̄ⲣⲟ (John 18:39). *Do you* (pl.) *want me to release the king to you?*
ⲟⲩⲱϣ ⲛ⸗ⲅ.ⲧⲛ̄ⲛⲟⲟⲩ ⲡⲉ⸗ⲕ.ϣⲏⲣⲉ (C.O. 257:6). *Be willing to send your son.*

409. The prenominal state of the verb ϭⲓⲛⲉ, ϭⲛ- is directly followed by the object clause without ϫⲉ when it occurs in a negative sentence with the meaning "*to ignore, not to understand*".
ⲛ̄.ϯ.ϭⲛ̄ ⲁⲛ ⲉⲣⲉ.ϫⲱ ⲙ̄ⲙⲟ⸗ⲥ ϫⲉ ⲟⲩ (Mark 14:68). *I don't understand what you* (f. sg.) *say.*

410. Some element of the object clause can be inserted as a cataphoric pronoun in the main clause, usually as its object.
ⲛ̄.ϯ.ⲥⲟⲟⲩⲛ ⲙ̄ⲙⲱ⸗ⲧⲛ̄ ⲁⲛ ϫⲉ ⲛ̄ⲧⲉⲧⲛ̄ ϩⲉⲛ.ⲉⲃⲟⲗ ⲧⲱⲛ (Luke 13:25). *I don't know (you) where you* (pl.) *come from.*

411. The entire object clause can also be substituted by a pronoun in the main clause. This is always the case with the verb ϫⲱ (*to say*).
ⲛⲓⲙ ⲡ.ⲉⲧ.ϫⲱ ⲙ̄ⲙⲟ⸗ⲥ ϫⲉ ⲁⲩⲉⲓ⸗ⲥ ⲧⲁ.ⲥⲱ (John 4:10). *Who is he who says (it): give it (= the water), so I can drink?*
ⲁ⸗ⲓ.ϩⲉ ⲉⲣⲟ⸗ⲥ ⲁ-ⲧⲉ⸗ⲕ.ⲛⲟⲩⲧⲉ ⲧⲁϩⲟ⸗ϥ (Aeg 17:8). *I have found (it) that your divinity has reached him.*

412. After verbs of incomplete predication, such as ⲕⲱ, *to let, leave*; ⲟⲩⲱⲛϩ ⲉⲃⲟⲗ, *to appear*; and in particular those expressing permanence or cessation, such as ⲗⲟ, *to stop, quit*; ⲟⲩⲱ, *to stop, finish*; 6ⲱ, *to continue, to persist; to stop, to cease*; ⲱⲥⲕ̄, *to delay, to continue*, the object clause can be expressed by a circumstantial clause.
ⲁ⸍ϥ.6ⲱ ⲉ.ⲛ.ϥ̄.ⲕⲓⲙ ⲁⲛ (Acts 27:41). *He remained immobile (while he was not moving).*

413. Another possible construction of the completive clause after these verbs is the future conjunctive (cf. 386), the causative infinitive (cf. 394) or the conjunctive.
ⲕⲁ-ⲛⲁⲓ ⲧⲏⲣ⸍ⲟⲩ ⲛ̄⸍ⲥⲉ.ⲃⲱⲕ ⲉⲃⲟⲗ (John 18:8). *Let all of these go.*

Subject clause

414. There is no special construction for the subject clause in Coptic. The subject clause can come after the main verb without a conjunction.

415. Every kind of sentence can function as a subject clause, including the conjunctive and the causative infinitive preceded by the preposition ⲉ-.

416. The grammatical subject of the main clause is normally the personal pronoun of the 3rd pers. f. sg. (with neutral meaning). The masculine pronoun is less often used in the main clause.

417. In that case the subject clause can be introduced by ⲭⲉ.

418. The expression ⲁ⸍ⲥ.ϣⲱⲡⲉ followed by a subject clause usually opens a new narrative unit. Literally it means "it happened that…", but ⲁ⸍ⲥ.ϣⲱⲡⲉ can usually remain untranslated.

ⲁ⸍ⲥ.ϣⲱⲡⲉ ⲇⲉ ⲁ⸍ϥ.ⲃⲱⲕ (Luke 7:11). *And he went (and it happened that he went).*
ⲛⲁⲛⲟⲩ⸍ⲥ ⲛⲁ⸍ϥ ⲉⲛⲉ.ⲩⲛ̄ ⲟⲩ.ⲱⲛⲉ ⲛ-ⲥⲓⲕⲉ ⲁϣⲉ ⲉ.ⲡ⸍ϥ̄.ⲙⲁⲕϩ (Mark 9:42). *It would be better for him that there was a grinding stone hanging around his neck.*
ⲉ⸍ⲥ.ϣⲁⲛ.ϣⲱⲡⲉ ⲇⲉ ⲛ̄⸍ⲥⲉ.ⲉⲓⲛⲉ ⲛⲁ⸍ϥ ⲛ̄-ϩⲉⲛ.ⲧⲃ̄ⲧ (Pach 5:1). *Because they used to bring him some fish (it used to happen that they brought…).*
ϥ.ⲟⲩⲟⲛϩ ⲉⲃⲟⲗ ⲭⲉ ⲉⲣⲉ-ⲡ.ⲇⲓⲕⲁⲓⲟⲥ.ⲛⲁ.ⲱⲛϩ ⲉⲃⲟⲗ ϩⲛ̄-ⲧ.ⲡⲓⲥⲧⲓⲥ (Gal 3:11). *It is manifest that the righteous one will live through faith.*

419. In a nominal sentence the subject ⲡⲉ/ⲧⲉ can be explicated through a completive clause introduced by ⲭⲉ, through a (causative) infinitive preceded by ⲉ-, or through a conjunctive.
ⲟⲩ.ⲁⲛⲁⲅⲕⲁⲓⲟⲛ ⲡⲉ ⲉ-ⲥⲉⲡⲥ̄ ⲛⲉ.ⲥⲛⲏⲩ (2Cor 9:5). *It is necessary to comfort the brothers.*

420. A certain number of 'impersonal predicates' (LAYTON 487) occur with a subject clause.

ⲁⲛⲁⲅⲕⲏ	*it's necessary*
ϩⲱ	*it's enough*
ϩⲁⲡⲥ̄	*it's necessary*
ϩⲛⲉ-/ϩⲛⲁ⸍	*it pleases*

ⲅⲉⲛⲟⲓⲧⲟ (negation: ⲙⲏⲅⲉⲛⲟⲓⲧⲟ)	*that… might (happen)*
ⲉⲝⲉⲥⲧⲓ (negation: ⲟⲩⲕⲉⲝⲉⲥⲧⲓ)	*it's possible, it's allowed*
(ⲉ)ϣϣⲉ (negation: ⲙⲉϣϣⲉ)	*it suits, it's becoming*
ϩⲁⲙⲟⲓ	*it would be good*

ⲁⲛⲁⲅⲕⲏ ⲅⲁⲣ ⲉ-ⲧⲣⲉ-ⲛⲉ.ⲥⲕⲁⲛⲇⲁⲗⲟⲛ ⲉⲓ (Matt 18:7). *For it is necessary that the scandals come.*

ϩⲱ ⲁⲛ ⲉⲣⲟ⸗ϥ ϫⲉ ⲁ⸗ϥ.ⲣ̄-ⲛⲟⲃⲉ (ShMiss 4 822:14). *It is not enough for him that he has sinned.*

ⲟⲩⲕⲉⲝⲉⲥⲧⲓ ⲛⲁ⸗ⲛ ⲉ-ⲙⲉⲩⲧ-ⲗⲁⲁⲩ (John 18:31). *We are not allowed (it is not allowed to us) to kill someone.*

421. A subject clause can be replaced by a final clause when it expresses a goal.

ⲥ.ⲣ̄-ⲛⲟϥⲣⲉ ⲛⲏ⸗ⲧⲛ̄ ϫⲉⲕⲁⲥ ⲁⲛⲟⲕ ⲉ⸗ⲓ.ⲉ.ⲃⲱⲕ (John 16:7). *It is useful to you* (pl.) *that I go.*

B. The temporal clause

422. The following constructions can be used to express a temporal relation with regard to the main clause.
– The precursive (cf. 355) expresses anteriority.
– The circumstantial conversion of ⲙ̄ⲡⲁⲧⲉ (cf. 322), meaning *before..* also expresses anteriority.
– The limitative conjugation base ϣⲁⲛⲧⲉ means *until…* (cf. 367).
– The circumstantial conversion can be used in a subordinate sentence with temporal meaning. Its connotation depends on the converted 'tense'.

423. Temporal clauses can also be introduced by a range of Coptic conjunctions, such as ϫⲓⲛ (*since*; with the focalising conversion of the past tense ϫⲓⲛⲧⲁ⸗ etc.), ⲙⲛ̄ⲛ̄ⲥⲁ (*after*), or Greek conjunctions such as ϩⲱⲥ, ϩⲟⲥⲟⲛ, ϩⲟⲧⲁⲛ (*when*).
The Greek conjunctions are often followed by a focalising conversion.

424. The preposition ⲙⲛ̄ⲛ̄ⲥⲁ (ⲉ-) with the causative infinitive expresses anteriority, the preposition ϩⲛ̄- with the causative infinitive expresses a synchronic action.
This construction is less often encountered with a simple infinitive.

425. If the conditional is used with temporal meaning (cf. 363), often introduced by the conjunction ϩⲟⲧⲁⲛ, it has a general sense with regard to a past tense (cf. 363).

ϫⲓⲛⲧⲁ-ⲛⲉ⸗ⲛ.ⲉⲓⲟⲧⲉ ⲅⲁⲣ ⲛ̄ⲕⲟⲧⲕ̄ ϩⲱⲃ ⲛⲓⲙ ⲙⲏⲛ ⲉⲃⲟⲗ ⲛ̄-ⲧⲉⲓ.ϩⲉ (2Pet 3:4). *For since our Fathers passed, everything remains like this (in this way).*

ϩⲟⲧⲁⲛ ⲉⲣⲉ.ⲡ.ϭⲟⲗ ⲛⲁ.ϣⲁϫⲉ ⲉ.ϣⲁ⸗ϥ.ϣⲁϫⲉ ⲉⲃⲟⲗ ϩⲛ̄-ⲛ.ⲉⲧⲉ.ⲛⲟⲩ⸗ϥ ⲛⲉ (John 8:44). *When the liar speaks, he (usually) speaks from what is his own.*

ⲙⲏ ⲟⲩⲛ̄-ϭⲟⲙ ⲉ-ⲧⲣⲉ⸗ⲩ.ⲛⲏⲥⲧⲉⲩⲉ ⲛ̄ϭⲓ-ⲛ̄.ϣⲏⲣⲉ ⲙ-ⲡ.ⲙⲁ ⲛ̄-ϣⲉⲗⲉⲉⲧ ϩⲟⲥⲟⲛ ⲉⲣⲉ-ⲡⲁ-ⲧ.ϣⲉⲗⲉⲉⲧ ⲛ̄ⲙⲙⲁ⸗ⲩ (Mark 2:19). *Can the children of the groom (the sons of the bridal chamber) fast while the groom is with them?*

ϨⲘ̄-Π.ⲦⲢⲀ.ⲤⲰⲦⲘ̄ (HM I 142:3). *While I was listening...*
Ⲁ⸗Ⲩ.ⲈⲒ ⲈⲂⲞⲖ ϨⲚ̄-ⲚⲈ.ⲘϨⲀⲀⲨ Ⲙ̄Ⲛ̄ⲚⲤⲀ-ⲦⲢⲈ⸗Ϥ.ⲦⲰⲞⲨⲚ (Matt 27:53). *They came out of the tombs after he was resuscitated.*
ϨⲞⲦⲀⲚ ⲈⲢϢⲀⲚ-Π.ⲢⲰⲘⲈ ⲘⲈⲢⲈ-Π.ⲚⲞⲂⲈ ϢⲀⲢⲈ-Π.ⲚⲞⲨⲦⲈ †-ϬⲞⲘ Ⲙ̄-Π.ⲚⲞⲂⲈ ⲈϨⲢⲀⲒ ⲈⲬⲰ⸗Ϥ (ShChass 68:30–35). *When man loves the sin, God gives the sin power over him.* (This sentence can also be understood as a conditional: *if he loves sin...*)
ϨⲘ̄-Π.ⲈⲒ ⲈⲂⲞⲖ Ⲙ̄-Π.Ⲓ̄ⲎⲖ̄ ϨⲚ̄-ⲔⲎⲘⲈ (Ps 113:1). *When Israel came forth from Egypt...* (literally: *in the coming forth from Israel...*)

426. After a temporal subordinate clause the main clause can be introduced by ⲦⲞⲦⲈ (*then*).
ϨⲞⲦⲀⲚ ⲄⲀⲢ Ⲉ⸗Ⲓ.ϢⲀⲚ.Ⲣ̄-ⲀⲦ.ϬⲞⲘ ⲦⲞⲦⲈ ϢⲀ⸗Ⲓ.ϬⲘ̄ϬⲞⲘ (2Cor 12, 10). *For when I am powerless, then I am powerful.*

C. The conditional clause

427. There are two sorts of adverbial clauses expressing a condition: the factual conditional clause and the contrafactual conditional clause. The first category embraces the *realis* and the *potentialis (eventualis)*, the latter the *irrealis*. The subordinate clause or protasis often precedes the main clause or apodosis. In the contrafactual conditional clause, the apodosis is correlated with the protasis.
Factual and contrafactual conditional clauses can be combined with one another.

The factual conditional clause

428. Within this group we can distinguish two sorts of conditional clauses: (1) those expressing a factual presupposition and (2) those expressing a general condition.
LAYTON (497) distinguishes a 3rd category: the *undifferentiated causal clause*. This type comes with some ambiguity with regard to its meaning and its translation. They cannot be formally designated as belonging to type 1 or 2.

429. A factual condition can be expressed with a conditional in the protasis, expressing an eventuality, often preceded by the conjunction ⲈϢⲰⲠⲈ or ⲈϢⲬⲈ.

430. The conditional can also have a temporal meaning. In this case it is often preceded by the conjunction ϨⲞⲦⲀⲚ (cf. 425).

431. It can be used in a concessive sense when it is preceded by the conjunction ⲔⲀⲚ (cf. 440).

432. Factual conditional clauses can consist of the conjunctions ⲈϢⲰⲠⲈ and ⲈϢⲬⲈ with the present, the future, a circumstantial conversion or a non-verbal construction.

433. A circumstantial phrase without conjunction can also express a factual condition.

ⲈⲢϢⲀⲚ-ⲠⲈ⸗Ⲕ.ⲂⲀⲖ ⲤⲔⲀⲚⲆⲀⲖⲒⲌⲈ Ⲙ̄ⲘⲞ⸗Ⲕ (Mark 9:47). *If your eye scandalizes you...*

ⲉϣϫⲉ ⲡⲉⲕ.ⲃⲁⲗ ⲥⲕⲁⲛⲇⲁⲗⲓⲍⲉ ⲙ̄ⲙⲟ⳽ⲕ ⲡⲟⲣⲕ⳽ϥ̄ (Matt 18:9). *If your eye scandalizes you, (then) pluck it out.*
ⲉ⳽ⲧⲉⲧⲛ̄.ⲡⲓⲥⲧⲉⲩⲉ ⲧⲉⲛ.(ⲛ)ⲁ.ϫⲓⲧ⳽ⲟⲩ (Matt 21:22). *If you (pl.) believe, you will receive them.*

The contrafactual conditional clause

434. The protasis of a contrafactual sentence usually has ⲉⲛⲉ- (circumstantial preterit conversion), the apodosis has the preterit conversion of the future, often with an invariable ⲡⲉ.

435. If the condition implies a present reality, ⲉⲛⲉ- can introduce a double conversion (circumstantial and preterit) of a durative sentence, or a nominal sentence, or an existential sentence with ⲟⲩⲛ̄-/ⲙⲛ̄- or an indicational sentence with ⲉⲓⲥ- (cf. 300).

436. If the condition implies a past reality ⲉⲛⲉ is accompanied by the focalising conversion of the past or by a negative past tense (without conversion).

437. The protasis can also be a preterit conversion of the present (introduced by ⲛⲉ). In that case, it expresses a connotation of irreality or regret.

ⲉⲛⲉ-ⲡⲉ⳽ⲧⲛ̄.ⲉⲓⲱⲧ ⲡⲉ ⲡ.ⲛⲟⲩⲧⲉ, ⲛⲉ⳽ⲧⲉⲧⲛ̄.ⲛⲁ.ⲙⲉⲣⲓⲧ ⲡⲉ (John 8:42). *If God were your Father, you (pl.) would love me.*
ⲉⲛⲉ.ⲙⲡ⳽ⲓ.ⲉⲓ ⲧⲁ.ϣⲁϫⲉ ⲛⲙ̄ⲙⲁ⳽ⲩ ⲛⲉ.ⲙ̄ⲙⲛ̄ ⲛⲟⲃⲉ ⲉⲣⲟ⳽ⲟⲩ ⲡⲉ (John 15:22). *If I had not come and talked to them, they wouldn't have any sin.*
ⲉⲛⲉ.ⲟⲩⲛ̄ ϭⲟⲙ ⲉϣϫⲉ ⲡⲉ ⲁ⳽ⲧⲉⲧⲛ̄.ⲡⲣ̄ⲕ ⲛⲉ⳽ⲧⲛ̄.ⲁⲗⲟⲟⲩⲉ (Gal 4:15). *If it would have been possible, you (pl.) would have plucked out your eyes.*

Some remarks

438. The apodosis is often introduced by ⲉⲓⲉ (ⲉⲉⲓⲉ) or, when it is a contrafactual condition, by ⲉϣϫⲉ, ⲉϣϫⲉ ⲡⲉ, ⲉϣϫⲡⲉ, ⲛⲉⲉⲓⲥⲡⲉ.
ⲉϣϫⲉ ⲛ.ⲉⲧ.ⲙⲟⲟⲩⲧ ⲛⲁ.ⲧⲱⲟⲩⲛ ⲁⲛ ⲉⲓⲉ ⲙ̄ⲡⲉ-ⲡⲉⲭ̄ⲥ̄ ⲧⲱⲟⲩⲛ (1Cor 15:13). *If the death will not be resuscitated, then Christ has not been resuscitated.*
ⲛ̄ⲥⲁⲃⲏⲗ ⲅⲁⲣ ϫⲉ ⲁ⳽ⲛ.ⲱⲥⲕ̄ ⲉϣϫⲉ ⲁ⳽ⲛ.ⲕⲟⲧⲛ̄ ⲙ̄-ⲡ.ⲙⲉϩ-ⲥⲡ-ⲥⲛⲁⲩ (Gen 43:10). *If we had not been delayed, we would have returned twice.*

439. The conjunctions ⲛ̄ⲥⲁⲃⲏⲗ ϫⲉ and ⲉⲓⲙⲏⲧ(ⲉ)ⲓ, often with a conjunctive, can be translated *if not* or *unless*.
ⲉⲓⲙⲏⲧⲓ ⲛ̄⳽ⲧⲉⲧⲛ̄.ⲕⲉⲧ ⲧⲏⲩⲧⲛ̄ (Matt 18:3). *If you (pl.) do not change yourselves.*

440. The concessive clause is introduced by the conjunctions ⲕⲁⲓⲡⲉⲣ, ⲕⲁⲓⲧⲟⲓ, ⲕⲁⲛ. A circumstantial conversion without conjunction can have the same connotation.
ⲕⲁⲛ ⲉ⳽ⲓ.ϣⲁⲛ.ⲙⲟⲩ ⲛ̄.ϯ.ⲛⲁ.ϫⲓ-ϯⲡⲉ ⲁⲛ ⲛ̄-ⲗⲁⲁⲩ ⲙ̄ⲡⲁⲧ⳽ϥ.ⲡ̄-ⲛⲁⲩ (ShChass 107). *Even if I die, I will not taste anything before the time has come.*
ⲉ.ⲁⲛⲅ ⲟⲩ.ⲥϩⲓⲙⲉ ⲛ̄.ⲥⲁⲙⲁⲣⲓⲧⲏⲥ (John 4:9). *Even though I am a Samaritan woman...*

441. The comparative conditional clause is introduced by the conjunction ϨⲰⲤ (ⲈϢⲬⲈ), followed by a circumstantial conversion. Alternatively, we can find a construction introduced by ⲈϢⲬⲈ, ⲚⲐⲈ ⲈϢⲬⲈ, ⲚⲐⲈ ⲬⲈ.
ϨⲰⲤ Ⲉ.Ⲁ⳱Ⲓ.ⲢⲀϢⲈ (Z 298:6). *As if I would have rejoiced.*

442. The non-inflected interjection (Ⲉ)ⲘⲘⲞⲚ, possibly accompanied by ⲈϢⲰⲠⲈ, ⲈϢⲬⲈ, ⲈⲚⲈ or Ⲉ, signifies *if not*.
ⲈⲘⲘⲞⲚ ⲈϢⲬⲈ Ⲁ⳱Ⲩ.ⲞⲠ⳱ⲞⲨ ⲠⲈ ϨⲰⲤ ϨⲀⲒⲢⲈⲦⲒⲔⲞⲤ (ShAmél II 341:7–8). *If not, they would have been considered as heretics.*

ⲈϢⲬⲈ Ⲛ.ⲈⲦ.ⲘⲞⲞⲨⲦ ⲚⲀ.ⲦⲰⲞⲨⲚ ⲀⲚ ⲈⲒⲈ ⲘⲠⲈ-ⲠⲈ.ⲬⲤ ⲦⲰⲞⲨⲚ (1Cor 15:13). *If the dead will not resuscitate, then Jesus has not been resuscitated.*
ⲈⲚⲈ.ⲘⲚ-ⲂⲀⲢⲂⲀⲢⲞⲤ ϢⲞⲞⲠ ⲞⲨ ⲠⲈ Ⲡ.ⲦⲀⲈⲒⲞ Ⲙ-Ⲡ.ⲘⲀⲦⲞⲒ ⲀⲨⲰ ⲠⲈ⳱Ϥ.ϢⲞⲨϢⲞⲨ (ShChass 70:20–24). *If there would be no barbarians, what would the honour and the pride of the soldier be?*

D. The causal clause

443. The causal clause can be introduced by the Coptic conjunctions ⲬⲈ, ⲈⲂⲞⲖ ⲬⲈ, ⲈⲦⲂⲈ ⲬⲈ, or by the Greek conjunctions ⲈⲠⲈⲒ, ⲈⲠⲈⲒⲆⲎ.

444. A circumstantial conversion without conjunction can also have a causal meaning.

ⲀⲘⲎⲒ⳱ⲦⲚ ⲬⲈ Ⲁ⳱ⲚⲔⲀ ⲚⲒⲘ ⲤⲞⲂⲦⲈ (Luke 14:17). *Come (pl.), for everything has been prepared.*
Ⲁ⳱Ⲛ.ⲤϬⲎⲢ Ⲉ-ⲦⲞⲨⲚ-ⲔⲨⲠⲢⲞⲤ ⲈⲦⲂⲈ ⲬⲈ ⲚⲈⲢⲈ-Ⲛ.ⲦⲎⲨ ϮⲞⲨⲂⲎ⳱Ⲛ (Acts 27:4). *We sailed to Cyprus, because the winds were against us.*
ⲈⲠⲈⲒ Ⲛ.ⲦⲀⲒ ⲀⲚ ⲦⲈ ⲦⲈ⳱Ϥ.ⲠⲒⲤⲦⲒⲤ (TT 110a:6). *Because this is not his faith.*

E. Final and consecutive clauses

445. Final and consecutive clauses might be expressed by the use of the conjunctive (cf. 371) or the future conjunctive (cf. 387) without conjunction.

446. The conjunction ⲬⲈ with the present (without conversion) can express consequence (especially in questions, TILL 360).

447. The final or consecutive clause can consist of the conjunction ⲬⲈ/ⲬⲈⲔⲀ(Ⲁ)Ⲥ (*in order that, so... that*) with the focalising conversion of the future (cf. 266) or with the optative (cf. 337).

448. In a final or consecutive clause the Greek conjunctions ϨⲰⲤⲦⲈ, ⲘⲎⲠⲰⲤ, and ⲘⲎⲠⲞⲦⲈ mostly occur with the conjunctive (cf. 129, 392).

449. The preposition Ⲉ- with the infinitive or causative infinitive can express a goal. This is also the case with ϨⲰⲤⲦⲈ Ⲉ- followed by the causative infinitive (cf. 392–393).

450. The limitative ϣⲁⲛⲧⲉ can be used with the meaning *in order that, so that* (cf. 364).

451. The circumstantial conversion without conjunction can have final or consecutive meaning.

ⲁ⸗ϥ.ϯ ⲛⲁ⸗ⲛ ⲛ̄-ⲟⲩ.ⲙⲛ̄ⲧ-ⲣⲙ̄ⲛ-ϩⲏⲧ ϫⲉ ⲉ⸗ⲛ.ⲉ.ⲥⲟⲩⲛ̄-ⲡ.ⲙⲉ (1John 5:20). *He gave us understanding, so that we may know the truth.*

ⲁⲩⲱ ⲡ.ⲇⲓⲁⲃⲟⲗⲟⲥ ⲙⲉⲛ ⲛⲉ.ϣⲁ⸗ϥ.ϫⲓ ⲙ-ⲡ.ϩⲣ̄ⲃ ⲛ-ⲧⲉ.ⲥϩⲓⲙⲉ ⲛ-ⲧⲉ.ⲩϣⲏ... ϫⲉⲕⲁⲥ ⲉ⸗ϥ.ⲛⲁ.ⲣ̄-ϩⲁⲗ ⲛⲛ-ⲁⲛⲧⲱⲛⲓⲟⲥ (V.A. 8:17–20). *And the devil usually took the appearance of a woman during the night… in order to deceive Antony.*

ⲁ⸗ⲩ.ⲙⲉϩ-ⲡ.ϫⲟⲉⲓ ⲥⲛⲁⲩ ϩⲱⲥⲧⲉ ⲉ-ⲧⲣⲉ⸗ⲩ.ⲱⲙⲥ̄ (Luke 5:7). *They filled two ships (so much) that they sank.*

ⲁ⸗ⲛ.ⲉⲓ ⲉ-ⲟⲩⲱϣⲧ̄ ⲛⲁ⸗ϥ (Matt 2:2). *We have come to worship him.*

See exercise 10

Relative clauses

A. The 'real' relative

452. The relative clause is always introduced by the converters ⲈⲦ, ⲈⲦⲈ, (Ⲉ)ⲚⲦⲀ.
If the relative clause has the aorist or a preterit conversion, it can alternatively have the relative converter ⲉ or ⲈⲦⲈ.

453. The antecedent of the relative clause is always definite. It can function as the subject or the relative clause or in any other grammatical function.

445. The relative converter is normally the first element of the relative clause. In some rare cases however, it can be preceded by another element in extraposition.
ⲠⲘⲀ ⲀⲚⲞⲔ Ⲉ.ϮⲚⲀⲂⲰⲔ ⲈⲢⲞ⸗ϥ (John 8:21). *The place I will go to.*

The antecedent is the subject of the relative clause

455. The converter ⲈⲦ is normally used when the antecedent is the subject of the relative clause.
ϢⲎⲢⲈ ϢⲎⲘ ⲚⲒⲘ ⲈⲦ.ϨⲚ̄-ⲂⲎⲐⲖⲈⲈⲘ (Matt 2:16). *All the little children, which are in Bethlehem.*

456. The converter ⲈⲦⲈ occurs with negative clauses, with ⲘⲠⲀⲦⲈ and ⲞⲨⲚ̄(ⲦⲈ) and with nominal sentences. ⲈⲦⲈ can also be used with the preterit conversion of the present or with the aorist.

457. The expression ⲈⲦⲈ ⲠⲀⲒ ⲠⲈ means *that is*.
Ⲡ.ⲬⲀⲒⲂⲈⲔⲈ ⲈⲦⲈ Ⲛ̄.ⲞⲨ.ϢⲰⲤ ⲀⲚ ⲠⲈ (John 10:12). *The mercenary who is not a shepherd.*
ϨⲀⲢⲈϨ ⲈⲢⲰ⸗ⲦⲚ̄ Ⲉ.ⲠⲈ.ⲐⲀⲂ ⲈⲦⲈ ⲦⲀⲒ ⲦⲈ ⲐⲨⲠⲞⲔⲢⲒⲤⲒⲤ (Luke 12:1). *Refrain* (pl.) *from the leaven, that is, the hypocrisy.*

458. The converter (Ⲉ)ⲚⲦⲀ is used as conjugation base for the relative past.
ⲠⲀ.ⲈⲤⲞⲞⲨ ⲈⲚⲦⲀ⸗ϥ.ⲤⲰⲢⲘ̄ (Luke 15:6). *My sheep that was lost.*

459. The antecedent can occur as the subject of the relative clause. This is always the case if the relative clause has a suffixally conjugated verboid or if it is a negative durative clause. Non-durative sentences always have the subject expressed.

460. The subject does not occur in relative clauses containing a durative sentence introduced by ⲈⲦ.

ⲠⲀ.ⲈⲤⲞⲞⲨ ⲈⲚⲦⲀ⸗ϥ.ⲤⲰⲢⲘ̄ (Luke 15:6) *My sheep that was lost.*

ⲚϨⲈⲐⲚⲞⲤ ⲈⲦⲈ Ⲛ̄-ⲤⲈ.ⲤⲞⲞⲨⲚ̄ ⲀⲚ Ⲙ̄-Ⲡ.ⲚⲞⲨⲦⲈ (K 9777 r° a 1). *The nations which do not know God.*
Ⲡ.ϢⲰⲤ ⲈⲦ.ⲚⲀⲚⲞⲨ⸗ϥ (John 10:11). *The good shepherd (the shepherd who is good).*

The antecedent is not the subject of the relative clause

461. When the antecedent is not the subject of the relative clause, the latter must contain a pronoun that refers to the antecedent. This anaphoric pronoun can only be omitted when the function of the antecedent in the relative clause is obvious.

462. The relative converters for this kind of clauses are the same as when the antecent functions as the subject of the relative clause. The suffixally conjugated verboids expressing qualities (cf. 150) however are introduced by the converter ⲈⲦⲈ.
Ⲧ.ⲘⲀⲀⲨ ⲈⲦⲈ ⲚⲀϢⲈ-ⲠⲈ⸗Ⲥ.ⲚⲀ (BG 71:6). *The mother whose mercy is great.*
Ⲡ.ⲘⲀ ⲈⲦⲈ ⲘⲚ̄-ϨⲞⲦⲈ Ⲛ̄ϨⲎⲦ⸗ϥ̄ (Ps 13:5). *The place where there is no fear.*

463. If the relative clause is a durative sentence, the pronominal subject is immediately attached to the relative converter (ⲈϮ, ⲈⲦ⸗Ⲕ, etc.).

464. The converter with a nominal subject has the form ⲈⲦⲈⲢⲈ-.
ⲠⲀⲒ ⲈϮ.ⲤⲰⲦⲘ̄ Ⲉ-ⲚⲀⲒ ⲈⲦⲂⲎⲎⲦ⸗ϥ̄ (Luke 9:9). *This one, about whom I hear these things.*
Ⲡ.ⲘⲀ ⲈⲦ⸗ⲞⲨ.Ⲛ̄ϨⲎⲦ⸗ϥ̄ (ShIII, 151). *The place where they are.*
Ⲡ.ⲘⲀ ⲈⲦⲈⲢⲈ-Ⲡ.ⲤⲰⲘⲀ ⲚⲀ.ϢⲰⲠⲈ Ⲙ̄ⲘⲞ⸗ϥ (Matt 24:28). *The place where the body will go.*

Some remarks

465. The grammatical antecendent of a relative clause might be a demonstrative pronoun that refers to the real antecedent, which precedes. In this construction the real antecedent might be indefinite.
ⲘⲀⲢⲒⲀ ⲦⲀⲒ ⲈⲚⲦⲀ⸗Ⲩ.ⲬⲠⲈ-Ⲓ̄Ⲥ̄ ⲈⲂⲞⲖ Ⲛ̄ϨⲎⲦ⸗Ⲥ ⲠⲀⲒ Ⲉ.ϢⲀ⸗Ⲩ.ⲘⲞⲨⲦⲈ ⲈⲢⲞ⸗ϥ ϪⲈ Ⲡ̄Ⲉ.Ⲭ̄Ⲥ̄ (Matt 1:16). *Mary, the one from whom Jesus was born, the one who is called the Christ.*
ⲞⲨ.ⲚⲞϬ Ⲛ̄-ⲢⲀϢⲈ ⲠⲀⲒ ⲈⲦ.ⲚⲀ.ϢⲰⲠⲈ Ⲙ̄-Ⲡ.ⲖⲀⲞⲤ ⲦⲎⲢ⸗ϥ̄ (Luke 2:10). *A great joy, the one that will come to be for the entire people.*

466. A relative clause can function as a noun if it is preceded by a determining pronoun (POLOTSKY, *Gl*, 8f.), which expresses its grammatical antecedent.
The substantivated relative clause might itself in its totality (with the determining pronoun) be considered as a noun. In that case it can have an article itself.
Ⲡ.ⲈⲦ.ϢⲰⲚⲈ *the sick one*
Ⲡ.ⲈⲦ.ⲚⲀⲚⲞⲨ⸗ϥ *the good*
ϨⲈⲚ.Ⲡ.ⲈⲦ.ⲚⲀⲚⲞⲨ⸗ϥ *good deeds*
Ⲡ.Ⲡ.ⲈⲦ.ⲞⲨⲀⲀⲂ *the saint*

467. Nouns derived from a relative clause often have a general meaning.

ⲡ.ⲉⲧ.ⲥⲟⲟⲩⲛ̄, *(every one) who knows*
ⲙⲛ̄ ⲡ.ⲉⲧ.ϩⲟⲃⲥ̄ (Mark 4:22). *There is nothing hidden*

468. Several relative clauses can be connected with one another with conjunctions or in an asyndetic way. When more than one relative sentence modify the same antecedent it is not necessary to repeat the converter.

469. The definite article does not have to be repeated when more than one substantivated relative clauses define the same element.
ⲡ.ⲉⲧ.ⲣⲁϣⲉ ⲛⲙ̄ⲙⲁ⸗ⲩ ⲏ ⲉⲧ.ⲥⲙⲟⲩ ⲉⲣⲟⲟⲩ (ShAmél I 8:4). *The one who rejoices with them and blesses them.*

470. A relative clause can be extended by an independent clause or by a conjunctive (cf. 373) or a circumstantial conversion.
ⲛ.ⲉⲛⲧⲁ⸗ⲛ.ⲛⲁⲩ ⲉⲣⲟ⸗ⲟⲩ ⲁⲩⲱ ⲁ⸗ⲛ.ⲥⲟⲧⲙ̄⸗ⲟⲩ (Acts 4:20). *What we have seen and heard.*
ⲛ.ⲉⲧ.ⲥⲟⲟⲩⲛ̄ ⲉ-ⲛⲉ⸗ⲩ.ϩⲃⲏⲩⲉ ⲛ̄⸗ⲥⲉ.ϩⲱⲡ ⲉϫⲱ⸗ⲟⲩ (ShAmél I 8:5s.). *Those who know their works and hide them.*

B. The circumstantial conversion

471. If the antecedent of a relative clause is indefinite, the circumstantial conversion introduced by ⲉ- is used instead of the relative conversion.
ⲟⲩ.ⲣⲱⲙⲉ ⲉ.ⲁ⸗ϥ.ϫⲟ ⲛ̄-ⲟⲩ.ϭⲣⲟϭ (Matt 13:24). *A man who has sown a seed.*

472. If the antecedent is a demonstrative noun, one might find a circumstantial conversion, although the relative conversion is more frequent (cf. 453).
ⲡⲁⲓ ⲉ.ⲁ-ⲇⲁⲩⲉⲓⲇ ⲁⲁ⸗ϥ (Luke 6:3). *That what David did.*

473. The circumstantial conversion can be used instead of the relative if the converted sentence has the aorist or a preterit conversion, even if the antecedent is definite.
ⲥⲉ.ⲛⲁ.ϭⲓⲛⲉ ⲙ̄-ⲡ.ϣⲏⲛ ⲉⲧ.ⲙ̄-ⲙⲁⲩ ⲉ.ⲁ⸗ⲩ.ⲡⲟⲣⲕ⸗ϥ (ShIII 141). *They will find that tree that they have plucked.*
ⲡⲁⲓ ⲉ.ϣⲁ⸗ⲩ.ⲙⲟⲩⲧⲉ ⲉⲣⲟ⸗ϥ ϫⲉ.ⲡⲉ.ⲭ̄ⲥ̄ (Matt 1:16). *The one who is called the Christ.*

474. In this case we alternatively find the relative converter ⲉⲧⲉ.
ϩⲉⲑⲛⲟⲥ ⲛⲓⲙ ⲛ̄-ⲣⲱⲙⲉ ⲉⲧⲉ.ⲙ̄ⲡ⸗ⲟⲩ.ⲥⲟⲩⲛ̄-ⲡ.ⲛⲟⲩⲧⲉ (ShChas 180). *Every nation of men, who have not come to know God.*

475. When the subject of the relative clause is different from the antecedent, the circumstantial conversion is often used with nominal sentences and negative durative sentences.
ⲡ.ϩⲉⲑⲛⲟⲥ ⲉ.ⲡ.ϫⲟⲉⲓⲥ ⲡⲉ ⲡⲉ⸗ϥ.ⲛⲟⲩⲧⲉ (Ps 42:12). *The nation of which the Lord is his God.*

476. If the defined antecedent expresses an element of time or manner the relative clause might alternatively be introduced by the relative converter or by the circumstantial converter. If the meaning is obvious, the anaphoric pronoun can be omitted.
ⲡ.ⲛⲁⲩ ⲉⲛⲧⲁ⸗ϥ.ⲙ̄ⲧⲟⲛ ⲛ̄ϩⲏⲧ⸗ϥ (John 4:52) *The hour, in which he was relieved.*
ⲛ̄-ⲛⲉ.ϩⲟⲟⲩ ⲅⲁⲣ ⲉ⸗ⲛ.ϩ︤ⲛ̄-ⲧ.ⲥⲁⲣⲝ (Rom 7:5) *The days that we are in the flesh.*

See exercise 11

Cleft Sentences

477. A cleft sentence is a sentence with focalising meaning. It consists of a focal point, the first term or expression in the sentence, followed by a topic element, a relative or circumstantial sentence that expands the focal point.
A Basic sentence is: ⲧⲉⲧⲛ̄.ⲛⲁ.ϫⲉ-ⲡⲁⲓ (Mark 13:11). *You shall say this.*
The corresponding cleft sentence is: ⲡⲁⲓ ⲡⲉⲧⲉⲧⲛⲁ-ϫⲟⲟ⸗ϥ (Mark 13:11). *It is* this *that you* (pl.) *shall say.*

478. A cleft sentence can be formed with the focal point + ⲡⲉ/ⲧⲉ/ⲛⲉ followed by a relative clause or by a circumstantial clause. ⲡⲉ/ⲧⲉ/ⲛⲉ can correspond to the focal point. In that case it is endophoric. Or it can correspond with the topic element and then introduces some new information. In that case it is presentative.
A sentence with endophoric ⲛⲉ is:
ⲛⲁⲓ ⲇⲉ ⲛ.ⲉⲧ.ϩⲁⲧⲛ-ⲧⲉϩⲓⲏ (Mark 4:15). *It is these that are along the path.*
ⲛⲉ.ⲛ̄ⲧⲟϥ ⲙⲁⲩⲁⲁ⸗ϥ ⲡⲉ ⲉ⸗ϥ.ⲁⲛⲁⲭⲱⲣⲉⲓ ϩⲙ̄-ⲡ.ⲙⲁ ⲉⲧⲙ̄ⲙⲁⲩ (ApophPatr 43:21–22). *It was he alone who was living as an anchorite in that place.*
A sentence with presentative ⲡⲉ is:
ⲟⲩⲣⲱⲙⲉ ⲛ̄-ⲣⲙ̄-ⲙⲁⲟ ⲡⲉ.ⲛⲧⲁ⸗ϥ-ⲧⲱϭⲉ ⲛ̄-ⲟⲩⲙⲁ ⲛ̄-ⲉⲗⲟⲟⲗⲉ (Matt 21:33). *There once was a rich man who planted a vineyard.*
ⲟⲩ.ⲣⲱⲙⲉ ⲡⲉ ⲉ⸗ϥ.ⲕⲱⲧ ⲛ-ⲟⲩ.ⲧⲟⲡⲟⲥ ⲉ-ⲧⲉ⸗ϥ.ⲭⲣⲓⲁ (ShIII 27:9). *There once was a man who was constructing a place for his own use.*

479. The form of ⲡⲉ/ⲧⲉ/ⲛⲉ is usually contracted with the relative marker ⲉⲧ or the circumstantial marker ⲉ. This is called the elided form: ⲡⲉⲧⲉ, ⲡⲉⲧⲉⲣⲉ-, ⲡⲉⲧ⸗, ⲡⲉⲧ-, ⲡⲉϣⲁ- (for ⲡⲉ.ⲉ.ϣⲁ) etc.

480. When the focal point of the cleft sentence is a personal independent pronoun (ⲁⲛⲟⲕ, ⲛ̄ⲧⲟⲕ, etc.), the relative topic element is connected without ⲡⲉ/ⲧⲉ/ⲛⲉ.
ⲛ̄ⲧⲟⲕ ⲉⲧ.ϫⲱ ⲙ̄ⲙⲟ⸗ⲥ (Matt 27:11) *It is you who say it.*

Part IV: Exercises

Exercises

The following exercises will allow you to control your understanding of the grammar and to repeat it by induction.

One should always start with the analysis of the forms in their components as it has been done in the examples in the grammatical exposition.

The last chapters have relatively few exercises. At this stage of the learning process the student should be able to read the texts in an increasing order of difficulty. The Coptic syntax can be appropriated inductively by translating the texts and refering back to the last chapter of Grammar, which does not have to be learned by heart.

All the words of the excercises are integrated in the Coptic and Greek glossaries.

Exercise 1

1. ⲡⲥⲁⲃⲉ
2. ⲙ̄ⲙⲁⲑⲏⲧⲏⲥ
3. ⲟⲩϩⲏⲕⲉ
4. ⲑⲩⲡⲟⲕⲣⲓⲥⲓⲥ
5. ⲛⲕⲟⲟⲩⲉ ⲧⲏⲣⲟⲩ
6. ⲧⲉⲑⲉⲱⲣⲓⲁ
7. ⲟⲩⲁⲣⲭⲱⲛ
8. ⲛⲉⲅⲣⲁⲫⲏ
9. ⲛⲉⲣⲣⲱⲟⲩ
10. ⲡⲉϩⲟⲟⲩ
11. ⲧⲉⲩϣⲏ
12. ⲟⲩⲣⲙ̄ⲙⲁⲟ
13. ϩⲉⲛϩⲓⲟⲟⲩⲉ
14. ⲟⲩϩⲏⲧ ⲛ̄ⲟⲩⲱⲧ
15. ⲛⲉϩⲃⲏⲩⲉ
16. ⲁⲃⲉⲗ ⲡⲇⲓⲕⲁⲓⲟⲥ
17. ⲙⲙⲉⲣⲁⲧⲉ
18. ⲡⲙⲁⲓϩⲏⲇⲟⲛⲏ
19. ⲛⲉϩⲓⲟⲙⲉ
20. †ⲣⲏⲛⲏ
21. ⲛⲉⲥⲟⲟⲩ
22. ϩⲉⲛⲕⲁⲧⲁ-ⲥⲁⲣⲝ
23. ⲥⲙⲟⲩ ⲛⲓⲙ ⲁⲣⲉⲧⲏ ⲛⲓⲙ ⲧⲁⲉⲓⲟ ⲛⲓⲙ
24. ⲟⲩϣⲁϫⲉ ⲛ̄ⲥⲃⲱ
25. ⲡⲗⲟⲅⲟⲥ ⲙ̄ⲡⲛⲟⲩⲧⲉ
26. ⲟⲩⲡ̄ⲛ̄ⲁ̄ ⲛⲱⲛϩ̄ ⲟⲩⲛⲟϭ ⲙ̄ⲙⲏⲏϣⲉ
27. ϣⲏⲣⲉ ⲛ̄ⲧⲉⲡⲟⲩⲟⲉⲓⲛ. ϣⲏⲣⲉ ⲛ̄ⲧⲉⲡⲕⲁⲕⲉ.
28. ⲛⲉⲩϩⲃⲏⲩⲉ ⲧⲏⲣⲟⲩ ⲛ̄ⲇⲓⲕⲁⲓⲟⲥⲩⲛⲏ
29. ⲛⲉϩⲃⲏⲩⲉ ⲙ̄ⲡⲕⲁⲕⲉ

30. ⲛϭⲓⲝ ⲛ̄ⲟⲩⲣⲱⲙⲉ ⲛ̄ⲥⲁⲃⲉ
31. ϣⲁϫⲉ ⲛⲓⲙ ⲙⲛ̄ϩⲱⲃ ⲛⲓⲙ ⲛ̄ⲁⲅⲁⲑⲟⲛ
32. ⲟⲩϩⲏⲅⲉⲙⲱⲛ ⲛ̄ⲧⲉⲛϩⲉⲑⲛⲟⲥ
33. ϣⲉ ⲛ̄ⲁⲓⲭⲙⲁⲗⲱⲧⲟⲥ
34. ⲟⲩϣⲏⲣⲉ ⲁⲩⲱ ⲛ̄ϣⲉⲉⲣⲉ ⲥⲛ̄ⲧⲉ
35. ⲧⲉⲡⲗⲁⲧⲟⲛⲓⲕⲏ ⲇⲓⲇⲁⲥⲕⲁⲗⲓⲁ
36. ⲡⲕⲁϩ ⲛ̄ⲣⲉϥϯ ⲕⲁⲣⲡⲟⲥ
37. ϯⲟⲩ ⲛ̄ϩⲟⲃⲟⲗⲟⲥ
38. ⲅⲉⲛⲟⲥ ⲛⲓⲙ ⲛ̄ϩⲉⲗⲗⲏⲛ ϩⲓϩⲁⲓⲣⲉⲧⲓⲕⲟⲥ
39. ⲥⲛⲁⲩ ⲥⲛⲁⲩ
40. ⲁⲛⲟⲛ ⲛⲉⲓⲭⲣⲓⲥⲧⲓⲁⲛⲟⲥ
41. ⲡⲉⲓⲅⲉⲛⲟⲥ ⲥⲛⲁⲩ
42. ⲡⲉⲛⲥⲧⲁⲩⲣⲟⲥ
43. ⲧⲉⲧⲛ̄ϩⲉⲗⲡⲓⲥ ⲧⲏⲣⲥ̄
44. ⲧⲁⲙⲛ̄ⲧⲕⲟⲩⲓ
45. ⲧⲱⲕ
46. ⲣⲱⲱ
47. ⲧⲁⲡⲥⲱⲧⲏⲣ
48. ⲧⲟⲟⲧ
49. ⲡⲉϥϩⲙ̄ϩⲁⲗ
50. ⲧⲁϩⲉ
51. ⲡⲁⲉⲓⲱⲧ
52. ⲛⲉⲓϣⲁϫⲉ
53. ⲟⲩϣⲉⲉⲣⲉ ϣⲏⲙ ⲛ̄ⲧⲁϥ
54. ⲟⲩⲧⲉⲓⲙⲓⲛⲉ
55. ⲛⲉⲓⲣⲱⲙⲉ ⲛ̄ϫⲁϫⲉ

Exercise 2

1. ⲁⲛⲅⲟⲩⲡⲟⲛⲏⲣⲟⲥ ⲛ̄ⲣⲱⲙⲉ (ShIII 123).
2. ⲛⲧⲉⲟⲩⲙⲁⲁⲩ ⲁⲛ (ShIII 22).
3. ⲁⲛⲟⲕ ϩⲱⲱⲧ (061) ⲁⲛⲅⲡⲉϥϩⲙ̄ϩⲁⲗ (ShIII 38).
4. ⲛⲧⲟⲕ ϭⲉ ⲛ̄ⲧⲕⲛⲓⲙ (John 1:22).
5. ⲡⲟⲩⲁ ⲡⲟⲩⲁ (163) ⲁⲛⲟⲛ ⲙ̄ⲙⲉⲗⲟⲥ ⲛ̄ⲛⲉⲛⲉⲣⲏⲩ (211) (Eph 4:25).
6. ⲧⲉϩⲣⲉ ⲙ̄ⲡⲣⲱⲙⲉ ⲡⲉ ⲟⲩⲟⲉⲓⲕ ⲙⲛ̄ⲟⲩⲙⲟⲟⲩ ⲙⲛ̄ⲛ̄ⲕⲉⲧⲣⲟⲫⲏ (Rossi II 3, 90b, 6–9).
7. ⲟⲩⲡⲟⲛⲏⲣⲟⲛ ⲡⲉ (ShChass 95).
8. ⲡⲉⲛⲁⲗⲟⲩ ϣⲏⲙ ⲡⲉ ⲛ̄ⲁⲧⲥⲟⲟⲩⲛ (P 130.1 133 329).
9. ⲟⲩ (023) ⲧⲉ ⲧⲉⲛϩⲉⲗⲡⲓⲥ (ShChass 82).
10. ⲡⲱⲕ (020) ⲡⲉ ⲡⲛⲟⲩⲃ ⲡⲱⲕ ⲡⲉ ⲡϩⲁⲧ ⲧⲱⲕ ⲧⲉ ⲧⲟⲓⲕⲟⲩⲙⲉⲛⲏ (ShIII 117).
11. ⲁⲅⲁⲑⲟⲛ ⲛⲓⲙ (024) ⲛⲟⲩϥ ⲛⲉ (ShIII 72).
12. ⲡⲉⲓⲏⲓ ⲅⲁⲣ ⲡⲁⲡⲣⲱⲙⲉ (019) ⲁⲛ ⲡⲉ ⲁⲗⲗⲁ ⲡⲁⲡⲛⲟⲩⲧⲉ ⲡⲉ (P 130,4)
13. ⲟⲩⲣⲱⲙⲉ ⲛ̄ⲟⲩⲱⲧ ⲉⲧⲉⲡⲛⲟⲩⲧⲉ ⲡⲉ ⲟⲩⲙⲁⲁⲩ ⲛ̄ⲟⲩⲱⲧ ⲉⲧⲉⲑⲓ̅ⲗ̅ⲏ̅ⲙ̅[1] ⲛ̄ⲧⲉⲡⲉ ⲧⲉ (ShIV 129).
14. ⲟⲩⲙⲟⲟⲩ ⲉⲙⲡⲱⲕ ⲁⲛ ⲡⲉ (ShOr 155).
15. ⲛⲉⲛⲁϣⲃⲉⲉⲣ ⲅⲁⲣ ⲛⲉ (ShChass 108).
16. ⲡϩⲱⲃ ⲛ̄ⲛ̄ⲇⲓⲕⲁⲓⲟⲥ ⲡⲉ ϩⲱⲃ ⲛⲓⲙ ⲛ̄ⲁⲅⲁⲑⲟⲛ ⲡϩⲱⲃ ⲛ̄ⲛⲁⲥⲉⲃⲏⲥ ⲡⲉ ϩⲱⲃ ⲛⲓⲙ ⲙ̄ⲡⲟⲛⲏⲣⲟⲛ (Wess 9,177b).
17. ⲛⲉⲡⲥⲁⲃⲃⲁⲧⲟⲛ ⲇⲉ ⲡⲉ ⲡⲉϩⲟⲟⲩ ⲉⲧⲙ̄ⲙⲁⲩ (John 5:9).
18. ⲁⲛⲟⲛ ⲛⲉϥϩⲙ̄ϩⲁⲗ ⲁⲩⲱ ⲛ̄ⲧⲟϥ ⲡⲉ ⲡⲉⲛⲁⲣⲭⲱⲛ ⲁⲩⲱ ⲡⲉⲛⲣ̄ⲣⲟ (ShIV 34).
19. ⲟⲩⲡⲟⲗⲓⲥ ⲉⲡⲉⲥⲣⲁⲛ (021) ⲡⲉ ⲛⲁⲍⲁⲣⲉⲑ (Luke 1:26).
20. ⲛⲁⲓ ⲛⲉ ⲧⲃⲱ ⲛ̄ϫⲟⲉⲓⲧ ⲥⲛ̄ⲧⲉ. (Rev 11:4).

---

[1] ⲑⲓ̅ⲗ̅ⲏ̅ⲙ̅ for ⲧ.ϩⲓⲉⲣⲟⲩⲥⲁⲗⲉⲙ : Jerusalem (cf. glossary of *nomina sacra*).

Exercise 3

1. ⲀⲚⲒⲤⲞⲨ ⲈⲠⲈⲒⲘⲀ (Luke 19:27).

2. ⲘⲀⲦⲀⲈⲒⲈ (138) ⲠⲈⲔⲈⲒⲰⲦ ⲘⲚ̄ⲦⲈⲔⲘⲀⲀⲨ (Matt 15:4).

3. ⲘⲠⲢ̄ⲈⲒ ⲈⲂⲞⲖ (Matt 24:26).

4. ϢⲰⲠⲈ Ⲛ̄ⲦⲀϨⲈ (Gal 4:12).

5. Ⲛ̄ⲦⲘⲈ Ϩ̄Ⲙ̄ⲠⲀⲒ ⲀⲚ (1John 2:4).

6. ⲤⲈⲤⲞⲞⲨⲚ ⲄⲀⲢ ϪⲈ ⲀⲄⲀⲐⲞⲚ ⲚⲒⲘ ⲚⲞⲨϤ (020) ⲚⲈ (ShIII 72).

7. ⲤⲈⲤⲰⲂⲈ Ⲛ̄ⲤⲰϤ Ⲛ̄ϬⲒⲚ̄ⲆⲀⲒⲘⲞⲚⲒⲞⲚ ⲈⲚϤⲤⲞⲞⲨⲚ ⲀⲚ (ShRE 10,164).

8. ⲦⲚ̄ⲢⲞⲔϨ̄ ⲦⲎⲢⲚ̄ Ϩ̄Ⲙ̄ⲠⲈⲚϨⲎⲦ ⲀⲨⲰ ⲦⲈⲦⲚ̄ⲚⲎⲨ ϨⲰ̄ⲦⲦⲎⲨⲦⲚ̄¹ (ShIII 24).

9. ⲠϢⲀϪⲈ ⲈⲦⲤⲎϨ (ShIII 153).

10. Ⲙ̄ⲠⲈϤⲘⲈⲈⲨⲈ ⲤⲞⲨⲦⲰⲚ ⲀⲚ ⲈϨⲞⲨⲚ ⲈⲠⲚⲞⲨⲦⲈ (ShIII 44).

11. ⲚⲈϤⲢ̄ⲠⲘⲈⲈⲨⲈ Ⲙ̄ⲠⲈϤⲐⲂ̄ⲂⲒⲞ Ⲙ̄ⲘⲒⲚ Ⲙ̄ⲘⲞϤ (291) (ShIII 95).

12. ⲈⲨϢⲰⲰⲦ Ⲙ̄ⲘⲞⲞⲨ Ⲛ̄Ⲛ̄ⲆⲀⲒⲘⲞⲚⲒⲞⲚ (ShAmél I 380).

13. Ⲛ̄ϮⲚⲀⲔⲀⲀⲔ ⲈⲂⲞⲖ ⲀⲚ ⲀⲖⲖⲀ ϮⲚⲀⲘⲒϢⲈ ⲞⲨⲂⲎⲔ Ⲛ̄ϨⲞⲨⲞ (ShIII 38).

14. ⲦⲈⲚⲀⲤⲞⲨⲰⲚⲞⲨ (ShIII 191).

15. ⲠϨⲀⲠ ⲈⲦⲈⲢⲈⲠϪⲞⲈⲒⲤ Ⲓ̄Ⲥ̄² ⲚⲀⲔⲢⲒⲚⲈ Ⲛ̄ⲚⲀⲒ Ⲛ̄ⲦⲈⲒⲘⲒⲚⲈ ⲚϨⲎⲦϤ̄ (Mun 99).

16. ⲈⲢⲈⲠϨⲞϤ ⲚⲀϢϨⲈⲖⲘⲞⲞⲨ³ ϢⲀⲦⲰⲚ (ShChass 28).

17. ⲢⲰⲘⲈ ⲄⲀⲢ ⲚⲒⲘ ⲞⲨⲈϢⲠⲰⲚϨ̄ ⲀⲨⲰ Ⲛ̄ⲤⲈⲞⲨⲰϢ ⲀⲚ ⲈⲘⲞⲨ (ShEnch 93).

18. ⲞⲨⲚ̄Ϩ̄ⲈⲚⲘⲎⲎϢⲈ ϮⲈⲞⲞⲨ ⲚⲀⲚ ϨⲒⲂⲞⲖ (ShIII 199).

19. Ⲙ̄Ⲛ̄ⲢⲀⲚ ⲞⲨⲆⲈ ⲤⲬⲎⲘⲀ ⲚⲀϢⲂⲞⲎⲐⲈⲒ ⲈⲢⲞⲚ (ShIV 3).

20. ⲤⲈⲞⲨⲀϢϤ̄ ϨⲒⲦⲚ̄Ⲛ̄ϨⲎⲔⲈ ⲤⲈⲘⲈ Ⲙ̄ⲘⲞϤ ϨⲒⲦⲚ̄Ⲛ̄ⲔⲈⲢ̄ⲢⲰⲞⲨ Ⲙ̄ⲘⲀⲒⲚⲞⲨⲦⲈ (ShChass 106).

21. ⲀⲚⲞⲚ ⲦⲚ̄Ⲛ̄ϨⲞⲨⲚ Ⲛ̄ⲚⲈⲚⲦⲞⲠⲞⲤ (ShIII 24).

22. ϮⲚⲘ̄ⲘⲀϤ Ϩ̄Ⲛ̄ⲦⲈϤⲐⲖⲒⲤⲒⲤ (Ps 90 (91):15).

---

1 ϨⲰⲦⲦⲎⲨⲦⲚ̄ is a form of ϨⲰⲰ⸗ (162) with the suffix of the 2nd pers. plural.
2 Ⲓ̄Ⲥ̄ for ⲒⲎⲤⲞⲨⲤ : Jesus (cf. Glossary of the *nomina sacra*).
3 Ϣ ist he short form of the auxiliary ⲈϢ, *to be able to, can*. ϨⲈⲖ- ist he prenominal form of the verb ϨⲰⲖ, *to throw, to bring*, followed by the object ⲘⲞⲞⲨ, *water*. W. E. Crum, *Coptic Dictionary* 666b, s.v. ϨⲰⲖ, suggests that one should understand 'poison' here.

23. ⲙⲡⲁϩⲁⲓ ⲅⲁⲣ ϩⲙⲡⲁⲏⲓ ⲁⲛ (Prov 7:19).

24. ⲡⲉⲧⲉⲣⲟⲟⲩ (ShIV 43, 28).

25. ϥϩⲛⲟⲩⲛⲟϭ ⲛⲉⲣⲅⲁⲥⲓⲁ (Wess 9,145).

26. ⲡⲣⲱⲙⲉ ⲉⲧⲉⲣⲉⲧⲉⲡⲗⲏⲅⲏ ϩⲓⲱⲱϥ (Wess 9,138).

27. ϥϩⲓϫⲁⲉⲓⲉ (Matt 24:26).

28. ⲑⲟⲧⲉ ⲙⲡⲛⲟⲩⲧⲉ ⲥⲛⲙⲙⲁⲕ ⲛⲟⲩⲟⲉⲓϣ ⲛⲓⲙ (ShIII 101).

29. ⲛⲉⲛϩⲛⲧⲉⲓϣⲁⲓⲣⲉ ⲛⲟⲩⲱⲧ ⲛⲙⲙⲏⲧⲛ (ShIII 220).

30. ⲉⲣⲉⲛⲉⲛⲕⲉⲉⲥ ⲧⲱⲛ (ShAmél I 212).

31. ⲡⲙⲁ ⲉⲧⲉⲣⲉⲧϣⲉⲗⲉⲉⲧ ⲙⲙⲁⲩ ⲉϥⲙⲙⲁⲩ ⲛϭⲓⲡⲛⲩⲙⲫⲓⲟⲥ (ShChass 138).

32. ⲉⲧⲃⲉⲛⲓⲙ ⲏ ⲉⲧⲃⲉⲟⲩ ⲉⲧⲃⲏⲏⲧ ⲛⲙⲙⲉ (Wess 9,112).

33. ⲉⲣⲉⲡⲙⲟⲩ ⲙⲛⲡⲱⲛϩ ϩⲛⲧϭⲓϫ ⲙⲡⲗⲁⲥ (Besa 85,23).

34. ⲛⲉⲓϩⲙⲡϣⲧⲉⲕⲟ ⲡⲉ (Matt 25:36).

Exercise 4

1. ⲛⲁϣⲉⲛⲉⲕⲗⲟⲟⲗⲉ (ShIII 31).
2. ⲛⲁⲛⲟⲩⲥ ⲛⲁⲛ ⲉⲙⲟⲩ ⲛ̄ϩⲟⲩⲟ (033) ⲉⲱⲛ̄ϩ ϩⲛ̄ϩⲉⲛⲑⲗⲓⲯⲓⲥ (Wess 9, 174).
3. ϩⲉⲛϩⲃⲏⲩⲉ ⲉⲛⲁⲛⲟⲩⲟⲩ ⲁⲛ (P 131,7 40).
4. ⲛⲑⲉ ⲉⲧⲉϩⲛⲏⲧⲛ̄ (ShIII 82).
5. ⲙⲛ̄ⲧⲉⲗⲁⲁⲩ ⲁⲅⲁⲡⲏ ⲉⲛⲁⲁⲁϥ ⲉⲧⲁⲉⲓ (John 15:13).
6. ⲧⲉⲩⲁⲅⲁⲡⲏ ⲉⲧⲉ ⲟⲩⲛ̄ⲧⲁⲩⲥ (ShIV 52, 20)
7. ⲁⲛⲟⲛ ⲟⲩⲛⲧⲁⲛⲥⲕ ⲙ̄ⲙⲁⲩ ϩⲱⲥ ⲉⲓⲱⲧ (Morgan 576, f. 2 v°, b :13–15).
8. ϩⲉⲛϣⲁϥⲧⲉ ⲧⲏⲣⲟⲩ ⲡⲉϫⲁⲩ ⲛⲉ (ShIII 118).

Exercise 5

1. ⲙ̄ⲙⲛ̄ ϩⲁϩ ⲛ̄ⲉⲩⲅⲉⲛⲏⲥ (1Cor 1:26).
2. ⲉⲓⲥϩⲏⲏⲧⲉ ϯⲛⲁϯⲗⲟⲅⲟⲥ ⲛⲁⲕ ϫⲉ ⲁϩⲓⲕⲱ ⲛ̄ⲥⲱⲉⲓ ⲙ̄ⲡⲁϩⲉⲓ (ExAn 128,35s.).
3. ⲟⲩⲛ̄ ⲟⲩⲁ ⲛⲁⲧⲟⲗⲙⲁ ⲉⲃⲟⲗ ⲛ̄ϩⲏⲧⲧⲏⲩⲧⲛ̄ (1Cor 6:1).
4. ⲉⲓⲥϩⲏⲧⲉ ⲇⲉ ⲉⲓⲥ ⲟⲩⲣⲱⲙⲉ ⲉϣⲁⲩⲙⲟⲩⲧⲉ ⲉⲣⲟϥ ϫⲉ ⲍⲁⲕⲭⲁⲓⲟⲥ (Luke 19:2).
5. ⲛⲉⲟⲩⲛ̄ ⲟⲩⲛⲟϭ ⲇⲉ ⲛ̄ⲟⲩⲟⲉⲓⲛ ⲉϥⲕⲱⲧⲉ ⲉⲣⲟⲟⲩ (ApocPeter 82,9s.).
6. ⲙⲛ̄ⲗⲁⲁⲩ ⲛ̄ϣⲃⲏⲣ ⲟⲩⲇⲉ ⲙⲛ̄ ⲥⲟⲛ ⲉⲣⲉⲡⲟⲩⲁ ⲡⲟⲩⲁ ϣⲓⲛⲉ ⲛ̄ⲥⲁ ⲧⲉϥⲛⲟϥⲣⲉ (Silv 98,3–5).
7. ⲉⲓⲥ ⲡⲉⲭ̄ⲥ̄ ⲡⲉϩⲓⲉⲓⲃ ⲙ̄ⲡⲛⲟⲩⲧⲉ (John 1:36).
8. ⲉⲓⲥ ⲡⲁⲓ ⲕⲏ ⲉⲩϩⲉ ⲙ̄ⲛ̄ⲟⲩⲧⲱⲟⲩⲛ ⲛ̄ϩⲁϩ ϩⲙ̄ⲡⲓⲏ̄ⲗ̄[1] (Luke 2:34).

---

1 ⲓ̄ⲏ̄ⲗ̄ for ⲓⲥⲣⲁⲏⲗ (cf. List of *nomina sacra*).

Exercise 6

1. ⲁϥⲧⲱⲟⲩⲛ ⲁϥⲁⲥⲡⲁⲍⲉ ⲙ̄ⲙⲟⲟⲩ ⲁϥⲥⲙⲟⲩ ⲉⲣⲟⲟⲩ (ShIV 198).

2. ⲁⲡⲉⲛϩⲏⲧ ϣⲟⲟⲩⲉ ⲁϩⲏⲧⲛ̄ ϣⲟⲟⲩⲉ ⲁⲛⲉⲛⲥⲁⲣⲝ̄ ϣⲟⲟⲩⲉ ⲙ̄ⲡⲉⲛ̄ⲛⲟⲃⲉ ⲣⲱ ⲙ̄ⲙⲓⲛⲉ ⲛⲓⲙ ⲙ̄ⲡϫⲁϫⲉ ⲛ̄ⲇⲁⲓⲙⲟⲛⲓⲟⲛ ϣⲟⲟⲩⲉ ϩⲣⲁⲓ ⲛ̄ϩⲏⲧⲛ̄ (ShIV 23).

3. ⲁⲛⲇⲁⲓⲙⲟⲛⲓⲟⲛ ⲥⲟⲩⲛ̄ⲡϫⲟⲉⲓⲥ ϩⲙ̄ⲡⲉⲓⲟⲩⲟⲉⲓϣ ⲁⲩⲡⲁϩⲧⲟⲩ ⲁⲩⲟⲩⲱϣⲧ̄ ⲛⲁϣ ⲁⲩⲁϣⲕⲁⲕ ⲉⲃⲟⲗ ϩⲛ̄ⲟⲩⲛⲟϭ ⲛ̄ⲥⲙⲏ (ShIII 85).

4. ⲁⲕⲙⲉⲣⲓⲧⲛ̄ ⲡⲁⲣⲁⲡⲉⲛⲙ̄ⲡϣⲁ ⲉⲁⲕϯ ⲙ̄ⲡⲉⲕⲙⲟⲛⲟⲅⲉⲛⲏⲥ ⲛ̄ϣⲏⲣⲉ ϩⲁⲣⲟⲛ (ShRE 10, 162a).

5. ⲛ̄ⲧⲁⲩⲣ̄ϣⲙ̄ⲙⲟ ⲉⲣⲱⲧⲛ̄ ⲉⲧⲃⲉⲛⲉⲩϩⲃⲏⲩⲉ ⲉⲑⲟⲟⲩ (124) (ShIII 143).

6. ϩⲱⲃ ⲛⲓⲙ ⲛ̄ⲧⲁϥⲁⲁⲩ (119) ⲛ̄ⲧⲁϥⲁⲁⲩ ⲧⲏⲣⲟⲩ ⲉⲧⲃⲉⲡⲉⲛⲟⲩϫⲁⲓ (ShAmél II 436).

7. ϣⲁⲣⲉⲡⲙⲟⲥⲧⲉ ⲅⲁⲣ ⲧⲟⲩⲛⲉⲥⲟⲩϯⲧⲱⲛ (ShIII 122).

8. ⲙⲉⲩⲉϣϭⲙ̄ϭⲟⲙ ⲉϣⲗⲏⲗ ⲛ̄ⲑⲉ ⲛ̄ⲟⲩϣⲏⲣⲉ ϣⲏⲙ (ShIV 52).

9. ϣⲁⲩϫⲟⲟⲥ ⲉⲧⲃⲉⲡϩⲟϥ ϫⲉϣⲁϥⲣ̄ϩⲟⲧⲉ ϩⲏⲧϥ̄ ⲙ̄ⲡⲣⲱⲙⲉ ⲉϥⲕⲏ ⲕⲁϩⲏⲩ (ShAmél I, 260).

10. ⲡⲙⲁ ⲉⲧⲉⲙⲉⲣⲉϫⲟⲟⲗⲉⲥ ⲟⲩⲧⲉ ϩⲟⲟⲗⲉ ⲧⲁⲕⲟ ⲛ̄ϩⲏⲧϥ̄ (ShAmél II 237 = Mt 6:20).

11. ⲙⲉⲩⲟⲩⲱϩ ϩⲛ̄ⲏⲓ ⲉⲙⲡⲁⲧⲟⲩⲕⲟⲧϥ̄ ⲁⲩⲱ ⲙⲉⲩⲕⲁϩⲉⲛϩⲛⲁⲁⲩ ⲛ̄ⲁⲛⲁⲅⲕⲁⲓⲟⲛ ⲛ̄ϩⲏⲧϥ̄ (ShAmél II, 147).

12. ⲥⲉⲟⲩⲱⲙ ⲙ̄ⲡⲁⲧⲟⲩⲃⲱⲕ ⲉⲧⲉⲡⲣⲟⲥⲫⲟⲣⲁ (ShChass 50).

13. ⲉⲧⲉⲧⲛ̄ⲉⲙⲟⲟϣⲉ ϩⲓⲡⲁϩⲟⲩ ⲛ̄ⲛⲉⲥⲛⲏⲩ (ShIV, 62).

14. ⲁϥϫⲟⲟⲣⲟⲩ ⲉⲃⲟⲗ ⲉⲛⲉⲭⲱⲣⲁ ϫⲉⲕⲁⲥ ⲉⲩⲉϣⲱⲡⲉ ϩⲛ̄ⲟⲩⲙⲛ̄ⲧϣⲙ̄ⲙⲟ ⲙⲛ̄ⲟⲩⲙⲛ̄ⲧϩⲏⲕⲉ (ShIII 99).

15. ⲛ̄ⲛⲉⲕⲱⲣⲕ̄ ⲛ̄ⲛⲟⲩϫ ⲉⲕⲉϯ ⲇⲉ ⲛ̄ⲛⲉⲕⲁⲛⲁϣ ⲙ̄ⲡϫⲟⲉⲓⲥ (ShIII 66).

Exercise 7

1. ⲁⲓⲣⲁϣⲉ ⲉⲙⲁⲧⲉ ⲛ̄ⲧⲉⲣⲓϫⲓ ⲛ̄ⲛⲉⲥϩⲁⲓ ⲛ̄ⲧⲉⲕⲙⲛ̄ⲧⲉⲓⲱⲧ (ShIII 13).

2. ⲁⲩϫⲓⲃⲟⲗ ⲅⲁⲣ ⲉⲓⲱⲥⲏⲫ[1] ϩⲙ̄ⲡⲏⲓ ⲙ̄ⲡⲣⲙ̄ⲛ̄ⲕⲏⲙⲉ ϣⲁⲛⲧϥ̄ⲉⲓ ⲉϩⲣⲁⲓ ⲉϩⲉⲛⲛⲟϭ ⲛ̄ⲑⲗⲓⲯⲓⲥ (ShIII 103).

3. ⲛⲉϥϣⲟⲟⲡ ⲇⲉ ϩⲙ̄ⲡⲙⲁ ⲉⲧⲙ̄ⲙⲁⲩ ϣⲁⲛⲧⲉϩⲏⲣⲱⲇⲏⲥ ⲙⲟⲩ (Matt 2:15).

4. ⲁⲛⲧⲱⲧ ⲛ̄ϩⲏⲧ ⲛ̄ⲧⲉⲣⲛ̄ⲥⲱⲧⲙ̄ ⲉⲛϣⲁϫⲉ ⲛ̄ⲧⲥⲟⲫⲓⲁ ⲙ̄ⲡⲛⲟⲩⲧⲉ (ShIII 14).

5. ⲉⲛϣⲁⲛⲉⲓⲣⲉ ⲅⲁⲣ ⲛ̄ⲧⲙⲉ ⲁⲛⲧⲁⲉⲓⲉⲧⲙⲉ ⲁⲛⲥⲱϣ ⲙ̄ⲡⲃⲟⲗ ⲉⲛϣⲁⲛⲉⲓⲣⲉ ⲇⲉ ⲙ̄ⲡⲛⲁ ⲁⲛⲧⲁⲉⲓⲉ ⲧⲙⲛ̄ⲧⲛⲁϩⲧ ⲁⲛⲥⲱϣ ⲛ̄ⲧⲙⲛ̄ⲧⲁⲧⲛⲁ (ShIII 112).

6. ⲉⲛϣⲁⲛⲧⲙ̄ⲙⲉⲓⲙⲉ ⲅⲁⲣ ⲉⲧⲁⲅⲁⲡⲏ ⲙ̄ⲡⲉⲭ̄ⲥ̄[2] ⲓ̄ⲥ̄ ϥⲛⲁϫⲡⲓⲟⲛ (ShRE 10, 164).

7. ϭⲱϣⲧ ⲛ̄ⲅⲛⲁⲩ ⲉⲧⲉⲓⲯⲩⲭⲏ (ShIV 200).

8. ⲥⲉⲣϩⲟⲧⲉ ϩⲏⲧϥ̄ ⲙ̄ⲡⲁⲅⲅⲉⲗⲟⲥ ϫⲉⲛⲛⲉϥⲡⲁⲧⲁⲥⲥⲉ ⲙ̄ⲙⲟⲟⲩ ⲁⲩⲱ ⲛϥ̄ⲙⲟⲟⲩⲧⲟⲩ (ShIV 21).

9. ϣⲁⲣⲉⲛ̄ⲥⲟⲟⲛⲉ ⲉⲓ ⲛ̄ⲥⲉⲥⲩⲗⲁ ⲙ̄ⲙⲟϥ ⲛ̄ⲥⲉϥⲉⲓ ⲙ̄ⲡⲉϥⲭⲣⲏⲙⲁ ⲧⲏⲣϥ̄ (ShIV 25).

10. ⲥⲉⲛⲏⲩ ⲇⲉ ⲛ̄ϭⲓϩⲉⲛϩⲟⲟⲩ ϩⲟⲧⲁⲛ ⲉⲩϣⲁⲛϥⲓ ⲙ̄ⲡⲁⲧϣⲉⲗⲉⲉⲧ ⲛ̄ⲧⲟⲟⲧⲟⲩ (Matt 9:15).

11. ⲙⲁⲣⲛ̄ⲡⲣⲟⲥⲉⲭⲉ ⲉⲛⲉϥϣⲁϫⲉ ⲧⲁⲣⲛ̄ⲉⲓⲙⲉ ⲉⲡⲉⲧⲛ̄ϣⲓⲛⲉ ⲛ̄ⲥⲱϥ (ShLefort 41).

12. ⲁⲙⲟⲩ ⲉⲧⲉⲕⲕⲗⲏⲥⲓⲁ ⲧⲁⲣⲉⲡⲛⲟⲩⲧⲉ ⲥⲙⲟⲩ ⲉⲣⲟⲕ ϩⲛ̄ⲧⲉⲕⲙⲛ̄ⲧⲣⲙ̄ⲙⲁⲟ (P 131.6 13).

13. ...ϣⲁⲛⲧⲉⲡⲥⲁⲧⲁⲛⲁⲥ ⲙⲉϩⲉⲓⲁⲧϥ̄ ⲙ̄ⲙⲱⲧⲛ̄ ⲁⲩⲱ ⲛϥ̄ϩⲱⲙ ⲉϫⲱⲧⲛ̄ (Besa 86,14).

14. ⲕⲁⲛ ⲉⲓϣⲁⲛⲙⲟⲩ ⲛ̄ϯⲛⲁϫⲓϯⲡⲉ ⲁⲛ ⲛ̄ⲗⲁⲁⲩ ⲙ̄ⲡⲁⲧϥ̄ⲣ̄ⲛⲁⲩ (ShChass 107).

15. ⲙⲛ̄ⲛ̄ⲥⲱⲥ ⲇⲉ ⲟⲛ ϯⲛⲁⲛⲁⲩ ⲉⲣⲱⲧⲛ̄ ⲛ̄ⲧⲉⲡⲉⲧⲛ̄ϩⲏⲧ ⲣⲁϣⲉ (John 16:22).

---

1 ⲉⲓⲱⲥⲏⲫ is a proper noun: Joseph.
2 ⲭ̄ⲥ̄ for ⲭⲣⲓⲥⲧⲟⲥ : Christ (cf. glossary of *nomina sacra*).

Exercise 8

1. ⲁⲕⲧⲣⲉⲛⲥⲟⲩⲱⲛⲅ (ShIII 90).

2. ⲁⲡⲉⲓⲣⲱⲙⲉ ⲏ ⲛⲉⲓⲣⲱⲙⲉ ⲣ̄ⲛⲟⲃⲉ ⲁⲩⲧⲣⲁⲣ̄ⲛⲟⲃⲉ ϩⲱ[1] (ShAmél I, 79).

3. ⲛ̄ⲛⲉⲩⲑⲗⲓⲃⲉ ⲛ̄ⲣⲱⲙⲉ ⲉⲧⲙ̄ⲧⲣⲉⲩⲧⲙ̄ⲙⲟϥ (ShIV 92).

4. ⲉⲓⲟⲩⲉϣⲟⲩ ⲛ̄ⲧⲟⲟⲧⲧⲏⲩⲧⲛ̄ ⲛ̄ⲥⲁⲧⲣⲉⲧⲛ̄ϯϩⲏⲩ ⲙ̄ⲙⲱⲧⲛ̄ (ShAmél I, 267).

5. ⲁⲛⲁⲩ ϫⲉϩⲛ̄ ϩⲁϩ ⲙ̄ⲙⲁ ϩⲛ̄ⲛⲉⲅⲣⲁⲫⲏ ⲁⲩϩⲱⲛ ⲉⲧⲟⲟⲧⲛ̄ ⲉⲧⲙ̄ⲧⲣⲉⲛⲱⲣⲕ ⲛ̄ⲗⲁⲁⲩ ⲛ̄ⲁⲛⲁϣ (ShIII 182).

6. ⲁⲩⲱ ⲛⲑⲉ ⲉⲧⲉⲧⲛ̄ⲟⲩⲉϣⲧⲣⲉⲣ̄ⲣⲱⲙⲉ ⲁⲁⲥ ⲛⲏⲧⲛ̄ ⲁⲣⲓⲥ ϩⲱⲧⲧⲏⲩⲧⲛ̄ ⲛⲁⲩ (Luke 6:31).

7. ⲛⲑⲉ ⲛ̄ⲟⲩⲟⲉⲓϣ ⲛⲓⲙ ϥⲛⲁⲁⲓⲁⲓ ⲟⲛ ⲧⲉⲛⲟⲩ ⲛ̄ϭⲓⲡⲉⲭ̄ⲥ̄ ϩⲙ̄ⲡⲁⲥⲱⲙⲁ ⲉⲓⲧⲉ ϩⲙ̄ⲡⲧⲣⲁⲱⲛ̄ϩ ⲉⲓⲧⲉ ϩⲙ̄ⲡⲧⲣⲁⲙⲟⲩ (Phil 1:20).

8. ⲁϥⲕⲧⲟ ⲛ̄ⲧⲉϥⲟⲣⲅⲏ ⲉⲡⲁϩⲟⲩ ⲉⲧⲙ̄ⲧⲣⲉϥⲕⲟⲗⲁⲍⲉ ⲙ̄ⲙⲟⲛ ϩⲛ̄ϩⲉⲛⲛⲟϭ ⲙ̄ⲡⲓⲣⲁⲥⲙⲟⲥ (ShIV 206).

---

1 ϩⲱ is a variant form of ϩⲱⲱⲧ (cf. W.E. CRUM, *Coptic Dictionary* 651b, s.v. ϩⲱⲱ≠).

Exercise 9

1. ϩⲁϩ ⲅⲁⲣ ⲛ̄ⲥⲟⲡ ϣⲁⲣⲉⲡⲃⲉⲣⲏϭ ⲱⲣⲃ̄ ⲉϩⲟⲩⲛ ⲛ̄ⲛⲉⲧϥ̄ⲙⲉⲉⲩⲉ ⲉⲣⲟⲟⲩ ⲉⲃⲟⲡⲟⲩ ⲁⲩⲱ ⲛ̄ϥ̄ⲡⲱⲧ ⲉϩⲣⲁⲓ ⲉϫⲱⲟⲩ ϩⲛ̄ⲧⲉϥϭⲟⲙ ⲛ̄ⲧⲁϩⲟⲟⲩ (ShIII 78).

2. ⲟⲩ ⲡⲉ ⲡⲛⲟⲃⲉ ⲏ ⲁϣ ⲡⲉ ⲡϫⲓⲛϭⲟⲛⲥ̄ ⲉⲛⲧⲁⲓϫⲓⲧⲏⲩⲧⲛ̄ ⲛ̄ϭⲟⲛⲥ̄ ⲛ̄ϩⲏⲧϥ̄ ⲛ̄ⲧⲱⲧⲛ̄ ⲛ̄ⲣⲉϥⲕⲣⲙ̄ⲣⲙ̄ ⲛ̄ⲣⲉϥϭⲛ̄ⲁⲣⲓⲕⲉ (ShIII 144).

Exercise 10

1. ⲁϥⲥⲟⲩⲱⲛϥ̄ ϫⲉⲡϫⲟⲉⲓⲥⲡⲉ (ShChass 69).

2. ⲙ̄ⲛ̄ⲁⲅⲁⲡⲏ ⲛ̄ϩⲏⲧⲟⲩ ⲉϩⲟⲩⲛ ⲉⲟⲩⲁ ⲛ̄ⲟⲩⲱⲧ ⲛ̄ⲛⲉⲧϯⲥⲃⲱ ⲛⲁⲩ (Wess 9, 162).

3. ϣⲱⲡⲉ ⲛ̄ⲧⲟⲕ ⲙ̄ⲡⲓⲥⲧⲟⲥ ⲉⲕⲟⲩⲁⲁⲃ[1] ⲁⲩⲱ ⲉⲕϣⲁⲛⲃⲱⲕ ϩⲁϩⲧⲏϥ ⲕⲛⲁⲛⲁⲩ ⲉⲡⲉⲟⲟⲩ ⲙ̄ⲡⲛⲟⲩⲧⲉ (ShIV 189).

Exercise 11

4. ⲛⲉⲧⲟ ⲛ̄ϣⲟⲣⲡ̄ ⲁⲩⲣ̄ϩⲁⲉ ⲉⲧⲃⲉⲧⲙⲛ̄ⲧⲁⲧⲥⲱⲧⲙ̄ ⲛⲉⲧⲟ ⲛ̄ϩⲁⲉ ⲁⲩⲣ̄ϣⲟⲣⲡ̄ ⲉⲧⲃⲉⲧⲙⲛ̄ⲧⲥϯⲙⲏⲧ (P 130.2).

5. ⲡⲉⲧⲛⲁϩⲁⲣⲉϩ ⲉϩⲉⲛⲕⲟⲩⲓ ⲛ̄ϣ̄ϣⲱⲡⲉ ⲉϥⲉⲛϩⲟⲧ ⲉⲣⲟⲟⲩ ϣⲁⲩϯϩⲉⲛⲛⲟϭ ⲉⲧⲟⲟⲧϥ̄ ⲛ̄ⲥⲉⲧⲁⲛϩⲟⲩⲧϥ̄ ⲉⲣⲟⲟⲩ (ShIV 113).

6. ⲉⲛⲉⲛⲧⲁⲓⲉⲓⲣⲉ ⲅⲁⲣ ⲛ̄ⲟⲩϩⲓ ⲛ̄ϭⲟⲛⲥ̄ ⲏ ⲟⲩϩⲱⲃ ⲉϥⲙ̄ⲡϣⲁ ⲙ̄ⲡⲙⲟⲩ ⲛⲉⲓⲛⲁⲡⲁⲣⲁⲓⲧⲓ ⲁⲛ ⲙ̄ⲡⲙⲟⲩ (Acts 25:11).

7. ⲙ̄ⲛ̄ⲣⲱⲙⲉ ⲉⲟⲩⲛ̄ⲧϥ̄ ⲛⲉⲥϩⲓⲟⲟⲩⲉ ⲛ̄ⲃⲱⲕ ⲉϩⲟⲩⲛ ϣⲁⲣⲟⲟⲩ ϫⲉⲥⲉⲥⲟⲃⲧⲉ ⲛⲁⲥ ⲛ̄ϩⲉⲛⲙⲁ ⲛ̄ϣⲱⲡⲉ ϩⲙ̄ⲡⲉⲩⲏⲉⲓ ⲛⲁⲣⲃϭⲣⲱϩ (Sh IV 17).

8. ⲁⲩⲉⲓⲙⲉ ⲅⲁⲣ ϫⲉⲛ̄ⲧⲁϥϫⲉⲧⲉⲓⲡⲁⲣⲁⲃⲟⲗⲏ ⲉⲧⲃⲏⲏⲧⲟⲩ (Mark 12:12).

---

1 ⲕⲟⲩⲁⲁⲃ.

Part V: Selection of texts

Selection of texts

The following texts belong to different domains of Coptic literature. Some texts are translated from a Greek original, others have been originally written in Coptic. This selection embraces biblical texts, monastic literature, homiletic and polemic texts and Gnostic writings.

Some grammatical elements are marked by references to the paragraphs of the grammar. Other particularities of the texts are treated in the footnotes.

Luke 15:11–32: the prodigal son

We reproduce the text from the edition of G. Horner, *The Coptic Version of the New Testament in the Southern Dialect otherwise called Sahidic and Thebaic*; vol. II, Osnabrück, 1969 (reprint of 1911–1924). In this edition you will also find an English translation of the Coptic text.

[11]ⲡⲉϫⲁϥ ϫⲉ ⲟⲩⲣⲱⲙⲉ ⲡⲉⲧⲉⲩⲛ̄ⲧⲁϥ (299) ⲙ̄ⲙⲁⲩ (155) ⲛ̄ϣⲏⲣⲉ ⲥⲛⲁⲩ. [12]ⲡⲉϫⲉ ⲡⲕⲟⲩⲓ ⲛ̄ϩⲏⲧⲟⲩ ⲙ̄ⲡⲉϥⲉⲓⲱⲧ. ϫⲉ ⲡⲁⲉⲓⲱⲧ ⲙⲁ (136) ⲛⲁⲓ ⲙ̄ⲡⲁⲙⲉⲣⲟⲥ ⲉⲧⲧⲁϩⲟ ⲙ̄ⲙⲟⲓ ϩⲛ̄ ⲧⲟⲩⲥⲓⲁ. ⲁϥⲡⲱϣ ⲇⲉ ⲉϫⲱⲟⲩ ⲛ̄ⲛⲉϥⲛ̄ⲕⲁ. [13]ⲙ̄ⲡⲁⲧⲉ (322) ϩⲁϩ ⲇⲉ ⲛ̄ϩⲟⲟⲩ ⲟⲩⲉⲓⲛⲉ. ⲁ ⲡⲕⲟⲩⲓ ⲛ̄ϣⲏⲣⲉ ⲥⲉⲩϩ̄ ⲛ̄ⲕⲁ ⲛⲓⲙ ⲉⲧⲛ̄ⲧⲁϥ. ⲁϥⲁⲡⲟⲇⲏⲙⲉⲓ ⲉⲩⲭⲱⲣⲁ ⲉⲥⲟⲩⲏⲩ[1]. ⲁϥϫⲱⲱⲣⲉ ⲉⲃⲟⲗ ⲙ̄ⲙⲁⲩ ⲛ̄ⲧⲉϥⲟⲩⲥⲓⲁ. ⲉϥⲙⲟⲟϣⲉ ϩⲛ̄ ⲟⲩⲙⲛ̄ⲧϣⲛ̄ⲁ (108). [14]ⲛ̄ⲧⲉⲣⲉϥϫⲉ ⲛ̄ⲕⲁ ⲛⲓⲙ ⲉⲃⲟⲗ ⲁⲩⲛⲟϭ ⲛ̄ϩⲉⲃⲱⲱⲛ ϣⲱⲡⲉ ϩⲛ̄ ⲧⲉⲭⲱⲣⲁ ⲉⲧⲙ̄ⲙⲁⲩ. ⲛ̄ⲧⲟϥ ⲇⲉ ⲁϥⲁⲣⲭⲉⲓ ⲛ̄ϣⲱⲱⲧ. [15]ⲁϥⲃⲱⲕ ⲁϥⲧⲟϭϥ̄ ⲉⲟⲩⲁ ⲛ̄ⲛ̄ⲣⲙ̄ⲧⲙⲉ (049) ⲛ̄ⲧⲉⲭⲱⲣⲁ ⲉⲧⲙ̄ⲙⲁⲩ. ⲁϥϫⲟⲟⲩϥ ⲉⲧⲉϥⲥⲱϣⲉ ⲉⲙⲟⲟⲛⲉ (449) ⲛ̄ϩⲉⲛⲣⲓⲣ. [16]ⲁⲩⲱ ⲛⲉϥⲉⲡⲓⲑⲩⲙⲉⲓ (238) ⲛ̄ϭⲓ ⲉⲃⲟⲗ ϩⲛ̄ ⲛ̄ϭⲁⲣⲁⲧⲉ ⲉⲧⲉⲣⲉ ⲛ̄ⲣⲓⲣ ⲟⲩⲱⲙ ⲙ̄ⲙⲟⲟⲩ. ⲁⲩⲱ ⲛⲉⲙⲛ̄ ⲗⲁⲁⲩ † ⲛⲁϥ. [17]ⲁϥⲙⲉⲕⲙⲟⲩⲕϥ ⲇⲉ ⲡⲉϫⲁϥ. ϫⲉ ⲟⲩⲛ̄ ⲟⲩⲏⲣ ⲛ̄ϫⲁⲓⲃⲉⲕⲉ ⲛ̄ⲧⲉ ⲡⲁⲉⲓⲱⲧ ⲥⲏⲩ ⲙ̄ⲡⲟⲉⲓⲕ (464). ⲁⲛⲟⲕ ⲇⲉ ⲉⲓⲛⲁⲙⲟⲩ ⲙ̄ⲡⲉⲓⲙⲁ ϩⲁ ⲡⲉϩⲕⲟ. [18]†ⲛⲁⲧⲱⲟⲩⲛ ⲧⲁⲃⲱⲕ (382) ϣⲁ ⲡⲁⲉⲓⲱⲧ ⲧⲁϫⲟⲟⲥ ⲛⲁϥ. ϫⲉ ⲡⲁⲉⲓⲱⲧ ⲁⲓⲣ̄ⲛⲟⲃⲉ ⲉⲧⲡⲉ ⲁⲩⲱ ⲙ̄ⲡⲉⲕⲙ̄ⲧⲟ ⲉⲃⲟⲗ. [19]ⲛ̄†ⲙ̄ⲡϣⲁ ⲁⲛ ϫⲓⲛ ⲧⲉⲛⲟⲩ ⲉⲙⲟⲩⲧⲉ ⲉⲣⲟⲓ ϫⲉ ⲡⲉⲕϣⲏⲣⲉ. ⲁⲁⲧ (119)[2] ⲛ̄ⲑⲉ ⲛ̄ⲟⲩⲁ ⲛ̄ⲛⲉⲕϫⲁⲓⲃⲉⲕⲉ.

---

1 Stative of ⲟⲩⲉ.
2 The prenominal form of the infinitive is used here instead of the imperative ⲁⲣⲓ.

²⁰ⲀϤⲦⲰⲞⲨⲚ ⲆⲈ ⲀϤⲈⲒ ϢⲀ ⲠⲈϤⲈⲒⲰⲦ. ⲈⲦⲒ ⲈϤⲘ̄ⲠⲞⲨⲈ³. Ⲁ ⲠⲈϤⲈⲒⲰⲦ ⲚⲀⲨ ⲈⲢⲞϤ. ⲀϤϢⲚ̄ϨⲦⲎϤ⁴ ⲈϨⲢⲀⲒ ⲈⲬⲰϤ. ⲀϤⲠⲰⲦ ⲀϤⲠⲀϨⲦϤ̄ ⲈⲬⲘ̄ ⲠⲈϤⲘⲀⲔϨ̄. ⲀϤϮⲠⲒ ⲈⲢⲰϤ. ²¹ⲠⲈϪⲈ ⲠⲈϤϢⲎⲢⲈ ⲚⲀϤ. ϪⲈ ⲠⲀⲈⲒⲰⲦ ⲀⲒⲢ̄ⲚⲞⲂⲈ ⲈⲦⲠⲈ ⲀⲨⲰ Ⲙ̄ⲠⲈⲔⲘ̄ⲦⲞ ⲈⲂⲞⲖ. Ⲛ̄ϮⲘ̄ⲠϢⲀ ⲀⲚ ϪⲒⲚ ⲦⲈⲚⲞⲨ ⲈⲘⲞⲨⲦⲈ ⲈⲢⲞⲒ ϪⲈ ⲠⲈⲔϢⲎⲢⲈ. ²²ⲠⲈϪⲈ ⲠⲈϤⲈⲒⲰⲦ ⲆⲈ Ⲛ̄ⲚⲈϤϨⲘ̄ϨⲀⲖ. ϪⲈ ϬⲈⲠⲎ ⲀⲚⲈⲒⲚⲈ ⲈⲂⲞⲖ Ⲛ̄ⲦⲈⲤⲦⲞⲖⲎ ⲈⲦⲚⲀⲚⲞⲨⲤ. Ⲛ̄ⲦⲈⲦⲚ̄ⲦⲀⲀⲤ (371) ϨⲒⲰⲰϤ. Ⲛ̄ⲦⲈⲦⲚ̄Ϯ Ⲛ̄ⲞⲨϨⲞⲨⲢ ⲈⲦⲈϤϬⲒϪ ⲀⲨⲰ ⲞⲨⲦⲞⲞⲨⲈ ⲈⲚⲈϤⲞⲨⲈⲢⲎⲦⲈ. ²³Ⲛ̄ⲦⲈⲦⲚ̄ⲈⲚ⁵ ⲠⲘⲀⲤⲈ ⲈⲦⲤⲀⲚⲀϢⲦ. Ⲛ̄ⲦⲈⲦⲚ̄ⲔⲞⲚⲤϤ̄. Ⲛ̄ⲦⲚ̄ⲞⲨⲰⲘ. Ⲛ̄ⲦⲚ̄ⲈⲨⲪⲢⲀⲚⲈ. ²⁴ϪⲈ (443) ⲠⲀϢⲎⲢⲈ ⲠⲀⲒ ⲈⲚⲈϤⲘⲞⲞⲨⲦ (472) ⲠⲈ. ⲀϤⲰⲚϨ̄. ⲚⲈϤⲤⲞⲢⲘ̄ ⲠⲈ. ⲀⲒϨⲈ ⲈⲢⲞϤ. ⲀⲨⲀⲢⲬⲈⲒ ⲆⲈ Ⲛ̄ⲈⲨⲪⲢⲀⲚⲈ. ²⁵ⲚⲈⲢⲈ ⲠⲈϤⲚⲞϬ ⲆⲈ Ⲛ̄ϢⲎⲢⲈ ϨⲚ̄ ⲦⲤⲰϢⲈ (263). ⲈϤⲚⲎⲨ ⲆⲈ ⲈϨⲢⲀⲒ ⲀϤϨⲰⲚ ⲈϨⲞⲨⲚ ⲈⲠⲎⲒ. ⲀϤⲤⲰⲦⲘ̄ ⲈⲨⲤⲨⲘⲪⲰⲚⲒⲀ ⲘⲚ̄ ⲞⲨⲬⲞⲢⲞⲤ. ²⁶ⲀϤⲘⲞⲨⲦⲈ ⲈⲞⲨⲀ Ⲛ̄Ⲛ̄ϨⲘ̄ϨⲀⲖ. ⲀϤϪⲚⲞⲨϤ ϪⲈ ⲞⲨ ⲚⲈ ⲚⲀⲒ. ²⁷Ⲛ̄ⲦⲞϤ ⲆⲈ ⲠⲈϪⲀϤ ⲚⲀϤ. ϪⲈ ⲠⲈⲔⲤⲞⲚ ⲠⲈⲚⲦⲀϤⲈⲒ (466). Ⲁ ⲠⲈⲔⲈⲒⲰⲦ ϢⲰⲰⲦ ⲈⲢⲞϤ Ⲙ̄ⲠⲘⲀⲤⲈ ⲈⲦⲤⲀⲚⲀϢⲦ. ϪⲈ (443) ⲀϤϨⲈ ⲈⲢⲞϤ ⲈϤⲞⲨⲞϪ (412). ²⁸ⲀϤⲚⲞⲨϬⲤ̄ ⲆⲈ Ⲙ̄ⲠϤ̄ⲞⲨⲰϢ ⲈⲂⲰⲔ ⲈϨⲞⲨⲚ. Ⲁ ⲠⲈϤⲈⲒⲰⲦ ⲈⲒ ⲈⲂⲞⲖ ⲀϤⲤⲈⲠⲤⲰⲠϤ̄. ²⁹Ⲛ̄ⲦⲞϤ ⲆⲈ ⲀϤⲞⲨⲰϢⲂ̄ ⲠⲈϪⲀϤ Ⲙ̄ⲠⲈϤⲈⲒⲰⲦ. ϪⲈ ⲈⲒⲤ ⲞⲨⲘⲎⲎϢⲈ Ⲛ̄ⲢⲞⲘⲠⲈ ϮⲞ Ⲛ̄ϨⲘ̄ϨⲀⲖ ⲚⲀⲔ. Ⲙ̄ⲠⲒⲔⲰ Ⲛ̄ⲤⲰⲒ ⲈⲚⲈϨ Ⲛ̄ⲞⲨⲈⲚⲦⲞⲖⲎ Ⲛ̄ⲦⲞⲞⲦⲔ. ⲀⲨⲰ Ⲙ̄ⲠⲔ̄Ϯ ⲚⲀⲒ Ⲛ̄ⲞⲨⲘⲀⲤ Ⲛ̄ⲂⲀⲀⲘⲠⲈ ⲈⲦⲢⲀⲈⲨⲪⲢⲀⲚⲈ (449) ⲘⲚ̄ ⲚⲀϢⲂⲈⲈⲢ. ³⁰Ⲛ̄ⲦⲈⲢⲈ ⲠⲈⲔϢⲎⲢⲈ ⲆⲈ ⲈⲒ. ⲠⲀⲒ ⲈⲚⲦⲀϤⲞⲨⲈⲘ ⲚⲈⲔⲚ̄ⲔⲀ ⲘⲚ̄ Ⲙ̄ⲠⲞⲢⲚⲞⲤ. ⲀⲔϢⲰⲰⲦ ⲈⲢⲞϤ Ⲙ̄ⲠⲘⲀⲤⲈ ⲈⲦⲤⲀⲚⲀϢⲦ. ³¹Ⲛ̄ⲦⲞϤ ⲆⲈ ⲠⲈϪⲀϤ ⲚⲀϤ. ϪⲈ ⲠⲀϢⲎⲢⲈ Ⲛ̄ⲦⲞⲔ Ⲕ̄ϢⲞⲞⲠ ⲚⲘ̄ⲘⲀⲒ⁶ Ⲛ̄ⲞⲨⲞⲈⲒϢ ⲚⲒⲘ. ⲀⲨⲰ ⲚⲞⲨⲒ (020) ⲦⲎⲢⲞⲨ ⲚⲞⲨⲔ ⲚⲈ. ³²ϢϢⲈ ⲆⲈ ⲈⲢⲞⲚ ⲈⲢⲀϢⲈ Ⲛ̄ⲦⲚ̄ⲈⲨⲪⲢⲀⲚⲈ. ϪⲈ ⲠⲈⲔⲤⲞⲚ ⲠⲀⲒ ⲈⲚⲈϤⲘⲞⲞⲨⲦ ⲠⲈ. ⲀϤⲰⲚϨ̄. ⲚⲈϤⲤⲞⲢⲘ̄ ⲠⲈ. ⲀⲒϨⲈ ⲈⲢⲞϤ.

---

3 ⲈϤ̣.Ⲙ̄-Ⲡ.ⲞⲨⲈ.
4 ϢⲚ-ϨⲎⲦ ⲈϪⲚ- means *to have pity, to have compassion*. Here we find the prepersonal form of ϨⲎⲦ (*heart*), which corresponds to the subject (Crum, *Coptic Dictionary*, 716b, s.v. ϨⲎⲦ).
5 ⲈⲚ- is the prenominal form of ⲈⲒⲚⲈ.
6 ⲚⲘ̄ⲘⲀ⸗ is the prepersonal form of ⲘⲚ̄- (*with*).

The apophthegmata patrum

We reproduce some passages from the edition of M. Chaîne, *Le manuscrit de la version copte en dialecte sahidique des « Apophtegmata patrum »*, Le Caire 1960. This edition is accompanied by a French translation.

3. ⲁⲟⲩⲥⲟⲛ ϫⲛⲉ ⲟⲩϩⲗⲗⲟ ϫⲉ[1] ⲡⲁⲉⲓⲱⲧ ⲉⲧⲃⲉ ⲟⲩ ⲁⲛⲟⲕ ⲡⲁϩⲏⲧ ⲛⲁϣⲧ ⲛϥⲣϩⲟⲧⲉ ⲁⲛ ⲛϩⲏⲧϥ ⲙⲡⲛⲟⲩⲧⲉ· ⲡⲉϫⲉ ⲡϩⲗⲗⲟ ⲛⲁϥ ϫⲉ ϯⲙⲉⲉⲩⲉ ϫⲉ ⲉⲣϣⲁⲛ ⲡⲣⲱⲙⲉ ⲁⲙⲁϩⲧⲉ ⲙⲡⲉϫⲡⲓⲟ ϩⲙ ⲡⲉϥϩⲏⲧ ϥⲛⲁϫⲡⲟ ⲛⲁϥ ⲛϩⲟⲧⲉ ⲙⲡⲛⲟⲩⲧⲉ· ⲡⲉϫⲉ ⲡⲥⲟⲛ ⲛⲁϥ ϫⲉ ⲟⲩ ⲡⲉ ⲡⲉϫⲡⲓⲟ· ⲡⲉϫⲉ ⲡϩⲗⲗⲟ ϫⲉⲕⲁⲥ ⲉⲣⲉ ⲡⲣⲱⲙⲉ ⲛⲁϫⲡⲓⲉ (256) ⲧⲉϥⲯⲩⲭⲏ ϩⲛ ϩⲱⲃ ⲛⲓⲙ ⲉϥϫⲱ ⲙⲙⲟⲥ ⲛⲁⲥ ϫⲉ ⲁⲣⲓⲡⲙⲉⲉⲩⲉ[2] ϫⲉ ϩⲁⲡⲥ ⲉⲣⲟⲛ ⲡⲉ ⲉⲧⲣⲉⲛⲁⲡⲁⲛⲧⲁ (134) ⲉⲡⲛⲟⲩⲧⲉ· ⲛϥϫⲟⲟⲥ ⲟⲛ ϫⲉ ⲁϩⲣⲟⲓ ⲁⲛⲟⲕ ⲙⲛ ⲣⲱⲙⲉ· ⲉⲣϣⲁⲛ ⲟⲩⲁ ⲇⲉ ⲙⲟⲩⲛ ⲉⲃⲟⲗ ϩⲛ ⲛⲁⲓ ⲥⲛⲏⲩ[3] ⲛⲁϥ ⲛϭⲓ (235) ⲑⲟⲧⲉ ⲙⲡⲛⲟⲩⲧⲉ.

5. ⲁⲩⲟⲁ ϫⲛⲉ ⲟⲩϩⲗⲗⲟ ϫⲉ ⲉⲧⲃⲉⲟⲩ ⲉⲓϩⲙⲟⲟⲥ (422) ϩⲙ ⲡⲁⲙⲁⲛϣⲱⲡⲉ[4] ⲡⲁϩⲏⲧ ⲕⲱⲧⲉ ⲥⲁⲥⲁ[5] ⲛⲓⲙ· ⲁϥⲟⲩⲱϣⲃ ⲛⲁϥ ⲛϭⲓ ⲡϩⲗⲗⲟ ϫⲉ ⲉⲃⲟⲗ ϫⲉ ⲉⲃⲟⲗϫⲉ ⲥⲉϣⲱⲛⲉ ⲛϭⲓ ⲛⲉⲕⲉⲥⲑⲏⲧⲏⲣⲓⲟⲛ[6] ⲉⲧϩⲓⲃⲟⲗ ⲧϭⲓⲛⲛⲁⲩ (051) ⲧϭⲓⲛⲥⲱⲧⲙ ⲧϭⲓⲛϣⲱⲗⲙ ⲧϭⲓⲛϣⲁϫⲉ ⲛⲁⲓ ϭⲉ ⲉϣⲱⲡⲉ ⲉⲕϣⲁⲛϫⲡⲟ (429) ⲛⲧⲉⲩⲉⲛⲉⲣⲅⲓⲁ ϩⲛ ⲟⲩⲙⲛⲧⲕⲁⲑⲁⲣⲟⲥ ϣⲁⲣⲉ ⲛⲕⲉⲉⲥⲑⲏⲧⲏⲣⲓⲟⲛ ⲉⲧϩⲓϩⲟⲩⲛ ϣⲱⲡⲉ ϩⲛ ⲟⲩϩⲣⲁϩⲧ ⲙⲛ ⲟⲩⲟⲩϫⲁⲓ.

6. ⲁⲟⲩⲁ ⲟⲛ ϫⲛⲉ ⲟⲩϩⲗⲗⲟ ϫⲉ ⲉⲧⲃⲉⲟⲩ ϯϩⲙⲟⲟⲥ ϩⲙ ⲡⲁⲙⲁⲛϣⲱⲡⲉ ϯϩⲁⲡⲗⲱⲡ· ⲁϥⲟⲩⲱϣⲃ ⲛⲁϥ ϫⲉ ⲉⲃⲟⲗϫⲉ ⲙⲡⲁⲧⲉⲕⲉⲓⲱⲣϩ ⲙⲡⲙⲧⲟⲛ ⲉⲧⲛϩⲉⲗⲡⲓⲍⲉ ⲉⲣⲟϥ (463) ⲟⲩⲇⲉ ⲧⲕⲟⲗⲁⲥⲓⲥ ⲉⲧⲛⲁϣⲱⲡⲉ· ⲉⲛⲉ ⲁⲕⲉⲓⲱⲣϩ (436) ⲛⲁⲓ ϩⲛ ⲟⲩⲱⲣϫ ⲁⲩⲱ ⲛⲧⲉ ⲡⲉⲕⲙⲁⲛϣⲱⲡⲉ ⲙⲟⲩϩ (371) ⲛⲃⲛⲧ ⲉⲣⲟⲕ

---

1 ϫⲉ can introduce an indirect discourse as well as a direct discourse.
2 Imperative of ⲣ-ⲙⲉⲉⲩⲉ.
3 ⲥ.ⲛⲏⲩ.
4 ⲙⲁ ⲛ-ϣⲱⲡⲉ: literally: *place of being.* The expression refers to the monk's cell.
5 (ⲛ-)ⲥⲁ-ⲥⲁ.
6 ⲉⲥⲑⲏⲧⲏⲣⲓⲟⲛ for the Greek αἰσθητήριον.

ϢΑΝΤΟΥΠⲰϨ ΕϨΡΑΙ ΕΠΕΚ[ΜΟΤΕ] ΝΕΚΝΑϬⲰ ΕϨΡΑΙ [ΝϨΗ]ΤΟΥ ΠΕ (253) ΝΓϬΙ (371) ϨΑΡ[ΟΟΥ] ΝΓΤⲘϨΛΟΠΛ[Π̄].

34. ΟΥϹΟΝ ΕϤϨΜΟΟϹ ϨⲚ Ⲛ̄ΡΙ ΜΑΥΑΑϤ ΑϤϢΤΟΡΤⲢ̄ ΑϤΒⲰΚ ΔΕ ϢΑ ΑΠΑ ΘΕⲰΔΟΡΟϹ Ⲛ̄ΤΕ ΠϨΕΡΜΗϹ[7] ΑϤΧΟΟϹ ΝΑϤ· ΠΕΧΕ ΠϨⲖⲖΟ ΔΕ ΝΑϤ ΧΕ ΒⲰΚ ΝΓΘΒΒΙΕ (371) ΠΕΚϨΗΤ ΝΓϬⲰ ΜⲚ ϨⲚΚΟΟΥΕ ΕΚϨΥΠΟΤΑϹϹΕ ΝΑΥ ΑϤΒⲰΚ ΔΕ ΑϤϬⲰ ΜⲚ ϨΟΙΝΕ ϨⲘ ΠΤΟΟΥ ΑϤΚΟΤϤ ΟΝ ΑϤΕΙ ϢΑ ΠϨⲖⲖΟ ΠΕΧΑϤ ΧΕ Ⲙ̄ΠΙⲘ̄ΤΟΝ ΕΙΟΥΗϨ ΜⲚ Ⲛ̄ΡⲰΜΕ· ΠΕΧΕ ΠϨⲖⲖΟ ΧΕ ΝΑϤ ΧΕ ΕϢⲰΠΕ Ⲙ̄ΠΕΚⲘ̄ΤΟΝ (432) ΜΑΥΑΑΚ ΟΥΔΕ ΟΝ ΕΚϢΟΟΠ ΜⲚ Ⲛ̄ΚΟΟΥΕ ΝΓΝΑⲘ̄ΤΟΝ ΑΝ ΕΤΒΕ ΟΥ ΑΚΕΙ ΕΒΟΛ ΕⲢ̄ΜΟΝΑΧΟϹ (449) ΧΕΚΑϹ ΑΝ ΕΚΝΑΤⲰΟΥΝ ϨΑ Ⲛ̄ΘΛΙΨΙϹ ΑΧΙϹ (136) ΕΡΟΙ ΧΕ ΕΙϹ ΟΥΗⲢ Ⲛ̄ΡΟΜΠΕ ΝΧΙ[8] Ⲛ̄ΤΑΚϯ Ⲙ̄ΠΕΙϹΧΥΜΑ[9] ϨΙⲰⲰΚ· ΠΕΧΑϤ ΧΕ ΕΙϹ ϢΜΟΥΝ Ⲛ̄ΡΟΜΠΕ· ΠΕΧΕ ΠϨⲖⲖΟ ΝΑϤ ΧΕ ΝΑΜΕ ΕΙϹ ϢϤΕ Ⲛ̄ΡΟΜΠΕ ΧΙΝΤΑΙⲢ̄ΜΟΝΑΧΟϹ Ⲙ̄ΠΙϬⲚ̄ ΟΥⲘ̄ΤΟΝ Ⲛ̄ΟΥϨΟΟΥ Ⲛ̄ΟΥⲰΤ ΑΥⲰ Ⲛ̄ΤΟΚ ΚΟΥⲰϢ ΕΕⲘΤΟΝ[10] ϨⲚ ΤΕΙϢΜΟΥΝΕ Ⲛ̄ΡΟΜΠΕ·

37. ΑϤΧΟΟϹ Ⲛ̄ϬΙ ΑΠΑ ΠΟΙΜΗΝ ΕΤΒΕ ΑΠΑ ΙⲰϨΑΝΝΗϹ ΠΚΟΛΟΒΟϹ ΧΕ ΑϤΤⲰΒϨ̄ Ⲙ̄ΠΝΟΥΤΕ ΑϤϤΙ Ⲙ̄ΠΟΛΥΜΟϹ ΕΒΟΛ Ⲙ̄ΜΟϤ ΑΥⲰ ΑϤϢⲰΠΕ Ⲛ̄ΑΜΕΡΙΜΝΟϹ· ΑϤΒⲰΚ ΔΕ ΑϤΧΟΟϹ Ⲛ̄ΟΥΑ Ⲛ̄ϨⲖⲖΟ ΧΕ ϯΝΑΥ ΕΡΟΙ ΜΑΥΑΑΤ ΧΕ ϯΜΟΤΝΕ[11] ΜⲚ ΠΟΛΥΜΟϹ ϨΙΧⲰΙ· ΠΕΧΕ ΠϨⲖⲖΟ ΝΑϤ ΧΕ ΒⲰΚ ΠΑΡΑΚΑΛΕΙ Ⲙ̄ΠΝΟΥΤΕ ΧΕΚΑϹ ΕΡΕ Ⲙ̄ΠΟΛΥΜΟϹ ΕΙ ΝΑΚ ϨΙΤⲚ̄ Ⲙ̄ΠΟΛΥΜΟϹ ΓΑΡ ΕϢΑΡΕ ΤΕΨΥΧΗ ΠΡΟΚΟΠΤΕΙ (330)· ΑΥⲰ Ⲛ̄ΤΕΡΕ ΠΠΟΛΥΜΟϹ ΤⲰΟΥΝ ΕΧⲰϤ Ⲙ̄ΠΕϤΚΟΤϤ ΕϢΛΗΛ ΕϤΙΤϤ̄ Ⲙ̄ΜΑΥ ΑΛΛΑ ΝΕϤΧⲰ Ⲙ̄ΜΟϹ ΧΕ ΠΧΟΕΙϹ ΕΚΕΤΑΑϹ (337) ΝΑΙ ΤΑϨΥΠΟΜΟΝΗ ϨⲘ ΠΠΟΛΥΜΟϹ·

---

7 This is a proper noun: Theodore of Phermes.
8 Ⲛ̄-ΧΙⲚ̄ΤΑ⸗Κ.ϯ: this is the conjunction ΧΙΝ (*since*), followed by the focalising conversion of the past cf. 423).
9 ϹΗΥΜΑ for the Greek σχῆμα.
10 ΕⲘΤΟΝ for Ⲙ̄ΤΟΝ.
11 ΜΟΤΝΕ for ΜΟΤⲚ, the stative of Ⲙ̄ΤΟΝ.

102. ⲉⲣⲉ ⲁⲡⲁ ⲙⲁⲕⲁⲣⲓⲟⲥ ⲙⲟⲟϣⲉ ⲛ̄ⲟⲩⲟⲉⲓϣ ⲙ̄ⲡⲕⲱⲧⲉ ⲙ̄ⲡϩⲉⲗⲟⲥ ⲉϥⲧⲱⲟⲩⲛ
ⲛ̄ϩⲛ̄ⲃⲏⲧ ⲁⲩⲱ ⲉⲓⲥ ⲡⲇⲓⲁⲃⲟⲗⲟⲥ ⲁϥⲧⲱⲙⲛ̄ⲧ ⲉⲣⲟϥ ϩⲛ̄ ⲧⲉϥϩⲓⲏ ⲉⲣⲉ ⲟⲩϩⲟϩⲥ̄
ⲛ̄ⲧⲟⲟⲧϥ̄ (100) ⲁⲩⲱ ⲉⲛⲉϥⲟⲩⲱϣ (241) ⲡⲉ ⲉⲣⲁϩⲧϥ̄ ⲙ̄ⲡⲉϥϣⲃ̄ϭⲟⲙ¹² ⲁⲩⲱ
ⲡⲉϫⲁϥ ⲛⲁϥ ϫⲉ ⲟⲩⲛⲟϭ ⲡⲉ ⲡⲁϫⲓⲛϭⲟⲛⲥ ⲉⲃⲟⲗ ⲙ̄ⲙⲟⲕ ϫⲉ ⲙⲛ̄ϭⲟⲙ ⲙ̄ⲙⲟⲓ ⲉⲣⲟⲕ·
ⲉⲓⲥ ϩⲏⲏⲧⲉ ⲅⲁⲣ ϩⲱⲃ ⲛⲓⲙ ⲉⲧⲉⲕⲉⲓⲣⲉ (463) ⲙ̄ⲙⲟⲟⲩ †ⲉⲓⲣⲉ ⲙ̄ⲙⲟⲟⲩ ϩⲱ¹³ ⲛ̄ⲧⲟⲕ
ϣⲁⲕⲛⲏⲥⲧⲉⲩⲉ ⲛ̄ϩⲛ̄ϩⲟⲟⲩ ⲁⲛⲟⲕ ⲇⲉ ⲙⲉⲓⲟⲩⲱⲙ ⲉⲡⲧⲏⲣϥ̄ ϣⲁⲕⲣ̄ ⲟⲩϣⲏ ⲛ̄ⲣⲟⲉⲓⲥ
ⲛ̄ϩⲛ̄ⲥⲟⲡ ⲁⲛⲟⲕ ⲇⲉ ⲙⲉⲓⲛ̄ⲕⲟⲧⲕ ⲉⲛⲉϩ ⲟⲩϩⲱⲃ ⲛ̄ⲟⲩⲱⲧ ⲡⲉⲧⲉⲕϫⲣⲁⲉⲓⲧ¹⁴ ⲉⲣⲟⲓ
ⲛ̄ϩⲏⲧϥ̄· ⲡⲉϫⲉ ⲁⲡⲁ ⲙⲁⲕⲁⲣⲓⲟⲥ ϫⲉ ⲟⲩ ⲡⲉ ⲛ̄ⲧⲟϥ ⲇⲉ ⲡⲉϫⲁϥ ϫⲉ ⲡⲉⲕⲑⲃ̄ⲃⲓⲟ
ⲡⲉ ⲁⲛⲟⲕ ⲇⲉ ⲙⲉⲓϭⲙ̄ϭⲟⲙ ⲉⲑⲃ̄ⲃⲓⲟⲓ ⲉⲛⲉϩ ⲉⲧⲃⲉ ⲡⲁⲓ ⲙ̄ⲡⲓϭⲙ̄ϭⲟⲙ ⲉⲣⲟⲕ·

126. ⲟⲩϩⲗ̄ⲗⲟ ⲇⲉ ⲛ̄ⲁⲛⲁⲭⲱⲣⲓⲧⲏⲥ ⲉϥⲥⲟⲣⲙ̄ ϩⲛ̄ ⲧⲉⲣⲏⲙⲟⲥ ⲁⲩⲱ ⲡⲉϫⲁϥ ϩⲣⲁⲓ
ⲛ̄ϩⲏⲧϥ̄ ϫⲉ ⲁⲓⲕⲁⲧⲟⲣⲑⲟⲩ ⲛ̄ⲧⲁⲣⲉⲧⲏ ⲁⲩⲱ ⲁϥϣⲗⲏⲗ ⲉⲡⲛⲟⲩⲧⲉ ⲉϥϫⲱ ⲙ̄ⲙⲟⲥ
ϫⲉ ⲟⲩⲡⲉϯϣⲁⲁⲧ ⲙ̄ⲙⲟϥ¹⁵ ⲧⲁⲗⲁϥ· ⲁϥⲟⲩⲱϣ ⲇⲉ ⲛ̄ϭⲓ ⲡⲛⲟⲩⲧⲉ ⲉⲑⲃ̄ⲃⲓⲉ
ⲡⲉϥⲙⲉⲉⲩⲉ ⲡⲉϫⲁϥ ⲛⲁϥ ϫⲉ ⲃⲱⲕ ϣⲁ ⲙⲉϣⲉⲛⲓⲙ¹⁶ ⲛ̄ⲁⲣⲭⲓⲙⲁⲇⲣⲓⲧⲏⲥ ⲁⲩⲱ
ⲡⲉⲧⲉϥⲛⲁϫⲟⲟϥ¹⁷ ⲛⲁⲕ ⲁⲣⲓϥ· ⲁ ⲡⲛⲟⲩⲧⲉ ⲇⲉ ϭⲱⲗⲡ̄ ⲉⲃⲟⲗ ⲙ̄ⲡⲓⲁⲣⲭⲓⲙⲁⲇⲣⲓⲧⲏⲥ
ⲉϥϫⲱ ⲙ̄ⲙⲟⲥ ϫⲉ ⲉⲓⲥ ⲙⲉϣⲉⲛⲓⲙ ⲛ̄ⲁⲛⲁⲭⲱⲣⲓⲧⲏⲥ ⲛⲏⲩ ϣⲁⲣⲟⲕ †
ⲟⲩⲫⲣⲁⲅⲉⲗⲗⲓⲟⲛ ⲛⲁϥ ⲛ̄ϥ̄ⲧⲣⲉϥⲙⲟⲟⲛⲉ (372, 133) ⲛ̄ⲛ̄ⲣⲓⲣ· ⲁϥⲉⲓ ⲇⲉ ⲛ̄ϭⲓ ⲡϩⲗ̄ⲗⲟ
ⲁϥⲕⲱⲗϩ̄ ⲉⲡⲣⲟ ⲁⲩⲱ ⲁϥⲃⲱⲕ ⲉϩⲟⲩⲛ ϣⲁ ⲡⲁⲡⲉ ⲛ̄ⲧⲥⲟⲟⲩϩⲥ̄ ⲁⲩⲁⲥⲡⲁⲍⲉ
ⲛ̄ⲛⲉⲩⲉⲣⲏⲩ (292) ⲁⲩϩⲙⲟⲟⲥ ⲁⲩⲱ ⲡⲉϫⲁϥ ⲛ̄ϭⲓ ⲡⲁⲛⲁⲭⲱⲣⲓⲧⲏⲥ ϫⲉ ⲟⲩ
ⲡⲉϯⲛⲁⲁⲁϥ ϫⲉ ⲉⲓⲉⲟⲩϫⲁⲓ· ⲡⲉϫⲁϥ ⲛⲁϥ ⲛ̄ϭⲓ ⲡⲁⲣⲭⲓⲙⲁⲇⲣⲓⲧⲏⲥ ϫⲉ
ⲡⲉϯⲛⲁϫⲟⲟϥ ⲛⲁⲕ ⲕⲛⲁⲁⲁϥ ⲛ̄ⲧⲟϥ ⲇⲉ ⲡⲉϫⲁϥ ϫⲉ ⲥⲉ ⲡⲉϫⲁϥ ⲛⲁϥ ϫⲉ ϥⲓ
ⲛ̄ⲧⲉⲓⲙⲁⲥⲧⲓⲅⲝ ⲛ̄ⲅⲙⲟⲟⲛⲉ ⲛ̄ⲛ̄ⲣⲓⲣ· ⲛⲉⲧⲥⲟⲟⲩⲛ ⲇⲉ ⲙ̄ⲙⲟϥ ⲁⲩⲛⲁⲩ ⲉⲣⲟϥ ⲉϥⲙⲟⲟⲛⲉ
ⲛ̄ⲛ̄ⲣⲓⲣ ⲛⲉⲩϫⲱ ⲙ̄ⲙⲟⲥ ϫⲉ ⲁⲛⲁⲩ ⲉⲡⲉⲓⲛⲟϭ ⲛ̄ⲁⲛⲁⲭⲱⲣⲓⲧⲏⲥ ⲉⲁⲡⲉϥϩⲏⲧ ⲡⲱϣⲥ̄
ⲁⲩⲱ ⲟⲩⲛ ⲟⲩⲇⲁⲓⲙⲱⲛ ϩⲓⲱⲱϥ ⲉϥⲙⲟⲟⲛⲉ ⲛ̄ⲉⲛⲣⲓⲣ¹⁸· ⲁϥⲛⲁⲩ ⲇⲉ ⲛ̄ϭⲓ ⲡⲛⲟⲩⲧⲉ

---

12 ⲙⲡ⸗ϥ.ϣ.ϭⲙ̄ϭⲟⲙ.
13 This is a variant of ϩⲱⲱ⸗ⲧ (cf. 162).
14 ϫⲣⲁⲉⲓⲧ is the stative of ϫⲣⲟ.
15 ⲟⲩ ⲡ.ⲉⲧ⸗ⲓ.ϣⲁⲁⲧ ⲙ̄ⲙⲟϥ (interrogative nominal sentence).
16 ⲙⲉϣⲉ (to ignore, cf. 157) + ⲛⲓⲙ (who): I don't know whom.
17 ⲡ.ⲉⲧ(ⲉ)⸗ϥ.ⲛⲁ.ϫⲟⲟ⸗ϥ.
18 ⲛ̄-ⲛ.ⲣⲓⲣ.

ⲉⲡⲉϥⲑⲃ̄ⲃⲓⲟ ϫⲉ ⲁϥϩⲩⲡⲟⲙⲓⲛⲉ (443) ⲛ̄ⲧⲉⲓϩⲉ ⲉⲡⲛⲟⲃⲛⲉϭ ⲛ̄ⲉⲛⲣⲱⲙⲉ[19] ⲁϥϫⲟⲟⲩϥ ⲟⲛ ⲉⲡⲉϥⲙⲁ·

145. ⲁⲩϫⲟⲟⲥ ⲉⲧⲃⲉ ⲟⲩⲁ ⲛ̄ⲛ̄ϩⲗ̄ⲗⲟ ϫⲉ ⲁϥϩⲙⲟⲟⲥ ϩⲛ̄ ⲧⲉϥⲣⲓ ⲉϥⲁⲅⲱⲛⲓⲍⲉ ⲁϥⲛⲁⲩ ⲉⲛ̄ⲇⲁⲓⲙⲱⲛ ϩⲛ̄ ⲟⲩⲱⲛϩ ⲉⲃⲟⲗ ⲁϥⲕⲟⲙϣⲟⲩ· ⲡⲇⲓⲁⲃⲟⲗⲟⲥ ⲇⲉ ⲁϥⲛⲁⲩ ⲉⲣⲟϥ ⲙⲁⲩⲁⲁϥ ϫⲉ ⲁϥϭⲱⲧⲡ̄ ϩⲏⲧϥ̄ ⲙ̄ⲡϩⲗ̄ⲗⲟ ⲁⲩⲱ ⲁϥⲉⲓ ⲁϥⲟⲩⲱⲛⲁϩ[20] ⲛⲁϥ ⲉⲃⲟⲗ ⲉϥϫⲱ ⲙ̄ⲙⲟⲥ ϫⲉ ⲁⲛⲟⲕ ⲡⲉ ⲡⲉⲭ̄ⲥ̄· ⲛ̄ⲧⲉⲣⲉϥⲛⲁⲩ ⲇⲉ ⲉⲣⲟϥ ⲛ̄ϭⲓ ⲡϩⲗ̄ⲗⲟ ⲁϥϩⲱⲭⲡ̄ ⲛ̄ⲛⲉϥⲃⲁⲗ· ⲡⲉϫⲁϥ ⲛⲁϥ ⲛ̄ϭⲓ ⲡⲇⲓⲁⲃⲟⲗⲟⲥ ϫⲉ ⲉⲧⲃⲉⲟⲩ ⲁⲕϩⲱⲭⲡ̄ ⲛ̄ⲛⲉⲕⲃⲁⲗ ⲁⲛⲟⲕ ⲡⲉⲡ ⲉⲭ̄ⲥ̄· ⲡⲉϫⲁϥ ⲇⲉ ⲛ̄ϭⲓ ⲡϩⲗ̄ⲗⲟ ϫⲉ ⲁⲛⲟⲕ ⲛ̄ϯⲟⲩⲱϣ ⲁⲛ ⲉⲛⲁⲩ ⲉⲡⲉⲭ̄ⲥ̄ ⲙ̄ⲡⲉⲓⲙⲁ· ⲁϥⲥⲱⲧⲙ̄ ⲇⲉ ⲉⲛⲁⲓ ⲛ̄ϭⲓ ⲡⲇⲓⲁⲃⲟⲗⲟⲥ [ⲁϥ]ⲣ̄ⲁⲧⲟⲩⲱⲛ[ϩ ⲉⲃⲟⲗ]·

208. ⲁ ϩⲉⲛⲙⲟⲛⲁⲭⲟⲥ ⲉⲓ ⲉⲃⲟⲗϩⲛ̄ ⲛⲉⲩⲣⲓ ⲁⲩⲥⲱⲟⲩϩ ⲉⲩⲙⲁ ⲛ̄ⲟⲩⲱⲧ ⲁⲩⲱ ⲁⲩⲕⲓⲙ ⲉⲡϣⲁϫⲉ ⲉⲧⲃⲉ ⲧⲁⲥⲕⲏⲥⲓⲥ ⲙⲛ̄ ⲧⲙⲛ̄ⲧⲣⲉϥϣⲙ̄ϣⲉⲛⲟⲩⲧⲉ[21] ⲁⲩⲱ ϫⲉ ϣ̄ϣⲉ ⲉⲣⲁⲛⲁϥ[22] ⲙ̄ⲡⲛⲟⲩⲧⲉ· ⲛⲁⲓ ⲇⲉ ⲉⲩϣⲁϫⲉ ⲛ̄ϩⲏⲧⲟⲩ ⲁⲩⲟⲩⲱⲛϩ ⲉⲃⲟⲗ ⲛ̄ϭⲓ ⲁⲅⲅⲉⲗⲟⲥ ⲥⲛⲁⲩ ⲛ̄ⲛⲁϩⲣⲉⲛ ϩⲟⲓⲛⲉ ⲛⲉⲛϩⲗ̄ⲗⲟ[23] ⲉⲧⲛ̄ϩⲏⲧⲟⲩ ⲉⲟⲩⲛ̄ ϩⲉⲛⲉⲡⲱⲙⲓⲥ[24] ⲛ̄ⲧⲟⲟⲧⲟⲩ ⲉⲩϯⲉⲟⲟⲩ ⲙ̄ⲡⲟⲩⲁ ⲡⲟⲩⲁ ⲉⲧϣⲁϫⲉ ⲉⲧⲃⲉ ⲧⲙⲛ̄ⲧⲣ̄ⲣⲟ ⲙ̄ⲡⲛⲟⲩⲧⲉ ⲁⲩⲱ ⲁⲩⲕⲁⲣⲱⲟⲩ ⲛ̄ϭⲓ ⲛⲉⲛⲧⲁⲩⲛⲁⲩ ⲉⲡϩⲟⲣⲟⲙⲁ· ⲙ̄ⲡⲉϥⲣⲁⲥⲧⲉ ⲁⲩⲥⲱⲟⲩϩ ⲉⲡⲙⲁ ⲉⲧⲙ̄ⲙⲁⲩ ⲁⲩⲕⲓⲙ ⲉⲩϣⲁϫⲉ ⲉⲧⲃⲉ ⲟⲩⲁ ⲛ̄ⲛⲉⲥⲛⲏⲩ ⲉⲁϥⲉⲣⲛⲟⲃⲉ[25] ⲁⲩⲱ ⲁⲩⲕⲁⲧⲁⲗⲁⲗⲓ ⲙ̄ⲙⲟϥ ⲁϥⲟⲩⲱⲛϩ ⲇⲉ ⲉⲃⲟⲗ ⲛ̄ⲛ̄ϩⲗ̄ⲗⲟ ⲛ̄ϣⲟⲣⲡ̄ ⲛ̄ϭⲓ ⲟⲩⲣⲓⲣ ⲉϥⲙⲉϩ ⲛ̄ⲥϯⲃⲱⲱⲛ ⲉϥⲟ ⲛ̄ⲁⲕⲁⲑⲁⲣⲧⲟⲛ ⲧⲏⲣϥ̄ ⲛⲉⲛⲧⲁⲩⲛⲁⲩ ⲇⲉ ⲉⲡϭⲱⲗⲡ̄ ⲉⲃⲟⲗ ⲛ̄ⲧⲉⲣⲟⲩⲉⲓⲙⲉ ⲉⲡⲛⲟⲃⲉ ⲉⲧϣⲟⲟⲡ ⲁⲩⲭⲱ ⲉⲛⲉⲥⲛⲏⲩ ⲙ̄ⲡⲉⲟⲟⲩ ⲡⲉ ⲉⲃⲟⲗϩⲛ̄ ⲛ̄ⲁⲅⲅⲉⲗⲟⲥ ⲙⲛ̄ ⲡⲉⲓⲛⲉ ⲙ̄ⲡⲣⲓⲣ·

---

19 ⲛ̄-ⲛ.ⲣⲱⲙⲉ.
20 ⲟⲩⲱⲛⲁϩ (ⲉⲃⲟⲗ) is the equivalent of ⲟⲩⲱⲛϩ (ⲉⲃⲟⲗ).
21 ⲧ.ⲙⲛ̄ⲧ-ⲣⲉϥ-ϣⲙϣⲉ-ⲛⲟⲩⲧⲉ (cf. 049, 051).
22 ⲣ̄-ⲁⲛⲁϥ.
23 ϩⲟⲓⲛⲉ ⲛ̄-ⲛ.ϩⲗ̄ⲗⲟ.
24 ϩⲉⲛ.ⲉⲡⲱⲙⲓⲥ.
25 ⲉ.ⲁϥ.ⲣ̄-ⲛⲟⲃⲉ.

240. ⲁ ⲁⲡⲁ ⲥⲁⲣⲁⲡⲓⲱⲛ ⲛⲁⲩ ⲉⲩⲡⲟⲣⲛⲏ ⲡⲉϫⲁϥ ϫⲉ ϯⲛⲏⲩ ϣⲁⲣⲟ ⲙ̄ⲡⲛⲁⲩ
ⲛ̄ⲣⲟⲩϩⲉ ⲥⲃ̄ⲧⲱⲧⲉ (007) ⲉⲃⲟⲗ ⲁⲩⲱ ⲛ̄ⲧⲉⲣⲉϥⲉⲓ ⲛⲁⲥ ⲉϩⲟⲩⲛ ⲡⲉϫⲁϥ ⲛⲁⲥ ϫⲉ
ϭⲱ ⲉⲣⲟⲓ ⲛ̄ⲟⲩⲕⲟⲩⲓ ϫⲉ ⲟⲩⲛ̄ⲧⲁⲓ ⲟⲩⲛⲟⲙⲟⲥ ⲙ̄ⲙⲁⲩ ϣⲁⲛϯϫⲟⲕϥ̄ ⲉⲃⲟⲗ· ⲛ̄ⲧⲟⲥ
ⲇⲉ ⲡⲉϫⲁⲥ ϫⲉ ⲕⲁⲗⲱⲥ ⲡⲁⲉⲓⲱⲧ· ⲛ̄ⲧⲟϥ ⲇⲉ ⲁϥⲁⲣⲭⲉⲓ ⲙ̄ⲯⲁⲗⲗⲉⲓ ϫⲓⲛ ⲡϣⲟⲣⲡ̄
ⲙ̄ⲯⲁⲗⲙⲟⲥ ϣⲁⲛⲧⲉϥϫⲱⲕ ⲉⲃⲟⲗ ⲙ̄ⲡϣⲉⲧⲁⲓⲟⲩ ⲙ̄ⲯⲁⲗⲙⲟⲥ ⲁⲩⲱ ⲕⲁⲧⲁ ⲥⲟⲡ²⁶
ⲛ̄ⲕⲁⲣⲱϥ ⲉⲃⲟⲗ ϣⲁϥⲉⲓⲣⲉ ⲛ̄ϣⲟⲙⲛ̄ⲧ²⁷ ⲛ̄ⲕⲗ̄ϫⲡⲁⲧ ⲛ̄ⲧⲟⲥ ϩⲱⲱⲥ ⲁⲥϭⲱ ⲉⲥϣⲗⲏⲗ
ϩⲓⲡⲁϩⲟⲩ ⲙ̄ⲙⲟϥ²⁸ ϩⲛ̄ ⲟⲩϩⲟⲧⲉ ⲙⲛ̄ ⲟⲩⲥⲧⲱⲧ· ⲁϥⲙⲟⲩⲛ ⲇⲉ ⲉⲃⲟⲗ ⲉϥϣⲗⲏⲗ
ϩⲁⲣⲟⲥ ⲧⲁⲣⲉⲥⲟⲩϫⲁⲓ (387) ⲁⲩⲱ ⲁ ⲡⲛⲟⲩⲧⲉ ⲥⲱⲧⲙ̄ ⲉⲣⲟϥ· ⲧⲉⲥϩⲓⲙⲉ ⲇⲉ
ⲁⲥⲡⲁϩⲧⲥ̄ ϩⲁⲣⲁⲧⲟⲩ ⲛ̄ⲛⲉϥⲟⲩⲉⲣⲏⲧⲉ ⲉⲥⲣⲓⲙⲉ ⲉⲥϫⲱ ⲙ̄ⲙⲟⲥ ϫⲉ ⲁⲣⲓ ⲧⲁⲅⲁⲡⲏ
ⲡⲁⲉⲓⲱⲧ ⲡⲙⲁ ⲉⲧⲉⲕⲥⲟⲟⲩⲛ ϫⲉ ϯⲛⲁⲟⲩϫⲁⲓ ⲛ̄ϩⲏⲧϥ̄ ϫⲓⲧ²⁹ ⲉⲙⲁⲩ ⲛ̄ⲧⲁ ⲡⲛⲟⲩⲧⲉ
ⲅⲁⲣ ⲧⲛ̄ⲛⲟⲟⲩⲕ (316) ϣⲁⲣⲟⲓ ⲉⲡⲁⲓ· ⲁⲩⲱ ⲁϥϫⲓⲧⲥ̄ ⲉⲩϩⲉⲛⲉⲉⲧⲉ ⲙ̄ⲡⲁⲣⲑⲉⲛⲟⲥ
ⲡⲉϫⲁϥ ⲇⲉ ⲛ̄ⲧⲙⲁⲁⲩ ⲛ̄ⲑⲉⲛⲉⲉⲧⲉ ϫⲉ ϫⲓ ⲛ̄ⲧⲉⲓⲥⲱⲛⲉ ⲁⲩⲱ ⲙ̄ⲡⲣ̄ⲧⲁⲗⲉ (142)
ⲛⲁϩⲃ̄ ⲉϫⲱⲥ ⲏ ⲉⲛⲧⲟⲗⲏ ⲁⲗⲗⲁ ⲛ̄ⲑⲉ ⲉⲧⲉⲥⲟⲩⲁϣⲥ̄ ⲙⲁⲣⲉⲥⲁⲁⲥ (349) ⲕⲁⲁⲥ ϩⲙ̄
ⲡϫⲟⲉⲓⲥ· ⲁⲩⲱ ⲙⲛ̄ⲛⲥⲁ ϩⲛ̄ⲕⲟⲩⲓ ⲛ̄ϩⲟⲟⲩ ⲡⲉϫⲁⲥ ϫⲉ ⲁⲛⲟⲕ ⲟⲩⲣⲉϥⲣ̄ⲛⲟⲃⲉ
ⲉⲓⲟⲩⲱϣ ⲉⲟⲩⲱⲙ ⲛ̄ⲟⲩⲥⲟⲡ ⲙ̄ⲙⲏⲛⲉ ⲙⲛ̄ⲛⲥⲁ ⲕⲉⲟⲩⲟⲉⲓϣ ⲟⲛ ⲡⲉϫⲁⲥ ϫⲉ
ⲉⲓⲟⲩⲱϣ ⲉⲟⲩⲱⲙ ⲛ̄ⲟⲩⲥⲟⲡ ⲕⲁⲧⲁ ⲥⲁⲃⲃⲁⲧⲟⲛ ⲙⲛ̄ⲛⲥⲱⲥ ⲟⲛ ⲡⲉϫⲁⲥ ϫⲉ ⲉⲡⲓⲇⲏ
ⲁⲓⲣ̄ ϩⲁϩ ⲛ̄ⲛⲟⲃⲉ ⲟⲡⲧ³⁰ ⲉϩⲟⲩⲛ ⲉⲩⲣⲓ ⲁⲩⲱ ⲡⲉϯⲛⲁⲟⲩⲟⲙϥ ⲧⲁⲁϥ ⲛⲁⲓ ϩⲛ̄
ⲟⲩϣⲟⲩϣⲧ ⲙⲛ̄ ⲡⲁϩⲱⲃ ⲛ̄ϭⲓϫ· ⲁⲩⲱ ⲁⲩⲉⲓⲣⲉ ϩⲓⲛⲁⲓ ⲁⲩⲱ ⲁⲥϩⲁⲛⲁϥ ⲙ̄ⲡⲛⲟⲩⲧⲉ
ⲁⲥⲉⲛⲕⲟⲧⲕ̄³¹ ⲇⲉ ϩⲙ̄ ⲡⲙⲁ ⲉⲧⲙ̄ⲙⲁⲩ ϩⲙ̄ ⲡϫⲟⲉⲓⲥ·

---

26 The Greek preposition κατά has a distributive meaning here: *every time*.
27 ϣⲙⲛ̄ⲧ-.
28 ϩⲓ-ⲡⲁϩⲟⲩ ⲙ̄ⲙⲟ≠ϥ: literally: *behind his buttocks*, meaning *behind him*.
29 ⲁ≠ϥ.ϫⲓⲧ≠ⲧ.
30 ⲟⲡⲧ≠ⲧ (= ⲟⲧⲡ≠ⲧ), see ⲱⲧⲡ.
31 ⲁ≠ⲥ.ⲛ̄ⲕⲟⲧⲕ̄.

A catechesis of Theodorus

The next text is taken from a catechetic fragment attributed to Theodorus, the coadjuvant of Horsiesis, Pachomius' successor in Tabbenese. We reproduce the texte from the edition of L. Th. Lefort, *Œuvres de S. Pachôme et de ses disciples*, Louvain 1956, 41:13–43:12. The French translation is published in a separate volume.

ετвεπαι μαρν̄ροεις ν̄τενϩαρεϩ[1] επεχαρισμα ενταϥει[2] εχων παραπενμ̄πωα ν̄νενϩвηγε, ν̄τενϩαρεϩ επνομος, ερεπογα πογα μ̄μον[3] ο ν̄κωτ μ̄πεϥερηγ (292) αγω ν̄ϩιη ν̄вωκ εϩογν επραωε ν̄τμν̄τερο[4] ν̄μπηγε (043). μαρεντ̄πενϩητбε[5] εμοοωε ϩμ̄πνομος τηρϥ ν̄τκοινωνια, ν̄τενωωμ̄ μ̄πκωϩτ̄ μν̄τκαταλαλια μν̄πεκρμ̄ρμ ϩν̄τбομ μ̄πεπνεγμα ετογααв, ετετμελετη[6] ν̄νωαχε μ̄πνογτε μ̄πεϩοογ μν̄τεγωη, αγω σοτε νιμ ν̄τεππονηρος ετχερο, ν̄τενбμбομ ϩμ̄πεθγρος ν̄τενπιστις, χεκας ερωανπκαιρος ωωπε ν̄τεπνογτε бμ̄πενωινε, ν̄σεϩε ερον ενσвτωτ ϩωστε ετρενχοος χεαιεγϕρανε μν̄νενταγχοος ναι χε μαρενвωκ ωαπηι μ̄πχοεις.

τν̄ωπ̄ϩμοτ ν̄τοοτϥ μ̄πνογτε πειωτ μ̄πενχοεις ιε πε̄χε̄, χεαϥααν ν̄μπωα ϩωστε ετρενρ̄πωвω̄ μ̄πενϩισε μν̄πενϩοχϩχ̄ ϩμ̄πεστ̄νογϥε ν̄τμν̄τσμητ μν̄ταχρο ν̄τπιστις ετταχρηγ ϩμ̄πνομος ν̄τκοινωνια ετογααв αγω μ̄με, ται επεσαρχηγος (472, 475) μν̄σαν̄αποστολοσπε απα παϩωμο[7], παι εντανσвτωτν̄ εκληρονομει ν̄νερητ εντα πνογτε ερητ μ̄μοογ ναϥ, ϩμ̄πτρενϩαρεϩ (134, 424) ενεϥεντολη, εντввηγ εвολ ϩν̄τωλμ̄ νιμ ν̄τετσαρξ μν̄πεπνεγμα, ενχωκ εвολ ν̄ογτввο ϩν̄θοτε μ̄πνογτε, ενο ν̄ατχροπ ν̄νενερηγ κατα σμοτ νιμ χινογωαχε ωαογϩωв, αγω ενο ν̄στ̄νογϥε ν̄νετϩιвολ ετρεγναγ ενενϩвηγε ετνανογογ ν̄σετ̄εοογ μ̄πενειωτ ετϩν̄μ̄πηγε, αγω ν̄τεογον νιμ ειμε,

---

1 ν̄τεν is an orthographic variant for ν̄τν̄.
2 εντα is an orthographic variant for ν̄τα.
3 ν̄-, μ̄μο⸗ can introduce a partitive genitive (cf. 178).
4 ερο is a variant for ρ̄ρο.
5 μαρε⸗ν.τ̄-πε⸗ν.ϩητ бε.
6 Elliptic construction for ετε (ται) τμελετη τε (cf. 457).
7 Pachomius was the founder of the monasteries of Tabbenese and Pbow.

ⲘⲚⲚⲈⲦⲤⲰϢϤ ⲚⲦⲈⲚⲀⲚⲀⲤⲦⲢⲞⲪⲎ ⲈⲦⲚⲀⲚⲞⲨⲤ, ϪⲈⲈⲚⲞⲨⲎϨ ⲀⲚ (405) ⲚⲤⲀϨⲈⲚϢⲀϪⲈ ⲚⲦⲞⲂⲦⲈ Ⲏ̄ ⲤⲞⲪⲒⲀ Ⲛ̄ⲢⲰⲘⲈ, ⲀⲖⲖⲀ ϪⲈⲠϪⲞⲈⲒⲤⲠⲈ ⲠⲈⲚⲈⲒⲰⲦ, ⲠϪⲞⲈⲒⲤⲠⲈ ⲠⲈⲚⲀⲢⲬⲰⲚ, ⲠϪⲞⲈⲒⲤⲠⲈ ⲠⲈⲚⲢ̄ⲢⲞ, ⲠϪⲞⲈⲒⲤ Ⲛ̄ⲦⲞϤ ⲠⲈⲦⲚⲀⲦⲀⲚϨⲞⲚ[8], ⲀⲨⲰ ⲈⲚⲦⲎⲦ Ⲛ̄ϨⲎⲦ ϨⲘ̄ϨⲞⲬϨ̄Ϫ̄ Ⲙ̄ⲠⲆⲒⲞⲔⲘⲞⲤ[9] ⲈⲚϪⲰ Ⲙ̄ⲘⲞⲤ ϪⲈⲚ̄ⲚⲀⲒ ⲦⲎⲢⲞⲨ ⲈⲚⲦⲀⲨⲈⲒ ⲈϨⲢⲀⲒ ⲈϪⲰⲚ Ⲙ̄ⲠⲈⲚⲢ̄ⲠⲈⲔⲰⲂϢ̄[10], ⲀⲨⲰ Ⲙ̄ⲠⲈⲚϪⲒⲚϬⲞⲚⲤ̄ ϨⲚ̄ⲦⲈⲔⲆⲒⲀⲐⲎⲔⲎ ⲞⲨⲆⲈ Ⲙ̄ⲠⲈⲠⲈⲚϨⲎⲦ ⲤⲀϨⲰⲰϤ ⲈⲠⲀϨⲞⲨ[11], ⲈⲚⲤⲞⲞⲨⲚ ϪⲈⲈⲚⲦⲀⲬⲀⲢⲒⲌⲈ[12] ⲚⲀⲚ ⲈⲠⲒⲤⲦⲈⲨⲈ ⲈⲠⲬ̄Ⲥ̄ Ⲙ̄ⲘⲀⲦⲈ ⲀⲚ, ⲀⲖⲖⲀ ⲈϢⲢ̄ϨⲒⲤⲈ[13] ⲞⲚ ⲈϪⲰϤ, ⲈⲚⲰⲠ Ⲛ̄ϨⲞⲬϨ̄Ϫ̄ ⲚⲒⲘ ϨⲒⲐⲖⲒⲮⲒⲤ (187) ⲚⲒⲘ ϪⲈⲈⲚⲖⲀⲀⲨⲚⲈ ϨⲒⲦⲘ̄ⲠⲈϨⲘⲞⲦ Ⲙ̄ⲠⲈⲦ†ϬⲞⲘ ⲚⲀⲚ ⲠⲈⲬ̄Ⲥ̄ Ⲓ̄Ⲥ̄ ⲠⲈⲚϪⲞⲈⲒⲤ, ⲈⲚⲘⲈⲈⲨⲈ ⲈⲂⲞⲖ ⲈⲚⲠⲈⲐⲞⲞⲨ (466) Ⲙ̄ⲚⲚϨⲒⲤⲈ ⲈⲚⲦⲀⲨⲀⲀⲨ Ⲙ̄ⲠⲈⲦⲘ̄ⲘⲀⲨ[14] ⲘⲚ̄ⲚⲈⲦⲞⲨⲀⲀⲂ ⲦⲎⲢⲞⲨ, ⲚⲀⲒ ⲈⲚⲦⲀⲨⲘⲞⲞϢⲈ ϨⲚ̄ϨⲈⲚⲂⲀⲖⲞⲦ ⲘⲚ̄ϨⲈⲚϢⲀⲀⲢ Ⲛ̄ⲂⲀⲀⲘⲠⲈ, ⲈⲨⲢ̄ϬⲢⲰϨ, ⲈⲨⲐⲖⲒⲂⲈ, ⲈⲨⲘⲞⲔϨ, ⲚⲀⲒ ⲈⲦⲈⲘ̄ⲠⲔⲞⲤⲘⲞⲤ Ⲙ̄ⲠϢⲀ Ⲙ̄ⲘⲞⲞⲨ ⲀⲚ, ⲀⲨⲰ ⲚⲈⲨⲢⲀϢⲈ ⲈⲘⲀⲦⲈ ⲈⲨⲤⲞⲞⲨⲚ ϪⲈⲈⲢⲈⲠⲈⲨⲞⲨϪⲀⲒ ϨⲚ̄ⲞⲨⲞⲨⲞⲈⲒϢ Ⲛ̄ⲐⲖⲒⲮⲒⲤ, ⲀⲨⲰ ⲠϨⲒⲤⲈ Ⲙ̄ⲠⲈⲞⲨⲞⲈⲒϢ ⲦⲈⲚⲞⲨ Ⲙ̄ⲠϢⲀ ⲀⲚ Ⲙ̄ⲠⲈⲞⲞⲨ ⲈⲦⲚⲀϬⲰⲖⲠ̄ ⲈⲢⲞⲚ.

ⲠⲈⲦⲈⲢⲈⲠϪⲞⲈⲒⲤ (464) ⲄⲀⲢ ⲘⲈ Ⲙ̄ⲘⲞϤ ϢⲀϤⲠⲀⲒⲆⲈⲨⲈ Ⲙ̄ⲘⲞϤ, ϢⲀϤⲘⲀⲤⲦⲒⲄⲞⲨ ⲆⲈ Ⲛ̄ϢⲎⲢⲈ ⲚⲒⲘ ⲈⲦϤ̄ⲚⲀϢⲞⲠⲞⲨ ⲈⲢⲞϤ, ⲀⲨⲰ ϪⲈⲤⲂⲰ ⲚⲒⲘ ⲠⲢⲞⲤⲦⲈⲨⲚⲞⲨ ⲘⲈⲚ ⲈϢϪⲈⲞⲨⲢⲀϢⲈ ⲀⲚ ⲠⲈ (432), ⲀⲖⲖⲀ ⲞⲨⲖⲨⲠⲎⲦⲈ, ⲘⲚ̄ⲚⲤⲰⲤ ϢⲀⲤ† ⲚⲞⲨⲔⲀⲢⲠⲞⲤ Ⲛ̄ⲎⲢⲎⲚⲒⲔⲞⲚ[15] Ⲛ̄ⲆⲒⲔⲀⲒⲞⲤⲨⲚⲎ Ⲛ̄ⲚⲈⲚⲦⲀⲨⲄⲨⲘⲚⲀⲌⲈ Ⲙ̄ⲘⲞⲞⲨ ⲈⲂⲞⲖ ϨⲒⲦⲞⲞⲦⲤ̄. ⲀⲢⲀ Ⲛ̄ⲦⲈⲚⲤⲞⲞⲨⲚ[16] ⲀⲚ Ⲛ̄ⲦⲄⲨⲘⲚⲀⲤⲒⲀ Ⲛ̄ⲚⲦⲂ̄ⲚⲞⲞⲨⲈ ϪⲈϢⲀⲨⲢ̄ⲞⲨ ⲚⲀⲨ, ⲈϢⲀⲨⲦⲤⲀⲂⲞⲞⲨ Ⲛ̄ⲐⲈ ⲈⲦⲈϨⲚⲈⲠⲈⲨϪⲞⲈⲒⲤ; ⲈⲀⲚⲈⲒⲘⲈⲆⲈ ⲈⲠⲤⲞⲞⲨⲚ ⲈⲦⲞⲨⲞⲬ[17] Ⲛ̄ⲦⲈⲚⲈⲄⲢⲀⲪⲎ ⲈⲦⲞⲨⲀⲀⲂ ⲘⲚ̄ⲦϬⲒⲚⲢ̄ϨⲰⲂ Ⲛ̄ⲦⲀⲠⲚⲞⲨⲦⲈ ⲠⲀⲒⲆⲈⲨⲈ Ⲛ̄ⲚⲈⲦⲞⲨⲀⲀⲂ Ⲛ̄ϨⲎⲦⲤ̄ ⲘⲚ̄ⲚⲈⲒⲞⲦⲈ Ⲛ̄ⲦⲔⲞⲒⲚⲰⲚⲒⲀ, Ⲙ̄ⲠⲢ̄ⲦⲢⲈⲚⲈⲄⲔⲀⲔⲈⲒⲆⲈ, ⲀⲖⲖⲀ ⲘⲀⲢⲈⲚϪⲞⲞⲤ ⲦⲎⲢⲚ̄ ϨⲘ̄ⲠⲈⲚϨⲎⲦ Ⲛ̄ⲚⲀϨⲢⲘ̄ⲠⲚⲞⲨⲦⲈ ⲀⲨⲰ ϨⲚ̄ⲦⲈⲚⲦⲀⲠⲢⲞ ϪⲈⲞⲨⲘⲞⲚⲞⲚ[18]

---

8 Ⲡ.ⲈⲦ.ⲚⲀ.ⲦⲀⲚϨⲞ⸗Ⲛ.
9 ⲆⲒⲞⲔⲘⲞⲤ for the Greek διωγμός.
10 Orthographic variant for Ⲙ̄Ⲡ⸗Ⲛ.Ⲣ̄-ⲠⲈ⸗ⲔⲰⲂϢ̄.
11 ⲤⲞⲞϨⲈ Ⲉ-ⲠⲀϨⲞⲨ : *to bow backwards* (literaly: *to erect backwards*).
12 Since the subject is not expressed, we can translate impersonally.
13 Ϣ- is an auxiliary (*to be able, can*, cf. Ⲉϣ).
14 Ⲙ̄-Ⲡ.ⲈⲦ.Ⲙ̄ⲘⲀⲨ
15 ⲎⲢⲎⲚⲒⲔⲞⲚ for the Greek εἰρηνικόν.
16 Read Ⲛ̄.ⲦⲚ̄.ⲤⲞⲞⲨⲚ.
17 ⲞⲨⲞⲬ is the stative of ⲞⲨϪⲀⲒ.
18 ⲞⲨⲘⲞⲚⲞⲚ for the Greek οὐ μόνον.

ⲉⲧⲣⲉⲩⲙⲟⲣⲛ̄, ⲁⲗⲗⲁ ⲉⲧⲣⲉⲛⲙⲟⲩ ⳉⲙ̄ⲙⲁ ⲛⲓⲙ ⳉⲁⲡⲣⲁⲛ ⲙ̄ⲡⲉⲛϫⲟⲉⲓⲥ ⲓ̄ⲥ̄ ⲡⲉⲭ̄ⲥ̄, ⲁⲩⲱ ⲛ̄ⲧⲉⲛϫⲟⲟⲥ[19] ⳉⲙ̄ⲡⲅⲟⲭⲥ̄ ⲛ̄ⲛⲁⲧⲉⲭⲣⲓⲁ[20] (019) ⲙ̄ⲡⲥⲱⲙⲁ ⲙⲛ̄ⲡⲛⲟϭⲛⲉϭ ⲛ̄ⲛⲉⲧⲛⲟϭⲛⲉϭ ⲙ̄ⲙⲟⲛ ⲉⲧⲃⲉⲡϣⲱⲱⲧ ⲙⲛ̄ⲡⲉⲙ̄ⲕⲁⳉ ϫⲉⲛⲓⲙ ⲡⲉⲧⲛⲁϣⲡⲟⲣϫⲛ̄ ⲉⲧⲁⲅⲁⲡⲏ ⲙ̄ⲡⲛⲟⲩⲧⲉ, ⲟⲩⲑⲗⲓⲯⲓⲥⲧⲉ, ⲏ̄ ⲟⲩⲗⲱⲭ̄ⳉ̄, ⲏ̄ ⲟⲩⲇⲓⲱⲅⲙⲟⲥ, ⲏ̄ ⲟⲩⳉⲕⲟ, ⲏ̄ ⲟⲩⲕⲱⲕⲁⳉⲏⲩ, ⲏ̄ ⲟⲩⲕⲓⲛⲇⲩⲛⲟⲥ, ⲏ̄ ⲟⲩⲥⲩⲃⲉ[21] ⲙⲛ̄ⲡⲕⲉⲥⲉⲉⲡⲉ[22], ⲕⲁⲧⲁ ⲧϭⲓⲛⲣ̄ⳉⲱⲃ ⲧⲏⲣⲥ̄ ⲙ̄ⲡⲁⲡⲟⲥⲧⲟⲗⲟⲥ, ⲡⲥⲱⲧⲡ̄ ⲙ̄ⲡⲛⲟⲩⲧⲉ, ⲡⲉⲛⲧⲁϥϫⲟⲟⲥ ⲛⲁⲛ ϫⲉⲧⲛ̄ⲧⲛ̄ⲑⲏⲩⲧⲛ̄[23] ⲉⲣⲟⲓ ⲕⲁⲧⲁⲑⲉ ⲉⲛⲧⲁⲓⲧⲛ̄ⲧⲱⲛⲧ̄ ⲉⲡⲉⲭ̄ⲥ̄, ⲉⲧⲉⲧⲉⲓϭⲓⲛⲣ̄ⳉⲱⲃ ⲛ̄ⲟⲩⲱⲧⲧⲉ ⲛ̄ⲛⲉⲧⲟⲩⲁⲁⲃ ⲧⲏⲣⲟⲩ ⲙⲛ̄ⲛ̄ⲉⲓⲟⲧⲉ ⲛ̄ⲧⲕⲟⲓⲛⲱⲛⲓⲁ ⲛⲁⲓ ⲉⲛⲧⲁⲩϫⲉⲕⲡⲉⲩⲁⲅⲱⲛ ⲉⲃⲟⲗ ⳉⲛ̄ⲟⲩⲙⲛ̄ⲧⲅⲉⲛⲛⲁⲓⲟⲥ, ⲉⲁⲩⲙ̄ⲧⲟⲛ ⲙ̄ⲙⲟⲟⲩ ⲉⲃⲟⲗ ⳉⲛ̄ⲛⲉⲩⳉⲓⲥⲉ ⳉⲙ̄ⲡⲧⲣⲉⲩⲃⲱⲕ ⲉⳉⲟⲩⲛ ⲉⲡⲉⲩⲙⲁ ⲛ̄ⲙⲧⲟⲛ ϣⲁⲉⲛⲉⳉ :-

---

19 Read ⲛ̄-ⲧⲛ̄.ϫⲟⲟⲥ.
20 ⲭⲣⲓⲁ for the Greek χρεία.
21 ⲥⲩⲃⲉ is a variant of ⲥⲏϥⲉ (from the Greek ξίφος).
22 ⲙⲛ̄-ⲡ.ⲕⲉ.ⲥⲉⲉⲡⲉ: *etcetera* (literally: *the rest also*).
23 ⲧⲛ̄ⲧⲛ̄-ⲑⲏⲩⲧⲛ̄ instead of ⲧⲛ̄ⲧⲱⲛ-ⲧⲛ̄ (for euphonic reasons).

The *Homily on the Church of the Rock*, attributed to Timothy Æluros

The homily on the Church of the Rock tells the story of a church consecrated to the Virgin Mary, situated on the east bank of the Nile. The legend retraces the history of the church to the dwelling of the Holy Family in Egypt. The passage we quote tells the story from the point of view of Mary. The text i staken from the edition of A. Boud'hors, *L'Homélie sur l'Église du Rocher attribuée à Timothée Ælure* (Patrologia Orientalis 49, 1, n° 217), Turnhout 2001. The text is published with a French translation.

[p̄]

ⲈⲒⲦⲀ ⲚⲦⲈⲢⲈⲚ
ⲤⲈⲈⲚⲦⲚ̄ⲤⲞⲞⲚⲈ[1]
ⲈⲂⲞⲖ ⲚⲞⲨⲔⲞⲨⲒ (107)
ⲀⲨⲰ ⲚⲦⲈⲢⲈⲠⲀ
ϢⲎⲢⲈ ϪⲈⲚⲀⲒ
ⲚⲀⲒ ⲌⲀⲠⲖⲨⲤ
ⲦⲎⲤ[2]· ⲀϤⲈⲒ
ⲘⲈ ⲈⲠⲀⲘⲞⲔ
ⲘⲈⲔ ⲠⲈϪⲀϤ
ⲚⲀⲒ· ϪⲈⲘⲀ
ⲢⲒⲀ ⲦⲀⲘⲀⲀⲨ
Ⲙ̄ⲠⲈⲢⲢ̄ⲔⲞⲨⲒ (142)
Ⲛ̄ϨⲎⲦ ⲈⲢⲞⲒ ϪⲈ (443)
ⲀⲒⲀⲚⲈⲒϪⲈ
ϢⲀⲚⲦⲈⲠ
ⲖⲨⲤⲦⲎⲤ ⲈⲢ
ⲚⲀⲒ ⲚⲀⲒ· Ⲙ̄
ⲘⲞⲚ ⲦⲞⲒⲔⲞ
ⲚⲞⲘⲒⲀ Ⲙ̄ⲠⲀ
ⲒⲰⲦ ⲈϪⲰⲒ ⲦⲀ

ϪⲰⲔ (382) ⲈⲂⲞⲖ
ϢⲀⲚⲦⲀⲠⲈ
ⲖⲈⳠⲠⲈⲒⲢⲀⲤⲘⲞⲤ (364)[3]
ⲚⲒⲘ Ⲛ̄ⲦⲈⲠⲈⲒ
ⲔⲞⲤⲘⲞⲤ· ϪⲈ
ⲠⲢⲰⲘⲈ Ⲛ̄ⲆⲒⲀ
ⲂⲞⲖⲒⲀ[4] ⲞⲨⲆⲒⲀ
ⲂⲞⲖⲞⲤⲠⲈ Ϩⲱ
ⲰϤ·
ⲦⲈⲚⲞⲨϬⲈ ⲰⲦ[5] ⲦⲀ
ⲘⲀⲀⲨ Ⲙ̄ⲠⲈⲢ
Ⲙ̄ⲔⲀϨ Ⲛ̄ϨⲎⲦ
ⲈⲦⲂⲈⲠⲈⲐⲂⲂⲒⲞ
Ⲛ̄ⲦⲀⲒϢⲞⲠϤ
ⲈⲢⲞⲒ ϨⲀⲦⲈⲚⲦⲞ
ⲖⲎ Ⲙ̄ⲠⲀⲈⲒⲰⲦ
ϨⲨⲠⲞⲘⲒⲚⲈ Ⲱ ⲦⲀ
ⲘⲀⲀⲨ Ⲛ̄ⲘⲘⲀⲒ
ⲈⲚⲈⲐⲖⲒⲮⲒⲤ
Ⲙ̄ⲠⲈⲒⲔⲞⲤ

---

1 ⲤⲈⲈⲚⲦ- for ⲤⲈⲚⲦ-, the prenominal state of the verb ⲤⲒⲚⲈ.
2 ⲖⲨⲤⲦⲎⲤ fort he Greek ληστής.
3 ⲠⲈⲖⲈϬ- for ⲠⲈⲖϬ-, the prenominal form of ⲠⲰⲖϬ.
4 The Greek noun διαβολία (*hostility*) is used with decriptive function (as an adjective, cf. 028). It could be translated *diabolical*.
5 ὦ introduces a Greek vocative..

ⲙⲟⲥ· ϫⲉⲛ̄ⲧⲟ (003)
ⲡⲉ ⲧⲡⲩⲗⲏ
ⲛ̄ⲑⲓ̄ⲗ̄ⲏ̄ⲙ̄[6]
ⲧⲁⲛⲉⲓϣⲁ (019) ⲉⲩ
ⲣⲟⲟⲩⲧ· ⲧⲁ
ⲛⲓⲥⲧⲟⲗⲏ ⲛⲁⲧ
ⲗⲱⲱⲙ·
ⲟⲩⲙⲏⲏϣⲉ ⲛ̄
ϣⲁϫⲉ ⲛⲥⲟⲗ
ⲥⲉⲗ[7] ⲁⲡⲁϣⲏ
ⲣⲉ ϫⲟⲟⲩ ⲉⲣⲟⲓ ϩⲓ
ⲧⲉϩⲓⲏ ϣⲁ
ⲡⲧⲟⲟⲩ ⲛⲕⲱⲥ[8]·
ⲉⲓⲧⲁ ⲛ̄ⲧⲉⲣⲛ̄
ϭⲟⲓⲗⲉ ⲉⲡⲧⲟ
ⲟⲩ ⲛ̄ⲕⲱⲥ·
ⲁⲛⲙⲟⲟϣⲉ
ⲕⲁⲧⲁⲙⲁ[9] ϩⲓ
ⲛⲉⲙⲁ[10] ⲛ̄ϭⲟⲓ
ⲗⲉ· ⲉⲓϣⲓⲛⲉ
ⲛ̄ⲥⲁⲟⲩⲙⲁ
ⲉⲛⲁⲛⲟⲩϥ

[ⲣ̄ⲁ̄]
ⲁⲡⲁϣⲏⲣⲉ ⲧⲉϫⲥ[11]
ⲧⲏⲏⲃⲉ ⲉⲣⲟⲓ
ⲉⲩⲙⲁ ⲛ̄ϭⲟⲓⲗⲉ
ϫⲉⲙⲁⲣⲟⲛ[12] ⲉ
ⲡⲉⲓⲙⲁ ⲱ ⲧⲁ
ⲙⲁⲁⲩ· ϫⲉⲡⲁⲧⲉⲫⲩⲗⲏ ⲛ̄
ⲓⲟⲩⲇⲁⲡⲉ· ⲧ
ⲛⲟⲩⲛⲉ ⲛ̄ⲧⲁⲓ
ϣⲁ ⲉⲃⲟⲗ ⲛ̄ϩⲏⲧⲥ̄
ϫⲉⲥⲉⲙ̄ⲡϣⲁ (443)
ⲙ̄ⲡⲁⲥⲙⲟⲩ
ⲙⲛ̄ⲡⲁϩⲙⲟⲧ
ⲙ̄ⲡⲁⲣⲁⲇⲁⲛ (032)[13]·
ⲛⲧⲉⲣⲉⲛϭⲟⲓⲗⲉ ⲉⲣⲟϥ
ⲁⲛϭⲓⲛⲉ ⲛⲟⲩⲥⲁ
ⲙ̄ⲡϣⲱⲓ· ⲉⲣⲉ
ⲟⲩϣⲟⲩϣⲧ ⲕ
ⲧⲏⲩ ⲉⲡⲉϥⲥⲁ
ⲛ̄ⲙϩⲓⲧ· ⲁⲛ

[ⲣ̄ⲃ̄]
ϭⲓⲛⲉ ⲛ̄ⲛⲉⲭⲣⲓⲁ
ⲧⲏⲣⲟⲩ· ⲛ̄ϣⲁ

---

6 ⲓ̄ⲗ̄ⲏ̄ⲙ̄ for ⲧ.ϩⲓⲉⲣⲟⲩⲥⲁⲗⲏⲙ, *Jerusalem* (cf. the glossary of *nomina sacra*).
7 ⲥⲟⲗⲥⲉⲗ is an orthographic variant for ⲥⲟⲗⲥⲗ.
8 Kôs is a toponym.
9 ⲕⲁⲧⲁ-ⲙⲁ : *from one place to the other* (κατά has a distributive meaning here).
10 Read ⲛ.ⲙⲁ.
11 ⲧⲉϫⲥ- is an orthographic variant for ⲧⲉⲕⲥ-, the prenominal form of the verb ⲧⲱⲕⲥ.
12 ⲙⲁⲣⲟⲛ is the absolute form of the conjugation base of the jussive (ⲙⲁⲣⲉ-). It is translated : *let us (go)* (Crum, *Coptic Dictionary* 182b).
13 Dan is the name of one of the 12 tribes of Israel.

ⲣⲉⲛⲉϩⲓⲟⲙⲉ ⲣ̄ⲭⲣⲓⲁ[14]
ⲙⲙⲟⲟⲩ ⲛ̄ⲥⲉϫⲱ
ⲕⲙ̄ ⲛ̄ⲛⲉⲩϣⲏ
ⲣⲉ· ⲧⲁⲉⲕⲁⲛⲏ
ⲙⲛ̄ⲧⲇⲁⲕⲟⲥ[15]
ⲙⲛ̄ⲡⲉⲕⲣⲁⲕ
ⲧⲏⲣ[16]· ⲁⲩⲱ ⲧ
ϣⲱⲧⲉ ⲙ̄ⲙⲟⲟⲩ·
....
ϩⲁⲡⲗⲱⲥ ⲁⲓⲣ̄
ⲥⲟⲟⲩ ⲛ̄ⲉⲃⲟⲧ
ⲉⲓϭⲁⲗⲏⲩ[17] ⲉⲡ
ⲧⲟⲟⲩ ⲉⲧⲙ̄
ⲙⲁⲩ ⲙⲛ̄ⲡⲁ
ϣⲏⲣⲉ· ϣⲁⲛ
ⲧⲉⲙⲱⲩⲥⲏⲥ[18]
ⲉⲓⲛⲉ ⲙ̄ⲡϣⲓ
ⲛⲉ ⲙⲡⲉϣⲧⲟⲣ
ⲧⲉⲣ ⲛⲁⲓ[19]· ⲁϥ
ⲉⲣⲁⲣⲭⲏ[20] ⲛ̄ⲧⲱ
ⲙⲉⲥ ϩⲙ̄ⲡⲧⲟ
ⲟⲩ ⲉⲧⲙ̄ⲙⲁⲩ
ⲁⲩⲱ ϣⲁϩⲣⲁⲓ

ⲉⲡⲟⲟⲩ ⲛ̄ϩⲟⲟⲩ[21]
[ⲣ̄ⲅ]
ⲁⲩⲱ ⲙⲡⲁⲧⲉ
ⲱⲥⲕ ϣⲱⲡⲉ
ϫⲓⲛⲉⲡⲉϣ
ⲧⲟⲣⲧⲉⲣ[22] ⲙ̄ⲙⲱ
ⲩⲥⲏⲥ· ϣⲁⲛ
ⲧⲉⲡϣⲙ̄ⲛⲟⲩ
ⲃⲉ[23] ⲛ̄ⲅⲁⲃⲣⲓⲏⲗ
ⲧⲁϩⲟⲛ· ⲛⲧⲁϥ
ⲥⲩⲙⲁⲛⲉ[24] ⲛⲁ[25]
ⲙ̄ⲡⲧⲁⲥⲥⲉ[26] ⲛ̄
ϩⲩⲣⲱⲇⲏⲥ[27]·
ⲁⲩⲱ ⲁⲛⲕⲱⲧⲛ̄
ⲉⲡⲉⲛⲕⲁϩ
ϣⲁⲡⲉϩⲟⲟⲩ ⲛ̄
ⲧⲁⲩⲥϯⲟⲩ[28] ⲙ̄ⲡⲁ
ϣⲏⲣⲉ ⲙ̄ⲙⲉⲣⲓⲧ
ⲧⲉⲛⲟⲩϭⲉ ⲱ ⲇⲓⲙⲟ
ⲑⲉⲟⲥ[29]· ⲁⲟⲩⲱⲛ ⲛ̄ⲧⲉⲥⲑⲩⲥⲓⲥ[30]
ⲙ̄ⲡⲉⲕϩⲏⲧ

---

14 The relative conversion is introduced by ⲛ̄ instead of ⲉⲧⲉ.
15 ⲇⲁⲕⲟⲥ for the Greek δάκος.
16 ⲕⲣⲁⲕⲧⲏⲣ for the Greek κρατήρ.
17 ϭⲁⲗⲏⲩ is the stative of ϭⲟⲉⲓⲗⲉ.
18 ⲙⲱⲩⲥⲏⲥ is a proper noun: Moses.
19 ⲛ̄-ⲛⲁⲓ.
20 ⲣ̄-ⲁⲣⲭⲏ. This verb can be translated with an adverbial locution: *since the beginning*. (Literally, it means: *he made a start with.*)

21 ⲡⲟⲟⲩ ⲛ̄-ϩⲟⲟⲩ: *until now*.
22 ϫⲓⲛⲉ is a variant of the preposition ϫⲓⲛ-.
23 ϣⲙ-ⲛⲟⲩⲃⲉ is an orthographical variant for ϣⲙ-ⲛⲟⲩϥⲉ (see ϣⲓⲛⲉ).
24 ⲥⲩⲙⲁⲛⲉ for the Greek σημαίνω.
25 ⲛⲁ≠ⲛ.
26 ⲧⲁⲥⲥⲉ for the Greek verb τάσσω. Used as a noun, it can mean *punishment*.
27 ϩⲩⲣⲱⲇⲏⲥ is a proper noun: Herod.
28 ⲥⲧⲁⲩⲣⲟⲩ for the Greek σταυρόω.
29 ⲇⲓⲙⲟⲑⲉⲟⲥ is a proper noun: Timothy.
30 ⲉⲥⲑⲩⲥⲓⲥ for the Greek αἴσθησις.

[ρ̄δ̄]
ⲛⲅⲉⲓⲙⲉ ⲉⲛⲉϯ
ϫⲱ (463) ⲙ̄ⲙⲟⲟⲩ ⲛⲁⲕ·
ⲛⲅⲥϩⲁⲓⲥⲟⲩ (006) ⲛⲟⲩ
ⲟⲛ ⲛⲓⲙ· ⲉⲩⲉⲣ

ⲡⲙⲉⲉⲩⲉ ⲛ̄ⲧⲁ
ϭⲓⲛⲟⲩⲱϩ ϩⲓϫⲛ̄
ⲧⲉⲓⲡⲉⲧⲣⲁ·

Anti-chalcedonian fragment

The following text is transmitted on a sheet of parchment from the 10th or 11th century. It belongs to the collection of the Université Catholique de Louvain. The fragment has been published by L. Th. Lefort, *Les manuscrits coptes de l'Université de Louvain*, t. 1: *Textes littéraires*, Louvain 1940, 140–143. This edition includes a French translation.

(flesh) p. 90 ⲡϨⲁⲓⲉ[1] ⲇⲉ ⲁϥⲛⲟⲭϥ̄ ⲉⲡⲉⲥⲏⲧ ⲉⲡⲉⲭⲁⲓⲟⲥ[2] ⲛ̄ⲛⲉϨⲟϥ· ⲙⲛ̄ⲛⲉⲟⲩⲟⲟϨⲉ:- ⲁⲛⲉⲛⲉⲓⲟⲧⲉ ϫⲟⲟⲥ ϫⲉⲁϥⲣ̄ⲙⲛ̄ⲧⲏ[3] ⲛ̄ⲣⲟⲙⲡⲉ Ϩⲙ̄ⲡⲙⲁ ⲉⲧⲙ̄ⲙⲁⲩ· ⲁⲗⲗⲁ ⲁⲡⲛⲟⲩⲧⲉ ϥⲓ ⲙ̄ⲡⲉϥⲉⲓⲛⲉ Ϩⲓϫⲙ̄ⲡⲉϥϨⲟ· ⲁϥϯ ⲛⲁϥ ⲛⲟⲩⲥⲙⲟⲧ ⲛ̄ⲣⲓⲣ ⲛ̄Ϩⲟⲟⲩⲧ ⲛ̄ⲧⲟⲟⲩ ⲙ̄ⲛⲟⲩⲗⲓⲃⲉ ⲛ̄ⲇⲁⲓⲙⲱⲛⲓⲟⲛ:- ⲁϥⲉⲓ ⲉⲃⲟⲗ Ϩⲙ̄ⲡⲡⲁⲗⲗⲁⲧⲓⲟⲛ ⲁϥⲃⲱⲕ [ⲉ]ⲛⲉⲙⲁⲛⲕⲁϣ [ⲙ]ⲛ̄ⲛⲉⲙⲁⲛⲕⲁⲙ [Ϩ]ⲓⲥⲟⲩⲣⲉ (187) ⲙⲛ̄ⲛⲉⲣⲏⲙⲓⲁ· ⲉϥⲉⲛⲕⲟⲧⲕ̄[4] Ϩⲛ̄ⲛⲉϨⲉⲗⲟⲥ ⲙⲛ̄ⲛⲁⲣⲟⲟⲩ[5] ⲛ̄ⲑⲉ ⲛ̄ⲛⲉⲣⲓⲣ· Ϩⲱⲥⲇⲉ[6] ⲛ̄ϥ̄ϯϨⲟⲧⲉ ⲛⲟⲩⲟⲛ ⲛⲓⲙ ⲉⲧϣⲟⲟⲡ Ϩⲙ̄ⲡⲙⲁ ⲉⲧⲙ̄ⲙⲁⲩ ⲉⲧⲃⲉⲛⲉⲣⲱⲙⲉ ⲙⲛ̄ⲛⲉⲑⲏⲣⲓⲟⲛ ⲉϥⲧⲁⲕⲟ ⲙ̄ⲙⲟⲟⲩ:- ⲛ̄ⲧⲉⲣⲉⲡⲛⲟⲩⲧⲉ ⲉⲣϨⲛⲁϥ ⲉⲥⲧⲟϥ ⲉⲧⲉϥⲁⲣⲭⲏ ⲛ̄ⲕⲉⲥⲟⲡ· ⲁϥϣⲓⲛⲉ ⲛ̄ⲥⲁⲡⲡⲉⲧⲟⲩⲁⲁⲃ ⲅⲣⲏⲅⲱⲣⲓⲟⲥ ⲁϥϨⲉ ⲉⲣⲟϥ ⲉϥⲟⲛ̄Ϩ ⲉⲃⲟⲗ ϫⲉⲉⲩϨⲁⲣⲉϨ (443) ⲉⲣⲟϥ Ϩⲓⲧⲙ̄ⲡⲛⲟⲩⲧⲉ:- ⲛ̄ⲧⲉⲩⲛⲟⲩ ⲛ̄ⲧⲁϥⲉⲛⲧϥ̄ ⲉϨⲣⲁⲓ Ϩⲙ̄ⲡⲙⲁ ⲉⲧⲙ̄ⲙⲁⲩ ⲁϥⲣ̄ϣⲡⲏⲣⲉ ⲙ̄ⲡⲉⲓⲛⲟϭ ⲛ̄ⲟⲩⲟⲉⲓϣ ⲛ̄ⲧⲁϥⲁⲁϥ[7] ⲙ̄ⲡⲉⲡⲉⲑⲟⲟⲩ (466) ⲧⲁϨⲟϥ:- ⲛ̄ⲧⲟϥ ⲇⲉ ⲁϥϣⲓⲛⲉ ⲛ̄ⲥⲁⲡⲣ̄ⲣⲟ ⲁⲩⲧⲁⲙⲟϥ ⲉⲡⲧⲱϣ ⲛ̄ⲧⲁϥϣⲱⲡⲉ ⲙ̄ⲙⲟϥ:- ⲛ̄ⲧⲉⲩⲛⲟⲩ (110) ⲁϥⲧⲱⲟⲩⲛ ⲁϥⲃⲱⲕ ⲉⲡⲙⲁ ⲉⲣⲡⲣ̄ⲣⲟ ⲉⲛⲕⲟⲧⲕ̄ ⲛ̄Ϩⲏⲧϥ̄· ⲁϥⲙⲟⲩⲧⲉ ϫⲉⲧⲉⲣⲏⲇⲁⲧⲏⲥ[8] ⲁⲙⲟⲩ (136) ⲉⲃⲟⲗ ⲛ̄ⲧⲛ̄ⲛⲁⲩ ⲉⲣⲟⲕ· Ϩⲓⲧⲛ̄ⲧϭⲟⲙ ⲙ̄ⲡⲁⲛⲟⲩⲧⲉ:- ⲛ̄ⲧⲉⲩⲛⲟⲩ ⲁϥⲉⲓ ⲉⲃⲟⲗ ⲉϥⲟⲩⲱϫⲡ̄ ⲛ̄ⲥⲁⲛⲕⲁⲙ ⲙⲛ̄ⲛⲥⲟⲩⲣⲉ ϣⲁⲛⲧⲉϥ *(hair)* p. 91 ⲉⲓ ϣⲁⲡⲡⲉⲧⲟⲩⲁⲁⲃ (466):- ⲡⲡⲉⲧⲟⲩⲁⲁⲃ ⲇⲉ ⲅⲣⲏⲅⲱⲣⲓⲟⲥ ⲁϥⲥⲫⲣⲁⲅⲓⲍⲉ ⲙ̄ⲙⲟϥ Ϩⲙ̄ⲡⲙⲁⲉⲓⲛ ⲙ̄ⲡⲉⲥ̄ϯⲟⲥ· ⲁⲡⲉⲓⲛⲉ ⲉⲑⲟⲟⲩ ⲡⲱⲧ ⲥⲁⲃⲟⲗ ⲙ̄ⲙⲟϥ· ⲁⲡⲉⲓⲛⲉ ⲙ̄ⲡⲛⲟⲩⲧⲉ ⲕⲟⲧϥ̄ ⲉⲣⲟϥ ⲛ̄ⲕⲉⲥⲟⲡ· ⲁϥϯⲉⲟⲟⲩ ⲙ̄ⲡⲛⲟⲩⲧⲉ:-

---

1 Ϩⲁⲓⲉ for Ϩⲁⲉ.
2 ⲭⲁⲓⲟⲥ for the Greek κατάγαιος.
3 ⲉⲓⲣⲉ with the meaning *to pass*.
4 ⲉϥⲉⲛⲕⲟⲧⲕ for ⲉϥⲛ̄ⲕⲟⲧⲕ.
5 ⲁⲣⲟⲟⲩⲉ.
6 Ϩⲱⲥⲇⲉ for the Greek ὥστε.
7 ⲣ̄-ⲟⲩⲟⲉⲓϣ: *to spend time*
8 ⲧⲉⲣⲏⲇⲁⲧⲏⲥ for the Greek τερατώδης or τερατίας.

ⲁⲕⲛⲁⲩ ⲧⲉⲛⲟⲩ ϫⲉⲡⲉⲧⲛⲁϯⲉⲟⲟⲩ ⲙ̄ⲡⲛⲟⲩⲧⲉ ϣⲁⲣⲉⲡⲛⲟⲩⲧⲉ ϯⲉⲟⲟⲩ ⲛⲁϥ ⲛϭ̄ⲕⲟ[9] ⲙ̄ⲡⲉϥⲉⲓⲛⲉ ⲉϥⲧⲏϭ (412) ⲉⲣⲟϥ:- ⲉⲣϣⲁⲛⲡⲣⲱⲙⲉ ϩⲱⲱϥ ϯⲡⲉϥⲟⲩⲟⲓ ⲉⲡⲇⲓⲁⲃⲟⲗⲟⲥ· ϣⲁⲣⲉⲡⲇⲓⲁⲃⲟⲗⲟⲥ ⲕⲱ ⲛ̄ⲛⲉϥⲥⲙⲟⲧ ⲉⲧⲑⲟⲟⲩ[10] ϩⲓϫⲱϥ ⲕⲁⲧⲁⲑⲉ ⲛ̄ⲧⲁⲕⲙⲉⲉⲩⲉ ⲉⲣⲟⲥ· ϩⲁⲛⲉⲓⲙⲓⲛⲉ ⲛ̄ϩⲓⲕⲱⲛ ⲛ̄ⲣⲱⲙⲉ ⲉⲧϣⲟⲃⲉ:- ⲁⲕⲛⲁⲩ ⲉⲭⲁⲙ[11] ⲛ̄ⲧⲁϥϫⲓ ⲙ̄ⲡⲥⲁϩⲟⲩ ⲙ̄ⲡⲉϥⲉⲓⲱⲧ· ⲁϥϣⲱⲡⲉ ⲛⲉϥϭⲱϣ ⲙⲛ̄ⲡⲉϥⲥⲡⲉⲣⲙⲁ ϣⲁϩⲣⲁⲓ ⲉⲡⲟⲟⲩ ⲛ̄ϩⲟⲟⲩ (110)[12]:- ⲧⲁⲓⲧⲉ ⲑⲉ ⲛ̄ⲛⲉⲓⲕⲉⲙⲏⲏϣⲉ ⲙ̄ⲙⲓⲛⲉ ⲛ̄ⲣⲱⲙⲉ ⲛ̄ⲧⲁⲩⲉⲛⲡϣⲓⲃⲉ ⲛⲁⲩ ⲙⲁⲩⲁⲁⲩ:-

ⲛⲁⲓ ⲇⲉ ⲛ̄ⲧⲉⲣⲉⲡⲉⲭⲁⲗⲕⲩⲧⲱⲛ[13] ⲥⲱⲧⲙ̄ ⲉⲣⲟⲟⲩ ⲡⲉϫⲁϥ ϫⲉⲉⲓⲥⲟⲩⲙⲏⲏϣⲉ ⲛ̄ϩⲟⲟⲩ ⲉϫⲓⲛ̄ⲧⲁⲡϩ[ⲟϥ] ⲗⲟϫⲧ̄· ⲙ̄ⲡⲉⲓ[ⲉⲙ]ⲧⲟⲛ ϩⲙ̄ⲡⲁϣ[ⲓ]ⲡⲉ ϣⲁϩⲣⲁⲓ [ⲉⲡⲟ]ⲟⲩ ⲛ̄ϩⲟⲟⲩ:- ⲡⲉϫⲉⲡⲉⲭⲁⲗⲕⲩⲧⲱⲛ ϫⲉⲙ̄ⲡⲉⲣϭⲱⲛⲧ ⲉⲣⲟⲓ ⲧⲁϣⲓⲛⲉ (382) ⲙ̄ⲙⲟⲕ ϩⲁⲡⲉⲓⲕⲉϩⲱⲃ ⲉⲣⲉⲧⲁⲯⲩⲭⲏ ⲉⲡⲉⲓⲑⲩⲙⲉⲓ ⲉⲣⲟϥ (472):- ⲉⲃⲟⲗ ϫⲉⲁⲓⲥⲱⲧⲙ̄ (443) ϫⲉⲁⲩϥⲓ ⲛ̄ⲧⲁⲡⲉ ⲛⲓⲱϩⲁⲛⲛⲏⲥ ⲡ̄ⲃⲁⲡⲧⲓⲥⲧⲏⲥ

---

9 *Sic* for ⲛϭ̄ⲕⲁ-.
10 *Sic* for ⲉⲑⲟⲟⲩ.
11 Proper noun: Cham.
12 ⲉⲡⲟⲟⲩ ⲛ̄ϩⲟⲟⲩ: (*everyday*) *up till today*.
13 ⲭⲁⲗⲕⲩⲧⲱⲛ, for the Greek χαλκηδωνικός.

Shenoute, on the Ethiopian invasions

The text is taken from the edition by J. Leipoldt and W. Crum, *Sinuthii archimandritae vita et opera omnia*, Leipzig, 1908, vol. III, text nr. 21: *De Aethiopum invasionibus II*. A separate volume has the Latin translation.

ⲦⲞⲨ ⲀⲨⲦⲞⲨ[1].

ⲚϢⲰⲬⲠ ⲚⲚϢⲀϪⲈ ⲘⲠⲈⲒⲬⲰⲰⲘⲈ Ⲏ ⲠⲔⲈⲤⲈⲈⲠⲈ ⲈⲚⲦⲀⲚⲬⲞⲞⲨ[2] ⲀⲨⲰ ⲀⲚⲤⲀϨⲞⲨ ϨⲚⲦⲘⲈϨⲢⲞⲘⲠⲈ ⲤⲚⲦⲈ (087), ⲘⲚⲚⲤⲀⲦⲢⲈⲚⲔⲰⲦ (134) ⲘⲠⲒⲎⲒ ϨⲘⲠⲔⲀⲒⲢⲞⲤ ⲈⲚⲦⲀⲚⲂⲀⲢⲂⲀⲢⲞⲤ ϢⲰⲖ ϢⲀⲚⲦⲞⲨⲂⲰⲔ ⲈϨⲞⲨⲚ ⲈⲦⲠⲞⲖⲒⲤ ⲈⲦⲞⲨⲘⲞⲨⲦⲈ ⲈⲢⲞⲤ ϪⲈⲔⲞⲈⲒⲤ[3], ϨⲘⲠⲤⲎⲨ ⲈⲚⲦⲀⲠⲈⲒⲚⲞϬ ⲘⲘⲎⲎϢⲈ ϬⲞⲈⲒⲖⲈ ⲈⲢⲞⲚ (461) ⲈⲨⲠⲎⲦ ϨⲎⲦⲞⲨ ⲚⲚⲈϬⲞⲞϢⲈ ⲈⲦⲘⲘⲀⲨ ⲈⲚⲦⲀⲨϢⲞⲨϢⲞⲨ ⲘⲘⲞⲞⲨ ϨⲚⲞⲨϬⲞⲘ ⲈⲦⲂⲈⲦⲘⲚⲦⲀⲦϬⲞⲘ ⲚϨⲈⲚⲔⲞⲘⲈⲤ[4] ⲚϨⲈⲖⲖⲎⲚ[5] ⲈⲚⲤⲈⲤⲞⲞⲨⲚ ⲢⲰ ⲀⲚ ϨⲚⲦⲈⲨⲘⲚⲦⲀⲠⲒⲤⲦⲞⲤ ⲘⲠⲈⲚⲦⲀϤⲦⲀⲘⲒⲞⲞⲨ ⲀⲨⲰ ⲠⲈⲦⲚⲀϮϬⲞⲘ ⲚⲀⲨ Ⲓ̅Ⲥ̅. ⲘⲀⲖⲖⲞⲚ ⲆⲈ ⲚⲈⲚⲚⲞⲂⲈ ⲈⲦⲢϨⲞⲨⲞ ⲔⲒⲘ ⲈⲦⲞⲒⲔⲞⲨⲘⲈⲚⲎ ⲚⲦⲞⲞⲨ ⲚⲈⲦⲢⲠⲔⲈⲦⲞⲨⲚⲞⲤ ⲘⲘⲞⲞⲨ ⲈϨⲢⲀⲒ ⲈϪⲰⲚ. ⲈⲘⲘⲞⲚ[6]. ϨⲈⲚⲞⲨ ϨⲰⲰϤⲚⲈ ⲈⲠⲦⲎⲢϤ ⲚⲚⲀϨⲢⲘⲠⲚⲞⲨⲦⲈ; Ⲏ ⲈϤⲦⲰⲚ[7] ⲠⲈⲦϤⲒⲢⲞⲞⲨϢ ϨⲀⲚⲈϨⲂⲎⲨⲈ ⲘⲠⲚⲞⲨⲦⲈ ⲠⲞⲨⲀ ⲠⲞⲨⲀ ⲔⲀⲦⲀⲦⲈϤⲘⲒⲚⲈ ϪⲈⲈϤⲚⲀϮϬⲞⲘ ⲚⲀⲚ; ⲚⲒⲘ ⲠⲈⲦⲈⲢⲈⲠϪⲞⲈⲒⲤ (463) ⲠⲚⲞⲨⲦⲈ ⲚⲀϪⲚⲞⲨϤ ϨⲘⲠⲈϨⲞⲞⲨ ⲘⲠϨⲀⲠ ⲚϤϮⲖⲞⲄⲞⲤ ϨⲀⲠⲈⲚⲦⲀⲨⲦⲞϢϤ ⲈⲢⲞϤ; ⲀⲚⲞⲔⲠⲈ Ⲏ ⲔⲈⲞⲨⲀ ⲚⲦⲀϨⲈ[8]. ϨⲈⲚⲔⲈⲢⲢⲰⲞⲨⲚⲈ ⲚⲈⲚⲦⲀⲨϪⲒⲚⲈ[9] ⲚϨⲈⲚⲀⲢⲬⲎ Ⲏ ϨⲈⲚⲈⲜⲞⲨⲤⲒⲀ. ⲘⲘⲀⲦⲞⲈⲒⲚⲈ ⲚⲈⲦⲀⲢⲬⲈⲒ ⲦⲎⲢⲞⲨⲚⲈ, ⲞⲨ ⲘⲞⲚⲞⲚ ϪⲈⲚⲈⲚⲦⲀⲨⲦⲀⲚϨⲞⲨⲦⲞⲨ ⲈϨⲈⲚϨⲂⲎⲨⲈ ⲀⲨⲰ ϨⲈⲚⲮⲨⲬⲎ, ⲀⲖⲖⲀ ϢⲀϨⲢⲀⲒ ⲞⲚ ⲈⲚⲖⲀⲞⲤ. ⲠⲦⲂⲂⲞ ⲘⲠⲈⲚⲤⲰⲘⲀⲠⲈ ⲀⲨⲰ ⲠⲈⲚϨⲎⲦ. ⲦⲘⲚⲦϢⲀⲨ ⲘⲠⲄⲀⲘⲞⲤⲦⲈ. ⲠⲢⲞⲤⲔⲀⲢⲦⲈⲢⲈⲒⲠⲈ ⲈⲠⲈϢⲖⲎⲖ ⲘⲚϨⲰⲂ ⲚⲒⲘ ⲈⲦⲈⲢⲈⲚⲈⲄⲢⲀⲪⲎ ϨⲰⲚ ⲈⲦⲂⲎⲎⲦⲞⲨ. ⲦⲀⲒⲦⲈ ⲐⲈ ⲈⲦⲈⲚⲀⲈⲒⲀⲦⲞⲨ ⲚⲚⲈⲦⲚⲀϬⲚⲞⲨⲠⲀⲢⲢⲎⲤⲒⲀ ⲘⲠⲚⲀⲨ ⲚⲦⲀⲚⲀⲄⲔⲎ. ⲞⲨⲞⲈⲒ[10]

---

1 Greek *incipit*, meaning *of the same*. This writing was preceded by another text from Shenoute in the Codex.
2 ⲈⲚⲦⲀ for Ⲛ̅ⲦⲀ.
3 ⲔⲞⲒⲤ is the Coptic name of the town Cynopolis (*town of the dog*).
4 *Comes* is a Latin title attributed to the high functionaries of the State.
5 The Greek word ἕλλην (derived from the adjective ἑλληνικός) refers to the Greek as well as to the pagans in Coptic. (The same usage is attested for Byzantine Greek.)
6 Ⲙ̅ⲘⲞⲚ.
7 ⲦⲰⲚ for ⲦⲰⲞⲨⲚ.
8 Ⲛ̅-ⲦⲀ.ϨⲈ: *like me* (literally: *in my way*).
9 Ⲛ.ⲈⲚⲦⲀⲨ.ϪⲒ ⲚⲈ.
10 ⲞⲨⲞⲈⲒ: cry of sorrow.

ⲇⲉ ⲛⲁⲛ ⲁⲛⲟⲛ ⲛⲣⲱⲙⲉ ⲉⲧϥⲟ[11] ⲁⲛ ⲛⲣⲟⲟⲩϣ ⲛⲁⲩ, ϫⲉⲥⲉⲛⲏⲩ ⲉϩⲣⲁⲓ ⲉⲛϭⲓϫ ⲙⲡⲛⲟⲩⲧⲉ ⲏ ϫⲉϥⲛⲁϫⲛⲟⲩⲛ {...

---

11 ϥⲟ for ϥⲓ.

Shenoute, On women's piety

The following text is taken from the edition of J. Leipoldt & E. W. Crum, *Sinuthii archimandritae vita et opera omnia*, t. IV, Louvain 1954, text nr. 52: *De pietate feminarum*. A separate volume has the Latin translation.

... ⲉⲧⲉ} ⲧⲛϣⲟⲡⲟⲩ ⲉⲡⲭⲓⲛϫⲏ, ⲉⲧⲉⲧⲛⲙⲏⲛ ⲉⲃⲟⲗ ϩⲛⲙⲙⲁ ⲉⲧⲙⲉϩ ⲛⲁⲡⲁⲧⲏ ⲛⲓⲙ ϫⲓⲛϩⲧⲟⲟⲩⲉ ϣⲁⲣⲟⲩϩⲉ, ⲉⲧⲉⲧⲛⲥⲓ ⲁⲛ ⲛⲥⲱⲧⲙ ⲁⲩⲱ ⲛⲛⲁⲩ ⲉⲛⲉⲧⲟ ⲛⲏⲧⲛ ⲛⲟⲥⲉ, ϣⲁϩⲣⲁⲓ ⲉⲛⲥⲕⲟⲡⲧⲓⲁ¹ ⲙⲛⲛⲑⲉⲁⲧⲣⲟⲛ. ⲧⲛⲟⲃϣ ⲇⲉ ϩⲱⲱϥ² ⲉⲛⲉϩⲃⲏⲩⲉ ⲙⲡⲉⲛⲱⲛϩ, ⲛⲁⲓ ⲉⲧⲛⲛⲁϭⲛⲧⲟⲩ ⲉⲣⲟⲛ ⲙⲡⲛⲁⲩ ⲛⲧⲁⲛⲁⲅⲕⲏ. ⲁⲛⲁⲩ ⲇⲉ ⲟⲛ ⲉⲑⲉ ⲉⲧⲉⲧⲛⲁⲙⲁϩⲧⲉ ⲙⲙⲱⲧⲛ ϩⲁⲧϩⲙⲙⲉ ⲙⲡⲧⲙϩⲟ ⲉⲧϩⲛⲛⲥⲓⲟⲟⲩⲛ ⲉⲧⲃⲉⲧⲟⲫⲉⲗⲓⲁ³ ⲛⲛⲥⲱⲙⲁ. ⲉⲛϣⲁⲛⲉⲓ ⲇⲉ ϩⲱⲱϥ ⲉⲛⲉⲕⲕⲗⲏⲥⲓⲁ, ⲡⲙⲁ ⲙⲡⲉⲓⲱ ⲉⲃⲟⲗ ⲛⲛⲉⲛⲛⲟⲃⲉ ⲁⲩⲱ ⲧⲟⲫⲉⲗⲓⲁ ⲛⲛⲉⲛⲯⲩⲭⲏ, ⲧⲉⲛⲟ⁴ ⲛϩⲏⲧ ϣⲏⲙ ⲉⲧⲙϥⲓ (118) ⲉⲣⲟⲛ, ϣⲁⲛⲧⲛⲥⲱⲧⲙ ⲉⲛⲗⲟⲅⲟⲥ ⲙⲡⲛⲟⲩⲧⲉ, ⲛⲁⲓ ⲉⲧϯⲕⲃⲟ ⲛⲛⲉⲛϩⲏⲧ. ⲁⲛⲁⲩ ⲉⲣⲟⲛ ⲉⲛⲟⲩⲱⲙ, ⲱ⁵ ⲛⲣⲱⲙⲉ, ⲉⲩϣⲁⲛⲧⲁϩⲙⲉⲛ ⲉⲩϯⲡⲛⲟⲛ⁶, ϫⲉⲛⲟ ⲛⲁϣ ⲛϩⲉ⁷. ⲛ̄ⲟⲩⲱⲙ ⲛⲟⲩⲱϣ ⲉϩⲁⲣⲡⲁⲍⲉ ⲛⲛⲕⲁ ⲛⲓⲙ ϩⲛⲟⲩⲙⲛⲧⲁⲧⲥⲓ. ⲕⲁⲛ⁸ ⲙⲁⲣⲛϣⲓⲡⲉ ϩⲏⲧⲟⲩ ⲛⲛⲓϣⲁϫⲉ ⲛⲧⲛϯⲡⲉⲛϩⲏⲧ ⲉⲛⲇⲓⲕⲁⲓⲱⲙⲁ ⲙⲡⲛⲟⲩⲧⲉ ⲁⲩⲱ ⲛⲉϥⲡⲣⲟⲥⲧⲁⲅⲙⲁ ⲙⲛⲛⲉϥⲛⲟⲙⲟⲥ ⲉⲧⲟⲩⲧⲱϩⲙ ⲙⲙⲟⲛ ⲉⲥⲱⲧⲙ ⲉⲣⲟⲟⲩ ϩⲛⲧⲉⲕⲕⲗⲏⲥⲓⲁ. ⲙⲡⲣⲧⲣⲉⲩⲡⲣⲟⲥⲉⲭⲉ ⲉⲣⲟⲛ ϩⲓⲧⲛⲛⲉⲧⲧⲱϩⲙ ⲛⲉⲃⲟⲗ⁹ ϩⲛⲧⲡⲉ ⲛⲥⲉϭⲛⲧⲛ ⲉⲣⲉⲛⲉⲛϩⲏⲧ ⲙⲛⲛⲉⲛⲯⲩⲭⲏ ϣⲟⲩⲉⲓⲧ ⲁⲩⲱ ⲉⲩϩⲕⲁⲉⲓⲧ ϩⲛⲛⲁⲙⲡⲏⲩⲉ. ⲕⲁⲓⲧⲟⲓ ⲛⲁϣⲱⲟⲩ ⲛϭⲓⲛⲁⲅⲁⲑⲟⲛ ⲉⲧⲕⲏ ⲉϩⲣⲁⲓ. ⲁⲛⲟⲛ ⲇⲉ ⲧⲉⲛⲁⲙⲉⲗⲉⲓ ⲉⲃⲟⲗ, ϫⲉⲉⲥⲉⲥⲟⲟⲩⲛ ⲛϭⲓⲛⲉⲧⲟⲩⲁⲁⲃ, ϫⲉⲛⲁϣⲉⲛⲉⲧⲛⲁ ⲉϩⲟⲩⲛ ⲉⲡⲏⲓ ⲙⲡⲛⲟⲩⲧⲉ, ⲉⲣⲉⲡⲉⲩϩⲏⲧ ⲥϭⲏⲣ, ⲉⲙⲉⲩⲡⲣⲟⲥⲉⲭⲉ ⲛⲟⲩⲉϩⲥⲁϩⲛⲉ ⲉⲧⲟⲩϩⲱⲛ ⲙⲙⲟⲟⲩ ⲉⲧⲟⲟⲧⲟⲩ. ⲙⲁⲣⲛⲥⲡⲟⲩⲇⲁⲍⲉⲃⲉ ⲉⲛⲉⲧⲛⲛⲁϯϩⲏⲩ ⲉⲣⲟⲟⲩ, ⲁⲩⲱ ⲙⲡⲣⲧⲣⲉⲡⲟⲩⲁ ⲡⲟⲩⲁ ⲙⲙⲟⲛ¹⁰ ϣⲓⲛⲉ ⲛⲥⲁϩⲉⲛⲗⲟⲉⲓϭⲉ, ϩⲱⲥ ⲛⲥⲣⲟϥⲧ ⲉϩⲉⲛⲡⲉⲧϣⲟⲩⲉⲓⲧ¹¹, ⲟⲩⲇⲉ

---

1 ⲥⲕⲟⲡⲧⲓⲁ is an unknown Greek word probably derived from σκέπτω, *to mock*. H. Wiesmann (CSCO, script. coptici 12) translates it by the Latin *ludibria* (*mockery*).
2 ϩⲱⲱϥ functions here as an adverb and means *even*.
3 ⲟⲫⲉⲗⲓⲁ for the Greek ὠφέλεια.
4 Read ⲧⲛ.ⲟ.
5 ὦ introduces a Greek vocative.
6 ϯⲡⲛⲟⲛ for the Greek δεῖπνον.
7 ϫⲉ introduces an indirect question here.
8 The editor suggests that we omit ⲕⲁⲛ (cf. 431), because it seems unappropriate before the jussive.
9 Sic. The editors suggest that we read ϩⲓⲧⲛⲛⲉⲧⲧⲁϩⲙⲛ ⲉⲃⲟⲗ.
10 ⲛ-, ⲙ̄ⲙⲟ⸗ can introduce a partitive genitive (cf. 183).

ⲘⲠⲢⲠⲀⲢⲀⲒⲦⲈⲒ ⲘⲠⲦⲰϨⲘ ⲈⲦⲤⲘⲞⲚⲦ ⲘⲠⲆⲒⲠⲚⲞⲚ[12] ⲘⲠⲈⲚⲞⲨϪⲀⲒ ⲈⲦⲂⲈⲠⲈⲘⲦⲞⲚ ⲘⲠⲔⲞⲤⲘⲞⲤ ⲈⲦⲚⲀⲦⲀⲔⲞ, ⲚⲐⲈ ⲚⲦⲀⲠⲈⲨⲀⲄⲄⲈⲖⲒⲞⲚ ϪⲞⲞⲤ, ϪⲈⲞⲨⲀ ⲘⲈⲚ ⲀϤⲠⲀⲢⲀⲒⲦⲈⲒ ⲈⲦⲂⲈϨⲈⲚⲤⲞⲈⲒϢ ⲚⲈϨⲈ, ⲔⲈⲞⲨⲀ ⲈⲦⲂⲈⲞⲨⲤⲰϢⲈ, ⲔⲈⲞⲨⲀ ϪⲈⲀⲒϨⲘⲞⲞⲤ ⲘⲚⲞⲨⲤϨⲒⲘⲈ. ⲠⲀⲒ ⲆⲈ ϯⲘⲈⲈⲨⲈ ϪⲈϤⲂⲀⲒⲎⲨ ⲚϨⲞⲨⲞ ⲈⲠⲔⲈⲤⲈⲠⲈ[13], ⲈⲂⲞⲖ ϪⲈⲠⲈⲦⲈϢϢⲈⲠⲈ (443) ⲈⲦⲢⲈϤϪⲒ ⲚⲦⲔⲈⲤϨⲒⲘⲈ ⲈⲠⲆⲒⲠⲚⲞⲚ· ⲚⲦⲞϤ ⲆⲈ ⲀϤϨⲞⲨⲢⲰϤ ⲘⲀⲨⲀⲀϤ ⲚⲚⲀⲄⲀⲐⲞⲚ ⲚϢⲀⲈⲚⲈϨ. ⲞⲨ ⲠⲈⲦⲞ ⲚϨⲢⲞⲠ ⲚⲀⲔ; ⲀϪⲒⲤ ⲈⲢⲞⲒ. ⲘⲎ ⲞⲨⲤⲰⲘⲀ ⲚⲞⲨⲰⲦ ⲀⲚⲠⲈ ⲠⲢⲰⲘⲈ ⲘⲚⲦⲈϤⲤϨⲒⲘⲈ; ⲀⲨⲰ ⲈⲦⲂⲈⲞⲨ ⲚⲄⲚⲀⲈⲒ ⲀⲚ ⲈⲠⲆⲒⲠⲚⲞⲚ, ⲚⲦⲞⲔ ⲀⲨⲰ ⲚⲦⲞⲤ: ⲀⲢⲀ ⲘⲈⲔⲞⲨⲰⲘ ϨⲚⲚⲒⲞⲈⲒⲔ ⲚⲞⲨⲰⲦ ⲚⲘⲘⲀⲤ ⲀⲨⲰ ⲚⲒϬⲒⲚⲞⲨⲰⲘ ⲚⲞⲨⲰⲦ; ⲈⲦⲂⲈⲞⲨ ⲚⲤⲚⲀⲈⲒ ⲀⲚ ⲚⲘⲘⲀⲔ ⲈⲠⲆⲒⲠⲚⲞⲚ ⲀⲨⲰ ⲠⲀⲢⲒⲤⲦⲰⲚ[14] ⲘⲠⲈⲬ̅Ⲥ̅; ⲀⲢⲀ ⲚⲤⲢⲬⲢⲒⲀ ⲀⲚ ⲚⲦⲞⲤ ⲈϢⲖⲎⲖ ⲀⲨⲰ ⲈⲤⲰⲦⲘ ⲈⲠⲖⲞⲄⲞⲤ ⲀⲨⲰ ⲈⲢⲈⲨⲤⲈⲂⲎⲤ ϨⲚϨⲰⲂ ⲚⲒⲘ; Ⲏ ⲈⲢⲈⲦⲘⲚⲦⲈⲢⲞ[15] ⲚⲘⲠⲎⲨⲈ ⲤⲂⲦⲰⲦ ⲚⲚϨⲞⲞⲨⲦ ⲘⲀⲨⲀⲀⲨ, ⲈⲚⲈⲤⲤⲂⲦⲰⲦ ⲀⲚ ⲚⲚⲈϨⲒⲞⲘⲈ ⲈⲦⲢⲈⲨⲂⲰⲔ ⲈϨⲞⲨⲚ ⲈⲢⲞⲤ; ⲘⲈϢⲀⲔ ⲚⲦⲞⲔ, ⲠⲈⲦⲈⲢⲈⲠⲈⲔϨⲎⲦ ϨⲞⲢϢ Ⲏ ⲈϤⲘⲈϨ ⲈⲦⲘⲦⲢⲈⲔⲞⲨⲰⲘ (449) ⲈⲂⲞⲖ ϨⲘⲠⲆⲒⲠⲚⲞⲚ ⲘⲠⲈⲬ̅Ⲥ̅, ⲈⲀⲔⲚⲦⲀϤⲞⲢⲘⲎ[16] ⲈϪⲚⲦⲈⲤϨⲒⲘⲈ. ⲚⲀⲘⲈ ⲚⲐⲈ ⲈⲦⲈⲞⲨⲚϨⲀϨ ⲚϨⲞⲞⲨⲦ ⲈϢⲀⲨϢⲰⲠⲈ ⲚϪⲰⲰⲢⲈ ⲔⲀⲦⲀⲔⲀⲒⲢⲞⲤ ⲀⲨⲰ ⲈⲚⲀϢⲈⲚϨⲒⲞⲘⲈ ⲈⲦⲢϬⲰⲂ, ⲞⲨⲚϨⲀϨ ⲞⲚ ⲚⲤϨⲒⲘⲈ ⲈϢⲀⲨⲢϪⲰⲰⲢⲈ ⲔⲀⲦⲀⲔⲀⲒⲢⲞⲤ ⲀⲨⲰ ⲚⲤⲈϪⲢⲞ, ⲚⲀϢⲈⲚϨⲞⲞⲨⲦ ⲞⲚ ⲈⲦⲞⲨϪⲢⲞ ⲈⲢⲞⲞⲨ (463) ⲀⲨⲰ ⲈⲦⲞ ⲚϬⲰⲂ. ⲠⲒⲀⲄⲰⲚ ⲚⲞⲨⲰⲦ ⲠⲈⲦⲔⲎ ⲈϨⲢⲀⲒ ⲚⲚϨⲞⲞⲨⲦ ⲘⲚⲚⲈϨⲒⲞⲘⲈ, ⲀⲨⲰ ⲠⲈⲔⲖⲞⲘ ⲈϤϢⲞⲞⲠ ϨⲒⲞⲨⲤⲞⲠ ⲚⲚϨⲞⲞⲨⲦ ⲘⲚⲚⲈϨⲒⲞⲘⲈ ⲈⲦⲚⲀⲘⲞⲨⲚ ⲈⲂⲞⲖ. ⲘⲠⲢⲦⲢⲈⲞⲨⲀ ⲤⲰⲦⲘ ⲈⲢⲞϤ ϨⲘⲠⲈⲨⲀⲄⲄⲈⲖⲒⲞⲚ, ϪⲈⲠⲈϪⲈⲔⲈⲞⲨⲀ, ϪⲈⲈⲦⲂⲈⲠⲀⲒ ⲀⲒϨⲘⲞⲞⲤ ⲘⲚⲞⲨⲤϨⲒⲘⲈ· ⲘⲘⲚϬⲞⲘ ⲘⲘⲞⲒ ⲈⲈⲒ. ⲚⲐⲈ ⲞⲚ ⲚⲦⲀⲠϪⲞⲈⲒⲤ ϪⲞⲞⲤ, ϪⲈⲔⲀⲦⲀⲐⲈ ⲚⲦⲀⲤϢⲰⲠⲈ ϨⲚⲚⲈϨⲞⲞⲨ ⲚⲚⲰϨⲈ[17], ⲈⲨϪⲒⲤϨⲒⲘⲈ ⲈⲨϨⲘⲞⲞⲤ ⲘⲚϨⲀⲒ, ⲚⲤⲈⲘⲈⲈⲨⲈ ϪⲈⲈϤⲤⲰϢ ⲘⲠϪⲒⲤϨⲒⲘⲈ ⲀⲨⲰ ⲈϤⲚⲞⲨϪ ⲈⲂⲞⲖ ⲘⲠⲄⲀⲘⲞⲤ· ⲚⲦⲞϤ ⲄⲀⲢ ⲠⲈⲚⲦⲀϤⲦⲀⲘⲒⲞ ϪⲒⲚⲚϢⲞⲢⲠ ⲚⲞⲨϨⲞⲞⲨⲦ ⲘⲚⲞⲨⲤϨⲒⲘⲈ· ⲀⲖⲖⲀ ⲀϤϪⲠⲒⲞ ⲚⲚⲈⲪⲀⲢⲒⲤⲤⲀⲒⲞⲤ

---

11 The substantivated relative Ⲡ.ⲈⲦ.ϢⲞⲨⲈⲒⲦ is considered as a noun and can thus have the indefinite article, ϨⲈⲚ.
12 ⲆⲒⲠⲚⲞⲚ for the Greek δεῖπνον.
13 ⲤⲈⲈⲠⲈ.
14 ⲀⲢⲒⲤⲦⲰⲚ for the Greek ἄριστον.
15 Ⲧ.ⲘⲚ̅Ⲧ-Ⲣ̅ⲢⲞ.
16 Ⲛ̅Ⲧ⸗ is the prenominal form of ⲈⲒⲚⲈ.
17 ⲚⲰϨⲈ is a proper noun: Noah.

ϢⲀϤϪⲞⲞⲤ, ϪⲈⲠⲈⲚⲦⲀϤⲤⲰⲚⲦ ϪⲒⲚⲚϢⲞⲢⲠ ⲚⲦⲀϤⲦⲀⲘⲒⲈⲞⲨϨⲞⲞⲨⲦ ⲘⲚⲞⲨⲤϨⲒⲘⲈ· ⲚⲦⲞϤ ⲄⲀⲢ ⲚⲀⲘⲈⲠⲈ ⲠⲆⲒⲘⲒⲞⲨⲢⲄⲞⲤ ⲘⲠⲦⲎⲢϤ, ⲈϤⲞ ⲚⲞⲨⲀ ⲚⲞⲨⲰⲦ ⲘⲚⲠⲈϤⲈⲒⲰⲦ ϪⲒⲚⲚϢⲞⲢⲠ. ⲀⲘⲈⲖⲈⲒ ϤϪⲰ ⲘⲘⲞⲤ ϪⲈⲠⲈⲚⲦⲀⲠⲚⲞⲨⲦⲈ ϢⲞⲚϤ[18] ⲘⲠⲢⲦⲢⲈⲢⲰⲘⲈ ⲠⲞⲢϪϤ. ⲀⲖⲖⲀ ⲈϤⲂⲚⲀⲢⲒⲔⲈ ⲈⲠⲈⲦⲞⲨⲀⲘⲀϨⲦⲈ ⲘⲘⲞϤ ϨⲒⲦⲚⲠⲞⲨⲰϢ ⲚⲚϨⲨⲆⲞⲚⲎ[19] ⲘⲠⲤⲰⲘⲀ, ⲈⲦⲘⲦⲢⲈϤⲈⲒ ⲈⲠⲀⲢⲒⲤⲦⲞⲚ ⲘⲘⲈ, ⲈⲂⲞⲖ ϪⲈⲠⲈⲦⲞ ⲘⲘⲞⲒϨⲨⲆⲞⲚⲎ[20] ⲚϤⲘⲠϢⲀ ⲀⲚ ⲘⲠⲆⲒⲠⲚⲞⲚ ⲈⲦⲘ̄ⲘⲀⲨ ⲞⲨⲆⲈ ⲚϤⲘⲠϢⲀ ⲀⲚ ⲘⲠⲈⲚⲦⲀϤⲤⲂⲦⲰⲦϤ ⲀⲨⲰ ⲠⲈⲦⲦⲰϨⲘ ⲘⲘⲞϤ ⲈⲢⲞϤ ⲒⲤ̄ ⲔⲀⲦⲀⲠⲈϤϢⲀϪⲈ ⲘⲘⲈ ⲘⲀⲨⲀⲀϤ. Ⲛ̄ⲐⲈ ⲚⲦⲀϤϪⲞⲞⲤ ⲚⲦⲞϤ ⲠϪⲞⲈⲒⲤ, ϪⲈⲚⲈⲦⲦⲀϨⲘ ⲚⲤⲈⲘⲠϢⲀ ⲀⲚ. ⲚⲀϢ ⲄⲀⲢ ⲚϨⲈ ⲈⲨⲚⲀⲢⲂⲞⲖ ⲈⲠⲈϪⲠⲒⲞ ⲚϬⲒⲚⲈⲦⲤⲰϢϤ ⲚⲦⲘⲚⲦⲤⲘⲚⲞⲤ[21] ⲘⲠⲄⲀⲘⲞⲤ; ⲀⲚⲀⲨ ⲈⲚⲈⲚⲦⲀⲨⲈⲢⲀⲚⲀϤ[22] ⲘⲠⲚⲞⲨⲦⲈ ϨⲚⲞⲨⲘⲈ. ⲈⲨⲔⲞⲒⲚⲞⲚⲈⲒ ⲈⲠⲄⲀⲘⲞⲤ ⲀⲨⲰ ⲤⲈⲦⲂⲀⲒⲞ ⲀⲚ ⲘⲠⲈⲬⲠⲈϢⲎⲢⲈ. ⲤⲈⲤⲘⲀⲘⲀⲀⲦ[23] ⲄⲀⲢ ϨⲚⲚⲈⲨϨⲂⲎⲨⲈ ⲦⲨⲢⲞⲨ, ⲈⲒⲦⲈ ⲈⲨϪⲒⲤϨⲒⲘⲈ, ⲈⲒⲦⲈ ⲈⲨϨⲘⲞⲞⲤ ⲘⲚϨⲀⲒ, ⲈⲒⲦⲈ ⲈⲨϪⲞ, ⲈⲒⲦⲈ ⲈⲨⲰⲖ, ⲈⲒⲦⲈ ϨⲚϨⲰⲂ ⲚⲒⲘ ⲚⲦⲀⲠⲚⲞⲨⲦⲈ ⲤⲞⲚⲦⲞⲨ ϪⲒⲚⲚϢⲞⲢⲠ. ⲀⲖⲖⲀ ϨⲚⲞⲨϢⲒ ⲘⲘⲈ. ϨⲈⲚⲈⲂⲒⲎⲚ ⲆⲈ ϨⲚϨⲰⲂ ⲚⲒⲘⲚⲈ ⲚⲀⲒ ⲈⲦⲚⲀⲈⲠⲒⲬⲈⲢⲒ ⲈⲚⲈⲦⲈⲘⲈϢϢⲈ (456), ϪⲈⲘⲠⲞⲨⲤⲞⲨⲚⲠⲚⲞⲨⲦⲈ ⲚⲦⲀϤⲦⲀⲘⲒⲞⲞⲨ, ⲚⲀⲒ ⲈⲦⲈⲞⲨⲚⲞⲨⲔⲀⲦⲀⲔⲖⲎⲤⲘⲞⲤ ⲚⲞⲢⲄⲎ ϨⲒϬⲰⲚⲦ ⲚⲀⲈⲒ ⲈϨⲢⲀⲒ ⲈϪⲰⲞⲨ, ⲚⲐⲈ ⲚⲚⲒⲀⲦⲚⲞⲨⲦⲈ ⲘⲠⲈⲨⲞⲈⲒϢ ⲚⲦⲀⲠⲔⲀⲦⲀⲔⲖⲎⲤⲘⲞⲤ ⲘⲘⲞⲞⲨ ⲈⲒ ⲀϤⲦⲀⲔⲞⲞⲨ.

---

18 ϢⲞⲚϤ⳿ϥ.
19 ϨⲨⲆⲞⲚⲎ for the Greek ἡδονή.
20 Ⲙ.ⲘⲀⲒ-ϨⲨⲆⲞⲚⲎ.
21 ⲤⲘⲚⲞⲤ for the Greek σεμνός.
22 ⲢⲢ̄-ⲀⲚⲀ⳿ϥ.
23 ⲤⲘⲀⲘⲀⲀⲦ is the stative of ⲤⲘⲞⲨ.

The three steles of Seth (NHC VII, 5)

The following Text has been taken from P. Claude, *Les trois stèles de Seth* (Bibliothèque Copte de Nag Hammadi, section Textes 8), Québec 1983. In this edition, the text is accompanied by a French translation.

P. 118

10 ΠΟΥѠΝϨ ΕΒΟΛ ΝΤΕ ΔѠCΙΘΕ
ΟC[1] ΝΤΕ ΤϢΟΜΤΕ[2] ΝCΤΗΛΗ
ΝΤΕ CΗΘ· ΠΙѠΤ ΝΤΕ ΤΓΕΝΕΑ
ΕΤΟΝϨ ΑΥѠ ΝΑΤΚΙΜ ΝΑΙ Ν
ΤΑϥΝΑΥ ΕΡΟΟΥ ΑΥѠ ΑϥCΟΥѠ

15 ΝΟΥ· ΑΥѠ ΕΤΑϥΟϢΟΥ ΑϥΡ
ΠΕΥΜΕΕΥΕ· ΑΥѠ ΑϥΤΑΑΥ
ΝΝΙCѠΤΠ ΕΥϢΟΟΠ ΜΠΙΡΗ
ΤΕ· ΚΑΤΑ ΘΕ ΕΤΕ ΝΕΥCϨ
ΟΥΤ[3] ΜΠΙΜΑ ΕΤΜΜΑΥ· ΟΥ

20 ΜΗΗϢΕ ΝCΟΠ ΑΕΙΡ ϢΒΗΡ Ν
ΤΕΟΟΥ[4] ΜΝ ΝΙϬΟΜ· ΑΥѠ ΑΙΡ
ΜΠϢΑ ΕΒΟΛ ϨΙΤΟΟΤΟΥ ΝΝΙ
ΜΝΤΝΟϬ ΝΑΤΤϢΙ ΕΡΟΟΥ·
ΕΥϢΟΟΠ ΔΕ ΝΤϨΕ· ΤϢΟ

25 ΡΠ ΝCΤΗΛΗ ΝΤΕ CΗΘ· ΤCΜΟΥ
ΕΡΟΚ ΠΙѠΤ ΠΙΓΕΡΑΔΑΜΑ[5]· Α
ΝΟΚ ϨΑ[6] ΠΕΤΕ ΠѠΚ ΝϢΗΡΕ·
ΕΜΜΑΧΑ CΗΘ· ΠΑΙ ΝΤΑΚΧΠΟϥ
ϨΝ ΟΥΜΝΤΑΤΜΙCΕ ΕΥCΜΟΥ

---

1 ΔѠCΙΘΕΟC is a proper name: Dositheos..
2 In this text the dialectical variants ΠΙ, Τ, ΝΙ φορ the definite article ΠΕ, ΤΕ, ΝΕ are used.
3 CϨΗΟΥΤ is a dialectal variant for CΗϨ.
4 Ν-Ν.Τ-ΕΟΟΥ.
5 ΓΕΡΑΔΑΜΑ is a proper noun: Geradamas.
6 ϨΑ signifies in this context *being, in the quality of*.

30 ⲛ̄ⲧⲉ ⲡⲉⲛⲛⲟⲩⲧⲉ ϫⲉ ⲁⲛⲟⲕ
ⲡⲉⲧⲉ ⲡⲱⲕ ⲛ̄ϣⲏⲣⲉ· ⲁⲩⲱ ⲛ̄

P. 119

ⲧⲟⲕ ⲡⲉ ⲡⲁⲛⲟⲩⲥ ⲡⲁⲓⲱⲧ· ⲁⲩⲱ
ⲁⲛⲟⲕ ⲙⲉⲛ ⲁⲉⲓϫⲟ ⲁⲩⲱ ⲁⲉⲓϫⲡⲟ
ⲛ̄ⲧⲟⲕ ⲇ[ⲉ] ⲁⲕ[ⲛ]ⲁⲩ ⲉⲛⲓⲙⲛ̄ⲧⲛⲟϭ
ⲁⲕⲁϩⲉⲣⲁⲧⲕ̄ [ⲉ]ⲕⲉ[7] ⲛ̄ⲁⲧⲱϫⲛ̄· †
5 ⲥⲙⲟⲩ ⲉⲣⲟⲕ [ⲡⲓ]ⲱⲧ· ⲥⲙⲟⲩ ⲉⲣⲟⲓ
ⲡⲓⲱⲧ· ⲉⲓϣ[ⲟ]ⲟⲡ ⲉⲧⲃⲏⲏⲧⲕ̄·
ⲉⲕϣⲟⲟⲡ ⲉ[ⲧ]ⲃⲉ ⲡⲛⲟⲩⲧⲉ· ⲉ
ⲧⲃⲏⲏⲧⲕ̄ †ϣⲟⲟⲡ ϩⲁⲧⲟⲟⲧϥ̄ ⲙ̄
ⲡⲏ ⲉⲧⲙ̄ⲙⲁⲩ· ⲛ̄ⲧⲕ̄ ⲟⲩⲟⲉⲓⲛ
10 ⲉⲕⲛⲁⲩ ⲉⲩⲟⲩⲟⲉⲓⲛ· ⲁⲕⲟⲩⲱ
ⲛ̄ϩ ⲛ̄ⲛⲟⲩⲟⲉⲓⲛ ⲉⲃⲟⲗ· ⲛ̄ⲧⲕ̄ ⲟⲩ
ⲙⲓⲣⲱⲑⲉⲁⲥ[8]· ⲛ̄ⲧⲟⲕ ⲡⲉ ⲡⲁⲙⲓⲣⲱ
ⲑⲉⲟⲥ· †ⲥⲙⲟⲩ ⲉⲣⲟⲕ ⲛ̄ⲑⲉ ⲛ̄
ⲟⲩⲛⲟⲩⲧⲉ· †ⲥⲙⲟⲩ ⲉⲧⲉⲕ
15 ⲙⲛ̄ⲧⲛⲟⲩⲧⲉ· ⲟⲩⲛⲟϭ ⲡⲉ ⲡⲓⲁ
ⲅⲁⲑⲟⲥ ⲛ̄ⲁⲩⲧⲟⲅⲉⲛⲏⲥ ⲉⲧⲁϥ
ϩⲉⲣⲁⲧϥ̄[9] ⲡⲛⲟⲩⲧⲉ ⲉⲧⲁϥⲣ̄ ϣⲟⲣⲡ̄
ⲛ̄ⲁϩⲉⲣⲁⲧϥ...

P. 121

ⲧⲛ̄ⲥⲙⲟⲩ ⲉⲣⲟⲕ ϩⲛ̄ {ⲟ}ⲩⲙⲛ̄ⲧϣⲁ
ⲉⲛⲉϩ· ⲧⲛ̄ⲥⲙⲟⲩ ⲉⲣⲟⲕ ⲉⲧⲁⲛ
ⲛⲟⲩϩⲙ̄ [ⲉⲃ]ⲟ[ⲗ] ϩⲁ ⲛⲓⲕⲁ{ⲧ}ⲁ ⲟⲩⲁ[10]

---

7 ⲉ is a dialectal variant of the stative of ⲉⲓⲣⲉ (ⲟ).
8 ⲙⲓⲣⲟⲑⲉⲁⲥ and ⲙⲓⲣⲱⲑⲉⲟⲥ are proper nouns.
9 In some dialects the form ⲉⲧ is used for the relative conversion of the past (instead of ⲛ̄ⲧⲁ-).
10 The expression ⲕⲁⲧⲁ ⲟⲩⲁ here means *individually*.

ⲛ̄ⲧⲉⲗⲓⲟⲥ· ⲛ̄[ⲧⲉ]ⲗⲓⲟⲥ ⲉⲧⲃⲏⲏ

5   ⲧⲕ̄· ⲛⲏ ⲉⲧⲁ[ⲩⲣ̄] ⲧⲉⲗⲓⲟⲥ ⲛ̄ⲙⲙⲁⲕ·
ⲡⲏ ⲉⲧϫⲏⲕ [ⲡ]ⲏ ⲉⲧⲉ ϣⲁϥϫⲱⲕ
ⲡⲓⲧⲉⲗⲓⲟⲥ ⲉⲃⲟⲗ ϩⲓⲧⲛ̄ ⲛⲁⲓ ⲧⲏⲣⲟⲩ·
ⲡⲁⲓ ⲉⲧⲉⲓⲛⲉ[11] ϩⲙ̄ ⲙⲁ ⲛⲓⲙ· ⲡⲓϣⲙ̄ⲛ̄ⲧ
ϩⲟⲟⲩⲧ· ⲁⲕⲁϩⲉⲣⲁⲧⲕ̄· ⲁⲕⲣ̄ ϣⲟ

10 ⲣ̄ⲡ̄ ⲛ̄ⲁϩⲉⲣⲁⲧⲕ̄· ⲁⲕⲡⲱϣ ϩⲙ̄ ⲙⲁ
ⲛⲓⲙ ⲁⲕϭⲱ ⲉⲕⲉ ⲛ̄ⲟⲩⲁ· ⲁⲩⲱ
ⲛⲏ ⲉⲧⲁⲕⲟⲩⲁϣⲟⲩ ⲁⲕⲛⲁϩⲙⲟⲩ·
ⲕⲟⲩⲱϣ ⲇⲉ ⲉⲧⲣⲉⲩⲛⲟⲩϩⲙ̄
ⲛ̄ϭⲓ ⲛⲏ ⲧⲏⲣⲟⲩ ⲉⲧⲙ̄ⲡϣⲁ· ⲛ̄ⲧⲕ̄

15 ⲟⲩⲧⲉⲗⲓⲟⲥ ⲛ̄ⲧⲕ̄ ⲟⲩⲧⲉⲗⲓⲟⲥ
ⲛ̄ⲧⲕ̄ ⲟⲩⲧⲉⲗⲓⲟⲥ: †ϣⲟⲣⲡ̄

    ⲛ̄ⲥⲧⲏⲗⲏ ⲛ̄ⲧⲉ ⲥⲏⲑ:

---

11 *Who is similar (to himself)*.

The Gospel of Mary (BG 1)

This text is taken from the edition by A. Pasquier, *L'Évangile selon Marie (BG 1)* (Bibliothèque copte de Nag Hammadi, section « textes » 10), Québec 1983. There is a French translation of the text in this volume.

P. 9

5 ⲚⲦⲀⲢⲈϤϪⲈ[1] ⲚⲀⲒ ⲀϤⲂⲰⲔ ⲚⲦⲞⲞⲨ ⲆⲈ
ⲚⲈⲨⲢⲖⲨⲠⲈⲒ ⲀⲨⲢⲒⲘⲈ ⲘⲠϢⲀ ⲈⲨ
ϪⲰ ⲘⲘⲞⲤ ϪⲈ ⲚⲚⲀϢ Ⲛ̄ⲤⲈ ⲈⲚⲚⲀⲂⲰⲔ
ϢⲀ Ⲛ̄ϨⲈⲐⲚⲞⲤ Ⲛ̄ⲦⲚ̄ⲦⲀϢⲈⲞⲈⲒϢ Ⲛ̄
ⲠⲈⲨⲀⲄⲄⲈⲖⲒⲞⲚ Ⲛ̄ⲦⲘⲚ̄ⲦⲈⲢⲞ[2] ⲘⲠϢⲎ
10 ⲢⲈ ⲘⲠⲢⲰⲘⲈ ⲈϢϪⲈ ⲠⲈⲦⲘ̄ⲘⲀⲨ Ⲙ̄
ⲠⲞⲨϮⲤⲞ ⲈⲢⲞϤ ⲚⲀϢ Ⲛ̄ϨⲈ ⲀⲚⲞⲚ ⲈⲨ
ⲚⲀϮⲤⲞ ⲈⲢⲞⲚ ⲦⲞⲦⲈ ⲀⲘⲀⲢⲒϨⲀⲘ[3] ⲦⲰ
ⲞⲨⲚ ⲀⲤⲀⲤⲠⲀⲌⲈ ⲘⲘⲞⲞⲨ ⲦⲎⲢⲞⲨ
ⲠⲈϪⲀⲤ Ⲛ̄ⲚⲈⲤⲤⲚⲎⲨ ϪⲈ ⲘⲠⲢ̄ⲢⲒⲘⲈ
15 ⲀⲨⲰ ⲘⲠⲢ̄ⲢⲖⲨⲠⲈⲒ ⲞⲨⲆⲈ ⲘⲠⲢ̄Ⲣ̄ ϨⲎⲦ
ⲤⲚⲀⲨ ⲦⲈϤⲬⲀⲢⲒⲤ ⲄⲀⲢ ⲚⲀϢⲰⲠⲈ
ⲚⲘⲘⲎⲦⲚ̄ ⲦⲎⲢ<Ⲧ>Ⲛ ⲀⲨⲰ ⲚⲤⲢ̄ⲤⲔⲈⲠⲀ
ⲌⲈ ⲘⲘⲰⲦⲚ̄ ⲘⲀⲖⲖⲞⲚ ⲆⲈ ⲘⲀⲢⲚ̄
ⲤⲘⲞⲨ ⲈⲦⲈϢⲘⲚ̄ⲦⲚⲞϬ ϪⲈ ⲀϤⲤⲂ
20 ⲦⲰⲦⲚ̄ ⲀϤⲀⲀⲚ Ⲛ̄ⲢⲰⲘⲈ Ⲛ̄ⲦⲀⲢⲈⲘⲀ
ⲢⲒϨⲀⲘ ϪⲈ ⲚⲀⲒ ⲀⲤⲔⲦⲈ ⲠⲈⲨϨⲎⲦ
[ⲈϨ]ⲞⲨⲚ ⲈⲠⲀⲄⲀⲐⲞⲚ ⲀⲨⲰ ⲀⲨⲢ̄ⲀⲢⲬⲈ
[ⲤⲐⲀⲒ] Ⲛ̄Ⲣ̄ⲄⲨⲘ[Ⲛ]ⲀⲌⲈ ϨⲀ ⲠⲢⲀ Ⲛ̄Ⲛ̄ϢⲀ
[Ϫ]Ⲉ Ⲙ̄Ⲡ̄[ⲤⲰⲢ]

---

1 Ⲛ̄ⲦⲀⲢⲈ is a dialectal variant for Ⲛ̄ⲦⲈⲢⲈ.
2 ⲘⲚ̄Ⲧ-Ⲣ̄ⲢⲞ.
3 ⲘⲀⲢⲒϨⲀⲘ is a proper noun: Mary.

P. 10

ⲡⲉϫⲉ ⲡⲉⲧⲣⲟⲥ ⲙⲙⲁⲣⲓϩⲁⲙ ϫⲉ ⲧⲥⲱ
ⲛⲉ ⲧⲛ̄ⲥⲟⲟⲩⲛ ϫⲉ ⲛⲉⲣⲉⲡⲥⲱ̄ⲣ ⲟⲩⲁϣⲉ
ⲛ̄ϩⲟⲩⲟ ⲡⲁⲣⲁ ⲡⲕⲉⲥⲉⲉⲡⲉ ⲛ̄ⲥϩⲓⲙⲉ
ϫⲱ ⲛⲁⲛ ⲛ̄ⲛ̄ϣⲁϫⲉ ⲙ̄ⲡⲥⲱ̄ⲣ ⲉⲧⲉⲉⲓⲣⲉ
5   ⲙⲡⲉⲩⲙⲉⲉⲩⲉ ⲛⲁⲓ ⲉⲧⲉⲥⲟⲟⲩⲛ ⲙ̄ⲙⲟ
ⲟⲩ ⲛ̄ⲛⲁⲛⲟⲛ ⲁⲛ ⲟⲩⲇⲉ ⲙⲡⲛ̄ⲥⲟⲧⲙⲟⲩ
ⲁⲥⲟⲩⲱϣⲃ̄ ⲛ̄ϭⲓ ⲙⲁⲣⲓϩⲁⲙ ⲡⲉⲇⲁⲥ
ϫⲉ ⲡⲉⲑⲏⲡ ⲉⲣⲱⲧⲛ̄ †ⲛⲁⲧⲁⲙⲁ[4] ⲑⲏⲩ
ⲧⲛ̄ ⲉⲣⲟϥ ⲁⲩⲱ ⲁⲥⲁⲣⲭⲉⲓ ⲛ̄ϫⲱ ⲛⲁⲩ
10 ⲛ̄ⲛⲉⲓϣⲁϫⲉ ϫⲉ ⲁⲓⲛⲟⲕ[5] ⲡⲉϫⲁⲥ ⲁⲓ
ⲛⲁⲩ ⲉⲡⲭ̄ⲥ ϩⲛ ⲟⲩϩⲟⲣⲟⲙⲁ ⲁⲩⲱ ⲁⲉⲓ
ϫⲟⲟⲥ ⲛⲁϥ ϫⲉ ⲡⲭ̄ⲥ ⲁⲓⲛⲁⲩ ⲉⲣⲟⲕ ⲙ̄
ⲡⲟⲟⲩ ϩⲛ ⲟⲩϩⲟⲣⲟⲙⲁ ⲁϥⲟⲩⲱϣⲃ ⲡⲉ
ϫⲁϥ ⲛⲁⲓ ϫⲉ ⲛⲁⲓⲁⲧⲉ ϫⲉ ⲛ̄ⲧⲉⲕⲓⲙ ⲁⲛ
15 ⲉⲣⲉⲛⲁⲩ ⲉⲣⲟⲉⲓ ⲡⲙⲁ ⲅⲁⲣ ⲉⲧⲉⲣⲉⲡⲛⲟⲩⲥ
ⲙ̄ⲙⲁⲩ ⲉϥⲙⲙⲁⲩ ⲛ̄ϭⲓ ⲡⲉϩⲟ[6] ⲡⲉϫⲁⲓ
ⲛⲁϥ ϫⲉ ⲡⲭ̄ⲥ ⲧⲉⲛⲟⲩ ⲡⲉⲧⲛⲁⲩ ⲉϥⲟ
ⲣⲟⲙⲁ ⲉϥⲛⲁⲩ ⲉⲣⲟϥ <ϩⲛ̄>ⲧⲉⲯⲩⲭⲏ <ⲏ>
ⲡⲉⲡ̄ⲛ̄ⲁ̄ ⲁϥⲟⲩⲱϣⲃ̄ ⲛ̄ϭⲓ ⲡⲥⲱ̄ⲣ ⲡⲉ
20 ϫⲁϥ ϫⲉ ⲉϥⲛⲁⲩ ⲁⲛ ϩⲛ̄ ⲧⲉⲯⲩⲭⲏ ⲟⲩ
ⲇⲉ ϩⲙ ⲡⲉⲡ̄ⲛ̄ⲁ̄ ⲁⲗⲗⲁ ⲡⲛⲟⲩⲥ ⲉⲧϣ[ⲟⲡ][7]
ϩⲛ ⲧⲉⲩⲙⲏⲧⲉ ⲙⲡⲉⲩⲥⲛⲁⲩ ⲛ̄ⲧⲟ[ϥ ⲡⲉⲧ]
ⲛⲁⲩ ⲉϥⲟⲣⲟⲙⲁ...

---

4 ⲧⲁⲙⲁ is a dialectal variant of ⲧⲁⲙⲟ.
5 ⲁⲓⲛⲟⲕ for ⲁⲛⲟⲕ.
6 ⲉϩⲟ is a dialectal variant of ⲁϩⲟ.
7 ϣⲟⲡ is a dialectal variant of ϣⲟⲟⲡ.

P. 17

7 ... ⲛⲧⲉⲣⲉⲙⲁⲣⲓϩⲁⲙ ϫⲉ
ⲛⲁⲓ ⲁⲥⲕⲁ ⲣⲱⲥ ϩⲱⲥⲧⲉ ⲛ̄ⲧⲁⲡⲥⲱ̄ⲣ
ϣⲁϫⲉ ⲛⲙ̄ⲙⲁⲥ ϣⲁ ⲡⲉⲉⲓⲙⲁ
10 ⲁϥⲟⲩⲱϣⲃ̄ ⲇⲉ ⲛ̄ϭⲓ ⲁⲛⲇⲣⲉⲁⲥ ⲡⲉϫⲁϥ
ⲛ̄ⲛⲉⲥⲛⲏⲩ ϫⲉ ⲁϫⲓ ⲡⲉⲧⲉⲧⲛ̄ϫⲱ
ⲙⲙⲟϥ ϩⲁ ⲡⲣⲁ ⲛ̄ⲛⲉⲛⲧⲁⲥϫ[ⲟ]ⲟⲩ
ⲁⲛⲟⲕ ⲙⲉⲛ ϯⲣ̄ⲡⲓⲥⲧⲉⲩⲉ ⲁⲛ ϫⲉ
ⲁⲡⲥⲱ̄ⲣ ϫⲉ ⲛⲁⲓ ⲉϣϫⲉ ⲛⲓⲥⲃⲟⲟⲩ
15 ⲉ ⲅⲁⲣ ϩⲛ̄ⲕⲉⲙⲉⲉⲩⲉ ⲛⲉ ⲁϥⲟⲩⲱ
ϣⲃ̄ ⲛ̄ϭⲓ ⲡⲉⲧⲣⲟⲥ ⲡⲉϫⲁϥ ϩⲁ ⲡⲣⲁ
ⲛⲛⲉⲉⲓϩⲃⲏⲩⲉ ⲛⲧⲉⲉⲓⲙⲓⲛⲉ ⲁϥ
ϫⲛⲟⲩⲟⲩ ⲉⲧⲃⲉ ⲡⲥⲱ̄ⲣ ϫⲉ ⲙⲏⲧⲓ
ⲁϥϣⲁϫⲉ ⲙⲛ̄ ⲟⲩⲥϩⲓⲙⲉ ⲛ̄ϫⲓⲟⲩⲉ
20 ⲉⲣⲟⲛ ϩⲛ ⲟⲩⲱⲛϩ ⲉⲃⲟⲗ ⲁⲛ ⲉⲛⲛⲁ
ⲕⲧⲟⲛ ϩⲱⲱⲛ ⲛ̄ⲧⲛ̄ⲥⲱⲧⲙ̄ ⲧⲏⲣⲛ̄
ⲛⲥⲱⲥ ⲛ̄ⲧ<ⲁ>ϥⲥⲟⲧⲡⲥ ⲛϩⲟⲩⲟ ⲉⲣⲟⲛ

P. 18

ⲧⲟⲧⲉ ⲁ[ⲙ]ⲁⲣⲓϩⲁⲙ ⲣⲓⲙⲉ ⲡⲉϫⲁⲥ ⲙ̄
ⲡⲉⲧⲣⲟⲥ <ϫⲉ> ⲡⲁⲥⲟⲛ ⲡⲉⲧⲣⲉ[8] ϩⲓⲉ ⲉⲕ
ⲙⲉⲉⲩⲉ ⲉⲟⲩ (401) ⲉⲕⲙⲉⲉⲩⲉ ϫⲉ ⲛ̄ⲧⲁⲓ
ⲙⲉⲉⲩⲉ ⲉⲣⲟⲟⲩ ⲙⲁⲩⲁⲁⲧ ϩⲙ̄ ⲡⲁ
5 ϩⲏⲧ ⲏ ⲉⲉⲓϫⲓ ϭⲟⲗ ⲉⲡⲥⲱ̄ⲣ ⲁϥⲟⲩ
ⲱϣⲃ̄ ⲛ̄ϭⲓ ⲗⲉⲩⲉⲓ[9] ⲡⲉϫⲁϥ ⲙⲡⲉⲧⲣⲟⲥ
ϫⲉ ⲡⲉⲧⲣⲉ ϫⲓⲛ ⲉⲛⲉϩ ⲕϣⲟⲡ[10] ⲛⲣⲉϥ
ⲛⲟⲩϭⲥ ϯⲛⲁⲩ ⲉⲣⲟⲕ ⲧⲉⲛⲟⲩ ⲉⲕⲣ̄

---

8 Πέτρε is the vocative of Πέτρος.
9 ⲗⲉⲩⲉⲓ is a proper noun: Levy.
10 ϣⲟⲡ for ϣⲟⲟⲡ.

ⲅⲩⲙⲛⲁⲍⲉ ⲉϩⲛ ⲧⲉⲥϩⲓⲙⲉ ⲛ̄ⲑⲉ ⲛ̄
10 ⲛⲓⲁⲛⲧⲓⲕⲉⲓⲙⲉⲛⲟⲥ ⲉϣϫⲉ ⲁⲡ
ⲥⲱⲧⲏⲣ ⲇⲉ ⲁⲁⲥ ⲛⲁⲝⲓⲟⲥ ⲛ̄ⲧⲕ̄ ⲛⲓⲙ
ⲇⲉ ϩⲱⲱⲕ ⲉⲛⲟϫⲥ ⲉⲃⲟⲗ ⲡⲁⲛⲧⲱⲥ
ⲉⲣⲉⲡⲥⲱⲧⲏⲣ ⲥⲟⲟⲩⲛ ⲙ̄ⲙⲟⲥ ⲁⲥ
ⲫⲁⲗⲱⲥ ⲉⲧⲃⲉ ⲡⲁⲓ ⲁϥⲟⲩⲟϣⲥ̄ ⲛ̄ϩⲟⲩ
15 ⲟ ⲉⲣⲟⲛ ⲙⲁⲗⲗⲟⲛ ⲙⲁⲣⲛ̄ϣⲓⲡⲉ ⲛ̄ⲧⲛ̄
† ϩⲓⲱⲱⲛ ⲙ̄ⲡⲣⲱⲙⲉ ⲛ̄ⲧⲉⲗⲓⲟⲥ
ⲛ̄ⲧⲛ̄ϫⲡⲟϥ ⲛⲁⲛ ⲕⲁⲧⲁ ⲑⲉ ⲛ̄ⲧⲁϥ
ϩⲱⲛ ⲉⲧⲟⲟⲧⲛ̄ ⲛ̄ⲧⲛ̄ⲧⲁϣⲉⲟⲉⲓϣ
ⲙ̄ⲡⲉⲩⲁⲅⲅⲉⲗⲓⲟⲛ ⲉⲛⲕⲱ ⲁⲛ ⲉϩⲣⲁⲓ
20 ⲛ̄ⲕⲉϩⲟⲣⲟⲥ ⲟⲩⲇⲉ ⲕⲉⲛⲟⲙⲟⲥ ⲡⲁ
ⲣⲁ ⲡⲉⲛⲧⲁⲡⲥ̄ⲱ̄ⲣ ϫⲟⲟϥ ⲛ̄ⲧⲉⲣⲉ

P. 19

[ⲗⲉ]ⲩ[ⲉⲓ ⲇⲉ ϫⲉ ⲛ]ⲁⲓ ⲁⲩⲱ ⲁⲩⲣ̄ⲁⲣⲭⲉⲓ ⲛ̄
ⲃⲱⲕ [ⲉⲧⲣⲉⲩⲧ]ⲁⲙⲟ ⲛ̄ⲥⲉⲧⲁϣⲉⲟⲉⲓϣ
ⲡ[ⲉ]ⲩⲁⲅⲅⲉⲗⲓⲟⲛ
ⲕⲁⲧⲁ
ⲙⲁⲣⲓϩⲁⲙⲙⲏ

Glossaries & Index

Coptic glossary

The Coptic words that appear in the examples, the exercises and the texts appear in this glossary following the order of the consonants. They are arranged in the same way as in the *Coptic Dictionary* by W. E. CRUM. For each verb the existing prenominal and prepersonal forms and the stative are given. Composite words and derivations figure under the original or the most characteristic word. The double consonants ⲑ, ⸰, ⲫ, ⲭ et ⲯ can be respectively found under Tϩ, ⲕⲥ, ⲡϩ, ⲕϩ and ⲡⲥ.

ⲁ

ⲁ: *precedes an approximate number* (cf. 088)
ⲁⲓⲁⲓ: to increase; to grow
ⲁⲗⲓ, ⲁⲗⲓⲧ⸗: *imper. of* ⲱⲗ
ⲁⲗⲟ⸗: *imper. of* ⲗⲟ
ⲁⲗⲟⲩ: child, youngster
ⲁⲗⲱ (f.), pl. ⲁⲗⲟⲟⲩⲉ: pupil, eye
ⲁⲙⲟⲩ, ⲁⲙⲏ, ⲁⲙϩⲉⲓⲧⲛ̄: *imper. of* ⲉⲓ
ⲁⲙⲁϩⲧⲉ: to prevail, to rule ; to embrace; to restrict, to detain
ⲁⲛ: *negation particle*
ⲁⲛ- (m.): chief of, great one
ⲁⲛⲁ⸗: pleasure, will
    ⲡ̄-ⲁⲛⲁ⸗: to please; to be pleased
ⲁⲛⲓ-: *imper. of* ⲉⲓⲛⲉ
ⲁⲛⲅ: *see* ⲁⲛⲟⲕ
ⲁⲛⲟⲕ, ⲁⲛⲅ-: *pers. pron.*: I
ⲁⲛⲟⲛ, ⲁⲛ(ⲛ̄)-: *pers. pron.*: we
ⲁⲛ(ⲉ)ⲓⲛⲉ: *imper. of* ⲉⲓⲛⲉ
ⲁⲛϭⲏⲃⲉ/ⲁⲛⲍⲏⲃⲉ (f.): school
ⲁⲛⲁⲩ: *imper. of* ⲛⲁⲩ
ⲁⲛⲁϣ (m.): oath
ⲁⲡⲁ: Apa, Father (*monastic title*)
ⲁⲡⲉ (f.), pl. ⲁⲡⲏⲩⲉ: head, chief
ⲁⲡⲟⲧ (m.), pl. ⲁⲡⲏⲧ: cup
ⲁⲡⲏⲩⲉ: *pl. of* ⲁⲡⲉ
ⲁⲣⲓ-: *imper. of* ⲉⲓⲣⲉ

ⲁⲡⲓⲕⲉ (m.): blame, fault
    ϭⲛ-ⲁⲡⲓⲕⲉ: to blame

ⲁⲡⲓⲡⲉ: *imper. of* ⲉⲓⲡⲉ

ⲁⲡⲟⲟⲩⲉ (*always pl..*): burr, thistle

ⲁⲡⲏⲭ(ⲛ̄)⸗: limit, end

-ⲁⲥⲉ: -six (cf. 085)

ⲁⲧ: *negation*: without
    ⲁⲧ.ϩⲏⲧ (ⲁⲑⲏⲧ): insensible
    ⲁⲧ.ⲛⲁⲩ ⲉⲣⲟ⸗ϥ: invisible

ⲁⲩⲉⲓ: *imper. particle*: give! bring hither! come!

ⲁⲩⲱ: *conj.*: and

ⲁⲩⲱⲛ-: *imper. of* ⲟⲩⲱⲛ

ⲁϣ: *interrogative pron.*: which ? what ? who?

ⲁϣⲁⲓ: to become many, to multiply; to be many

ⲁϣⲉ: *see* ⲉⲓϣⲉ

ⲁϣⲕⲁⲕ: *see* ⲱϣ

-ⲁϥⲧⲉ: -four (cf. 085)

ⲁϩⲉ: *see* ⲱϩⲉ

ⲁϩⲟ (m.), pl. ⲁϩⲱⲱⲣ: treasury

ⲁϩⲱⲱⲣ: *pl. of* ⲁϩⲟ

ⲁϩⲣⲟ⸗: what about... ? why?

ⲁϫⲓ-: *imper. of* ϫⲱ

ⲁϫⲛ-, ⲁϫⲛ̄ⲧ⸗ (*sometimes* ⲉϫⲛ̄-): *prep.*: without

B

ⲃⲱ (f.): tree
    ⲃⲱ ⲛ̄-ⲕⲛ̄ⲧⲉ: fig tree
    ⲃⲱ ⲛ̄-ⲉⲗⲟⲟⲗⲉ: vine

ⲃⲱⲕ, ⲃⲏⲕ†: to go

ⲃⲉⲕⲉ (m.): salary, remuneration
    ϫⲁⲓ-ⲃⲉⲕⲉ: who receives a salary, mercenary

ⲃⲟⲗ (m.), ⲃⲗ̄(ⲛ̄)-, ⲃⲁⲗⲗⲁ⸗: the outside
    ⲛ̄ⲃⲗ̄-, ⲛ̄ⲃⲁⲗⲗⲁ⸗: *prep.*: beyond, except
    ⲣ̄-ⲃⲟⲗ: to be liberated; to escape

ⲃⲱⲗ, ⲃⲉⲗ-, ⲃⲟⲗ⸗, ⲃⲏⲗ†: to loosen, to untie; to set free
    ⲉⲃⲟⲗ: *adv.*: outside
    ⲥⲁⲃⲟⲗ: *prep.*: outside of, externally
    ϣⲁⲃⲟⲗ: *prep.*: towards the outer side

ϨⲀⲂⲞⲖ: *prep.*: from
    ϨⲒⲂⲞⲖ: *prep.*: outside, except, before
ⲂⲀⲖⲞⲦ (f.): skin garment; skin bag
ⲂⲀⲀⲘⲠⲈ (m./f.): goat
ⲂⲰⲰⲚ (m.), ⲂⲞⲞⲚⲈ (f.): evil, bad
ⲂⲞⲞⲚⲈ: *see* ⲂⲰⲰⲚ
ⲂⲚⲦ (m./f.): *see* ϥⲚⲦ
ⲂⲢ̄ⲢⲈ: new, young
ⲂⲎⲦ (m.): palm leaf
ⲂⲎⲦ: *see* ⲂⲰⲦⲈ
ⲂⲞⲦⲈ (f.): spiteful thing, abomination
ⲂⲰⲦⲈ, ⲂⲈⲦ-/ⲂⲞⲦ-, ⲂⲎⲦ⸗, ⲂⲎⲦ†: pollute; detest; *stative*: to be hated, damned

Ⲉ

Ⲉ-, ⲈⲢⲞ⸗: *direction:* toward, for, against
ⲈⲂⲞⲖ: *see* ⲂⲰⲖ
ⲈⲂⲒⲎⲚ (m./f.): poor
ⲈⲂⲞⲦ (m.): month
ⲈⲖⲞⲞⲖⲈ (m.): grape
    ⲘⲀ Ⲛ̄-ⲈⲖⲞⲞⲖⲈ: vineyard
ⲈⲘⲀⲦⲈ: *adv.*: very, much
ⲈⲘⲀⲨ: *adv.*: there *(with movement)*
ⲈⲚⲈ: *circonst. conversion of the preterit conversion* (cf. 241, 434)
ⲈⲚⲚⲈ: *variant form for the optative* (cf. 336)
ⲈⲚⲈϨ (m.): eternity; *adv.*: always, eternally
    ϢⲀ-ⲈⲚⲈϨ: eternal(ly); forever
    ⲘⲚ̄Ⲧ.ϢⲀ-ⲈⲚⲈϨ: eternity
ⲈⲠⲈⲤⲎⲦ: *adv.*: downward
ⲈⲢⲞ⸗: *see* Ⲉ-
ⲈⲢⲀⲦ⸗: *see* ⲢⲀⲦ⸗
ⲈⲢⲎⲦ: vow, promise, devote; *nn m.* (pl. ⲈⲢⲀⲦⲈ): vow, promise
ⲈⲢⲀⲦⲈ: *pl. of* ⲈⲢⲎⲦ
ⲈⲢⲎⲨ: *expresses reciprocity* (cf. 292)
ⲈⲤⲞⲞⲨ (m.): sheep
ⲈⲦⲂⲈ-, ⲈⲦⲂⲎⲎⲦ⸗: *prep.*: because of, concerning
ⲈⲦⲂⲎⲎⲦ⸗: *see* ⲈⲦⲂⲈ-
ⲈⲞⲞⲨ (m.): honour, glory
    †-ⲈⲞⲞⲨ: to give glory, to glorify; to praise; *nn m.*: glory
ⲈϢ-: can, to be able to

ⲉϣⲱⲡⲉ: *conj.*: if (cf. 429, 442)
ⲉϣϣⲉ: *see also* ϣϣⲉ: it is fitting, right
ⲉϣⲝⲉ: *conj.*: if (cf. 429, 438, 442)
ⲉϣⲝⲉⲡⲉ: *used in the apodosis of a contra-factual conditional sentence* (cf. 438)
ⲉϩⲉ (m./f.): bull, cow
ⲉϩⲟⲩⲛ: *adv.*: inside
ⲉϩⲣⲁⲓ: *adv.*: upside; downside; *adv. strengthening the preceding prep. or verb*
ⲉϩⲟⲩⲟ ⲉ-, ⲉϩⲟⲩⲉ: more than, *see* ϩⲟⲩⲟ
ⲉϫⲛ-: *see* ⲁϫⲛ-
ⲉϭⲱϣ, ⲉϭⲟⲟϣⲉ (m./f.): Ethiopian, black

Ⲏ

Ⲏⲓ (m.): house
Ⲏ(ⲏ)ⲡⲉ: *see* ⲱⲡ
Ⲏⲣⲡ (m.): wine

ⲉⲓ/ⲓ

ⲉⲓ, ⲛⲏⲩ†: to go; to come
ⲉⲓⲁ, ⲉⲓⲁⲧ⸗: eye, sight
    ϩⲁⲉⲓⲁⲧ⸗: before
ⲉⲓⲉ: *interrogative particle* (cf. 399): if, either; *particle introducing an apodosis*: then, unless, without (cf. 438); *interjection strengthening the following word*: well then, surely
ⲉⲓⲱ (ⲉⲃⲟⲗ), ⲉⲓⲁ-, ⲉⲓⲁⲁ⸗, ⲉⲓⲏ†: to wash
ⲉⲓⲙⲉ: to know, to understand
ⲉⲓⲛⲉ, (ⲉ)ⲛ-, ⲛⲧ⸗: to bring, to carry
ⲉⲓⲛⲉ: to resemble, to be like; *nn m.*: aspect, likeness; resemblance
ⲉⲓⲉⲡ-: *see* ⲉⲓⲟⲡⲉ
ⲉⲓⲟⲡⲉ (f.): work
    ⲉⲓⲉⲡ-ϣⲉ: wooden, timber
    ⲉⲓⲉⲡ-ϣⲱⲧ: commerce, merchandise
ⲉⲓⲟⲟⲣ (m.): canal
    ϫⲓⲟⲟⲣ: to ferry over, to ford river, to cross
ⲉⲓⲣⲉ, (ⲉ)ⲣ-, ⲁⲁ⸗, ⲟ†: to do; to become; *stative*: to be
ⲉⲓⲱⲣϩ, ⲉⲓⲉⲣϩ-/ⲉⲓⲁⲣϩ-, ⲉⲓⲟⲣϩ⸗: to see, to perceive; *nn m.*: vision, view
ⲉⲓⲥ: behold! *Introduces existential sentences* (cf. 300–307)
    ⲉⲓⲥ ϩⲏ(ⲏ)ⲧⲉ: behold!
ⲉⲓⲁⲧ⸗: *see* ⲉⲓⲁ
ⲉⲓⲱⲧ (m.), pl. ⲉⲓⲟⲧⲉ: father

ⲉⲓⲟⲧⲉ: *pl. of* ⲉⲓⲱⲧ
ⲉⲓϣⲉ, ⲁϣⲧ-/ⲉϣⲧ-, ⲁϣⲧ⸗, ⲁϣⲉ†: to hang
ⲉⲓⲱϩⲉ (m.): field
    ⲉⲓⲉϩ-ⲉⲗⲟⲟⲗⲉ: vineyard
    ⲉⲓⲉϩ-ϣⲏⲛ: orchard

Ⲕ

⸗ⲕ, ⲕ- (m.): *pers. pron.*: you
ⲕⲉ (m.), ⲕⲉⲧⲉ (f.), pl. ⲕⲟⲟⲩⲉ: *indef. pron.*: other, also (cf. 024)
ⲕⲱ, ⲕⲁ-, ⲕⲁⲁ⸗, ⲕⲏ† (ⲉⲃⲟⲗ): to put; to allow; to let; to leave; to forgive
    ⲕⲱ ⲛ̄ⲥⲁ-: to put, to leave behind; to renounce
    ⲕⲁ ⲣⲱ⸗, ⲕⲁⲣⲁⲉⲓⲧ†: to be silent
    ⲕⲁ-ⲣⲱ⸗ϥ (m.): silence
ⲕⲃⲟ, ⲕⲃⲉ-, ⲕⲏⲃ⸗: to be cold; to freeze; *nn m.*: cold, freshness
    † ⲕⲃⲟ: to refresh, to make cold
ⲕⲱⲕ, ⲕⲏⲕ† (often with ⲁϩⲏⲩ): to peal, to strip naked
    ⲕⲱⲕⲁϩⲏⲩ: *nn m.*: nudity
ⲕⲁⲕⲉ (m.): darkness
ⲕⲁⲕⲓⲁ: *same meaning as* ⲕⲁⲕⲉ
ⲕⲗⲟⲟⲗⲉ (f.): cloud
ⲕⲗⲟⲙ (m.), pl. ⲕⲗⲟⲟⲙ: crown
ⲕⲗⲟⲟⲙ *pl. of* ⲕⲗⲟⲙ
ⲕⲱⲗϩ, ⲕⲗϩ-, ⲕⲟⲗϩ⸗, ⲕⲟⲗϩ†: to beat, to strike, to knock
ⲕⲱⲗϫ, ⲕ(ⲉ)ⲗϫ-, ⲕⲟⲗϫ⸗: to bend
    ⲕⲗϫ-ⲡⲁⲧ: genuflexion
ⲕⲁⲙ (m.): reed, rush
ⲕⲓⲙ, ⲕⲉⲙⲧ-, ⲕⲉⲙⲧ⸗: to move; to be moved
    ⲁⲧ.ⲕⲓⲙ: immovable
ⲕⲏⲙⲉ (f.): Egypt
ⲕⲱⲙϣ, ⲕⲙϣ-, ⲕⲟⲙϣ⸗: to sneer; to mock; to contemn; *nn m.*: mockery; contempt
ⲕⲱⲛⲥ, ⲕⲉⲛⲥ-, ⲕⲟ(ⲟ)ⲛⲥ⸗, ⲕⲟⲛⲥ†: to pierce, to slay
ⲕⲟⲩⲛ(ⲧ)⸗, ⲕⲟⲩⲟⲩⲛ⸗: bosom
ⲕⲛⲧⲉ (m.): fig
ⲕⲣⲙⲣⲙ: to murmur; to be vexed; *nn m.*: murmuring, complaint
ⲕⲉⲉⲥ (pl.): bones
ϫⲟⲩⲣ (m.): ring
ⲕⲱⲧ, ⲕⲉⲧ-, ⲕⲟⲧ⸗: to construct, to build, to form; *nn m.*: construction; edification
ⲕⲉⲧⲉ; *see* ⲕⲉ

ⲔⲰⲦⲈ, ⲔⲈⲦ-, ⲔⲞⲦ⸗, ⲔⲎⲦ†: to turn, to go round; to look for; (*with* Ⲉ-) to surround; *nn m.*: turning round, circuit, surroundings
ⲔⲦⲞ, ⲔⲦⲈ-, ⲔⲦⲞ⸗, ⲔⲦⲎⲨ†: to turn, to surround; to return
ⲔⲞⲞⲨⲈ: *see* ⲔⲈ
ⲔⲞⲨⲒ: little, small
    Ⲣ̄-ⲔⲞⲨⲒ: to be little, to be few, to be little time
ⲔⲀϢ (f.): reed
    ⲘⲀ Ⲛ̄-ⲔⲀϢ: bed, plantation of reeds
ⲔⲀϨ (m.): land, earth
ⲔⲰϨⲦ (m.): fire, flame

Ⲗ

ⲖⲞ: to stop, to cease
ⲖⲒⲂⲈ, ⲖⲈⲂⲦ⸗, ⲖⲞⲂⲈ†: to be mad; *nn m.*: madness
ⲖⲰⲔⲤ/ⲖⲰⲬ, ⲖⲬ-, ⲖⲞⲬ⸗, ⲖⲞⲬ†: to bite, to pierce, to stab
ⲖⲒⲔⲦ⸗: veil, covering
    Ⲛ̄-ⲖⲒⲔⲦ⸗: on top of, covering
ⲖⲰ(Ⲱ)Ⲙ(Ⲉ), ⲖⲞ(Ⲟ)ⲘⲈ⸗/ⲖⲀⲀⲘ(Ⲉ)⸗: to wither, to fade; to be filthy *nn m.*: filth, witheredness
    ⲀⲦ.ⲖⲰⲰⲘ(Ⲉ): unfading; immaculate
ⲖⲀⲤ (m.): tongue
ⲖⲀⲀⲨ: *adv.*: in nothing, no way
ⲖⲀⲀⲨ: *indef. pron.*: someone, something; *adv.*: at all
ⲖⲰⲬϨ, ⲖⲈⲬϨ-, ⲖⲞⲬϨ⸗, ⲖⲞⲬϨ†: to be crushed, effaced; to be sticky, adhesive *nn m.*: anguish, oppression
ⲖⲞ(Ⲉ)ⲒϬⲈ (f.): cause; excuse

Ⲙ

ⲘⲀ (m.): place
    Ⲉ-Ⲡ.ⲘⲀ Ⲉ-: instead of
ⲘⲀ: *imper. of* ϯ
ⲘⲀⲒ-: *part. cstr. of* ⲘⲈ: loving
    ⲘⲀⲒ-ⲚⲞⲨⲦⲈ: God-loving, pious
ⲘⲈ (f.): truth
ⲘⲈ, ⲘⲈⲢⲈ-, ⲘⲈⲢⲒⲦ⸗: to love
    ⲘⲈⲢⲒⲦ, pl. ⲘⲈⲢⲀⲦⲈ: beloved
ⲘⲞⲨ, ⲘⲞⲞⲨⲦ†: to die; *nn m.*: death
ⲘⲞⲨⲒ (m./f.): lion
ⲘⲀⲀⲂ, ⲘⲀⲀⲂⲈ, ⲘⲀⲂ-: thirty

ⲙⲟⲕⲙⲉⲕ, ⲙⲉⲕⲙⲟⲩⲕ⸗: to think, to ponder; to meditate, to intend; *nn m.*: thought
ⲙⲁⲕϩ̄ (m.): neck
ⲙ̄ⲟⲩⲕϩ, ⲙⲟⲕϩ⸗, ⲙⲟⲕϩ†: to afflict, to oppress
ⲙ̄ⲕⲁϩ: to be painful, difficult; to be grieved; *nn m.*: pain, difficulty, grief, suffering
    ⲣ̄-ⲙ̄ⲕⲁϩ: to be pained, grieved
ⲙ̄ⲙⲟ⸗: *see* ⲛ̄-
(ⲙ̄)ⲙⲛ̄: there isn't; *introduces a negative durative sentence with indefinite subject* (cf. 267)
ⲙ̄ⲙⲟⲛ: *adv.*: verily
ⲙ̄ⲙⲟⲛ: *negation*: not (cf. 442)
ⲙ̄ⲙⲏⲛⲉ: *adv.*: every day, daily
ⲙ̄ⲙⲓⲛⲙⲙⲟ⸗: *reflexivity marker* (cf. 291)
(ⲙ̄)ⲙⲛ̄ⲧⲉ-, (ⲙ)ⲙⲛ̄ⲧⲁ⸗: to have not
ⲙⲙⲁⲧⲉ: *adv.*: only, exclusively
ⲙ̄ⲙⲁⲩ: *adv.*: there
ⲙⲛ̄-, ⲛⲙ̄ⲙⲁ⸗: *prep.*: with; and
ⲙⲁⲉⲓⲛ (m.): sign
    ϫⲓ-ⲙⲁⲓⲉⲛ: to predict
    ⲣⲉϥ.ϫⲓ-ⲙⲁⲉⲓⲛ: fortune-teller
ⲙⲟⲩⲛ(ⲉ), ⲙⲏⲛ(ⲉ)⸗, ⲙⲏⲛ† (ⲉⲃⲟⲗ): to continue; to remain; to keep on doing
ⲙⲓⲛⲉ (f.): sort, quality, manner
ⲙⲟⲟⲛⲉ, ⲙⲉⲛⲉ-, ⲙⲁⲛⲟⲩ(ⲟⲩ)⸗: to pasture, to feed
ⲙⲛ̄ⲧ: *to build abstract nouns* (cf. 049)
ⲙⲛ̄ⲧ-: *see* ⲙⲏⲧ
ⲙⲛ̄ⲧⲣⲉ (m.): witness; testimony
    ⲣ̄-ⲙⲛ̄ⲧⲣⲉ: to be a witness, to testify
ⲙ̄ⲡⲣ̄-: *negation of the imper.* (cf. 142)
ⲙ̄ⲡⲱⲣ (ⲉ-): *negation of the imper.* (cf. 143)
ⲙ̄ⲡϣⲁ: to be worthy; *nn m.*: worth, desert, fate
ⲙ̄ⲡϣⲁ: *adv.*: very
ⲙⲟⲩⲣ, ⲙ(ⲉ)ⲣ-, ⲙⲟⲣ⸗, ⲙⲏⲣ†: to bind, to gird, to tie; *nn m.*: band, girth, strap
ⲙⲉⲣⲉ-: *negative aorist* (cf. 325)
ⲙⲉⲣⲓⲧ: *see* ⲙⲉ
ⲙⲉⲣⲁⲧⲉ: *see* ⲙⲉ
ⲙⲁⲥ: *see* ⲙⲓⲥⲉ
ⲙⲁⲥⲉ: *see* ⲙⲓⲥⲉ
ⲙⲓⲥⲉ, ⲙⲁⲥ-/ⲙⲉⲥ-, ⲙⲁⲥⲧ⸗/ⲙⲉⲥⲧ⸗: to bear, to bring forth; *nn m.*: offspring, generation
    ⲁⲧ.ⲙⲓⲥⲉ: unborn
    ⲙⲛ̄ⲧ.ⲁⲧ.ⲙⲓⲥⲉ: the fact of not being born
    ⲙⲁⲥ (m) young

ⲘⲀⲤ Ⲙ̄-ⲘⲞⲨⲒ: lion cup
    ⲘⲀⲤⲈ (m.): young animal; calf, bull
ⲘⲀⲤⲦ-: *part. cstr. of* ⲘⲞⲤⲦⲈ
    ⲘⲀⲤⲦ-ⲚⲞⲨⲦⲈ: God-hating, impious
ⲘⲞⲤⲦⲈ, ⲘⲈⲤⲦⲈ-, ⲘⲈⲤⲦⲰ⸗: to hate; *nn m.*: hatred
ⲘⲤⲞⲞⲨ *pl. of* Ⲙ̄ⲤⲀϨ
Ⲙ̄ⲤⲀϨ (m.), pl. ⲘⲤⲞⲞⲨ: crocodile
ⲘⲎⲦ, ⲘⲎⲦⲈ, ⲘⲚ̄Ⲧ-: ten
ⲘⲀⲦⲞⲒ (m.): soldier
ⲘⲎⲦⲈ (f.): middle
ⲘⲞⲦⲈ (m.): neck
ⲘⲞⲨⲦⲈ: to call, to speak
ⲘⲦⲞ (m.): face, presence
ⲘⲦⲞⲚ, ⲘⲞⲦⲚ†: to rest; to be calm; *nn m.*: rest
ⲘⲀⲀⲨ (f.): mother
ⲘⲞⲞⲨ (m.): water
ⲘⲀⲨⲀⲀ(Ⲧ)⸗: alone, only
ⲘⲈⲈⲨⲈ: to think; *nn m.*: thought, memory
    Ⲣ̄-ⲘⲈⲈⲨⲈ, Ⲣ̄ Ⲙ̄-Ⲡ.ⲘⲈⲈⲨⲈ: to remind, to remember
ⲘⲞⲨⲞⲨⲦ, ⲘⲈⲨⲦ-, ⲘⲞⲞⲨⲦ⸗: to kill
ⲘⲈϢⲈ-, ⲘⲈϢⲀ⸗: to ignore
    ⲘⲈϢⲀⲔ: maybe
ⲘⲎⲎϢⲈ (m.): multitude, mass
ⲘⲒϢⲈ, ⲘⲈϢ-/ⲘⲀϢ-, ⲘⲀϢ⸗: to fight; to attack
ⲘⲞⲞϢⲈ: to wander, to walk
ⲘⲈϢⲀⲔ: *see* ⲘⲈϢⲈ-
ⲘⲈϢϢⲈ: *negation of* (Ⲉ)ϢϢⲈ
ⲘⲀϨ (m.): nest, shelter
ⲘⲈϨ- : *used to build ordinal numbers* (cf. 091)
ⲘⲞⲨϨ, ⲘⲈϨ/ⲘⲀϨ-, ⲘⲀϨ⸗/ⲘⲞϨ⸗, ⲘⲈϨ†: to fill; to be full
ⲘⲞⲒϨⲈ (f./m.): miracle
ⲘϨⲒⲦ (m): Nord
ⲘϨⲀⲀⲨ (m.): tomb
ⲘⲀⲀϪⲈ (m.): ear

N

Ⲛ̄-, Ⲙ̄ⲘⲞ⸗: *locative, temporal, instrumental preposition; connection with direct object; genitive; preposition expressing identity; introduces the object; partitive genitive*
Ⲛ̄-, ⲚⲀ⸗: *prep. dative*

Ⲛⲁ: *precedes an approximate number* (cf. 089)
Ⲛⲁ: to have pity, mercy; *nn m.*: pity, charity
    ⲁⲧ.Ⲛⲁ: without compassion
    ⲘⲚ̄Ⲧ.ⲁⲧ.Ⲛⲁ: lack of compassion
    ⲘⲚ̄Ⲧ.Ⲛⲁ: alms
Ⲛⲁ: to go
Ⲛⲁⲁ-/Ⲛⲁⲉ-, Ⲛⲁⲁ(ⲁ)⸗: to be great
ⲚⲞⲨⲂ (m.): gold
ⲚⲞⲂⲈ (m.): sin
    ⲁⲧ.ⲚⲞⲂⲈ: without sin
    Ⲣ̄-ⲚⲞⲂⲈ: to sin
    ⲢⲈϤ.Ⲣ̄-ⲚⲞⲂⲈ: sinner
ⲚⲔⲀ (m.): thing
ⲚⲔⲞⲦⲔ: to sleep
ⲚⲒⲘ: *indef. pron./art.*: each, every (cf. 024, 169, 172)
    ⲞⲨⲞⲚ ⲚⲒⲘ: everyone
ⲚⲒⲘ: *interrogative pron.*: who?
ⲚⲘ̄ⲘⲀ⸗: *see* ⲘⲚ̄-
ⲚⲀⲚⲞⲨ-, ⲚⲀⲚⲞⲨ⸗: to be good
    Ⲡ.ⲈⲦ.ⲚⲀⲚⲞⲨ⸗ϥ: the Good
ⲚⲞⲨⲚⲈ (f.): root
ⲚⲈⲤⲈ-, ⲚⲈⲤⲰ⸗: to be beautiful
ⲚⲈⲤⲂⲰⲰ⸗: to be smart, intelligent
Ⲛ̄ⲤⲀⲂⲎⲖ: *conj.*: if not; *adv.* outside of; except
ⲚⲈⲈⲒⲤⲠⲈ: *introduces the apodosis after a contra-factual condition* (cf. 438)
ⲚⲀϨⲦ: *part. cstr.* of Ⲛⲁ: pity, compassion, charity
    ⲘⲚ̄Ⲧ.ⲚⲀϨⲦ: pity; charity
ⲚⲀⲒⲀⲦ⸗: to be blessed
Ⲛ̄ⲦⲈ-, Ⲛ̄Ⲧⲁ⸗: *prep. genitive*
Ⲛ̄ⲦⲞ, Ⲛ̄ⲦⲈ (f.sg.): *pers. pron.*: you
ⲚⲞⲨⲦⲈ (m.), ⲚⲦⲰⲢⲈ (f.): God, Goddess
Ⲛ̄ⲦⲞⲔ, Ⲛ̄ⲦⲔ- (m.sg.): *pers. pron.*: you
Ⲛ̄ⲦⲰⲢⲈ: *see* ⲚⲞⲨⲦⲈ
Ⲛ̄ⲦⲞⲤ: *pers. pron.*: she
Ⲛ̄ⲦⲰⲦⲚ̄, Ⲛ̄ⲦⲈⲦⲚ̄- (pl.): *pers. pron.*: you
Ⲛ̄ⲦⲞⲞⲨ (m./f. pl.): *pers. pron.*: they
Ⲛ̄ⲦⲞϤ, ⲚⲦϤ̄-: *pers. pron.*: he
ⲚⲀⲨ: to see; to look; *nn m.*: sight, view, vision
ⲚⲀⲨ (m.): hour, time
ⲚⲎⲨ: *stative of* ⲈⲒ

ⲚⲀϢⲈ-, ⲚⲀϢⲰ⸗: to be many, much
ⲚϢⲞⲦ, ⲚⲀϢⲦ†: to be hard, strong, difficult
ⲚⲈϥⲢ̄-: to be good
ⲚⲞϤⲢⲈ (f.): good, profit, advantage
    Ⲣ̄-ⲚⲞϤⲢⲈ: to be useful
ⲚⲈϨ (m.): oil
ⲚⲀϨⲂ (m.): yoke
ⲚⲀϨⲂ (f.): shoulders, back, neck
ⲚⲞⲨϨⲘ, ⲚⲈϨⲘ-/ⲚⲀϨⲘ-, ⲚⲀϨⲘ⸗, ⲚⲀϨⲘ†: to be saved, safe; to escape from; to save, to preserve; *nn m.*: safety
Ⲛ̄ϨⲞⲨⲚ: *prep.*: in, within
Ⲛ̄ⲀϨⲢⲚ: *see* ϨⲞ
Ⲛ̄ϨⲎⲦ⸗: *see* ϨⲚ̄-
ⲚⲀϨⲦⲈ, ⲚϨⲞⲦ⸗, ⲚϨⲀⲦ†: to have faith, to believe
    ⲘⲚ̄Ⲧ.ⲚⲀϨⲦ: belief
Ⲛ̄ϨⲞⲨⲞ Ⲉ-, Ⲛ̄ϨⲞⲨⲈ: more than, *see* ϨⲞⲨⲞ
ⲚⲞⲨϪ: lying, false, pseudo-
ⲚⲞⲨϪ: *see* ⲚⲞⲨϪⲈ
ⲚⲞⲨϪⲈ, ⲚⲈϪ, , ⲚⲞϪ⸗/ⲚⲀϪ⸗, ⲚⲎϪ†: to throw, to cast
ⲚⲞϬ: great, big
    ⲘⲚ̄Ⲧ.ⲚⲞϬ: greatness
ⲚⲈϬⲰ⸗: to be ugly
ⲚⲞϬⲚⲈϬ, ⲚⲈϬⲚⲈϬ-, ⲚⲈϬⲚⲞⲨϬ⸗: to reproach, to mock; *nn m.*: reproach
ⲚⲞⲨϬⲤ, ⲚⲈⲔⲤ-, ⲚⲞϬⲤ⸗: to be wroth, to be angry
    ⲢⲈϤ.ⲚⲞⲨϬⲤ : wrathful person

Ⲟ

Ⲟ (Ⲛ̄-) (*stative of* ⲈⲒⲢⲈ): to be
ⲞⲂϢ: *see* ⲰⲂϢ
ⲞⲈⲒⲔ (m.): bread
ⲞⲚ: again, too
ⲞⲠⲦ: *see* ⲰⲦⲠ
ⲞⲤⲈ (f.): loss, damage
    Ⲧ̄-ⲞⲤⲈ: to suffer loss, hurt, to be fined
ⲞⲦⲠ: *see* ⲰⲦⲠ
ⲞⲈⲒϢ: *see* ⲦⲀϢⲈ ⲞⲈⲒϢ
ⲞϨⲤ (m.): sickle

ⲡ

ⲡⲁ, ⲧⲁ, ⲛⲁ: *poss. pron.* (cf. 019)
ⲡⲁⲓ, ⲧⲁⲓ, ⲛⲁⲓ: *dem. pron.* (cf. 013)
ⲡ(ⲉ), ⲧ(ⲉ), ⲛ(ⲉ): *def. art.* (cf. 016, 054)
ⲡⲉ, ⲧⲉ, ⲛⲉ: *dem. pron.* (cf. 014)
ⲡⲉ (f.), pl. ⲡⲏⲩⲉ: heaven
ⲡⲏ, ⲧⲏ, ⲛⲏ: *dem. pron.* (cf. 013)
ⲡ(ⲉ)ⲓ (f.): kiss

    ϯ- ⲡ(ⲉ)ⲓ: to kiss

ⲡⲉⲓ, ⲧⲉⲓ, ⲛⲉⲓ: *dem. art.* (cf. 015)
ⲡⲱ⸗, ⲧⲱ⸗, ⲛⲟⲩ⸗: *poss. pron.* (cf. 020)
ⲡⲱⲗϭ/ⲡⲱⲗⲕ, ⲡ(ⲉ)ⲗϭ-/ⲡⲉⲗⲕ-, ⲡⲟⲗϭ⸗/ⲡⲟⲗⲕ⸗/ⲡⲁⲗϭ⸗: to be agreed, to reach satisfaction, to decide; *with* ⲉⲃⲟⲗ: to reach conclusion, to make an end
ⲡⲱⲱⲛⲉ, ⲡ(ⲉ)ⲉⲛⲉ-, ⲡⲟⲟⲛⲉ⸗, ⲡⲟⲟⲛⲉ†: to change, to turn
ⲡⲱⲣⲕ, ⲡ(ⲉ)ⲣⲕ-, ⲡⲟⲣⲕ⸗: to be plucked out, destroyed; to pluck out
ⲡⲱⲣϫ, ⲡⲉⲣϫ-, ⲡⲟⲣϫ⸗, ⲡⲟⲣϫ†: to divide, to separate; to be divided, separated
ⲯⲓⲥ/ⲯⲓⲧ, ⲯⲓⲧⲉ/ⲯⲓⲥⲉ: nine
ⲯⲁⲓⲧ-: *see* ⲡⲥⲧⲁⲓⲟⲩ
ⲡⲥⲧⲁⲓⲟⲩ, ⲯⲁⲓⲧ-: ninety
ⲡⲁⲧ (f.): knee
ⲡⲱⲧ, ⲡⲏⲧ†: to escape; to persecute; to run

    ⲙⲁ ⲛ̄-ⲡⲱⲧ: refuge

ⲡⲟⲟⲩ: today
ⲡⲏⲟⲩⲉ: *pl. of* ⲡⲉ
ⲡⲱϣ(ⲉ), ⲡⲉϣ-, ⲡⲟϣ⸗, ⲡⲏϣ†: to divide; to separate; to part
ⲡⲱϣⲥ, ⲡⲉϣⲥ-, ⲡⲟϣⲥ⸗, ⲡⲟϣⲥ†/ⲡⲟⲥϣ†: to be amazed, beside oneself; to amaze; to turn aside
ⲡⲱϩ, ⲡⲉϩ-, ⲡⲟϩ⸗, ⲡⲏϩ†: to break, to burst, to tear; *nn m.*: division; piece; part
ⲡⲱϩ, ⲡⲉϩ-, ⲡⲏϩ⸗: to reach, to attain to
ⲡⲁϩⲣⲉ (m.): medicament, drug, remedy

    ⲣ̄-ⲡⲁϩⲣⲉ: to use drugs, to heal

ⲡⲱϩⲧ, ⲡⲉϩⲧ-, ⲡⲁϩⲧ⸗, ⲡⲁϩⲧ†: to bend; to fall; to kneel
ⲡⲁϩⲟⲩ (m., pl.): buttocks; back

    ϩⲓ-ⲡⲁϩⲟⲩ: *prep.*: behind

ⲡⲉϫⲉ-, ⲡⲉϫⲁ⸗: to say (to have said)

ⲣ

ⲣⲁ (m.): state, condition; *conferring a local or generic sense to the following noun*
    ϩⲁ-ⲡ.ⲣⲁ: concerning

ⲣⲁ-: *component in the formation of nouns*: part of
    ⲣⲁ-ⲧⲏⲩ: sky

ⲣⲓ (f.): cell (of a monk); room

ⲣⲟ, ⲣⲛ̄-, ⲣⲱ⸗: mouth; door, gate
    ⲕⲁ ⲣⲱ⸗: to be silent
    ⲡⲁ-ⲡ.ⲣⲟ: doorkeeper
    ⲉⲣⲛ̄-, ⲉⲣⲱ⸗: *prep.*: toward, to, upon; against
    ϩⲁⲣⲛ̄-, ϩⲁⲣⲱ⸗: *prep.*: beneath; before
    ϩⲓⲣⲛ̄-, ϩⲓⲣⲱ⸗: *prep.*: at, upon

ⲣⲱ-; *see* ⲣⲟ

ⲣⲱ: emphatic or explicative particle

ⲣⲟⲕϩ̄, ⲣⲟⲭ: to burn

ⲣⲙ̄-: *see* ⲣⲱⲙⲉ

ⲣⲱⲙⲉ (m.), ⲣⲙ̄(ⲛ)-: man
    ⲣⲙ̄-ⲙⲁⲟ: rich
    ⲣⲙ̄.ⲛ̄-ⲕⲏⲙⲉ: Egyptian
    ⲣⲙ̄.ⲛ̄-ⲛⲟⲩⲧⲉ: pious
    ⲣⲙ̄-ⲣⲁⲕⲟⲧⲉ: Alexandrian

ⲣⲓⲙⲉ: to weep; *nn m.*: tear

ⲣⲙⲉⲓⲏ (f.): tear

ⲣⲟⲙⲡⲉ (f.), ⲣⲙ̄ⲡⲉ-, pl. ⲣⲙ̄ⲡⲟⲟⲩⲉ: year

ⲣⲙ̄ⲡⲟⲟⲩⲉ: *see* ⲣⲟⲙⲡⲉ

ⲣⲛ̄-: *see* ⲣⲟ

ⲣⲁⲛ (m.), ⲣⲉⲛ-, ⲣⲛ̄ⲧ⸗: name

ⲣⲛ̄ⲧ⸗: *see* ⲣⲁⲛ

ⲣ̄ⲡⲉ (m.), pl. ⲣ̄ⲡⲏⲩⲉ: temple

ⲣ̄ⲡⲏⲩⲉ: *see* ⲣ̄ⲡⲉ

ⲣⲓⲡ (m.): pig

ⲣ̄ⲣⲟ (m.), pl. (ⲡ)ⲣⲱⲟⲩ: king
    ⲙⲛ̄ⲧ.ⲣ̄ⲣⲟ: kingdom

ⲣⲟⲉⲓⲥ: to be awake; to watch

ⲣⲁⲥⲧⲉ (m.): morrow

ⲣⲁⲧ⸗ (m.): foot
    ⲉⲣⲁⲧ⸗: *prep.*: to (*mostly of persons*)
    ϩⲁⲣⲁⲧ⸗: *prep.*: beneath
    ϩⲓⲣⲁⲧ⸗: *prep.*: toward

ⲣⲏⲧⲉ (m.): manner, fashion, likeness

ⲢⲞⲞⲨⲦ: *see* ⲞⲨⲢⲞⲦ
ⲢⲞⲞⲨϢ: to have care for, to be intent on; *nn m.*: care, attention, anxiety
    ϤⲒ-ⲢⲞⲞⲨϢ: to take care of
ⲢⲀϢⲈ: rejoice; *nn m.*: gladness, joy
ⲢⲰϢⲈ, ⲢⲈϢⲦ-/ⲢⲀϢⲦ-, ⲢⲀϢ(Ⲧ)⁼: to suffice, to be enough
ⲢⲈϤ: man who (cf. 051)
ⲢⲞⲨϨⲈ (m.): evening
ⲢⲰϨⲦ, ⲢⲈϨⲦ-, ⲢⲀϨⲦ⁼/ⲢⲞϨⲦ⁼, ⲢⲀϨⲦ†: to strike; to cast; to be struck; to fall; *nn m.*: stroke, blow

Ⲥ

⁼Ⲥ, Ⲥ-: *pers. pron.*: she, her
ⲤⲀ: man of; maker of; dealer in
    ⲤⲀ Ⲛ̄-ⲚⲈϨ: oil seller
    ⲤⲀ Ⲛ̄-ϪⲒ-ϬⲞⲖ: liar
ⲤⲀ: side, part
    Ⲛ̄ⲤⲀ-, Ⲛ̄ⲤⲰ⁼: behind, after; against
ϢⲈ, ⲤⲈ-, ⲤⲈⲦ-: sixty
ⲤⲈ-: *pers. pron.*: they
ⲤⲈ: *affirmative particle; in answers*: yes
Ⲥ(Ⲉ)Ⲓ, ⲤⲎⲨ⁼, ⲤⲎⲨ†: to be filled, satisfied; enjoy
    ⲀⲦ.ⲤⲒ: insatiate
    ⲘⲚ̄Ⲧ.ⲀⲦ.ⲤⲒ: unsatedness, greed
ⲤⲞ: *nn m., occurs only in the expression* ϯ-ⲤⲞ
    ϯ-ⲤⲞ (Ⲉ-): to spare; to refrain; *nn m.*: forebearance; abstinence
ⲤⲞ(Ⲉ): *see* ⲤⲞⲞⲨ
ⲤⲀⲂⲈ (m.), ⲤⲀⲂⲎ (f.): wise
ⲤⲰⲂⲈ: to laugh; to mock
ⲤⲂⲰ (f.), pl. ⲤⲂⲞⲞⲨⲈ/ⲤⲂⲰⲞⲨⲈ: doctrine, teaching
    ϪⲒ-ⲤⲂⲰ: to get teaching; to be taught
ⲤⲂ̄ⲂⲈ, ⲤⲂⲂⲈ-, ⲤⲂⲂⲎⲦ-, ⲤⲂⲂⲎⲨ⁼: circumcise; *nn m.*: circumcision
ⲤⲂⲞⲔ: to become small, to be small; to make less
ⲤⲀⲂⲎⲖ: *see* Ⲛ̄ⲤⲀⲂⲎⲖ
ⲤⲞⲂ̄Ⲧ (m.): wall, fence
ⲤⲞⲂⲦⲈ, ⲤⲂⲦⲈ-, ⲤⲂⲦⲰⲦ⁼, ⲤⲂⲦⲰⲦ†: to prepare, to set in order; to be ready
ⲤⲂⲞⲞⲨⲈ, ⲤⲂⲰⲞⲨⲈ: *pl. of* ⲤⲂⲰ
ⲤⲒⲔⲈ, ⲤⲈⲔⲦ-, ⲤⲀⲔⲦ⁼, ⲤⲞ(Ⲟ)ⲔⲈ†: to grind, to pound
    ⲰⲚⲈ Ⲛ̄-ⲤⲒⲔⲈ: grinding stone
ⲤⲞⲖⲤⲖ̄, ⲤⲖ̄ⲤⲖ-, ⲤⲖ̄ⲤⲰⲖ⁼, ⲤⲖ̄ⲤⲰⲖ†: to be comforted; to comfort; *nn m.*: consolation

ⲥⲙⲏ (f.): voice, sound
ⲥⲙⲟⲩ, ⲥⲙⲁⲙⲁⲁⲧ⸗/ⲥⲙⲁⲁⲧ⸗: to bless; to praise
ⲥⲙⲓⲛⲉ, ⲥⲙ(ⲉ)ⲛ-, ⲥⲙⲛⲧ⸗, ⲥⲙⲟⲛⲧ†: to be established, set right; to establish, to construct; *nn m.*: confirmation, agreement, adornment
ⲥⲙⲏⲧ: *see* ⲥⲱⲧⲙ
ⲥⲙⲟⲧ (f.): form; character; likeness; pattern
ⲥⲁⲉⲓⲛ (m.): physician
ⲥⲟⲛ (m.), ⲥⲱⲛⲉ (f.), pl. ⲥⲛⲏⲩ: brother; sister; sibling
ⲥⲓⲛⲉ, ⲥⲛ-/ⲥ(ⲉ)ⲛⲧ-/ⲥⲁ(ⲁ)ⲧ-, ⲥⲁ(ⲁ)ⲧ⸗/ⲥⲟ(ⲟ)ⲧ⸗/ⲥⲛⲧ⸗: to pass by, through; *nn m.*: passing, decline (of day)
ⲥⲟ(ⲟ)ⲛⲉ (m.): robber
ⲥⲱⲛⲉ: *see* ⲥⲟⲛ
ⲥⲱ(ⲱ)ⲛⲧ, ⲥ(ⲉ)ⲛⲧ-, ⲥⲟ(ⲟ)ⲛⲧ⸗, ⲥⲟⲛⲧ†: to be created; to create; *nn m.*: creature; creation
ⲥⲛ̄ⲧⲉ: *see* ⲥⲛⲁⲩ
ⲥⲛⲁⲩ, ⲥⲛ̄ⲧⲉ-: two
-ⲥⲛⲟⲟⲩⲥ (m.), -ⲥⲛⲟⲟⲩⲥⲉ (f.): - two (cf. 086)
ⲥⲛⲏⲩ: *pl. of* ⲥⲟⲛ
ⲥⲁⲁⲛϣ, ⲥⲁⲁⲛϣ-, ⲥⲁⲛⲟⲩϣ⸗, ⲥⲁⲛⲁϣⲧ†: to make live; to be alive; to nourish; *stative*: to be nourished, well fed
ⲥⲉⲡ-: *see* ⲥⲟⲡ
ⲥⲟⲡ, ⲥⲉⲡ-, pl. ⲥⲟⲟⲡ, ⲥⲱⲱⲡ: occasion, time, turn
    ϩⲓ-ⲟⲩ.ⲥⲟⲡ: at one time, together
ⲥⲟⲟⲡ, ⲥⲱⲱⲡ: *pl. of* ⲥⲟⲡ
ⲥⲉⲉⲡⲉ: to remain over, to be remainder; to leave remaining, to spare; *nn m.*: remainder
ⲥⲟⲡⲥ, ⲥⲉⲡⲥ-: to pray; to comfort
ⲥⲟⲡⲥⲡ, ⲥⲡⲥⲱⲡ-, ⲥ(ⲉ)ⲡⲥⲱⲡ⸗, ⲥⲉⲡⲥⲱⲡ†: to pray; to entreat; to comfort
ⲥⲡⲟⲧⲟⲩ (m., pl.): lips
ⲥⲟⲩⲣⲉ (f.): thorn, spike, dart
ⲥⲱⲣⲙ, ⲥⲉⲣⲙ-, ⲥⲟⲣⲙ-, ⲥⲟⲣⲙ⸗: to go astray, to err; to lose; *nn m.*: error
ⲥⲣϥⲉ/ⲥⲏⲣϥⲉ, ⲥⲣⲟϥⲧ†: to be at leisure, inoccupied; *with* ⲉ-: to have leisure for, to be occupied with
ⲥⲉⲧ-: *see* ⲥⲉ
ⲥⲁⲧⲉ (f.): fire
ⲥⲓⲧⲉ, ⲥⲉⲧ-/ⲥⲁⲧ-/ⲥⲓⲧ-, ⲥⲁⲧ⸗/ⲥⲉⲧ⸗/ⲥⲓⲧ⸗, ⲥⲏⲧ† (ⲉ-): to throw, to sow; to put
    ⲥⲟⲧⲉ (m./f.), pl. ⲥⲟⲟⲧⲉ: arrow, dart
ⲥⲱⲧⲉ, ⲥⲉⲧ-/ⲥⲟⲧ-, ⲥⲟ(ⲟ)ⲧ⸗/ⲥⲁ(ⲁ)ⲧ⸗: to redeem, to rescue, to save
ⲥϯ-: *see* ⲥⲧⲟⲓ
ⲥⲧⲟ: *see.* ⲧⲥⲧⲟ
ⲥⲧⲟⲓ (m.), ⲥϯ-: smell
    ⲥϯ-ⲃⲱⲱⲛ: bad smell, stench
    ⲥϯ-ⲛⲟⲩϥⲉ: perfume

ⲥⲱⲧⲙ̄, ⲥⲉⲧⲙ-, ⲥⲟⲧⲙ⸗: to hear; to listen
    ⲥ†ⲙⲏⲧ, ⲥⲙⲏⲧ: obedient (*for* ⲥⲉⲧⲙ-ϩⲏⲧ)
    ⲙⲛ̄ⲧ.ⲥ†ⲙⲏⲧ, ⲙⲛ̄ⲧ.ⲥⲙⲏⲧ: obedience
    ϭⲓⲛ-ⲥⲱⲧⲙ̄: hearing report
ⲥⲱⲧⲡ, ⲥⲉⲧⲡ-, ⲥⲟⲧⲡ⸗: to choose; *nn m.*: chosen, elect
ⲥⲧⲱⲧ: tremble; *nn m.*: trembling
ⲥⲏⲩ: *see* ⲥⲉⲓ
ⲥⲏⲩ (m.): time, season
ⲥⲟⲟⲩ, ⲥⲟ(ⲉ): six
ⲥⲓⲟⲟⲩⲛ (f.): bath
ⲥⲟⲩⲉⲛ (m.), ⲥⲟⲩⲛ̄ⲧ⸗: value, price, worth
ⲥⲟⲟⲩⲛ̄, ⲥⲟⲩ(ⲉ)ⲛ-, ⲥⲟⲩⲱⲛ⸗: to know; *nn m.*: knowledge
    ⲁⲧ.ⲥⲟⲟⲩⲛ: without knowledge, ignorant
ⲥⲟⲩⲉⲛⲧ⸗: *see* ⲥⲟⲩⲉⲛ
ⲥⲟⲟⲩⲧⲛ, ⲥⲟⲩⲧⲛ-, ⲥⲟⲩⲧⲱⲛ⸗, ⲥⲟⲩⲧⲱⲛ†: to be straight, upright; to stretch; to straighten
ⲥⲱⲟⲩϩ, ⲥⲉⲟⲩϩ-, ⲥⲟⲟⲩϩ⸗, ⲥⲟⲟⲩϩ†: to be gathered, collected; to gather, to collect
    ⲥⲟⲟⲩϩⲥ (f.): congregation; collection
ⲥⲁϣ (f.): *see* ⲥⲱϣ
ⲥⲟⲉⲓϣ (m.): pair
    ⲥⲟⲉⲓϣ ⲛ-ⲉⲛⲉϩ: yoke; yoking animal
ⲥⲱϣ, ⲥⲉϣ-/ϣⲉⲥ-, ⲥⲟϣ⸗: to strike
    ⲥⲁϣ, ⲥϣ-, ⲥϣⲛ̄- (f.): blow, stroke, sore
    ⲥϣ ⲛ̄-ⲁⲁⲥ: blow (with hand)
    ϣⲥⲛ̄-ⲗⲟⲅⲭⲏ: lance stab
ⲥⲱϣ, ⲥⲉϣ-/ϣⲉⲥ-, ⲥⲟϣ⸗/ϣⲟⲥ⸗, ⲥⲏϣ†/ϣⲏⲥ†: to be despised, humbled; to despise *nn m.*: shame, contempt
    ⲥⲱϣϥ, ⲥⲉϣϥ-, ⲥⲟϣϥ⸗, ⲥⲟϣϥ†: to be despised, scorned
ⲥⲱϣⲉ (f.): field
ⲥⲁϣϥ̄, ⲥⲁϣϥⲉ: seven
ⲥⲱϣϥ: *see* ⲥⲱϣ
ⲥϣϥⲉ: seventy
ⲥⲏϥⲉ (f.): sword; knife
ⲥⲁϩ (m.): writer
ⲥⲏϩ: *stative of* ⲥϩⲁⲓ
ⲥⲟⲟϩⲉ, ⲥⲁϩⲉ-, ⲥⲁϩⲱ(ⲱ)⸗: to be set up, upright; to set up
ⲥϩⲁⲓ, ⲥⲉϩⲁⲓ-/ⲥϩⲉ-, ⲥϩⲁⲓ(ⲥ/ⲧ)⸗/ⲥⲁϩ(ⲧ)⸗/ⲥⲉϩⲧ⸗, ⲥⲏϩ†: to write; *nn m*: writing; letter
ⲥϩⲓⲙⲉ (f.), pl. ϩⲓⲟⲙⲉ: woman
ⲥⲁϩⲛⲉ: to provide; to supply
    ⲟⲩⲉϩ-ⲥⲁϩⲛⲉ: to command
ⲥⲁϩⲟⲩ, ⲥϩⲟⲩ(ⲉ)ⲣ-, ⲥϩⲟⲩⲱⲣ⸗: to curse; *nn m.*: curse

ⲥϭⲏⲣ: to sail
ⲥϭⲣⲁϩⲧ: to rest, to pause, to be quiet; *nn m.*: quiet, rest

ⲧ

ⲧⲁⲓ: *adv.*: here
    ⲉⲧ.ⲧⲁⲓ: who is here
ⲧⲁ(ⲉ)ⲓⲟ, ⲧⲁ(ⲉ)ⲓⲉ-, ⲧⲁ(ⲉ)ⲓⲟ⸗, ⲧⲁ(ⲉⲓ)ⲏⲩ⸗: to honour; to pay respect; to adorn *nn. m.*: honour
ⲧⲉ- (f.): *pers. pron.*: you (f. sg.)
-ⲧⲏ: - five (cf. 086)
†-: *pers. pron.*: I
†, †-, ⲧⲁⲁ⸗: to give
    † ⲛ̄ⲁ-: to give to
    † ϩⲓ-, ϩⲓⲱⲱ⸗: to lay on; to clothe
†(ⲉ): *see* †ⲟⲩ
ⲧⲏⲏⲃⲉ (m.): finger
ⲧⲱⲱⲃⲉ, ⲧⲉⲃⲉ-, ⲧⲟⲟⲃ⸗/ⲧⲃⲃⲟ⸗: to repay, to requite
ⲧⲃⲁ (m.): ten thousand
ⲧⲃⲃⲟ, ⲧⲃⲃⲉ-, ⲧⲃⲃⲟ⸗, ⲧⲃⲃⲏⲩ†: to become pure, to be pure; purify; *nn m.*: purity; purification
ⲧⲃⲛⲏ, pl. ⲧⲃⲛⲟⲟⲩⲉ: beast
ⲧⲃ̄ⲧ (m.): fish
ⲧⲟⲃⲧⲃ, ⲧⲃⲧ(ⲉ)ⲃ-, ⲧⲃⲧⲱⲃ⸗: to form, to compound; to invent; *nn m.*: mix, compound
ⲧⲱⲃϩ, ⲧ(ⲉ)ⲃϩ-, ⲧⲟⲃϩ⸗: to pray, to entreat; to console
ⲧⲁⲕⲟ, ⲧⲁⲕⲉ-, ⲧⲁⲕⲟ⸗: to destroy; *nn m.*: destruction
    ⲁⲧ.ⲧⲁⲕⲟ: indestructible
    ⲙⲛ̄ⲧ.ⲁⲧ.ⲧⲁⲕⲟ: indestructibility
ⲧⲱⲕⲥ, ⲧⲉⲕⲥ-, ⲧⲟⲕⲥ⸗, ⲧⲟⲕⲥ†: to pierce; to bite; to be pierced; to be studded (with nails)
    ⲧⲉⲕⲥ-ⲧⲏⲏⲃⲉ: to point finger at; to show
ⲧⲁⲗⲟ, ⲧⲁⲗⲉ-, ⲧⲁⲗⲟ⸗, ⲧⲁⲗⲏⲩ†: to lift, to offer up; to set up; to go up, to mount
ⲧⲱⲗⲙ, ⲧⲟⲗⲙ⸗, ⲧⲟⲗⲙ⸗: to be defiled, besmirched; to defile; *nn m.*: stain, pollution
ⲧⲙ: *negation*: not (cf. 118, 132)
ⲧⲁⲙⲓⲟ, ⲧⲁⲙⲓⲉ-, ⲧⲁⲙⲓⲟ⸗, ⲧⲁⲙⲓⲏⲩ†: to make; to create; *nn m.*: thing made; creation
ⲧⲁⲙⲟ, ⲧⲁⲙⲉ-, ⲧⲁⲙⲟ⸗: to tell, to inform
†ⲙⲉ (m.): town, village
ⲧⲙ̄ⲙⲟ, ⲧⲙ(ⲙ)ⲉ-, ⲧⲙ(ⲙ)ⲟ⸗/ⲧⲙ(ⲙ)ⲉ⸗: to nourish
ⲧⲱⲙⲛⲧ: *see* ⲧⲱⲙⲧ
ⲧⲱⲙⲥ, ⲧ(ⲉ)ⲙⲥ-, ⲧⲟⲙ(ⲉ)ⲥ⸗, ⲧⲟⲙⲥ†: to bury; to be buried
ⲧⲱⲙⲧ, ⲧⲟⲙⲛⲧ⸗: to meet, to befall; *nn m.*: meeting, event

Coptic glossary   161

ⲦⲘϨⲞ, ⲦⲘϨⲈ-, ⲦⲘϨⲞ⸗: to set on fire, to kindle; to burn; *nn m.*: burning; heat

Ⲧ̄Ⲛ-: *pers. pron.*: we

Ⲧ̄Ⲛ-: *see* ⲦⲰⲢⲈ

ⲦⲰⲚ: *interrogative adv.*: where? wherefrom? how?

ⲦⲰⲚ (m.): dispute, strife

ϯ-ⲦⲰⲚ: to dispute, to quarrel; *nn m.*: dispute; fight

ⲦⲈⲚⲞⲨ: *see* ⲞⲨⲚⲞⲨ

ϯ ⲚⲀ-: *see* ϯ

ⲦⲰⲚⲞⲨ, ⲦⲰⲚⲈ: *adv.*: very, greatly

Ⲧ(Ⲛ̄)ⲚⲀⲨ: *adv.*: when?

Ⲧ̄ⲚⲚⲞⲞⲨ, Ⲧ(Ⲛ)ⲚⲈⲨ-, ⲦⲚ(Ⲛ)ⲞⲞⲨ⸗/ⲦⲚⲚⲞⲨⲦ⸗: to send

ⲦⲞⲚⲦⲚ, Ⲧ(Ⲉ)ⲚⲦⲚ-, ⲦⲚⲦⲰⲚ⸗, ⲦⲚⲦⲰⲚ†/ⲦⲚⲦⲞⲚⲦ†: to be like; to liken; to estimate; to speculate ; *nn m.*: likeness, similitude; oracle

ⲦⲀⲚϨⲞ, ⲦⲀⲚϨⲈ-, ⲦⲀⲚϨⲞ⸗, ⲦⲀⲚϨⲎⲨ†: *caus. of* ⲰⲚϨ: to make alive, to keep alive; to be alive; *nn m.*: keeping alive; saving

ⲦⲀⲚϨⲞⲨⲦ, ⲦⲀⲚϨⲈⲦ-, ⲦⲀⲚϨⲞⲨⲦ⸗, ⲦⲀⲚϨⲎⲦ†: to trust, to believe

ϯⲠⲈ (f.): taste

ϪⲒ-ϯⲠⲈ: to taste

ⲦⲀⲠⲢⲞ (f.): mouth

ⲦⲎⲢ⸗: all, whole, every

ⲦⲢⲈ-: *used to build a caus. inf.* (cf. 130)

ⲦⲰⲢⲈ (f.), Ⲧ̄Ⲛ-, ⲦⲈ-, ⲦⲞⲞⲦ⸗: hand

Ⲛ̄Ⲧ̄Ⲛ- (Ⲛ̄ⲦⲈ-), Ⲛ̄ⲦⲞⲞⲦ⸗: *prep.*: in; by hand of, by; with; beside; from

ϨⲀⲦ̄Ⲛ-, ϨⲀⲦⲞⲞⲦ⸗: *prep*: under the hand of; beside; with

ϨⲒⲦ̄Ⲛ-, ϨⲒⲦⲞⲞⲦ⸗: *prep.*: by the hand of; through, by; from

ⲦⲤⲞ, ⲦⲤⲈ-, ⲦⲤⲞ⸗: to give to drink

ⲦⲤⲀⲂⲞ, ⲦⲤⲀⲂⲈ-, ⲦⲤ(Ⲁ)ⲂⲞ⸗: to make wise; to teach; to show

ⲦⲤ̄ⲂⲔⲞ, ⲦⲤⲂⲔⲈ-, ⲦⲤⲂⲔⲞ⸗: to make small, to diminish

(Ⲧ)ⲤⲦⲞ, (Ⲧ)ⲤⲦⲈ-, (Ⲧ)ⲤⲦⲞ⸗, (Ⲧ)ⲤⲦⲎⲨ†: to bring; to pay back; to repeat

ⲦⲞⲈⲒⲦ: to mourn; *nn m.*: mourning, lament

ⲦⲞⲞⲦ⸗: *see* ⲦⲰⲢⲈ

ⲦⲰⲦ, ⲦⲈⲦ-, ⲦⲞⲦ⸗, ⲦⲎⲦ†: to be joined; to be persuaded; to be agreeable; to make equal

ⲦⲦⲞ, ⲦⲦⲈ-, ⲦⲦⲞ⸗: to make give, to require

ⲦⲈⲦⲚ̄-: *pers. pron.*: you (pl.)

ϯⲦⲰⲚ: *see* ⲦⲰⲚ

ⲦⲀⲒⲞⲨ: fifty

ⲦⲎⲨ (m.): wind

ϯⲞⲨ, ϯ(Ⲉ): five

ⲦⲞⲞⲨ (m.): mountain, mountainous country

ⲦⲞⲞⲨ, ⲦⲈⲨ-, ⲦⲞⲞⲨ⸗: to buy

ⲦⲞⲞⲨⲈ (m.): shoe, (pair of) shoes

ⲧⲟⲩⲱ⸗: see ⲧⲟⲩⲛ̄-
ⲧⲟⲩⲛ̄-, ⲧⲟⲩⲱ⸗: bosom
    ⲉ-ⲧⲟⲩⲉⲛ-: *prep.*: toward (to the bosom of)
ⲧⲱⲟⲩⲛ̄/ⲧⲱ(ⲱ)ⲛ, ⲧⲟⲩⲛ̄-, ⲧⲟⲩⲱⲛ⸗/ⲧⲱ(ⲱ)ⲛ⸗: to arise; to raise; to carry
ⲧⲟⲩⲛⲟⲥ, ⲧⲟⲩⲛⲉⲥ-/ⲧⲟⲩⲛⲟⲩⲥ, ⲧⲟⲩⲛⲟⲥ⸗: to wake; to raise; to stand up; to be resuscitated; to set up; *nn m.*: raising, resurrection
ⲧⲱϣ, ⲧⲉϣ-/ⲧⲟϣ-, ⲧⲟϣ⸗, ⲧⲏϣ†: to be boundary, to be fixed; to limit; to determine; *nn m.*: ordinance; destiny; affair; fashion
ⲧⲁϣⲟ, ⲧⲁϣⲉ-, ⲧⲁϣⲟ⸗: to increase
    ⲧⲁϣⲉ-ⲟⲉⲓϣ: to proclaim, to preach
ⲧⲱϩ, ⲧⲏϩ-/ⲧⲁϩ-, ⲧⲁϩ⸗, ⲧⲏϩ†: to be mixed, disturbed, clouded; to mix, to stir
ⲧⲁϩⲟ, ⲧⲁϩⲉ-, ⲧⲁϩⲟ⸗, ⲧⲁϩⲏⲩ†: to make to stand, to set up; to attain, to reach; to assign to; to be able
ϯϩⲉ, ⲧⲁϩⲉ†: to become drunken, to be drunken
ⲧϩⲏ⸗: see ϩⲏⲧ
ⲑⲁⲃ (m.): leaven
ⲑ̄ⲃⲃⲓⲟ, ⲑ̄ⲃⲃⲓⲉ-, ⲑ̄ⲃⲃⲓⲟ⸗: to humiliate; to be humble; *nn m.*: humility
ⲧⲱϩⲙ, ⲧⲉϩⲙ-/ⲧⲁϩⲙ⸗, ⲧⲁϩⲙ⸗, ⲧⲁϩⲙ†: to nock, to summon, to invite; *nn m.*: calling, convocation
ⲧϩ̄ⲙⲕⲟ, ⲧϩ̄ⲙⲕⲉ-, ⲧϩ̄ⲙⲕⲟ⸗: to ill use; to afflict; to humiliate; *nn m.*: ill treatment; affliction
ⲧⲁϫⲣⲟ, ⲧⲁϫⲣⲉ-, ⲧⲁϫⲣⲟ⸗, ⲧⲁϫⲣⲏ(ⲟ)ⲩ†/ⲧⲁϫⲣⲁⲉⲓⲧ†: to make strong, firm, fast; to be strengthened, decided; *nn m.*: firmness, strength, solidity
ⲧⲱϭⲉ, ⲧⲉϭ-, ⲧⲟ(ⲟ)ϭ⸗, ⲧⲏϭ†: to be fixed, joined; to plant
(ⲧ)ϭⲁ(ⲉ)ⲓⲟ, (ⲧ)ϭⲁ(ⲉ)ⲓⲉ-, (ⲧ)ϭⲁ(ⲉ)ⲓⲟ⸗, (ⲧ)ϭⲁ(ⲉ)ⲓⲏⲩ†: to make ugly; to disgrace; to condemn; to be disgraced, condemned

ⲟⲩ

ⲟⲩ: *indef. art.*: a (cf. 064)
ⲟⲩ: *interrogative pron.*: what?
ⲟⲩⲁ: *indef. pron.*: someone
ⲟⲩⲁ (m.): blasphemy
    ϫⲓ-ⲟⲩⲁ: to speak blasphemy
ⲟⲩⲁ, ⲟⲩⲉⲓ: one
ⲟⲩⲁⲁ(ⲧ)⸗: alone
ⲟⲩⲉ, ⲟⲩⲏ(ⲏ)ⲩ⸗/ⲟⲩⲏⲟⲩ⸗, ⲟⲩⲏⲩ†: to be distant, far-reaching; *nn m.*: distance
ⲟⲩⲉⲓ: see ⲟⲩⲁ
ⲟⲩⲟ(ⲉ)ⲓ (m.): rush, course, swift movement; progress, impetuosity
    ϯ-ⲟⲩⲟ(ⲉ)ⲓ: to go about seeking, to seek; to go forward
ⲟⲩⲱ: to cease; to stay; to stop; to finish

Coptic glossary

ⲟⲩⲁⲁⲃ†: to be pure; to be saint ; *see* ⲟⲩⲟⲡ
    ⲡ.ⲉⲧ.ⲟⲩⲁⲁⲃ: saint
ⲟⲩⲃⲉ-, ⲟⲩⲃⲏ⸗: *prep.*: opposite; toward; against
ⲟⲩⲁⲙ-: *part. cstr. of* ⲟⲩⲱⲙ
    ⲟⲩⲁⲙ-ⲣⲱⲙⲉ: cannibal
ⲟⲩⲱⲙ, ⲟⲩ(ⲉ)ⲙ-/ⲟⲩⲱⲙ-/ⲟⲩⲟⲙ-, ⲟⲩⲟⲟⲙ⸗: to eat; to bite
    ϭⲓⲛ-ⲟⲩⲱⲙ: food
ⲟⲩⲛ̄-: there is/are
ⲟⲩⲛ̄-: *used in the durative sentence with indefinite subject* (cf. 267)
ⲟⲩⲟⲛ: someone; something
ⲟⲩⲟⲉⲓⲛ (m.): light
ⲟⲩⲱⲛ, ⲟⲩⲏⲛ⸗: to open
ⲟⲩⲉⲓⲛⲉ: to pass by
ⲟⲩⲛ̄ⲧⲉ-, ⲟⲩⲛ̄ⲧⲁ⸗: to have
ⲟⲩⲛⲟⲩ (f.): hour; moment
    ⲛ̄-ⲧⲉ.ⲩⲛⲟⲩ: *adv.*: immediately
    ⲧⲉⲛⲟⲩ: *adv.*: now
ⲟⲩⲱⲛϣ (m.): wolf
ⲟⲩⲱⲛϩ̄ (ⲉⲃⲟⲗ), ⲟⲩⲉⲛϩ-, ⲟⲩⲟⲛϩ⸗, ⲟⲩⲟⲛϩ†: to reveal; to be revealed; to appear; *nn m.* revelation; apparition
    ⲁⲧ.ⲟⲩⲱⲛϩ ⲉⲃⲟⲗ: invisible
ⲟⲩⲟⲡ: to be pure, innocent
ⲟⲩⲏⲣ: *interrogative pron.*: how many? how much?
ⲟⲩⲣⲟⲧ, ⲣⲟⲟⲩⲧ†: to be glad, eager, ready; *stative*: to be glad, fresh, flourishing; *nn m.* gladness; abundance; zeal
ⲟⲩⲉⲣⲏⲧⲉ (f./pl.): foot, feet
ⲟⲩⲱⲧ: single; alone; any; one and same
ⲟⲩⲧⲉ-, ⲟⲩⲧⲱ⸗: *prep*: between, among
ⲟⲩⲏⲩ: *stative of* ⲟⲩⲉ
ⲟⲩⲟⲉⲓϣ (m.): time, occasion
ⲟⲩⲱϣ, ⲟⲩⲉϣ-, ⲟⲩⲁϣ⸗: to desire, to love; *nn m.*: desire, love
ⲟⲩϣⲏ (f.): night
    ⲣ̄-ⲟⲩϣⲏ: to pass night
ⲟⲩⲱϣⲃ, ⲟⲩⲉϣⲃ-, ⲟⲩⲟϣⲃ⸗: to answer
ⲟⲩⲱϣⲧ: to worship; to great; to kiss
ⲟⲩⲱϩ, ⲟⲩⲉϩ-, ⲟⲩⲁϩ⸗, ⲟⲩⲏϩ†: to put, to set; to add; to be placed; to dwell; *with* ⲛ̄ⲥⲁ-: to put after; to follow
    ⲟⲩⲉϩ-ⲥⲁϩⲛⲉ: to command, to order
    ϭⲓⲛ-ⲟⲩⲱϩ: act of dwelling; manner of life
ⲟⲩⲟⲟϩⲉ (f.): scorpion
ⲟⲩϫⲁⲓ, ⲟⲩⲟϫ†: to be whole, safe, sound; *nn m.* : health, safety; weal

ⲟⲩⲱϫⲡ: *see* ⲟⲩⲱϭⲡ
ⲟⲩⲱϭⲡ, ⲟⲩⲉϭⲡ-, ⲟⲩⲟϭⲡ⸗, ⲟⲩⲟϭⲡ†: to break; to be broken

ⲱ

ⲱ(ⲱ): to conceive; *nn m.*: conception
ⲱⲃϣ, ⲉⲃϣ-, ⲟⲃϣ⸗, ⲟⲃϣ†: to forget; to be forgotten; to sleep; *nn m.*: forgetfulness; oblivion; sleep
    ⲣ̄-(ⲡ.)ⲱⲃϣ: to be forgetful; to be forgotten
ⲱⲗ, ⲟⲗ-/ⲱⲗ-, ⲟⲗ⸗, ⲏⲗ†: to hold, to contain, to enclose; to take, to lay hold of; to gather; to harvest; *nn m.*: gathering; harvest
ⲱⲙⲥ, ⲉⲙⲥ-/ⲁⲙⲥ-, ⲟⲙⲥ⸗, ⲟⲙⲥ†: to be sunk, submerged; to sink, to dip; to baptize; to be baptized; *nn m.*: sinking, dipping; baptism
ⲱⲛⲉ (f.): stone
ⲱⲛϩ, ⲟⲛϩ⸗: to live; *nn m.*: life
ⲱⲡ, ⲉⲡ-, ⲟⲡ⸗/ⲁⲡ⸗, ⲏⲡ†: to count; to esteem; to consider; *nn m.*: reckoning
    ⲏ(ⲏ)ⲡⲉ (f.): number
ⲱⲣⲃ̄, ⲉⲣⲃ̄-, ⲟⲣⲃ⸗, ⲟⲣⲃ†: to be enclosed, apart; to be quiet; to restrict; to surround; *nn m.*: seclusion; quietude
ⲱⲣⲕ, ⲱⲣⲕ-, ⲟⲣⲕ⸗: to swear; *nn m.*: swearing
ⲱⲣϫ, ⲱⲣϫ-, ⲟⲣϫ⸗, ⲟⲣ(ⲉ)ϫ†: to be firm, secure, fastened; to confirm, to fasten; to imprison; *nn m.*: firmness, assurance; deed of security; lock
ⲱⲥⲕ, ⲟⲥⲕ†: to delay; to continue, to be prolonged; to be delayed; *nn m.*: duration; delay
ⲱⲧⲡ, ⲉⲧⲡ-, ⲟⲡⲧ⸗, ⲟⲧⲡ†/ⲟⲡⲧ†: to shut, to enclose, to imprison; *nn m.*: seclusion, imprisonment
ⲱϣ, ⲉϣ-/ⲱϣ-/ⲁϣ-, ⲟϣ⸗: to cry, to announce; to sound; to read; to promise; to vow
    ⲁϣ-ϣⲕⲁⲕ (ⲁϣⲕⲁⲕ): to cry out
ⲱϣⲙ, ⲉϣⲙ-, ⲟϣⲙ⸗, ⲟϣⲙ†: to be quenched, dried up; to quench
ⲱϩⲉ, ⲁϩⲉ†: to stand; to stay; to wait
    with ⲡⲁⲧ⸗: to reap; to mow; *nn m.* reaping, harvest
    ⲟϩⲥ (m.): sickle
ⲱϫⲛ, ⲉϫⲛ(ⲉ)-/ⲱϫⲛ-, ⲟϫⲛ⸗: to cease, to perish; to make cease, to destroy; *nn m.*: ceasing, destruction
    ⲁⲧ.ⲱϫⲛ: unceasing

ϣ

ϣ: *see* ⲉϣ
ϣⲁ (m.), ϣⲁⲛⲧ⸗: nose
ϣⲁ-, ϣⲁⲣⲟ⸗: prep: to, toward (*of persons*); to, at (*of places*)
    ϣⲁϩⲣⲁⲓ: *see* ϩⲣⲁⲓ

ϢΑ: to rise (*of the sun*); *nn m.*: rising (*of the sun*); feast, festival
ϢΕ (m./f.): wood
ϢΕ: hundred
ϢΙ, ϢΙ-, ϢΙΤ⸗, ϢΗΥ†: to measure; to weigh; *nn m.*: measure; weight
    ΑΤ.ϢΙ: immeasurable
    Ϯ-ϢΙ: to set measure; to restrict
ϢΟ: thousand
ϢΩΙ (m.): what is high, above
ϢΒΕ: *see* ϢϥΕ
ϢΙΒΕ, ϢΒ-/Ϣ(Ε)ΒΤ-, Ϣ(Ε)ΒΤ⸗, ϢΟ(Ο)ΒΕ†: to change; to be changed; *nn m.*: change; difference
ϢΒΗΡ (m.): friend, comrade
    ϢΒΡ̄-: companion in
ϢΚΑΚ: to cry, to shout; *nn m.*: cry
ϢΩΛ, ϢΕΛ-, ϢΟΛ⸗/ϢΑΛ⸗: despoil; *nn m.*: spoil, booty
ϢΛΗΛ: to pray; *nn m.*: prayer
ϢΩΜ: to smell
    ϬΙΝ-ϢΩΜ (f.): sense, power of smell
ϢΕΛΕΕΤ (f.): bride; marriage
    ΠΑ-ϢΕΛΕΕΤ: bridegroom
ϢΗΜ: small; few; young; humble
ϢΩΜ (m.): summer
ϢΜ̄ΜΟ: stranger
ϢΜΟΥΝ, ϢΜΟΥΝΕ: eight
ϢΟΜΝ̄Τ (m.), ϢΟΜΤΕ (f.): three
ϢΟΜΤΕ: *see* ϢΟΜΝ̄Τ
ϢΜϢΕ, ϢΜϢΕ-, ϢΜϢΗΤ⸗: to serve; to worship; *nn m.*: service; worship
    ΡΕϤ.ϢΜϢΕ: server; worshipper
ϢΝ̄-: *see* ϢΗΡΕ
ϢΗΝ (m.): tree
ϢΝΑ (m.): profligate; prodigal
    ΜΝ̄Τ.ϢΝΑ: profligacy; intemperance
ϢΙΝΕ, ϢΕΝ(Τ)-, ϢΝΤ⸗: to seek; to ask; *nn m.*: inquiry; news; report
    ϢΙΝΕ Ε-: to visit; to inquire for; to greet; to bid farewell
    ϢΙΝΕ Ν̄ΣΑ-: to inquire for; to seek after
    ϢΜ-ΝΟΥϤΕ: good news
    ϬΜ-Π.ϢΙΝΕ: to visit
ϢΩΝΕ: to be sick, weak; *nn m.*: sickness, disease
ϢΩΝΒ: *see* ϢΩΝϤ
ϢΑΝΤ⸗: *see* ϢΑ

ϣⲱⲛϥ/ϣⲱⲛⲃ, ϣⲉⲛϥ-/ϣⲉⲛⲃ, ϣⲟⲛϥ⸗/ϣⲟⲛⲃ⸗, ϣⲟⲛϥ†: to join; to come together; *nn m.*: union, unity

ϣⲱⲡ, ϣ(ⲉⲡ)-, ϣⲟⲡ⸗, ϣⲏⲡ†: to receive; to contain; to take

ϣⲓⲡⲉ: to be ashamed; to shame, to make shamed; *nn m.*: shame

ϣⲱⲡⲉ, ϣⲟⲟⲡ†: to become, to befall; *stative*: to exist, to be

ϣⲡⲏⲣⲉ (f.): wonder, amazement

    ⲣ̄-ϣⲡⲏⲣⲉ: to be amazed; to marvel at, to admire

ϣⲁⲁⲣ (m.): skin

ϣⲁⲓⲣⲉ (f.): couch; cohabitation; sheepfold

ϣⲁⲣⲟ⸗: *see* ϣⲁ-

ϣⲉⲉⲣⲉ: *see* ϣⲏⲣⲉ

ϣⲏⲣⲉ (m.), ϣⲉⲉⲣⲉ (f.), ϣⲡⲏⲩ (pl.): child; son; daughter

    ϣⲛ̄-, ϣⲡ̄-: child of

        ϣⲛ̄-ⲥⲟⲛ: nephew (son of a brother)

        ϣⲡ̄-ⲃⲱⲱⲛ: bad son

ϣⲱⲣⲡ, ϣ(ⲉ)ⲣⲡ-, ϣⲟⲣⲡ⸗, ϣⲟⲣⲡ(ⲉ)†: to be early; to be first; *nn m.*: morning

ϣⲡⲏⲩ: *pl. of* ϣⲏⲣⲉ

ϣⲉⲥ-, ϣⲟⲥ⸗, ϣⲏⲥ†: *see* ⲥⲱϣ

ϣⲱⲥ (m.), pl. ϣⲟⲟⲥ/ϣⲱⲱⲥ: herd, shepherd

ϣⲥⲛ̄-: *see* ⲥⲱϣ

ϣⲏⲧ: two hundred

ϣⲱⲧ (m.): trader, merchant

ϣⲱⲱⲧ, ϣ(ⲉ)(ⲉ)ⲧ-, ϣⲁ(ⲁ)ⲧ⸗, ϣⲁⲁⲧ†: to cut, to slay; to be cut short, to want, to lack; *nn m.*: thing cut; sacrifice; need; shortage

ϣⲱⲧⲉ (f.): well, cistern, pit

ϣⲧⲉⲕⲟ (m.), pl. ϣⲧⲉⲕⲱⲟⲩ: prison

ϣⲧⲉⲕⲱⲟⲩ: *pl. of* ϣⲧⲉⲕⲟ

ϣⲧⲟⲣⲧⲣ, ϣⲧⲣⲧⲣ-, ϣⲧⲣⲧⲱⲣ⸗, ϣⲧⲣⲧⲱⲣ†: to be disturbed, troubled, in haste; to disturb, to cause to hasten; *nn m.*: disturbance, trouble, haste, confusion

ϣⲁⲩ, ϣⲟⲩ- (m.): use; value; *as adj.*: useful, fitting

    ⲙⲛⲧ.ϣⲁⲩ: usefulness; propriety; modesty

    ϣⲟⲩ-ⲙⲉⲣⲓⲧ⸗ϥ̄: amiable

ϣⲟⲟⲩⲉ, ϣⲟⲩⲱⲟⲩ†: to be dry

ϣⲟⲩⲟ, ϣⲟⲩⲉ-, ϣⲟⲩⲟ⸗: to flow; to pour; to discharge, to empty

ϣⲟⲩⲉⲓⲧ: empty

ϣⲟⲩⲱⲟⲩ: *stative of* ϣⲟⲟⲩⲉ

ϣⲟⲩϣⲟⲩ: to boast, to pride oneself; *nn m.*: boast, pride

ϣϣⲉ: it is fitting, right; *negation*: ⲙⲉϣϣⲉ

ϣⲟⲩϣⲧ (m.): window; niche, alcove

ϣϥⲉ/ϣⲃⲉ/ⲥϣϥⲉ, ϣϥⲉ-: seventy

ϣⲁϥⲧⲉ (m.): iniquitous, impious person or thing

ϢⲀϪⲈ: to speak, to say; *nn m.*: word, saying
    ϬⲒⲚ-ϢⲀϪⲈ (f.): speech; saying; tale
ϢⲞϪⲚⲈ: to take counsel, to consider; *nn m.*: counsel, design
    ϪⲒ-ϢⲞϪⲚⲈ: to advise; to take counsel
    ⲢⲈϤ.ϪⲒ-ϢⲞϪⲚⲈ: adviser, counseler
ϢⲰϪⲠ, ϢⲈϪⲠ-, ϢⲞϪⲠ⸗, ϢⲞϪⲠ†: to be over, to remain over; to leave over, behind; *nn m.*: remainder, rest
ϢϬⲞⲘ: *see* ϬⲞⲘ

Ϥ

⸗Ϥ, Ϥ-: *pers. pron.*: he, him
ϤⲀⲒ-: *part. cstr. of* ϤⲒ
    ϤⲀⲒ-ⲚⲀϨⲂ: yoking beast
    ϤⲀⲒ-ϢⲒⲚⲈ: ship
ϤⲒ, ϤⲒ-, ϤⲒⲦ⸗: to bear, to carry, to take
    ϤⲒ ϨⲀ-: to bear under, to support, to tolerate
ϤⲚⲦ (m./f.): worm
ϤⲦⲞ(Ⲉ): *see* ϤⲦⲞⲞⲨ
ϤⲦⲞⲞⲨ (m.), ϤⲦⲞ(Ⲉ) (f.): four

Ϩ

Ϩⲁ-, ϨⲀⲢⲞ⸗: *prep.*: under; in; at; from; by reason of; in respect of; toward
ϨⲀⲈ: last
ϨⲀⲒ (m.): husband
ϨⲈ (f.): manner
ϨⲈ: to fall; to light upon; to find; *nn m.*: fall; destruction
ϨⲎ (f.), ϨⲎⲦ⸗: fore part; beginning
ϨⲎ (f.), ϨⲎⲦ⸗: belly; womb
    ϨⲀ-ⲐⲎ: *prep./conj.*: before
    ϨⲎⲦ⸗: *prep.*: before, in front of
    Ⲛ̄ϨⲎⲦ⸗ *(see* ϨⲚ̄-*)*: *prep.*: in
ϨⲎ, ϨⲈ- (m.): season
    ϨⲈ-ⲂⲰⲰⲚ: bad season; famine
ϨⲒ-, ϨⲒⲰ(Ⲱ)⸗: on; at; in
ϨⲒⲈ: *particle, see* ⲈⲒⲈ
ϨⲒⲎ (f.), pl. ϨⲒⲞⲞⲨⲈ: road; path
ϨⲒⲰⲰ⸗: *see* ϨⲒ-

ϩΟ (m.), ϩΡΝ̄-/ϩΝ̄-, ϩΡΑ⸗: *prep.*: face; side, edge
    Є-ϩ(Ρ)Ν̄-, Є-ϩΡΑ⸗: *prep.*: toward face of; to; among
    ΝΑ-ϩΡΝ̄-, ΝΑ-ϩΡΑ⸗: *prep.*: in presence of; before
ϩⲰ: to suffice, to be enough
ϩⲰⲰ⸗: self; also; but, on other hand
ϩΙЄΙΒ (m.): lamb
ϩⲰΒ (m.), pl. ϩΒΗΥЄ: thing; work; matter; event
    Ρ̄-ϩⲰΒ: to do work, to be zealous
    ϬΙΝ-Ρ̄-ϩⲰΒ (f.): work
ϩΙΒЄ, ϩΟΒЄ†: to be low, to be short;
    ϩΒ̄ΒЄ (m.): low part, place
ϩΒ̄ΒЄ: *see* ϩΙΒЄ
ϩЄΒⲰⲰΝ: *see* ϩΗ
ϩⲰΒⲤ, ϩ(Є)ΒⲤ-, ϩΟΒⲤ⸗, ϩΟΒⲤ†: to cover; to be covered; to hide
ϩΒΗΥЄ: *pl. of* ϩⲰΒ
ϩΗΚЄ: poor
ϩΚΟ, ϩΚΑЄΙΤ†/ϩΚΟЄΙΤ†: to be hungry; *nn m.*: hunger; famine
ϩΑΛ: *with* Ρ̄-: to deceive
ϩⲰΛ, ϩ(Є)Λ-/ϩΟΛ-, ϩΟΛ⸗: to throw; to bring
ϩΟΟΛЄ (f.): moth
ϩΛ̄ΛΟ (m.), ϩΛ̄ΛⲰ (f.): old person
    ΜΝ̄Τ.ϩΛ̄ΛΟ: (old) age
ϩΛ̄ΛⲰ: *see* ϩΛ̄ΛΟ
ϩⲰΛЄΜ, ϩЄΛЄΜ-, ϩΟΛΜ⸗: to seize
ϩΛΟΠΛ(Є)Π, ϩΑΠΛⲰΠ⸗, ϩΛΟΠΛⲰΠ†: to be weary, despondent; *nn m.*: weariness, distress
ϩΑΛϬ-: *part. cstr. of* ϩΛΟϬ
    ϩΑΛϬ-ϢΑϪЄ: eloquent
ϩΛΟϬ, ϩΟΛϬ†: to be sweet; to take delight
ϩΑΜ-: craftsman
    ϩΑΜ-ϢЄ: carpenter
    ϩΑΜ-ΝΟΥΒ: goldsmith
ϩⲰΜ, ϩЄΜ-, ϩΟΜ⸗, ϩΗΜ†: to tread, to trample; to beat
ϩΑΜΟΙ: *interj.*: would, o that! (cf. 420)
ϩΜЄ, ϩΜЄ-, ϩΜ̄Τ-: forty
ϩΙΟΜЄ: *pl. of* ⲤϩΙΜЄ
ϩΜΟΜ, ϩΗΜ†: to be hot; *nn m.*: heat; fever
ϩΜΜЄ (f.): heat; fever (*see* ϩΜΟΜ)
ϩΜЄΝЄ, ϩΜ(Є)ΝЄ-, ϩΜЄΝЄΤ-: eighty
ϩΜЄΝЄΤ-: *see* ϩΜЄΝЄ

ϩⲙⲟⲟⲥ: to sit; to remain; to dwell
ϩⲙⲧ-: *see* ϩⲙⲉ
ϩⲙⲟⲧ (m.): grace; gift
    ϣⲡ-ϩⲙⲟⲧ (ⲛⲧⲛ̄-): to give thanks to (*literally*: to receive grace from)
ϩⲙ̄ϩⲁⲗ (m./f.): servant
    ϣⲃⲣ-ϩⲙ̄ϩⲁⲗ: fellow slave
ϩⲛ̄-: *see* ϩⲟ
ϩⲛ̄-, ⲛ̄ϩⲏⲧ⸗: *prep.*: in; at; on; by; with; from
    ⲉ-ϩ(ⲉ)ⲛ-: *prep.*: toward; against
ϩⲉⲛ: *indef. art. pl.* (cf. 064)
ϩⲱⲛ, ϩⲱⲛⲉ, ϩⲛ-, ϩⲟⲛ⸗, ϩⲏⲛ†: to approach, to be nigh; to comply with
ϩⲱⲛ, ϩⲟⲛ⸗: to bid, to command
ϩⲛⲉ-, ϩⲛⲁ⸗: to will, to desire; *impersonal*: it pleases
    ⲣ̄-ϩⲛⲁ: to be willing, to desire
ϩⲟ(ⲉ)ⲓⲛⲉ: some, certain
ϩⲱⲛⲉ: *see* ϩⲱⲛ
ϩⲉⲛⲉⲉⲧⲉ (f.): monastery
ϩⲛⲁ(ⲁ)ⲩ, ϩⲛ(ⲟ)ⲟⲩ (m.): vessel, pot, receptacle; thing
ϩⲁⲡ (m.): judgment, inquest
    ⲣ̄-ϩⲁⲡ: to give judgment; to avenge; to go to law
    ϯ-ϩⲁⲡ: to give judgment
    ⲣⲉϥ.ϯ-ϩⲁⲡ: judge
    ϫⲓ-ϩⲁⲡ: to receive judgment; to go to law
ϩⲱⲡ, ϩⲉⲡ-, ϩⲟⲡ⸗, ϩⲏⲡ†: to be hidden; to hide
ϩⲁⲡⲥ: it is needful, necessary
ϩⲣⲁⲓ: upper part; lower part; *often as adv. or with prep.*
    ⲉϩⲣⲁⲓ: *adv.*: to above, upward; downward
    ϣⲁϩⲣⲁⲓ: *adv.*: upward; downward
ϩⲁⲣⲟ⸗: *see* ϩⲁ-
ϩⲣⲁ⸗: *see* ϩⲟ
ϩⲣⲁ⸗: *see* ϩⲣⲟⲟⲩ
ϩⲣⲉ (f./m.), pl. ϩⲣⲏⲩⲉ, ϩⲣⲉⲟⲩⲉ, ϩⲣⲉⲟⲟⲩ: food
ϩⲣⲃ (m.): form; likeness
ϩⲣⲟⲟⲩ (m.), ϩⲣⲟⲩⲛ̄-, ϩⲣⲁ⸗: voice; sound
ϩⲣⲟϣ, ϩ(ⲉ)ⲣϣ-, ϩⲟⲣϣ⸗: to be heavy, slow, difficult; to make heavy; *nn m.*: weigh, burden
ϩⲁⲣⲉϩ (ⲉ-): to keep; to guard; to restrain
ϩⲓⲥⲉ, ϩⲁⲥⲧ-, ϩⲁⲥⲧ⸗/ϩⲟⲥⲧ⸗/ϩⲓⲥⲧ⸗, ϩⲟⲥⲉ†: to toil, to be troubled, difficult; to trouble, to weary; *nn m.*: labour, product of labour; weariness; suffering
ϩⲁⲧ (m.): silver

ϨΗΤ (m.), (Ϩ)ΤЄ-, (Ϩ)ΤN̄-, ϨΤΗ⸗: heart; mind
    ΑΘΗΤ: foolish, insensible
    P̄Μ.N̄-ϨΗΤ: understanding
    ϢN-ϨΗΤ: pitiful
    P̄-ΚΟΥΙ N̄-ϨΗΤ: to be faint-hearted
    P̄-ϨΗΤ CNΑΥ: to be of two minds, doubtful
    †-ϨΤΗ⸗: to pay head; to observe
    ϨΑ(Ϩ)ΤN̄/ϨΑ(Ϩ)ΤЄ-, ϨΑ(Ϩ)ΤΗ⸗: *prep.*: below heart of; with; beside

ϨΗΤ (m.), ΤϨΗ⸗: tip; edge
ϨΗ(Η)ΤЄ: *see* ЄΙC
ϨΟΤЄ (f.): fear
    Ο N̄-ϨΟΤЄ: to be afraid
    P̄-ϨΟΤЄ: to be afraid
    †-ϨΟΤЄ: to give fear, to terrify
    ϪΙ-ϨΟΤЄ: to bring fear, to frighten

ϨΤЄ-: *see* ϨΗ
ϨΤЄ-: *see* ϨΗΤ
ϨΤΗ⸗: *see* ϨΗΤ
ϨΤΟ (m.): horse
ϨⲰΤB̄, ϨЄΤB-, ϨΟΤB⸗, ϨΟΤB†: to kill; *nn m.*: slaughter, murder
ϨΤN̄-: *see* ϨΗΤ
ϨΤΟΟΥЄ (m.): dawn, morning
ϨΗΥ (m.): profit; usefulness
    †-ϨΗΥ: to give profit; to benefit
ϨΟΟΥ (m.): day
    ΠЄΘΟΟΥ: who, what is evil; wickedness
ϨΟΟΥ†: to be putrid, bad, wicked
ϨΙΟΥЄ, ϨΟΥ-, ϨΙΤ⸗: to be struck, whetted; to strike; to cast; to lay
ϨΙΟΟΥЄ: *pl. of* ϨΙΗ
ϨΟΥΟ (m.): greater part, greatness; *with* N̄-/Є-... Є-: more than (cf. O33)
    P̄-ϨΟΥΟ: to have more, to exceed
ϨΟΥΡЄ-/ϨΟΥΡⲰ-, ϨΟΥΡ(Ⲱ)Ⲱ⸗/ϨΟΥΡΟ⸗: to deprive
ϨΟΥЄΙΤ(Є): first
ϨΟΟΥΤ (m.): male; husband
ϨⲰϢ, ϨЄϢ-/ϨΟϢ-, ϨⲰϢ⸗, ϨΗϢ†: to be in distress; *nn m.*: distress, straits
ϨΟϤ (m.), ϨⲰϤ (f.): serpent
ϨⲰϤ: *see* ϨΟϤ
ϨΑϨ: many, much
ϨⲰϪΠ, ϨЄϪΠ-, ϨΟϪΠ⸗, ϨΟϪΠ†: *to shut*

ϨⲞⲬϨⲬ, Ϩ(Ⲉ)ⲬϨⲬ-, ϨⲈⲬϨⲰⲬ⸗, ϨⲈⲬϨⲰⲬ†: to be distressed, restricted, narrow; to straighten, to compel; *nn m.*: distress, need

Ⲭ

ⲬⲀⲓ-: *cstr. part. of* Ⲭⲓ
    ⲬⲀⲓ-ⲂⲈⲔⲈ: one who receives a salary; mercenary
ⲬⲀⲈⲓⲈ (m.): desert
ⲬⲈ: *conj.*: introduces a completive, causal or final sentence (###, ###, ###); introduces direct or indirect speech
ⲬⲎ (m.): emptiness; vanity
    Ⲭⲓⲛ-ⲬⲎ/Ϭⲓⲛ-ⲬⲎ: emptiness; vanity
Ⲭⲓ, Ⲭⲓ-/ⲬⲈ-, Ⲭⲓⲧ⸗: to receive; to take; to bring; to accept
ⲬⲞ, ⲬⲈ-/ⲬⲞ-, ⲬⲞ⸗, ⲬⲎⲨ†: to sow; to plant
ⲬⲞ/ⲬⲰ, ⲬⲈ-/Ⲭⲓ-, ⲬⲞ⸗: to put; to send forth; to spend
ⲬⲞ(Ⲉ)ⲓ (m.): ship, boat
ⲬⲰ⸗: *see* Ⲭⲛ-
ⲬⲰ, ⲬⲈ-/Ⲭⲓ-, ⲬⲞⲞ⸗/Ⲭⲓⲧ⸗: to speak, to tell
ⲬⲀⲓ-ⲂⲈⲔⲈ: *see* Ⲭⲓ
ⲬⲰⲔ (ⲈⲂⲞⲖ), ⲬⲈⲔ-/ⲬⲀⲔ-, ⲬⲞⲔ⸗, ⲬⲎⲔ†: to be completed, full; to end; to complete, to finish; to fulfil; *nn m.* completion; end; total; fulfilment
ⲬⲰⲔⲘ(Ⲉ), ⲬⲈⲔⲘ-, ⲬⲞⲔⲘ⸗/ⲬⲀⲔⲘ⸗, ⲬⲞⲔⲘ†: to wash; to wet; *nn m.*: washing; cleansing; baptism
    Ϯ-ⲬⲰⲔⲘ: to give washing; to baptize
    Ⲭⲓ-ⲬⲰⲔⲘ: to take washing; to be baptised
ⲬⲈⲔⲀ(Ⲁ)Ⲥ: that, in order that (cf. 447)
ⲬⲞⲞⲖⲈⲤ (f.): moth; putrefaction
ⲬⲰⲰⲘⲈ (m.): sheet; roll of papyrus; book
Ⲭⲛ (ⲬⲈⲛ, Ⲭⲓⲛ): *conj.*: or
Ⲭⲛ̄- (m.), ⲬⲰ⸗: head
    ⲈⲬⲚ̄-, ⲈⲬⲰ⸗: upon, over; for, on account of; against; to
    ϨⲓⲬⲚ̄-, ϨⲓⲬⲰ⸗: on head of; upon, over; on; at; beside; through
Ⲭⲓⲛ-: *prep.*: from (onward); while yet; since
    ⲬⲓⲛⲦⲀ⸗: Ⲭⲓⲛ + *focalising conversion of the past tense* (cf. 423)
ⲬⲚⲞⲨ, ⲬⲚⲈ-/ⲬⲚⲞⲨ-, ⲬⲚⲞⲨ⸗: to ask, to question, to require; to tell, to say; *nn m.*: questioning, inquiry
ⲬⲓⲛⲬⲎ (m.): *see* ⲬⲎ
ⲬⲓⲛϬⲞⲚⲤ: *see* ϬⲞⲚⲤ
Ⲭ(Ⲉ)Π- (m./f.): hour
ⲬⲠⲓⲞ, ⲬⲠⲓⲈ-, ⲬⲠⲓⲞ⸗, ⲬⲠⲓⲎⲦ†: to blame, to upbraid; *stative*: to be ashamed, modest; *nn m.*: blame; modesty

ⲭⲡⲟ, ⲭⲡⲉ-/ⲭⲡⲟ-, ⲭⲡⲟ⸗, ⲭⲡⲁⲉⲓⲧ†: to beget; to bring forth; to acquire; *nn m.*: birth; begetting

ⲭⲓⲟⲟⲣ: *see* (ⲉ)ⲓⲟⲟⲣ

ⲭⲱⲱⲣ(ⲉ): *see* ⲭⲣⲟ

ⲭⲱⲱⲣⲉ, ⲭⲉ(ⲉ)ⲣⲉ-, ⲭⲟⲟⲣ⸗, ⲭⲟⲟⲣⲉ†: to scatter, to disperse; *nn m.*: scattering, dissolution

ⲭⲉⲣⲟ, ⲭⲉⲣⲉ-, ⲭⲉⲣⲟ⸗: to blaze; to burn; to kindle

ⲭⲣⲟ, ⲭⲣⲁⲉⲓⲧ†: to become *or* to be strong, firm, victorious; *nn m.*: victory; strength

    ⲭⲱⲱⲣⲉ, ⲭⲱⲱⲣ†: to be strong, hard, bold

ⲭⲱⲣⲡ: to stumble, to trip

    ⲭⲣⲟⲡ (m.): obstacle, impediment

    ⲁⲧ.ⲭⲣⲟⲡ: unimpeded

ⲭⲟⲉⲓⲥ (m.): lord

ⲭⲁⲥⲓ: *cstr. part. of* ⲭⲓⲥⲉ

    ⲭⲁⲥⲓ-ϩⲏⲧ: high-hearted; arrogant

ⲭⲓⲥⲉ, ⲭⲉⲥⲧ-, ⲭⲁⲥⲧ⸗/ⲭⲓⲥⲧ⸗, ⲭⲟⲥⲉ†: to become *or* to be high; to exalt

ⲭⲟⲉⲓⲧ (m.): olive tree; olive

ⲭⲟⲟⲩ, ⲭⲉⲩ-/ⲭⲟⲟⲩ-, ⲭⲟ(ⲟ)ⲟⲩ⸗/ⲭⲁⲩⲟⲩ⸗: to send

ⲭⲓⲟⲩⲉ: to steal; *nn m.*: theft, fraud; *nn m./f.*: stolen; secret

    ⲛ-ⲭⲓⲟⲩⲉ: *adv.*: secretly; unbeknown to

    ⲣⲉϥ.ⲭⲓⲟⲩⲉ: thief

ⲭⲟⲩⲧ-: *see* ⲭⲟⲩⲱⲧ

ⲭⲟⲩⲱⲧ (m.), ⲭⲟⲩⲱⲧⲉ (f.), ⲭⲟⲩⲧ-: twenty

ⲭⲱϩ, ⲭⲏϩ⸗: to touch

ⲭⲱϩⲙ, ⲭⲉϩⲙ-, ⲭⲁϩⲙ⸗, ⲭⲁϩⲙ†: to be defiled; to defile, pollute; *nn m.*: uncleanness; pollution

ⲭⲁⲭ (m.): sparrow

ⲭⲱⲭ: head; capital

    ⲁⲛ-ⲭⲱⲭ: chief, captain

ⲭⲁϫⲉ (m.): enemy

    ⲙⲛ̄ⲧ.ⲭⲁϫⲉ: enmity

ϭ

ϭⲉ: *enclitic particle*: then, therefore, but; again, once more

ϭⲉ: *indef. pron.*: other

ϭⲁ(ⲉ)ⲓⲟ: *see* ⲧϭⲁ(ⲉ)ⲓⲟ

ϭⲱ, ϭⲉⲉⲧ†/ϭⲏⲏⲧ†: to continue; to persist; to desist; to stop

ϭⲱⲃ: *see* ϭⲃⲃⲉ

ϭⲃⲃⲉ, ϭⲁⲃ, ϭⲟⲟⲃ⸗/ϭⲟⲟϥ⸗: to become *or* to be feeble, timid; *nn m.*: weakness

    ϭⲱⲃ: weak person

ϭⲟⲗ (m.): lie; liar
    ϫⲓ ϭⲟⲗ: to lie; to speak lie
    ⲣⲉϥ.ϫⲓ-ϭⲟⲗ: liar
ϭⲟ(ⲉ)ⲓⲗⲉ, ϭⲁⲗⲉ-, ϭⲁⲗⲱⲱ⸗, ϭⲁⲗⲏⲩ(ⲧ)†/ϭⲁⲗⲟⲟⲩⲧ†: to dwell; to visit; *nn m.*: sojourn
    ⲙⲁ ⲛ̄-ϭⲟ(ⲉ)ⲓⲗⲉ: dwelling place; station
ϭⲱⲱⲗⲉ, ϭⲉ(ⲉ)ⲗⲉ-/ϭⲗ-, ϭⲟⲟⲗ⸗, ϭⲟⲟⲗⲉ: swathe, clothe; surround; cover; *nn m.*: covering; cloak
ϭⲱⲗⲡ, ϭ(ⲉ)ⲗⲡ-, ϭⲟⲗⲡ⸗, ϭⲟⲗⲡ†: to uncover; to open; to reveal
ϭⲱⲗⳉ, ϭⲟⲗⳉ⸗, ϭⲟⲗⳉ⸗: to be entwined, implicated
ϭⲟⲙ (f.): power, strength
ϭⲙ: *auxiliary*: to find power; to be strong, able
ϭⲛ̄ϭⲟⲙ: to find power; to be strong, able
ϭⲓⲛ-: *forming noun of action*
    ϭⲓⲛ-ϣⲁϫⲉ (f.): word; conversation; story
    ϭⲓⲛ-ϣⲱⲛⲉ (f.): sickness
ϭⲓⲛⲉ, ϭⲛ-, ϭ(ⲉ)ⲛⲧ⸗: to find; to understand
ϭⲟⲛⲥ (m.): might; violence
    ϫⲓ ⲛ̄-ϭⲟⲛⲥ: to use violence; to do evil; *nn m.*: violence, iniquity
ϭⲱⲛⲧ, ϭⲟⲛⲧ†: to be wroth; *nn m.*: wrath
    ⲣ̄-ϭⲱⲛⲧ: to be angry
    ϯ-ϭⲱⲛⲧ: to cause anger; to provoke
ϭⲓⲛϫⲏ (m.): *see* ϫⲏ
ϭⲉⲡⲏ: to hasten
ϭⲏⲡⲉ (f.): cloud
ϭⲱⲡ(ⲉ), ϭⲱⲡ-/ϭⲟⲡ-, ϭⲏⲡ⸗, ϭⲏⲡ†: to seize, to take
ϭⲁⲣⲁⲧⲉ: *see* κεράτιον
ϭⲣⲱϩ, ϭⲣⲟϩ†: to be in want, needy, diminished; *nn m.*: want; need
ϭⲣⲁϩⲧ: *see* ⲥϭⲣⲁϩⲧ
ϭⲉⲣⲏϭ (m.): hunter
ϭⲱⲣϭ: to waylay; to hunt; *nn m.*: snare
ϭⲣⲟ(ⲟ)ϭ (m.): seed
ϭⲟⲥ, ϭⲉⲥ- (m.): half
ϭⲟⲧ (f.): size; age; form
ϭⲱⲧⲡ, ϭⲉⲧⲡ-, ϭⲟⲧⲡ⸗, ϭⲟⲧⲡ†: to be defeated, overcome; to defeat, to overcome
ϭⲱⲧϩ, ϭⲟⲧϩ⸗, ϭⲟⲧϩ†: to wound, to pierce; to intrude; *nn m.* pierced place, hole
ϭⲱⲟⲩ, ϭⲟⲟⲩ⸗, ϭⲏⲩ†: to be narrow; to make narrow
ϭⲱϣⲧ, ϭⲟϣⲧ⸗: to look, to see; to look out, to wait for; *nn m.*: look, glance
ϭⲓϫ (f.): hand

Greek glossary

This list contains all the Greek words encountered in the examples, the exercises and the texts. They are arranged in the Greek alphabetical order. The orthography of Greek words can be slightly deviant in Coptic. The initial aspiration (ϩ) is rendered in Greek by the use of the *spiritus asper* above the first vowel or diphtongue of the word. Sometimes we find aspirations in Coptic where the Greek original has none. There is moreover a tendency to confuse ι/η/γ, ο/ⲱ and, more rarely, κ/ϭ.

A
τὸ ἀγαθόν (n.): the Good
ἀγαθός, -ή, -όν: good
ἡ ἀγάπη (f.): love, charity
ὁ ἄγγελος (m.): messenger, angel
ὁ ἀγῶν (m.): fight; combat; competition
ἀγωνίζομαι, ⲁⲅⲱⲛⲓⲍⲉ: to fight
ὁ Αἰγύπτιος (m.): Egyptian
αἱρετικός, -ή, -όν, ϩⲁⲓⲣⲉⲧⲓⲕⲟⲥ: heretic
αἴσθησις (f.), ⲉⲥⲑⲩⲥⲓⲥ: (sense) perception
τὸ αἰσθητήριον (n.), ⲉⲥⲑⲏⲧⲏⲣⲓⲟⲛ: organ of sense
αἰχμάλωτος, -ον: prisoner (of war), captive
ἀκάθαρτος, -ον: unclean, impure, foul
ὁ ἀλέκτωρ (m.): cock
ἀληθινός, -ή, -όν: real, true, truthful
ἀλλά: *conj.*: but, on the other hand
ἄλλος, -η, -ο: other
    ἄλλο... ἄλλο...: on the one hand..., on the other...
ἀμέλει: *adv.*: really, truly
ἀμελέω, ⲁⲙⲉⲗⲉⲓ (ⲉⲃⲟⲗ): to have no care for; to be neglectful of; to allow
ἀμέριμνος, -ον: free from care; unconcerned
ἀναγκαῖος, -α, -ον: necessary
ἡ ἀνάγκη (f.): necessity
ἡ ἀνάστασις (f.): resurrection
ἡ ἀναστροφή (f.): return; mode of life, behaviour
ὁ ἀναχωρητής (m.), ⲁⲛⲁⲭⲱⲣⲓⲧⲏⲥ: anchoret; hermit
ἀνέχω, ⲁⲛⲉⲓⲭⲉ: to hold up; to uphold; to maintain
ἀντί: *prep.*: opposite; instead of
ἀντικείμενος, -η, -ον: concurrent; enemy
ἄξιος, -α, -ον: worthy
ἀπαντάω, ⲁⲡⲁⲛⲧⲁ: to meet, to encounter

ἀπαρνέομαι, ⲁⲡⲁⲣⲛⲁ: to deny, to refuse
ἀπατάω, ⲁⲡⲁⲧⲁ: to deceive; to lead astray
ἡ ἀπάτη (f.): fraud, deceit, guile
ἄπιστος, -ον: unfaithful
    ⲙⲛⲧ.ⲁⲡⲓⲥⲧⲟⲥ: infidelity; unbelief
ἁπλῶς, ϩⲁⲡⲗⲱⲥ: *adv.* : simply; absolutely; in a word
ἀποδημέω, ⲁⲡⲟⲇⲏⲙⲉⲓ: to be away from home, abroad; to go abroad
ἀποκαθίστημι, ⲁⲡⲟⲕⲁⲑⲓⲥⲧⲁ: to restore; to hand over
ὁ ἀπόστολος (m.): apostle
ἆρα: *interrogative particle* (cf. 399)
ἡ ἀρετή (f.): virtue
τὸ ἄριστον (n.), ⲁⲣⲓⲥⲧⲱⲛ: breakfast
ἁρπάζω, ϩⲁⲣⲡⲁⲍⲉ: to snatch away; to carry off; to seize, to ravish
ἀρχαῖος, -α, -ον: old
    ⲛ̄-ⲁⲣⲭⲁⲓⲟⲥ: in the past
ἡ ἀρχή (f.): beginning, origin; principle; government, power
ὁ ἀρχηγός (m.): cause; founder, author
ἄρχομαι, ⲁⲣⲭⲉⲓ: to begin
ὁ ἀρχιμανδρίτης (m.), ⲁⲣⲭⲓⲙⲁⲇⲣⲓⲧⲏⲥ: archimandrite
ὁ ἄρχων (m.): governor, chief, archon
ἀσεβής, -ές: impious
ἡ ἄσκησις (f.): exercise; training; ascesis
ἀσπάζομαι, ⲁⲥⲡⲁⲍⲉ: to kiss, to embrace; to great
ἀσφαλής, -ές: firm, safe, secure
ἀσφαλῶς: *adv.*: safely; without faltering
αὐτεξούσιος, -ον: free; in one's own power
ὁ αὐτογενής (m.): autogenes (self-produced)
αὐτός, -ή, -όν: self, same; *as dem. pron.*: he, him; she, her
    τοῦ αὐτοῦ: from (*or* by) the same (*genitive*)
ἡ ἀφορμή (f.): starting-point; occasion; resources

Β
τὸ βάπτισμα (n.): baptism
βάρβαρος, -ον: barbarian, non-Greek
βοηθέω, ⲃⲟⲏⲑⲉⲓ: to help

Γ
ὁ γάμος (m.): marriage
γάρ: *enclitic conj.*: for
ἡ γενεά (f.): race; family; descent; generation
γενναῖος, -α, -ον: high-born, noble, excellent
γένοιτο: (might it happen) that (*expresses a wish*); *negation*: μὴ γένοιτο (cf. 420)
τὸ γένος (n.): race; offspring; generation; kind

ἡ γνῶσις (f.): knowledge
ἡ γραφή (f.): writing; Scripture
γυμνάζω, ⲅⲨⲘⲚⲀⲌⲈ: train, exercise; *with* ϨⲀ: to dispute about
ἡ γυμνασία (f.): exercise, practice

D
ὁ δαίμων (m.): demon
τὸ δαιμόνιον (n.), ⲆⲀⲒⲘⲰⲚⲒⲞⲚ: demon, devil
δέ: *enclitic conj.*: and; but; (*with* μέν) on the other hand
τὸ δεῖπνον (n.), ⲆⲒⲠⲚⲞⲚ, ϮⲠⲚⲞⲚ: meal
ὁ δημιουργός (m.), ⲆⲒⲘⲒⲞⲨⲢⲄⲞⲤ: architect, demiurge, creator
ἡ διαβολία (f.): enmity; aversion
ὁ διάβολος (m.): devil
ἡ διαθήκη (f.): disposition; covenant; testament
διακονέω, ⲆⲒⲀⲔⲞⲚⲈⲒ: to serve, to minister
ἡ διδασκαλία (f.): doctrine; teaching
δίκαιος, -α, -ον: just, righteous
δικαίως: *adv.*: with reason
ἡ δικαιοσύνη (f.): justice
τὸ δικαίωμα (n.): judgement; verdict; justification
ὁ διωγμός (m.), ⲆⲒⲞⲔⲘⲞⲤ: hunt; persecution

E
Ἑβραῖος, -α, -ον: Hebrew
   ⲘⲚ̄Ⲧ.ϨⲈⲂⲢⲀⲒⲞⲤ: Hebrew
ἐγκακέω, ⲈⲄⲔⲀⲔⲈⲒ: to lose heart; to grow tired
τὸ ἔθνος (n.), ϨⲈⲐⲚⲞⲤ: people, nation; *pl.* gentiles, pagans
ἡ εἰκών (f.), ϨⲒⲔⲰⲚ: image, statue, representation
εἰμήτι (Ⲉ-): *prep.*: except for; *conj.*: if not
ἡ εἰρήνη (f.), ⲒⲢⲎⲚⲎ: peace; rest
εἰρηνικός, -ή, -όν, ⲎⲢⲎⲚⲒⲔⲞⲤ: peaceful
εἶτα: *conj.*: then, next
εἴτε... εἴτε: *conj.*: either... or
ἡ ἐκκλησία (f.): assembly; church
ὁ ἕλλην, ϨⲈⲖⲖⲎⲚ: Greek; gentile, pagan
ἑλληνικός, -ή, -όν: Greek, Hellenic
τὸ ἕλος (n.), ϨⲈⲖⲞⲤ: marsh-meadow
ἐλπίζω, ϨⲈⲖⲠⲒⲌⲈ: to hope
ἡ ἐλπίς, ϨⲈⲖⲠⲒⲤ (f.): hope
ἡ ἐνέργεια (f.): activity
ἐνιαύσιος: *adv.*: yearly; during a year
ἡ ἐντολή (f.): commandment, order
ἔξεστι (n) *impersonal verb*: it is possible; it is allowed; *negation*: οὐκ ἔξεστι

ἡ ἐξουσία (f.): authority; power
ἐπεί, ἐπειδή, ⲉⲡⲓⲆⲎ: when; since
ἐπιθυμέω, ⲉⲡⲓⲑⲨⲘⲈⲒ, ⲉⲡⲉⲓⲑⲨⲘⲈⲒ: to desire
ἡ ἐπιθυμία (f.): desire
ἡ ἐπιστολή (f.), pl. ⲉⲡⲓⲤⲦⲞⲖⲞⲞⲨⲈ: letter
ἐπιχειρέω, ⲉⲡⲓⲬⲈⲢⲈⲒ: to put one's hand to; attempt; attack
ἡ ἐπωμίς (f.): (monastic) scapular
ἡ ἐργασία (f.): work; occupation; effort; function
ἡ ἐρημία (f.): desert; desolate place; solitude
ἔρημος, -ον: desolate, abandoned; *nom m.*: desert
ἔτι: yet, still
τὸ εὐαγγέλιον (n.): good news; Gospel
εὐσεβής, -ές: pious; faithful
εὐφραίνω, εὐφραίνομαι, ⲉⲨⲫⲢⲀⲚⲈ: to rejoice; to be happy; to make happy

Z

H
ἤ: *conj.*: or
ὁ ἡγεμών (m.): chief, leader
ἡ ἡδονή (f.), ϨⲎⲆⲞⲚⲎ, ϨⲨⲆⲞⲚⲎ: pleasure

Θ
τὸ θέατρον (n.): theatre, spectacle
ἡ θεωρία (f.): exam, inquiry; theory
τὸ θηρίον (n.): wild animal
θλίβω, ⲐⲖⲒⲂⲈ: to oppress (*in Coptic also*: to be oppressed)
ἡ θλίψις (f.): oppression, affliction; pressure
ὁ θυρεός (m.), ⲐⲨⲢⲞⲤ: shield
ἡ θυσία (f.): offering, sacrifice; offering festival

I
Ἰουδαῖος, -α, -ον, ⲒⲞⲨⲆⲀⲒ: Jew(ish)

K
ὁ κάδος (m.): jar, vessel; urn
καθαρός, -ά, -όν: pure
 ⲘⲚ̄Ⲧ-ⲔⲀⲐⲀⲢⲞⲤ: purity
ὁ καιρός (m.): (right) moment, occasion
καίτοι, ⲔⲈⲦⲞⲒ: and indeed, and further; and yet

καλός, -ή, -όν: beautiful
καλῶς: *adv.*: good, well
κἄν: *conj.*: even if
ὁ καρπός (m.): fruit
κατά: *prep.*: downwards; toward; in accordance with; after; according to
κατάγαιος, -ον, ⲭⲁⲓⲟⲥ: subterranean; on the ground
ὁ κατακλυσμός (m.), ⲕⲁⲧⲁⲕⲗⲏⲥⲙⲟⲥ: destruction, inundation, deluge
καταλαλέω, ⲕⲁⲧⲁⲗⲁⲗⲓ: to blame; to rail at
ἡ καταλαλία (f.): evil report, slander
καταφρονέω, ⲕⲁⲧⲁⲫⲣⲟⲛⲉⲓ: to look down upon, to despise; to disregard
κατορθόω, ⲕⲁⲧⲟⲣⲑⲟⲩ: to make right; to correct; to be right, perfect
τὸ κεράτιον (n.), ⲑⲁⲣⲁⲧⲉ: pod
κηρύσσω, ⲕⲩⲣⲓⲥⲥⲁⲓ: to announce
ὁ κίνδυνος (m.): danger, risk
ἡ κιννύρα (f.), ⲃⲓⲛⲏⲣⲁ: lyre
κληρονομέω, ⲕⲗⲏⲣⲟⲛⲟⲙⲓ: to inherit, to receive
κοινωνέω, ⲕⲟⲓⲛⲟⲛⲉⲓ: participate; join
ἡ κοινωνία (f.): (monastic) community
κολάζω, ⲕⲟⲗⲁⲍⲉ: to chastise; to punish; to reprove
ἡ κόλασις (f.): chastisement, punishment; correction
ὁ κόμης (m.): magistrate (*from the Latin "comes"*)
κοσμικός, -ή, -όν: cosmic; belonging to the world
ὁ κόσμος (m.): cosmos
ἡ κρατήρ (m.): vessel, bowl
κρίνω, ⲕⲣⲓⲛⲉ: to judge
ἡ κρίσις (f.): judgement

Λ
ὁ λαός (m.): people
ἡ λεκάνη (f.): dish; pot; pan
ὁ ληστής (m.), ⲗⲩⲥⲧⲏⲥ: robber; thief
ὁ λόγος (m.): Logos; reason; Word; history
ἡ λόγχη (f.): lance, spear
λυπέομαι, ⲗⲩⲡ(ⲉ)ⲓ: to be sad, afflicted; to suffer
ἡ λύπη (f.): affliction; suffering; sadness

Μ
ἡ μαγία (f.): magic, magic trick
ὁ μαθητής (m.): pupil, disciple
     ϢⲂⲢ̄-ⲘⲀⲐⲎⲦⲎⲤ: classmate
μᾶλλον: *adv.*: more; rather
μαστιγόω, ⲘⲀⲤⲦⲒⲄⲞⲨ: to whip; to flog
ἡ μάστιξ (f.), ⲘⲀⲤⲦⲒⲚⲄⲜ: whip; scourge

ἡ μελέτη (f.): care; exercise
τὸ μέλος (n.): member, limb
μέν: *enclitic particle*: indeed; *with* δέ: on the one hand
τὸ μέρος (n.): part
μετανοέω, **ⲘⲈⲦⲀⲚⲞⲈⲒ**: to convert; to repent
ἡ μετάνοια (f.): repentance
μή: *interrogative particle*: not? (cf. 399)
μητι: *interrogative particle* (cf. 399)
μήποτε: *conj.*: lest ever
μήπως: *conj.*: in order not to; lest in any way
μόγις: *adv.*: scarcely; hardly
μοναχός, -ή, -όν: alone; solitary; *noun*: monk, nun
μονογενής, -ές: monogenes (the only-born)
μόνον: *adv.*: only
μόνος, -η, -ον: alone
τὸ μυστήριον (n.): mystery, secret

N

νηστεύω, **ⲚⲎⲤⲦⲈⲨⲈ**: to fast
ὁ νόμος (m.): law
    ⲀⲬⲚ̄-ⲚⲞⲘⲞⲤ: illegally
ὁ νοῦς (m.): intellect, spirit
ὁ νυμφίος (m.): husband

Ξ

ἡ ξένη (f.): foreign country
τὸ ξίφος (n.), **ⲤⲒϤⲈ, ⲤⲎϤⲈ, ⲤⲨⲂⲈ**: sword

O

ὁ ὀβολός (m.), **ϨⲞⲂⲞⲖⲞⲤ**: obol
ἡ οἰκονομία (f.): household; government; Economy (of Salvation); design
ὁ οἰκονόμος (m.): manager; administrator; house-steward
ὁ οἶκος (m.): house
ἡ οἰκουμένη (f.): (inhabited) world
ὅλος, -η, -ον, **ϨⲞⲖⲞⲤ**: complete, whole
ὅλως, **ϨⲞⲖⲰⲤ**: *adv.*: completely
ἡ ὀργή (f.): anger; wrath
τὸ ὅρομα (n.), **ϨⲞⲢⲞⲘⲀ**: vision
τὸ ὅρος (m.), **ϨⲞⲢⲞⲤ**: limit; border; definition; rule
ὅσον: *conj.*: so far as; so much as; as long as
ὅταν, **ϨⲞⲦⲀⲚ**: *conj.*: when; whenever
οὐ: *particle of negation*: not

οὐδέ: *conj.*: and not, neither
ἡ οὐσία (f.): being; substance; property
οὔτε: *conj.*: and not, neither

Π

παιδεύω: to educate
τὸ παλάτιον (n.), ΠΑΛΛΑΤΙΟΝ: palace
πάντως: *adv.*: completely; certainly; absolutely
παρά, ΠΑΡΑΡΟ⸗: *prep.*: next to; in comparison with; beyond
ἡ παραβολή (f.): comparison; parable
παράγω, ΠΑΡΑΓΕ: to transport; to pass
παραδίδωμι, ΠΑΡΑΔΙΔΟΥ: to hand over, to deliver; to betray
παραιτέομαι, ΠΑΡΑΙΤΕΙ: to beg; obtain (a favour); decline, reject
παρακαλέω, ΠΑΡΑΚΑΛΕΙ: to invoke; to pray; to exhort
παρθένος (f.): young girl; virgin
ἡ παρρησία (f.): freedom of speech; frankness; freedom
πατάσσω, ΠΑΤΑϹϹΕ: to beat; to knock; to strike; to smite
ὁ πατριάρχης (m.): patriarch
πειράζω, ΠΕΙΡΑΖΕ: to tempt
ὁ πειρασμός (m.): temptation; trial
περίχωρος, -ον (f.), ΠΕΡΙΧΟΡΟϹ: the country round about
ἡ πέτρα (f.): rock
ἡ πηγή (f.): source
πιστεύω, ΠΙϹΤΕΥΕ: to believe
ἡ πίστις (f.): faith; belief; trust
πιστός, -ή, -όν: faithful
τὸ πλάσμα (n.): thing moulded or fashioned; figure
πλατωνικός, -ή, -όν, ΠΛΑΤΟΝΙΚΟϹ: platonic
ἡ πληγή (f.): blow, stroke; plague
τὸ πνεῦμα (n.): spirit
ὁ πόλεμος, ΠΟΛΥΜΟϹ (m.): war, combat, fight
πολεμέω, ΠΟΛΥΜΕΙ: to be at war; to make war; to fight
ἡ πόλις (f.): city
πολλάκις: *adv.*: often
πονηρός, -ά, -όν: evil, bad; criminal
ἡ πόρνη (f.): prostitute; adulterous woman
ὁ πόρνος (m.): fornicator; idolater
προκόπτω, ΠΡΟΚΟΠΤΕΙ: to advance; to be advanced
πρός, ΠΡΟϹΡΟ⸗: *prep.*: toward; across; against; around; for
προσέχω, ΠΡΟϹΕΧΕ: to be intent on; to be on one's guard against; to attach oneself to
προσκαρτερέω, ΠΡΟϹΚΑΡΤΕΡΕΙ: to persist in; to devote oneself to; to wait for
τὸ πρόσταγμα (n.): ordinance, command
ἡ προσφορά (f.): offering; application
ὁ προφήτης (m.): prophet

ἡ πύλη (f.): door; gate; entrance
πῶς: *adv.*: how? In any way, at all

Ρ

Σ
τὸ σάββατον (n.): sabbat; week
Σαμαρίτης, -ες: Samaritan
σαρκικός, -ή, -όν: fleshly, bodily
ἡ σάρξ (f.): flesh
σεμνός, -ή, -όν, ⲤⲘⲚⲞⲤ: honourable; solemn, exalted; worthy
    ⲘⲚ̄Ⲧ-Ⲥ(Ⲉ)ⲘⲚⲞⲤ: dignity; sacredness
σημαίνω, ⲤⲨⲘⲀⲚⲈ: to indicate; to give signs; to appear; to be manifest; signify; declare
σκανδαλίζω, ⲤⲔⲀⲚⲆⲀⲖⲒⲌⲈ: scandalise; to be an obstacle
τὸ σκάνδαλον (n.): obstacle; scandal
σκεπάζω, ⲤⲔⲈⲠⲀⲌⲈ: to cover; to shelter; to protect
ἡ σοφία (f.): wisdom
σοφός, -ή, -όν: wise
τὸ σπέρμα (n.): semen, seed
σπουδάζω, ⲤⲠⲞⲨⲆⲀⲌⲈ: to be eager; to pay attention; to do hastily; to pursue zealously
ἡ σπουδή (f.): haste; speed; zeal
ὁ σταυρός (m.): cross
σταυρόω, ⲤⲦⲀⲨⲢⲞⲨ: to crucify
ἡ στήλη (f.): stele
τὸ στιχάριον (n.): tunic
ἡ στολή (f.): robe, garment
συλάω, ⲤⲨⲖⲀ: to strip off; to plunder; to take off
ἡ συμφωνία (f.): harmony; music
ὁ σύνδουλος (m.): co-slave
σφραγίζω, ⲤⲪⲢⲀⲄⲒⲌⲈ: to seal; to certify; to confirm
τὸ σχῆμα (n.), ⲤⲬⲨⲘⲀ: form; figure; (fashion of) dress
τὸ σῶμα (n.): body
σωματικῶς: *adv.*: bodily, physically
ὁ σωτήρ (m.): saviour

Τ
τάσσω, ⲦⲀⲤⲤⲈ: to arrange; to order; to rule; to impose
τέλε(ι)ος, -α, -ον: complete, accomplished, perfect
ὁ τερατίας (m.), ⲦⲈⲢⲎⲆⲀⲦⲎⲤ (?): thaumaturge, worker of miracles
τερατώδης, -ες, ⲦⲈⲢⲎⲆⲀⲦⲎⲤ (?): miraculous, prodigious, monstrous
τολμάω, ⲦⲞⲖⲘⲀ: to dare, to have the courage

ὁ τόπος (m.): place
τότε: *adv.*: then, at that moment
ἡ τροφή (f.): food

Υ
ἡ ὑπόκρισις (f.): hypocrisy
ὑπομένω, ϨΥⲠⲞⲘⲒⲚⲈ: to abide, to await; to be patient; to endure
ἡ ὑπομονη (f.): patience, endurance, perseverance
ὑποτάσσω, ϨΥⲠⲞⲦⲀⲤⲤⲈ: to place under; to submit; to be obedient

Φ
ὁ φαρισαῖος (m.), ⲪⲀⲢⲒⲤⲤⲀⲒⲞⲤ: pharisee
τὸ φραγέλλιον (n.): whip
ἡ φυλή (f.): tribe

Χ
χαρίζομαι, ⲬⲀⲢⲒⲌⲈ: to grant a favour
ἡ χάρις (f.): grace
τὸ χάρισμα (n.): charisma; gift; grace
ὁ χιλίαρχος (m.): commandant
ὁ χορός (m.): dance
ὁ χόρτος (m.): meadow, prairie; garden; grass
ἡ χρεία (f.), ⲬⲢⲒⲀ: need; commodity
     Ⲣ̄-ⲬⲢⲒⲀ: to need, to be needy
τὸ χρῆμα (n.): thing; possession; money; richness
ὁ χριστιανός (m.): Christian
ἡ χῶρα (f.): region; country; countryside, province (in Egypt)
χωρίς: *prep.*: without

Ψ
ψάλλω, ⲮⲀⲖⲖⲈⲒ: to sing (to a harp), to psalm
ὁ ψαλμός (m.): Psalm
ἡ ψυχή (f.), pl. ⲮⲨⲬⲞⲞⲨⲈ: soul

Ω
ὡς, ϨⲰⲤ: *conj.*: since; when; *prep.*: like
ὥστε, ϨⲰⲤⲦⲈ: *conj.*: so as, so that; in order that; *prep.*: like
ἡ ὠφέλεια (f.), ⲞⲪⲈⲖⲒⲀ: help, aid; profit, advantage

Glossary of proper nouns

This list contains all the proper nouns you'll find in the examples, the exercises and the texts. They are presented in the 'normal' alphabetical order, that is, taking the vowels in account.

ⲁⲃⲉⲗ: Abel
ⲁⲛⲇⲣⲉⲁⲥ: Andrew
ⲁⲛⲧⲟⲛⲓⲟⲥ: Antony
ⲁⲡⲟⲗⲗⲱⲛ: Apollon
ⲃⲁⲣⲁⲃⲃⲁⲥ: Barabbas
ⲃⲏⲑⲗⲉⲉⲙ: Betlehem
ⲅⲁⲃⲣⲓⲏⲗ: Gabriel
ⲅⲁⲗⲓⲗⲁⲓⲁ: Galilee
ⲅⲉⲣⲁⲇⲁⲙⲁ: Geradama
ⲅⲣⲏⲅⲱⲣⲓⲟⲥ: Gregory
ⲇⲁⲛ: Dan
ⲇⲁⲩⲉⲓⲇ: David
ⲇⲓⲙⲟⲩⲉⲟⲥ: Timothy
ⲇⲱⲥⲓⲑⲉⲟⲥ: Dositheus
ⲉⲙⲙⲁⲭⲁ: Emmacha
ⲑⲉⲱⲇⲟⲣⲟⲥ: Theodore
ⲓⲁⲕⲱⲃⲟⲥ: James
ⲓⲏⲥⲟⲩⲥ: Jesus
ⲓⲟⲣⲇⲁⲛⲏⲥ: Jordan
ⲓⲟⲩⲇⲁ: Juda
ⲉⲓⲱⲥⲏϥ: Joseph
ⲓⲱϩⲁⲛⲛⲏⲥ: John
ⲓⲱϩⲁⲛⲛⲏⲥ ⲡ.ⲃⲁⲡⲧⲓⲥⲧⲏⲥ: John the baptist
ⲓⲱϩⲁⲛⲛⲏⲥ ⲡ.ⲕⲟⲗⲟⲃⲟⲥ: John of Kolobos
ⲕⲁⲛⲁ: Cana
ⲕⲏⲙⲉ: Egypt
ⲕⲩⲡⲣⲟⲥ: Cyprus
ⲕⲱⲥ: Kôs
ⲗⲉⲩⲉⲓ: Levy
ⲙⲁⲕⲁⲣⲓⲟⲥ: Macarius
ⲙⲁⲣⲓⲁ: Mary

ⲙⲁⲣⲓⲁ ⲧ.ⲙⲁⲅⲇⲁⲗⲏⲛ· Mary Magdalene
ⲙⲁⲣⲓϩⲁⲙ(ⲙ): Mary
ⲙⲁⲑⲑⲁⲓⲟⲥ: Matthew
ⲙⲓⲣⲱⲑⲉⲁⲥ: Mirôtheas
ⲙⲓⲣⲱⲑⲉⲟⲥ: Mirôtheos
ⲙⲱⲩⲥⲏⲥ: Moïse
ⲛⲁⲍⲁⲣⲉⲑ: Nazareth
ⲡⲁⲩⲗⲟⲥ: Paul
ⲡⲁϩⲱⲙⲟ: Pachomius
ⲡⲉⲧⲣⲟⲥ: Peter
ⲡⲟⲓⲙⲏⲛ: Poimen
ⲡϩⲉⲣⲙⲏⲥ: Phermes
ⲥⲁⲙⲁⲣⲓⲁ: Samaria
ⲥⲁⲟⲩⲗ: Saul
ⲥⲁⲣⲁⲡⲓⲱⲛ: Serapion
ⲥⲁⲧⲁⲛⲁⲥ: Satan
ⲥⲏⲑ: Seth
ⲧⲉⲣⲧⲓⲟⲥ: Tertius
ⲭⲁⲙ: Cham
ϩⲏⲣⲱⲇⲏⲥ: Herod
ϩⲓⲉⲣⲟⲩⲥⲁⲗⲏⲙ: Jerusalem
ϩⲩⲣⲱⲇⲏⲥ: Herod

Glossary of nomina sacra

Nomina sacra are abbreviations of important Christian names and titles.

ⲓ̅ⲥ̅: ⲓⲏⲥⲟⲩⲥ: Jesus
ⲓ̅ⲏ̅ⲗ̅: ⲓⲥⲣⲁⲏⲗ: Israel
ⲑⲓ̅ⲗ̅ⲏ̅ⲙ̅: ⲧ.ϩⲓⲉⲣⲟⲩⲥⲁⲗⲏⲙ: Jerusalem
ⲡ̅ⲛ̅ⲁ̅: ⲡⲛⲉⲩⲙⲁ: Spirit
ⲡⲭ̅ⲥ̅: ⲡ.ϫⲟⲉⲓⲥ: the Lord
ⲥ̅ⲱ̅ⲣ̅: ⲥⲱⲧⲏⲣ: Saviour
ⲭ̅ⲥ̅: ⲭⲣⲓⲥⲧⲟⲥ: Christ

Grammatical index

absolute bound state
    nouns 046–047
adjective 027
    see attribution
    construct participle 052
adverb 103, 104–106, 377
    adverbial predicate 225, 260–266, 271
        conversions 263–266
        negation 261–262
    greek 105, 426
    interrogative 402
    noun 110
    prepositional locution 067, 107–109
anaphroric
    see pronoun
antecedent
    see circumstantial and relative conversion
aorist 324–330, 456, 473
    negation 325–326
apodosis
    see conditional clause
appellative 159
apposition 158–163
    subject 158, 209–213, 235–237
approximation 250
article 034, 041, 159, 200, 466
    definite 016, 054–062, 469
    demonstrative 015–016
    indefinite 064–068
    possessive 021
    zero-determiner 069–074, 160, 163, 166
assimilation 055
asyndeton 371, 395, 409, 414, 445, 468
attribution 026, 164, 176–177
    with n̄- 086, 092, 101–102, 161, 165–172
    without n̄- 173–175
bipartite construction
    see durative sentence
bound state
    see noun, preposition, verb, prenominal bound state, prepersonal bound state
cataphoric
    see pronoun
causal clause 349, 390, 443–444

causative infinitive 129–134, 379, 389–394, 415, 424, 449
    negation 132
    noun 392–394
    verb 133, 390
circumstance 357
circumstantial conversion 146, 422, 433, 440–441, 443, 451, 470, 471–476
    after the imperative 140
    antecedent 471–472
    before conjunctive 373
    cleft sentence 477–480
    durative sentence 228, 242, 254, 264, 273, 277
    nominal sentence 197–198, 204, 216–217
    non-durative sentence: 314, 328, 340
    preterit 241, 343–436
    suffixically conjugated verboid 296, 298–299
    verbs of incomplete predication 412
cleft sentence
    see circumstantial and relative conversion
comparative 032–033
completive clauses
    object clause 405–413
    subject clause 213, 414–421
    with conjunctive 376
concessive clause 440
conditional 358–363, 425
conditional clause 361–362, 427–442
    apodosis 434, 438
    comparative 441
    contrafactual 434–437
    factual 428–433
    protasis 429–437
conjunction
    apodotic 397, 438
    completive 405–407, 417, 419
    disjunctive 189, 403
    enclitic 233
    nominal coordination 186–190
    paratatic 371, 395, 396, 468
    subordinate clause c. 362, 374–375, 423–425, 429–432, 439–442, 443, 446–448

conjunctive 352, 368–379, 382, 408, 415, 419, 445, 448, 470
    with verb 371–373, 413
    without verb 374–379
consecutive clause 371, 445–448, 450–451
conversions 144
    see circimstantial c., focalising c., preterit c., relative c.
construct participle
    see adjective
coordination
    see asyndeton, conjunctions
dative
delocutive
    see nominal sentence
demonstrative
    see article, pronoun
    ⲉⲧⲙ̄ⲙⲁⲩ 017
denotative function 027–028, 040
deprivation 070
descriptive function 028–029, 052
determiner 075–079
    see article
direct speech 405
disjunctive
    see conjunction
doubr 399
dual 045
durative sentence 223–292
    see adverbial predicate, future, present
    before conjunctive 373
    conversions 227–230, 435, 459–460
    indefinite subject 152–153, 267–277
        conversions 272–277
    negation 226
    object 278–292
    predicate 126, 225
    subject 005
endophoric
    see pronoun
enumeration 071
exhortative 349
existential sentence 300, 302, 304, 435
    conversions 306
extraposition 454
    see apposition, nominal sentence
fear 407
final clause 371, 387, 406, 421, 445, 447–451
focalising conversion 148, 423, 447
    durative sentence 230, 244, 256–259, 266, 276, 333–334, 338

non-durative sentence 316–318, 330, 436
question 402
suffixically conjugated verboid 298–299
future 247–259
    auxiliary ⲛⲁ 225, 271
    before conjunctive 372
    conversions 251–259, 434, 447
    negation 248, 475
    subject 233–237
future conjunctive 380–388, 445
general truth 326
genitive 178–179
    explicative 181
    partitive 183
    possessed nouns 048
    with ⲛ̄- 048, 050, 180–183
    with ⲛ̄ⲧⲉ- 184–185
goal
    see final clause
habit 326
identity 161, 219
ignore 409
imperative 135–141
    before conjunctive 372
    negation 142–143
impersonal predicate 420
incapacity 326
incomplete predication
    see verb
indefinite
    see article, pronoun
indicational sentence 300–301, 303, 305, 307, 435
indirect speech 405
infinitive 111–113, 225, 271, 449
    see causative infinitive, verb
    before conjunctive 372, 379
    negation 118
intention 259
interjection 442
interlocutive
    see nominal sentence
interrogative
    see adverb, particle, pronoun, question
invariable ⲡⲉ 207, 240, 253, 263, 321, 434
irrealis 427
irreality 205, 437
    see conditional clause
iteration
    noun 163
    predicate 219

jussive 342–350
   negation 345–348
lexeme 025–026
limitative 364–367, 422, 450
narration 312, 387, 395, 418
negation 070
nominal sentence 191–222
   conversions 196–199, 204–205, 435, 475
   delocutive 191, 206–218
   extraposition 202–203, 209–213, 215, 217, 221
   interlocutive 191, 200–205
   negation 195
   periphrastic construction 194
   predicate 068, 192–194
   subject 004, 191, 200, 207, 220
   three members 209–213
non-durative sentence 308–388
   see aorist, conditional, conjunctive, future conjunctive, jussive, limitative, 'not yet', optative, past, precursive
   before conjunctive 372, 373
   subject 007
   subordinate clause bases 351–354
non-existence 070
'not yet' 319–323, 456
   conversions 321–323, 422
noun 025–026, 233
   see adverb
   abstract 065
   bound state 046–048, 049, 100
   common 213
   composite 049–053, 056, 069
   expressing time 057–058
   gender 034–040, 059
   gendered 027–030, 166
   greek 030–031, 037, 044, 167
   inanimates 031
   infinitive 038, 111, 391
   material 066
   non-gendered 027, 028, 030, 052
   number 034, 041–045, 059
   prefix 051
   proper nouns 060–061, 160, 213
numerals
   approximate 088
   cardinal 080–088
   ordinal 089–092
   two 087
object
   see durative sentence, prepositions, sternjernstedt
optative 331–341, 413
   negation 335–336, 340–341, 384, 447
order 337, 349, 385
particle 377, 399
past 310–318, 357, 395
   conversions 313–318, 436, 458
   negation 311, 436
perspective 259
plural
   see noun-number
possessive
   see article, noun, pronoun, suffixically conjugated verboids
   confusion between article and pronoun 022, 048
potentialis 427
precept 337
precursive 355–357, 422
prediction 337
prenominal bound state
   nouns 046, 048, 049
   numerals 082
   prepositions 093–096
   verbs 119–120, 149, 279, 283, 308
prepersonal bound state
   conjunctive 369
   nouns 046, 048, 182
   prepositions 094–097
   verbs 119–120, 149, 286, 308, 334
prepositions
   see attribution, genitive, dative, object
   attributive 168
   bound states 093–094, 096–097
   composite 048, 100
   defective 101–102
   greek 099
   object 278, 280–281, 282, 286
   prepositional locution
      see adverb
   simple 098–099
   with adverb 103
   with causative infinitive 392–394
   with independent personal pronoun 002
   with personal suffix 007
   with zero-determiner 072–074
present 231
   conversions 238–246, 437
   negation 232
   subject 233–237

preterit conversion 145, 357, 473
   durative sentence 227, 238–240, 251–253, 263, 272, 277, 434, 437, 456
   nominal sentence 196, 205, 214–215
   non-durative sentence 313, 321, 327
   possession 299
   verbs of quality 149, 295
prohibition 337
promise 337, 385
pronoun
   anaphoric 207, 210, 461, 476
   cataphoric 211
   demonstrative 012–014, 054, 192–193, 465, 472, 477–480
   determinative 466
   elided form 479
   endophoric 207, 478
   indefinite 024, 063, 192–193
   interrogative 023, 192–193, 402
   personal
      independent 001–004, 191, 193, 200, 202, 208, 480
      prefixed 005–006, 224
      suffix 007–011, 048, 097
         second suffix 287, 289
   possessive 018–020, 193
   presentative 478
   proleptic 410
   with ⲭⲱ 411
protasis
   see conditional clause
question 387, 398–404
   deliberative 388, 400
   direct and indirect 404
   partial 401
   rhetorical 385, 399
realis 427
reassurance 385
reciprocity 292
reflexivity 290–291
regret 437
relative conversion 147, 452–470
   antecedent 453, 455, 459, 461–462, 465–466, 472, 476
   before conjunctive 373, 470
   cleft sentence 477–480

   durative sentence 229, 243, 255, 265, 274, 277, 463
   nominal sentence 199, 218
   non-durative sentence 315, 323, 329, 341
   substantivated 053, 466–467, 469
   suffixically conjugated verboid 297–299, 462
relative time 351
repeated action 326
result
   see consecutive clause
rhetorical question
   see question
semanteme 025–026
singular event 357
stative 121–128, 225, 271
stern-jernstedt rule 279–281
subject clause
   see completive clause
suffixically conjugated verboids 149–157, 293–299
   conversions 295–299, 462, 459
   double object 157
   negation 294
   periphrastic construction 293
   possession 154–157, 299, 456
   quality 150, 295, 462
superlative 032
supposition 259
temporal clause 361, 363, 367, 422–426
tripartite conjunction
   see non-durative sentence
'until' 367
verb 025, 111–157
   bound states 119–120, 278
   causative 114, 285
   composite 115
   greek 116–117, 120
   incomplete predication 386, 394, 412–413
   movement 123
   periphrastic locution 126
vocative 062
wish 337, 349
wonder 399
zero-determiner
   see article

Concordances & Paradigms

Concordance with some existing grammars

paragraph	LAYTON	PLISCH	TILL	VERGOTE
001–011	75–90	F	183–200	129–135
012–017	56, 58	D	201–202	127–128
018–022	54	E1–2	203–208	136–137
023	91–140	H1	209–217	145
024	50, 51, 60		218–232	141–144
025–026	91–93, 126		74	79–80
027–031	104, 113		147–149	189
032–033	95		151–155	
035–040	105–107, 117	B1	75–76	81, 112
041–045	108	B1	81–86	113, 173, 176
046–048	138–140			174–177
049–053	109–112, 118–122	B2	123–146	86–89
054–062	43, 52, 159–167	C	87–91, 94–99	121–122
063–068	162, 168	C	92–93, 100–102	123
069–074	47, 59		103–108	126
075	51, 55			
080–088	66–70	I1	156–168	147–152
089–092	112, 123	I2	169–173	153–154
093–097	200–201, 205, 214		233–234, 236	
098–099	202–205	K1, K3, K4	235, 237, 239	174, 177
100–102	208–213	K2		175
103	206		238	176
104–106	215			
107–109	216–219, 212		240	176
110	220			
111–120	159–161, 167	O1	253–256	90–91, 93–94
121–128	162, 168	O2	257	92
129–134	359	U	335	161,6
135–143	163, 365–369	W	297–300	
144–148	395–396	X	327–331	162–168
149–153	373–382	V	281–288	169–170
154–157	383–392	R	289–296	170.8
158–162	149		110	188
163	97		109	
165–172	96–100, 102, 116	N	114–119	189
173–175	101		121	
180–183	147	N	111–112	190
184–185	148		113	190

paragraph	LAYTON	PLISCH	TILL	VERGOTE
186–190	145		374–377	178
191			242	
192			242	
200–205	259–264	P1	243	194
206–208	265–267, 280–283	P1	244–245	193, 195–196
209–213	268–270	P2	246	197–199
214–218	256	P3		
219	273–274			
221	279		248	
222	257			
223–226	305–311			
227–230		S5		
231–237	317–318	S1	251, 303	158
238–246	320		303, 317	163.1, 164.1, 165.1
247–250	317–318	S3	252, 306	158
251–259	320		306, 318	163.2, 164.2, 165.2
260–262	317–318	S	249–250	192
263–266	320			
267–271	322			192
272–277	324			
278–281	171	S2	258–259	186.1
282			263–264	
283–284	171		260	
285–289	172–173			
290–291	176		262	
292	177		206	
293–299	373–382	V	281–296	169–170
300–307	476–485	Q	387	183
308–309 general	325	T	301–302	159
310–312	334	T1	313–315	159.1
313–318	334		316, 327–328	163–166
319–320	336	T1	320	159.2
321–323	336		327–328	163–166
324–326	337	T1	304–305	159.3
327–330	337		327–328	163–166
331–338	338	T1	308–309	159.4
339–341	338		327–328	163–166
342–350	340	T3	310	160.2
351–354	342–343	T2		161
355–357	344–345	T2	319	161.3
358–363	346–348	T2	447–448	161.5
364–367	349	T2	312	161.4
368–370	350–351	T2	321	161.1

paragraph	LAYTON	PLISCH	TILL	VERGOTE
371–373	352–353, 355		322	161.1
374–379	354		323–324	161.1
380–388	357–358	T3	311	161.2
389	359	U	335	161.5
390	360–361			
391–394	362–363		338, 351	
395–397	234–237		371–373	179
398–404		X4	430–446	201.5
405–413			413–420	209
414–421			421–422	208
422–426	493		428–429	211.1
427–433	495–497		447–460	212.1–2
434–437	498		456–458	212.3–5
438–442	494, 500–501		425–426, 447–455, 459–460	211.5, 212.6
443–444	493		427	211.2
445–451	502–504		423–424	211.3–4
452–454	399–402	X2	461–463	210
455–460	405		464–468	
461–464	407		469–474	
465–470	411		476–481	
471–476	404, 430	X1	475	210
477–480	461–475	X3, X4		

Concordance of grammatical terms

Pronouns and determiners

demonstrative article: *demonstrative adjective*

independent personal pronoun: *absolute personal pronoun*

personal suffixes: *suffix pronouns*

possessive article: *possessive adjective*

prefixed personal pronoun: *prefix pronouns*

Verbs

conversions: *transpositions*

focalising conversion: *second tenses*

prenominal state: *nominal state*

prepersonal state: *pronominal state*

stative: *the qualitative*

suffixically conjugated verboids: *suffixconjugation*

The nominal sentence

interlocutive sentence

delocutive sentence

The durative sentence: *adverbial sentence, bipartite pattern*

present: *present I*

preterit of the present: *imperfect*

focalising conversion of the present: *present II*

future: *future I*

preterit of the future: *imperfect of the future*

focalising conversion of the future: *future II*

durative sentence with adverbial predicate: *adverbial sentence*

The non-durative sentence: *verbal sentence, tense-base conjugation, tripartite pattern*

past: *perfect I*

focalising conversion of the past: *perfect II*

"not yet": *negative completive*

aorist: *praesens consuetudinis*

optative: *future III, energetic future*

jussive: *optative, causative imperative*

precursive: *temporalis*

limitative: *"until"*

future conjunctive: *finalis, causative conjunctive*

Grammatical paradigms

A. Pronouns

Personal pronouns

Independent personal pronouns, emphatic form

	sg.	pl.
1	ⲁⲛⲟⲕ	ⲁⲛⲟⲛ
2 m.	ⲛ̄ⲧⲟⲕ	ⲛ̄ⲧⲱⲧⲛ̄
2 f.	ⲛ̄ⲧⲟ	
3 m.	ⲛ̄ⲧⲟϥ	ⲛ̄ⲧⲟⲟⲩ
3 f.	ⲛ̄ⲧⲟⲥ	

Independent personal pronouns, reduced form

	sg.	pl.
1	ⲁⲛⲅ	ⲁⲛ(ⲛ̄)
2 m.	ⲛ̄ⲧⲕ	ⲛ̄ⲧⲉⲧⲛ̄
2 f.	ⲛ̄ⲧⲉ	
3 m.	ⲛ̄ⲧϥ̄	(ⲛ̄ⲧⲟⲟⲩ)
3 f.	(ⲛ̄ⲧⲟⲥ)	

Prefixed personal pronouns

	sg.	pl.
1	ϯ	ⲧⲛ̄
2 (m)	ⲕ (ⲅ)	ⲧⲉⲧⲛ̄
2 (f)	ⲧⲉ (ⲧⲣ)	
3 (m)	ϥ	ⲥⲉ
3 (f)	ⲥ	

Personal suffixes

1	⸗ⲓ	⸗ⲛ
	⸗ⲧ	
2 m.	⸗ⲕ	⸗ⲧⲛ̄
2 f.	Ø	⸗ⲧⲏⲩⲧⲛ̄
	⸗ⲉ	
	⸗ⲧⲉ	
3 m.	⸗ϥ	⸗ⲟⲩ
3 f.	⸗ⲥ	

Demonstrative and possessive pronouns and articles

Demonstrative pronouns

m.	f.	pl.
ⲡⲁⲓ	ⲧⲁⲓ	ⲛⲁⲓ
ⲡⲏ	ⲧⲏ	ⲛⲏ
ⲡⲉ	ⲧⲉ	ⲛⲉ

Demonstrative articles

m.	f.	pl.
ⲡⲉⲓ	ⲧⲉⲓ	ⲛⲉⲓ
ⲡⲓ	†	ⲛⲓ
ⲡ/ⲡⲉ	ⲧ/ⲧⲉ	ⲛ/ⲛⲉ

Possessive pronouns

m.	f.	pl.
ⲡⲁ-	ⲧⲁ-	ⲛⲁ-
ⲡⲱ⸗	ⲧⲱ⸗	ⲛⲟⲩ⸗

Possessive articles

	m.	f.	pl.
1	ⲡⲁ	ⲧⲁ	ⲛⲁ
2 m.	ⲡⲉⲕ	ⲧⲉⲕ	ⲛⲉⲕ
2 f.	ⲡⲟⲩ	ⲧⲟⲩ	ⲛⲟⲩ
3 m.	ⲡⲉϥ	ⲧⲉϥ	ⲛⲉϥ
3 f.	ⲡⲉⲥ	ⲧⲉⲥ	ⲛⲉⲥ
1.	ⲡⲉⲛ	ⲧⲉⲛ	ⲛⲉⲛ
2	ⲡⲉⲧⲛ̄	ⲧⲉⲧⲛ̄	ⲛⲉⲧⲛ̄
3	ⲡⲉⲩ	ⲧⲉⲩ	ⲛⲉⲩ

B. Conjugation bases

Durative sentences

Present-based conjugations

	present	focalising present	preterite present
1	ϯ	ⲉⲓ	ⲛⲉⲓ
2 m.	ⲕ	ⲉⲕ	ⲛⲉⲕ
2 f.	ⲧⲉ/ⲧ(ⲉ)ⲣ	ⲉⲣ(ⲉ)	ⲛⲉⲣⲉ
3 m.	ϥ	ⲉϥ	ⲛⲉϥ
1	ⲧⲛ̄	ⲉⲛ	ⲛⲉⲛ
2	ⲧⲉⲧⲛ̄	ⲉⲧⲉⲧⲛ̄	ⲛⲉⲧⲛ̄
3	ⲥⲉ (ⲥⲟⲩ)	ⲉⲩ	ⲛⲉⲩ
noun	/	ⲉⲣⲉ	ⲛⲉⲣⲉ

Future-based conjugations

	future	focalising future	preterit future
1	ϯⲛⲁ	ⲉⲓⲛⲁ	ⲛⲉⲓⲛⲁ
2 m.	ⲕⲛⲁ	ⲉⲕⲛⲁ	ⲛⲉⲕⲛⲁ
2 f.	ⲧⲉⲛⲁ	ⲉⲣⲉⲛⲁ	ⲛⲉⲣⲉⲛⲁ
3 m.	ϥⲛⲁ	ⲉϥⲛⲁ	ⲛⲉϥⲛⲁ
3 f.	ⲥⲛⲁ	ⲉⲥⲛⲁ	ⲛⲉⲥⲛⲁ
1	ⲧⲛ̄ⲛⲁ	ⲉⲛⲛⲁ	ⲛⲉⲛⲛⲁ
2	ⲧⲉⲧⲛ̄(ⲛ)ⲁ	ⲉⲧⲉⲧⲛ̄(ⲛ)ⲁ	ⲛⲉⲧⲛ̄(ⲛ)ⲁ
3	ⲥⲉⲛⲁ	ⲉⲩⲛⲁ	ⲛⲉⲩⲛⲁ
noun	/	ⲉⲣⲉ- ⲛⲁ	ⲛⲉⲣⲉ- ⲛⲁ

Non-durative sentences

Main clause conjugation bases

	affirmative past	negative past	focalising past
1	ⲁⲓ	ⲙ̄ⲡⲓ	ⲛ̄ⲧⲁⲓ
2 m.	ⲁⲕ	ⲙ̄ⲡⲉⲕ	ⲛ̄ⲧⲁⲕ
2 f.	ⲁⲣ(ⲉ)	ⲙ̄ⲡⲉ	ⲛ̄ⲧⲁⲣⲉ
3 m.	ⲁϥ	ⲙ̄ⲡⲉϥ	ⲛ̄ⲧⲁϥ
3 f.	ⲁⲥ	ⲙ̄ⲡⲉⲥ	ⲛ̄ⲧⲁⲥ
1	ⲁⲛ	ⲙ̄ⲡⲛ̄	ⲛ̄ⲧⲁⲛ
2	ⲁⲧⲉⲧⲛ̄	ⲙ̄ⲡⲉⲧⲛ̄	ⲛ̄ⲧⲁⲧⲉⲧⲛ̄
3	ⲁⲩ	ⲙ̄ⲡⲟⲩ	ⲛ̄ⲧⲁⲩ
noun	ⲁ-	ⲙ̄ⲡⲉ-	ⲛ̄ⲧⲁ-

	not yet
1	Μ̄πατ︤
2 m.	Μ̄πατκ
2 f.	Μ̄πατε
3 m.	Μ̄πατϥ̄
3 f.	Μ̄πατς̄
1	Μ̄πατν̄
2	Μ̄πατετν̄
3	Μ̄πατογ
noun	Μ̄πατε-

	affirmative aorist	*negative aorist*
1	ϣαι	μει
2 m.	ϣακ	μεκ
2 f.	ϣαρ(ε)	μερε
3 m.	ϣαϥ	μεϥ
3 f.	ϣας	μες
1	ϣαν	μεν
2	ϣατετν̄	μετετν̄
3	ϣαυ	μευ
noun	ϣαρε-	μερε-

	affirmative optative	*negative optative*
1	ειε	ν̄να
2 m.	εκε	ν̄νεκ
2 f.	ερε	ν̄νε
3 m.	εϥε	ν̄νεϥ
3 f.	εςε	ν̄νες
1	ενε	ν̄νεν
2	ετετνε	ν̄νετν̄
3	ευε	ν̄νευ
noun	ερε- (ε)	ν̄νε-

	affirmative jussive	*negative jussive*	*(= negative caus. inf.)*
1	μ̄αρι	μ̄π̄ρτρα	
3 m.	μαρεϥ	μ̄π̄ρτρεϥ	
3 f.	μαρες	μ̄π̄ρτρες	
1	μαρν̄	μ̄π̄ρτρεν	
3	μαρου	μ̄π̄ρτρευ	
noun	μαρε-	μ̄π̄ρτρε-	

Subordinate clause conjugation bases

precursive

1	ⲚⲦⲈⲢⲒ
2 m.	ⲚⲦⲈⲢⲈⲔ
2 f.	ⲚⲦⲈⲢⲈ
3 m.	ⲚⲦⲈⲢⲈϤ
3 f.	ⲚⲦⲈⲢⲈⲤ
1	ⲚⲦⲈⲢⲚ̄
2	ⲚⲦⲈⲢⲈⲦⲚ̄
3	ⲚⲦⲈⲢⲞⲨ
noun	ⲚⲦⲈⲢⲈ-

conjunctive

1	ⲚⲦⲀ/ⲦⲀ
2 m.	Ⲛ̄Ⲅ
2 f.	ⲚⲦⲈ
3 m.	Ⲛ̄Ϥ
3 f.	Ⲛ̄Ⲥ
1	ⲚⲦⲚ̄
2	ⲚⲦⲈⲦⲚ̄
3	Ⲛ̄ⲤⲈ
noun	ⲚⲦⲈ-

conditional

1	ⲈⲒϢⲀⲚ
2 m.	ⲈⲔϢⲀⲚ
2 f.	ⲈⲢ(Ⲉ)ϢⲀⲚ
3 m.	ⲈϤϢⲀⲚ
3 f.	ⲈⲤϢⲀⲚ
1	ⲈⲚϢⲀⲚ
2	ⲈⲦⲈⲦⲚ̄ϢⲀⲚ
3	ⲈⲨϢⲀⲚ
noun	ⲈⲢ(Ⲉ)ϢⲀⲚ-

future conjunctive

1	ⲦⲀ/ⲦⲀⲢⲒ
2 m.	ⲦⲀⲢⲈⲔ
2 f.	ⲦⲀⲢⲈ
3 m.	ⲦⲀⲢⲈϤ
3 f.	ⲦⲀⲢⲈⲤ
1	ⲦⲀⲢⲚ̄
2	ⲦⲀⲢⲈⲦⲚ̄
3	ⲦⲀⲢⲞⲨ
noun	ⲦⲀⲢⲈ-

limitative

1	ϢⲀⲚⲦⲒ/ϢⲀⲚⲦⲀ
2 m.	ϢⲀⲚⲦⲔ
2. f.	ϢⲀⲚⲦⲈ
3 m.	ϢⲀⲚⲦϤ̄
3 f.	ϢⲀⲚⲦⲤ̄
1	ϢⲀⲚⲦⲚ̄
2	ϢⲀⲚⲦⲈⲦⲚ̄
3	ϢⲀⲚⲦⲞⲨ
noun	ϢⲀⲚⲦⲈ-